Educational and Cultural Challenges of the European Sustainability Model

María Dolores Sánchez Galera

Educational and Cultural Challenges of the European Sustainability Model

Breaking Down Silos in the Legal Domain

Springer

María Dolores Sánchez Galera
Public Law Department
Carlos III University of Madrid
Madrid, Spain

ISBN 978-3-030-38715-0 ISBN 978-3-030-38716-7 (eBook)
https://doi.org/10.1007/978-3-030-38716-7

This Springer imprint is published by the registered company Springer Nature Switzerland AG.
The registered company address is: Gewerbestrasse 11, 6330 Cham, Switzerland

Preface

> [O]ne can hardly believe there has been a revolution in all history so rapid, so extensive, so complete. Through it the face of the earth is making over, even as to its physical forms; political boundaries are wiped out and moved about, as if they were indeed only lines on a paper map; population is hurriedly gathered into cities from the ends of the earth; habits of living are altered with startling abruptness and thoroughness; the search for the truths of nature is infinitely stimulated and facilitated and their application to life made not only practicable, but commercially necessary. Even our moral and religious ideas and interests, the most conservative because the deepest-lying things in our nature, are profoundly affected. That this revolution should not affect education in other than formal and superficial fashion is inconceivable.[1]

This book purports to bring to light that is actually possible and urgent to address systemic solutions and institutional interventions in the fields of culture and education. Conceptual tools, legal frameworks, experiences and best practices are at the disposal of policy makers to build a new, different notion of education integrated in the Anthropocene.

I have decided to devote the following pages to draft a research agenda to generate discussion in a field that has been unfortunately highly neglected by legal scholarship. What I want is to generate further discussions and study on the topic that would go beyond the boundaries of legal scholarship to foster solutions capable to tackle the most urgent cultural and educational challenges of our era.

I am submitting the draft of this monographic work closely after the disclosure of 2019's Nobel prize awards. The Nobel Prize in Economic Science has been awarded to Dr. Banerjee, Dr. Duflo and Dr. Kremer. They have been working on the importance of understanding one of the most significant question in economics: why do some countries in the world stay poor while others grow rich? This might be one of the most important question in economics and a hard one to answer. Years of pioneering experimental research in the field with an important focus on health and

[1] **John Dewey.** "The School and Social Progress." Chapter 1, *The School and Society*. Chicago: University of Chicago Press (1907): 19-44.

education issues have driven three researchers of the Massachusetts Institute of Technology to draft some conclusions to improve action to fight poverty. Their experimental approach provide useful material for politicians to widen their range of available solutions for the alleviation of global poverty today. Still, the solution is not easy, because the problem is huge and dramatically extended, and because the problem is huge and dramatically extended, and also because it is not just an economic issue: politics and policies at the heart of the origins and of the possible solutions.

Poverty alleviation continues to be one of the most pressing problems of the world. Today, a global agenda that has found global consensus to delineate a concrete framework of action involving a vast quantity of actors in their shared responsibility to transform the world is pressing for action but we still need further awareness on the importance of endemic failures in our political, research and institutional agendas.

Today we are facing a deep change in the learning and cultural environments, threatened by the devastating and gloomy shapes of global pressing problems such as poverty, hunger, population growth, nature depravation, natural disasters and wars.

Fast urban development and demanding consequences of these global endemic failures need rapid answers also in regional and local contexts where development models seem to have reached a greater equilibrium among the social, the economic and the environmental dimensions. Although according to indicators radical changes within society, economy and the education system seems an impossible challenge. The transition to a sustainable society has proved to be more effective when we take advantage of open governance mechanism where our scope for action takes place in our spheres of influence, as individuals, citizens and members of local communities. Still, the need to provide a fertile institutional basis for people empowerment to establish a just world that is more ecologically sounded should aim at streamlining its cultural and education systems. A systemic change is needed if we want to take seriously the challenges of sustainability which puts at risk the survival of human life and planet earth. The explosion of technological and digital tools should be at the service of human values to contrast nature and human depravation, and legal practice and research should be more concerned with the upgrading of the proactive role of law in those issues.

Nowadays, the playground of our kids is mostly shaded by the new forms of communication and societal complexities. Complexities arise from every social field, and this should draw our attention further away than the simple construction of a legal framework for the protection of nature (either at European, global, national or local level). I have felt the need to take a glance at the wider picture, and speak out the absence of critical legal approaches in educational and cultural issues. There is a need for more awareness on how Europe (with its leading global role) is pursuing sustainable development as the supreme frontier of environmental protection hailing social concerns, but also as the supreme flag of action hiding business as usual, without addressing loftiest challenges.

I have heard many times at every scientific forum how much we need educational and cultural changes, but at the practical and policy level courageous solutions and real awareness by public authorities are missing. Curiously enough, legal scholarship has neglected for so long these two important social transformation yardsticks: education and culture. I am interested on both concerns and their inextricable link, understanding how important the intersection and integration of both is for the attainment of a successful return to a healthy and dreamful playground for our kids where they could find beauty, natural landscapes and hopefully find the strength for healthy growth and healthy communication channels again.

This has nothing to do with the ideal context of natural education that Rousseau described in his *Èmile*, or other ideas on social education that are part of our cultural traditions. The present book has to do with transformations, as envisaged in the UN 2030 Global Agenda for Sustainable Development: Transforming our World (UN 2015). I make the case for Europe, in a moment of deep European identity crisis. I make the case for the dissenting visions from mainstreaming economics and for those who want to work for institutional transformations, ecology, peace, justice, poverty eradication and social inclusion. I also make the case for those who want to abandon the business as usual vision in their daily lives. I want to discuss of a real change of paradigm through a multidisciplinary analyses that puts on the air the alarming concern for action in the education and cultural fields if we want a real and effective sustainable development, a more integrated Europe and, perhaps, a more habitable world. I will not cling to a 'retrotopy', nor to the past but striving for a better future for those kids who are always at the centre of our discourses, but still remain at the bottom of our political decisions and our public policies.

Tony Wagner has written that politicians do not address educational topics because they are so self-concerned with their own positions. Obviously, they earned such positions thanks to the existing educational system. Thus, they have failed to consider systemic transformations as urgent matters. I believe this is certainly the truth.

Europe needs more changes and needs to be there claiming for a European sustainability identity with a stronger social pillar for future generations. Europe needs to keep building healthy international relations, welfare policy and migration policies that are inclusive and integrative despite of the social complexities. Fortunately, considering the relevance of the economy for the issue of sustainability, there are already many valuable contributions in the field, providing for transformative tool kits and pioneering practices in which people, communities and their welfare are at the heart of the system.

Nevertheless, the economic paradigm has been overwhelmingly influential, and it still stands behind political decisions. I believe the commons, and other innovative approaches in our legal structures and, more broadly, on our decision-making processes, can counter-balance the marketisation and the economisation of the public sphere. Joseph Stiglitz has been recently speaking in different public discussions of devolving competencies to the state to meliorate our welfare systems and steal the super powers the enormous market has accumulated. In Europe, we must believe that we can still do it; but it is not sufficient anymore: we must take a further step which would make us stop believing and start acting. In any case, what is crucial is to leave behind the powerful economic ideas that are ruling the world, 'gains', 'capital' and 'economic assets' and start devoting attention to 'transformational paths' that take cultural initiative as fundamental engine for social change and inspiration, and incorporates an improved version of our education systems. Further than that, we must believe in our own power for transforming the societies to which we belong.

Unfortunately, we need more institutional means to facilitate the upgrading of our public education system abandoning the logics of the market and by ceasing to see educational and cultural ambitions as a simple scale of economic value and accountability measures. We have ended up 'standardising' academic objectives in function of a technically designed curriculum created in a decade where social, environmental and, most of all, demographic problems and complexities were not so evident in the wealthiest part of the world. Plato and many other thinkers of our western philosophical tradition reserved a more egregious position to the educational and cultural role in society. Our ancestors devoted to culture and education the highest instrumental position to build justice and fair virtuous societies. This book humbly tries to bring them back to present times.

Madrid, Spain
December 2019

María Dolores Sánchez Galera

Acknowledgements

My amazing family needs to be mentioned in the first place. I must thank my loving and patient husband and my three kids for their constant support and amorous encouragements. My kids have been often confronted with an absent-minded and frustrated mom with permanent lack of sleep and missing during holiday time, but their wonderful and sweet cooperation has been all my strength. The book is in fact dedicated to them and all those desiring to contribute to a good society striving to propose an alternative lifestyle to the dominant unsustainable standards of living missing out cultural, spiritual and educational values.

This book is the result of the efforts of several years of work in the topic of law and sustainability, thanks to the UC3M and the European Commission through the Marie-Sklodowska Curie COFUND action connecting excellence. My personal project on sustainability was hosted by Pascual Madoz Institute on Environment, Land, Urbanism and Environment in the Carlos III University. The idea and main arguments of this book were conceived at the end of the project understanding the urgent need of a new approach with educational and cultural issues at the forefront of a sustainability discussion.

I am deeply indebted to Luciano Parejo Alfonso for his supervision work during all these years. His endorsement, inspiration and continuous encouragement helped me to take the challenge of breaking silos into the legal domain for the sake of discussing cultural and educational issues under the paradigm of sustainability. Luciano lent his support to develop my ideas into a book. I am also thankful to Jesús Prieto de Pedro, Miguel Beltrán de Felipe, Marcos Váquer Caballeria, Francisco Javier Sanz Larruga, Elisa Morgera, Xira Ruiz Campillo, Teresa Parejo Navajas, Esin Örucü, Sheila Foster, Pietro Masala and Luis Jimena Quesada for their support, inspiration and comments on earlier versions of this work. I am also thankful to my dear friend Migle Laukyte, Timothy John Murphy, Antonio Descalzo, Isabel Hernandez, Antonio Estella de Noriega, Esther Torrecilla,

Mercedes Pardo Buendía, Agustín de Asís, Javier Ansuátegui and Mercedes Ortiz for their friendship and support. I am also grateful to the several people who helped me to revise and amend the earlier versions of this book, and I am not naming. A warm thank you also to the staff of Springer who so kindly and efficiently helped to bring this project to a good end, with a special thanks to Brigitte for believing in my project.

Contents

Chapter 1
Introduction

Abstract This book analyses the notion of sustainability, its contents and the public policies related to it as part of the global governance scenario. It attempts to be a renewed enquiry of the (almost worn-out) issue of sustainable development by shedding light into methodological difficulties of traditional disciplinary approaches when addressing the neglected cultural and educational aspects of sustainability. More fundamentally, the book tries to provide legal, political, social, culture and education scholars, guidance for a future research agenda on the necessary systemic changes in education and cultural institutions for a real transformation of society under the premises of the UN Global Agenda 2030. The topic has been neglected by legal scholarship so far, but sustainability policies are bound to fail without addressing educational and cultural systemic adjustments. The book opens with an introduction. Chapter 2 focuses on a critical outline of sustainability, and stands up for new methodological approaches. Chapter 3 consists of a critical overview of the European Union sustainability model, examining its normative and political basis grounded on a strong environmental integration of sectorial policies, neglecting more transformative systemic and social dimensions of sustainability. The common's discourse and the ecological aspects are brought into conversation with other governance approaches that are instrumental and crucial to face cultural and educational challenges today. Chapter 4 tries to present education and culture as drivers for a deep transformation illustrating the growing recognition of this idea in some international agreements. Chapter 5 puts together sustainability concept and sustainability policies and the cultural and educational ideas behind those strategies. It shows the fragmented policy scenario and it tries to demonstrate that despite strong international consensus in the role education and culture have for ecological transition, there remains space for legal scholarship to engage in more subversive discourses prompting the necessary legal framework for a systemic change. Some case studies bring evidence of this. Chapter 6 closes the analysis with some concluding remarks.

M. D. Sánchez Galera, *Educational and Cultural Challenges of the European Sustainability Model*, https://doi.org/10.1007/978-3-030-38716-7_1

Few people can deny that education is inextricably linked with culture just as culture is considered to be the underlying dimension of sustainability.[1] It is no coincidence then that the UNESCO (2015) booklet suggests a reorientation of the purpose of education (under the premises of sustainability), and goes so far as to say that education, while traditionally oriented towards inculturation and adaptation, can also be oriented towards transformation. The power of transformation is indeed the most prominent aspect of the pedagogical theories of two of the most important thinkers on education of our time, Paolo Freire and Jean Piaget.

In recent years, the shift towards sustainability as the only possible development strategy has invaded every scientific and political discourse. However, no consensus has yet been reached on identifying the most pressing challenges for a sustainable future. Education and culture have not been recognised by global actors as pressing challenges. In contrast with such lack of recognition, this book makes the case for such an argument. I approach the conceptualisation of a strong sustainability model that has been slowly embedded by the European integration process entrenched in the global governance complexity. In such global complex scenario, the word 'transformation' has colonised the 'imaginary' of this era in many different disciplines dealing with sustainability challenges. In September 2015, the heads of UN states when adopting the 2030 Agenda for Sustainable Development, referred to the 'Agenda' as the Agenda *'Transforming our World'*. The 17 sustainable development goals (SDGs) that were agreed map out where this transformation is supposed to lead.

For some decades now, and increasingly since the Agenda was adopted, culture has often been understood and, more recently, highlighted as the fourth pillar of the traditional sustainable development temple formed by the three classical components: (E)conomy, (E)nvironment, (E)quity. I am not adopting such a view and I prefer to stick to Brundtland's classic definition of sustainable development which not only acknowledges the three previously mentioned aspects, but it also adds the institutional (or governance) one.[2] In fact, the governance issue is crucial to face the current 2030 Agenda for Sustainable Development. The Agenda enhances social empowerment for action in the monitoring processes, making the case for a broader spectrum of actors. It introduces the foundations for systemic institutional changes by providing action mechanisms for the civil society at large to build a strong sustainability approach within 'ecological' boundaries. Today, we know that peace and prosperity cannot be achieved without joint ventures involving governments, international organisations and non-governmental ones, the business community and civil society, all at once. The interdependence of humanity has been recognised (at least on a theoretical level) by all of the nations of the world.

The beginning of my analysis deals with the conceptualisation of sustainability, its contextualisation and the evolution of the sustainability paradigm worldwide. I

---

[1] See Gerner (2018).

[2] I choose this definition because it is widely accepted for its criticalities as much as for its potential instrumental character to reach global consensus, as I will explain further in these lines.

address some methodological questions needed to understand the limited role of traditional disciplinary approaches when dealing with sustainability issues concerning a field that has gained overarching existence in the widely accepted geological epoch of the Anthropocene. Still, I argue that the role of legal science is important in accepting its position for transformative systemic changes needed to build the future of our generations within ecological limits. In fact, the analysis provides an extensive survey of the relevant literature from a range of disciplines, and gives an account of alternative methodological approaches operating outside the realm of legal scholarship when facing sustainability issues and its challenges.

In the third chapter of the book, I will be focusing on the European context specifically. The evolution of the European Union Sustainability Model (from now onwards EUSM) resembles the unfinished and open-ended aspect of the EU process of integration, as well as its legal framework. I draw on the conceptual and historical evolution of sustainability, and the new trends of legal authority in the field of international law claiming planetary scope that have brought international lawyers to think that they have a crucial role to play to contrast the unsustainability practices of our current production systems in the Anthropocene, but not only to combat externalities but to promote systemic changes.

There are references to the so-called ‘global law’ and the ambitious 2030 Agenda for Sustainable Development launched by the United Nations which aims to contrast the risks posed by humans in this new geological era. All such trends are defining paradigms of action under regional governance such as the EU experience. I argue how to address, consequently, future generations’ challenges of the next millennium. This takes me to discuss some foundational concepts of the commons. The commons pictured as a crucial element for transformations in Europe, as well as in other parts of the world, are experiencing pioneering local transforming realities that contribute to strengthening an incipient European sustainability model.

The following chapters of the book and the concluding remarks are the heart of the argument and will be devoted to educational and cultural issues as the neglected foundations of sustainability. There is an accurate analysis of how the role of law should be re-endorsed on the education and cultural policy fields to drive more transformative systemic and social dimensions of sustainability. Having defined the scope of action of the EU sustainability agenda, it is easier to find concrete critical aspects. Based on that, I try to suggest an innovative action trying to address the right legal, political, social, economic, pedagogical mechanisms at hand to increase awareness, especially among legal scientist and policy makers to drive institutions towards systemic transformation and society changes. I argue that legal mechanisms pursuing a strong sustainability approach should address education, training and cultural questions and ideas rooted on fundamental society queries. Or perhaps, it would be most adequate to refer to what sociologists have called ‘imaginary’ to capture the notion of transforming something more than ideas, to include a set of values, laws, institutions and symbols with which people imagine their social whole (Göpel, 2016).

The present research agenda tries to give an answer to the following questions: How is Europe introducing sustainability ‘concerns’ in the educational and cultural fields whilst these fields remain part of the national identity of the Member States? Can the European sustainability model respond to the cultural and educational challenges of the future and advance systemic transformations? For the purpose of the analysis, I am fully aware of the benefits and the limitations that legal analysis brings to a discussion of this nature. Sustainability problems require integrated concepts and integrated solutions, and we must bear in mind that we do not necessarily need to follow a unique or predetermined theoretical path to build strong arguments to face cultural and educational challenges. I am providing working definitions of sustainability, culture and education, and referring eventually to legal definitions, when applicable. However, definitions in this book are given for the sake of operationalising them during the analysis.

This volume does not intend to be a treatise on education or the transformative power of education and cultural enhancement, rather it tries to outline a research agenda to make the case for the necessary transformations of our societies to face future challenges for a sustainable future in line with the 2030 Agenda for Sustainable Development.

The unexplored conceptual frameworks of education and culture beyond disciplinary boundaries that are presented in the book try to be a departing point for a future investigation and policy action that takes account of these issues outside rhetorical disquisitions acknowledging methodological, conceptual and empirical complexities. Future policy action should integrate them based on their necessary role for a systemic transformation needed to build the sustainability model required by our current and future generations. This analysis also seeks a link between culture and education, and raises awareness of their neglected position as transformation drivers despite of their increasing relevance in different International Law documents, declarations, conventions, and agreements. Their increased recognition in the international sphere should trigger policy, individual and community action.

I believe that only educational and cultural systemic changes could bring the real kind of 'mindshift',[3] and people empowerment required within European societies to embrace a strong sustainability model. At the European institutional level, culture and education issues are short of competences, but still, both issues have gained bigger relevance in late times in the EU political agenda, and the EU coordinating role could be more prominent regarding sustainability concerns without necessarily invading national primary legal competence on such issues. The problem is, although educational matters stand as an essential yardstick of the European social model, they have been fairly dismissed within the context of the sustainability policy. The same has happened to culture so far, despite of the early entrance of sustainability concerns in cultural heritage and landscape issues through the Council of Europe normative framework. Today, social policy concerns to which culture and education belong are the weakest pillar of the current sustainability model.

The way we understand educational planning and the way it is managed today should change. Education is one of the social domains that has evolved less

[3]See further Göpel (2016).

in the last century, at institutional level and in the most formal sense of the term. Still, the act of education planning is quite a recent policy phenomenon, and it is now the most concrete expression of educational administration whether by the State or by one of its constituents (region, province, local authority). The discouraging part of such planning activity is that the majority of European education systems planning processes are almost entirely disconnected from the reality where formal education takes place, it is disconnected from people and society needs. In fact, legislation on education and culture is often concentrated on issues pertaining to the state's desire to penetrate educational and cultural institutions and are characterised by closures, lack of openness and resistance to any outside influence. European States need to rethink their educational system due to the necessity to adapt to a changing world constantly accelerating at fast speed in a global interconnected scenario, but with specific needs and resources associated to the local contexts. The need to draw attention to the current disconnection between the school system and the natural world is worrying, as well as the excessive attention placed on STEMS and technological engagement of kids.

This book indeed sheds light on how to face such challenges that should start by contrasting institutional stiffness to address major changes in education and culture to build a better world. For some evidence on this, some case studies will be briefly presented as part of the work.

References

Gerner, M. (2018). Managing cultural sustainability: Safe haven, cultural property, and sustainability in best practice. In E. Lagrange, S. Oeter, & R. Uerpmann-Wittzack (Eds.), *Cultural heritage and international law objects, means and ends of international protection* (pp. 175–208). Cham, Switzerland: Springer.

Göpel, M. (2016). *The great mindshift. How a new economic paradigm and sustainability transformations go hand in hand.* Springer Open.

Chapter 2
Conceptual and Methodological Premise: Breaking Silos Into the Legal Domain

Abstract The notion of sustainability has been widely discussed in the last two decades. This chapter briefly sums up these debates and tries to present a new concept that combines the prevailing normative perspective and new contents from other fields, particularly from education and culture. Today's sustainability discussions should suggest theoretical frameworks that provide new (or old) epistemologies that empower people and help policy action to face challenges which are mostly global, interconnected and systemic (see Sect. 2.1). The world needs more than ever deep cultural transformations, awareness and civil society engagement to preserve planet Earth for future generations in the Anthropocene but there has been little engagement of legal scholarship in alternative interdisciplinary dialogues dealing with education and culture as part of sustainability. Under these premises, the role of law cannot be any longer disconnected from other knowledge systems and should redesign legal and institutional intervention allowing future generations 'access' to justice nurturing bottom-up approaches best operationalised from cultural and educational realms (see Sect. 2.2). New methodological and integrated approaches are prevailing today, while sustainability science has also emerged as a scientific field departing from traditional academic approaches and breaking silos into the existing scientific domains. This does not imply dismissing the role of specific knowledge fields: it means that fields such as legal science should reflect the new systemic thinking of contemporary science (see Sect. 2.3).

2.1 Conceptual and Methodological Premise: Breaking Silos Into the Legal Domain

Sustainability has originally been introduced as an ecological paradigm contrasting the traditional extractive and aggressive model of fostering social well-being and economic growth. However, this change of paradigm can be insufficient in itself if not combined with a different way of looking at the world and organising knowledge to resolve our disconnection with the Earth system, which sustainability helps to bring into the horizon of our growth model. Thankfully, things are changing. Now we look at the world in its global complexity and try to grasp the interconnected

M. D. Sánchez Galera, *Educational and Cultural Challenges of the European Sustainability Model*, https://doi.org/10.1007/978-3-030-38716-7_2

nature of future challenges. It has been widely assumed that in the Anthropocene,[1] there are growing dangers caused by men since the beginning of the first Industrial Revolution. Human activity, and its ecological footprint, is provoking devastating effects to the biosphere, and the main challenge is to foster a cultural transformation impinging on education and knowledge transfer. The challenges for today's societies are huge, on top of that, the scientific world needs to connect with society and build bridges of knowledge for transformation.

The argument of this study is at the crossroad between European law, international law and international relations, global environmental law, ecology and sustainability sciences, education law and educational studies, cultural studies and comparative law. This is why the title announces 'breaking silos', because the analysis is substantially based on interdisciplinary-based bibliographical research. It also scrutinises thoroughly several levels of the legal system that today interact horizontally in what it has been called an 'inter-legality'[2] dynamic trying to provide effective regulatory solutions under sustainable development premises. Furthermore, it surveys the most relevant aspects of the EU sustainability model embedded in the global governance narrative. I break 'silos' into the legal clusters in an attempt to bring a more critical overview of the topic. This is, I go for a truly multidisciplinary approach, substantial to a contribution that examines the European sustainability model embracing global trends amidst the plurality of regulatory orders, exploring and suggesting conceptual paths to face cultural and educational challenges of such model. I consider the contribution of sociology, culture and ecology and sustainability sciences, economic sciences and pedagogy relevant and substantial to the issues raised.

Based mainly on literature review of the many different disciplines at play under sustainability premises, this chapter intends to shed light on three main aspects that are key instruments for the rest of the analysis and for the research agenda that I am proposing: (1) The blurry conceptual nature of Sustainability. Sustainability is still a slippery concept because it requires us to connect different aspects of our lives and of our world that are often separated. Sustainability thus poses a key challenge for knowledge that needs some clarification for a richer legal approach considering its highly recognised normative existence and its central role not only limited to Governments[3]; (2) The missing scholarly narrative about the consideration of law as an additional component of sustainable development seems to be less relevant than the missing attention given to educational and cultural components in the temple of sustainable development; and (3) The importance to accept new methodological approaches to unbundle the full potential of the normative existence of

[1]Viñuales (2018) refers to the term Anthropocene, as an advent in which "[h]umans have become an Earth-shaping force of geological proportions or, more specifically, that they have caused a lasting change in the Earth system", for further bibliographical reference on this geological era, see Viñuales (2018).

[2]See further on this topic, Kabblers and Palombella (2019).

[3]See for instance, Pope Francis I (2015).

sustainability considering the little attention given to transdisciplinary research and Earth system approach by lawyers outside the boundaries of environmental and ecological concerns.

2.2 Sustainability and the Blurry Normative Nature of an Open-Ended Concept of Multidisciplinary Existence

I do not intend to deal with definitions under this paragraph. However, before grasping the core of the argument, it is important to draw a distinction between the ecologist and the environmental approaches to sustainable development. It becomes relevant for a legal discourse in sustainability: "The ecologist approach is critical of growth and favours ecological sustainability ('strong sustainability'). The environmental approach assumes the validity of growth and places equal importance on environmental sustainability, social justice and economic prosperity ('weak sustainability'). The difference between them is not just gradual, but fundamental, as it becomes clearer when we follow the sustainability debate throughout the 1980s and 1990s" Bosselmann (2008).

I guess this initial distinction, which has also separated different political and economic schools of thought within the field, explains how and why sustainability becomes a blurry normative concept with a short-sighted existence if considered without a historical perspective. Sustainability, during its sequential conceptual life has normally been presented by international agreements and the academic world in general in the normative top-down version of 'Sustainable Development', most commonly known as the Brundtland definition (from *Our Common Future*): "*sustainable development is development that meets the needs of the present without compromising the ability of future generations to meet their own needs*".

The definition has never been a problem in itself, nor its command and control normative existence. However, the fact that *Our Common* future initially defends the idea of ecological limits and criticises economic growth for creating environmental harm, the degradation of nature, pollution, and the overconsumption of resources in the industrialised world, but then later, after having referred to the environmental damage caused by the rapid economic growth after the Second World War, presses upon the need for a "new era of economic growth" seems sort of controversial, if we look at it with the intention of purely embracing its most ecological version.[4]

We can clearly see that the history of the 'blurry' concept of the sustainability and its subsequent 'normative version' persists today. Sustainable development departs

[4]Bosselmann (2008), pp. 26–27 argues that "growth critics such as Edward Goldsmith, Mesarovic, Eduard Pestel, Dennnis Meadows, Rudolf Bahro (1994) or Herman Daly, have always been opposed to sustainable development; while authors like Wilfred Beckermann, K. Arrow, Peter Bartelmus, David Pearce or William Nordhaus saw growth as an inherent part of the new concept of sustainable development.

from this point, and accurately reflects the complexities surrounding 'the future' under the 'sustainability paradigm'. In fact, historians have referred to the Brundtland report, as the most 'paradoxical' or 'blatantly contradictory' part of the whole conceptual existence of sustainability (Caradonna, 2015).

In reality, there would be so much to say under this paragraph. However, to make a long story short, I will talk about this in the next chapter and I will just draw attention to the brilliant analyses of 'sustainability' offered by professor Bosselmann in his landmark work *The Principle of Sustainability. Transforming Law and Governance.*[5] His work is inspired by the ecological roots of the thought of the green philosopher, Rudolf Bahro. The result of his analysis is a wonderfully meticulous multidisciplinary study on sustainability and its transformative potential.

The European sustainability model, as it is now, adheres to the 'normative version' outlined within International Conventions and agreements in the field of environmental law (that is to say a weak version) which goes hand in hand with economic prosperity and market integration objectives. SD in such normative conceptual framework, such as other normative idea, i.e. equality, justice, democracy, etc., has been written into specific legal norms that touch upon many different context and sectors and deploying laws for developing appropriate institutions and institutional arrangements to further sustainability. Still its conceptual existence is somehow slippery from a legal standpoint.

The conceptual version labelled in the Lisbon Treaty as "sustainable development" (in Article 3 of the Treaty on the European Union)[6] seeks the broadest political acceptance among Member States as it happened with the Brundtland Report. However, when taking a closer look at the wording of the article there is room for improvement of the strongest sustainability version with concerns for more policy and institutional integration at cross-sectorial level and more participatory and localised participatory approaches for which we make the case. In fact, Article 3 of the TEU, by integrating the idea of a social market, gives signs of fostering the social and ecology value-based model that the EU needs to face future challenges. On top of that, on its accepted version of Brundtland's definition, Europe is recognising as part of 'sustainable development' an ecological concept of justice that concerns intragenerational justice or equity caring for the poor; and intergenerational justice regarding a concern for future generations. Seemingly, on accepting the definition provided by the Brundtland Report, the key issue of decisional and institutional integration is embedded in the conceptual framework of the EUSM. Thus, any additional subsidiary principle connected with the achievement of sustainable development that has been subsequently added to the definition becomes part of the normative narrative of the EUSM, including: the right to development; inter and intra-generational equity; the precautionary principle; the polluter pays principle;

[5]Bosselmann (2008).

[6]From now onwards (TEU).

and greater transparency, access to information, and participation in environmental decision-making.[7]

Nowadays in Europe (and this has been the norm for a long time now), as well as in the rest of the world, the growing awareness of environmental depredation has led many economists to distance themselves from an economic model based on growth, or any sort of development that is not based on local knowledge and empowerment (ecological economists), but this trend has not affected as much in other scholarly field. We hardly find legal scholars addressing alternative disciplinary approaches to radically change epistemology, neither to believe in education and culture as the main architects of a 'sustainable future'. However, we are still fortunate that 'ecological' awareness has helped lawyers build a substantial body of environmental law at a transnational level and in some instances to shift the widely recognised attention of environmental law based on defensive protection and rights to duties. In addition to that, environmental law and policy concerns created the conditions for broadening awareness of the philosophy of sustainability although, as it has been pointed from a historical point of view, "sustainability is not the outcome of the environmental movement, but at the same time it could not have existed without it. Environmentalism facilitated the integrated systems thinking of sustainability that truly began to take shape in the 1980s" (Caradonna, 2015, p. 106).

Thus, somehow, an increased human awareness has helped the activism of the environmental movement to have an impact on our societies, our economic systems and our scientific approaches. It is exactly there where we can find the original tripartite composition of the sustainability concept that has fluently circulated across the different scientific fields. It has some merit, because it already interconnects three systemic realities: economic, social and environmental. As Caradonna (2015) rightly affirms, the environmental and social movements of the 1960s and early 1970s are the direct predecessors of the inspiration for the modern sustainability movement with a specific lineage that brought about a wide range of current practices, concepts and concerns rooted first and foremost in the elaboration of an ecological sense of production. This ecological awareness that underpins the 'sustainability' concept itself necessarily helps sustainability to be associated with "a complex relationship between humans, human technology, and the built environment, on the one hand and the ecosystem use and degradation, on the other" (Caradonna, 2015, p. 110) this gives, consequently, an integrated systems thinking that provides the essential background to approach the idea of sustainability that we need and lawyers have so far dismissed.

It was in the eighties when the legal component made its appearance, and also when the three 'Es' (Economy, Ecology, Equity) appeared as the basic model for sustainability, and it was then when 'sustainability' became the core of international agreements, with a relevant proliferation. Indeed, sustainability found its greatest supporter in the United Nations that recasts sustainability as "sustainable development" and integrated its principles into international agreements. Thereafter it

[7]On this, see further, Humphreys (2017), Chapter 3.

became part of the global political agenda, triggering multidisciplinary approaches in an integrated and fragmented manner, but surely spreading the Earth system approach that was already outlined in the writings of the club of Rome and it is increasingly becoming popular among international lawyers (Kotzé & Kim, 2019).

It is only later that a fourth element: 'governance', came out as the other crucial component of sustainability. Governance today symbolises not only peace and justice when associated with the concept of SD, but also represents the yardstick of sustainability action, empowerment and participation of civil society as main builders of a sustainable future. At this point, taking a global perspective the current interregional configuration of the world and the ambitious UN 2030 global agenda should help us to overcome the dichotomy between international legal boundaries and municipal ones under the old premise of 'our common future' where intra generational and intergenerational justice take form. In the age of globalisation, the separation between both spheres is withering somewhat, and it is within this context that cultural and educational concerns become crucial. Such concerns despite of not being considered elements of the sustainability concept are embedded into the notion as part of its intrinsic existence.

In effect to affirm that many civilisations of the world would have had no need for ecological movements if the 'western' way of production and consumption had not been imposed on certain local realities by global dynamics. These global dynamics have taken civilisations to overcome the traditional dichotomy between the international and the municipal legal sphere. Monitoring these changing aspects affecting adversely certain sectors of societies has been the main target of International Human Rights which have been a tough challenge considering our diversity and cultural traditions (Sen, 1999). Unfortunately, those have not emerged at the same speed as the westernised ways of living and production that have quickly spread over.[8]

Still the environment which is global by nature has helped to bridge cultural (with emphasis added) dialogues between different parts of the world creating scientific and normative dialogues among several cultures enshrining the functions of the Earth's ecological systems felt everywhere beyond any cultural identity. This is the cultural intrinsic nature of SD that I am assuming but hardly emerges. Unfortunately, cultural homogenisation has not only privileged ecological concerns, it has also favoured destructive behaviours. Today, as it was 'forecasted' by Schumacher (1973), what capitalism has achieved in terms of cultural 'homogenisation' no other movement has ever achieved! Although Schumacher was adopting a critical approach towards the way development policies were conducted, he would always

[8]On this argument, Sen (1999) in Chapter 6 of his book *Development as Freedom*, he makes a striking introduction of how honey collectors in the Bay of Bengal (at the southern edge of Bangladesh in India, where there is the Sundarban and lives the famous Royal Bengal tiger and famous also for its honey) risk their lives running the risk to be attacked by the (protected, in risk of extinction) Bengal tiger for the sake of their economic needs (fifty cents for selling a bottle of honey). Sen argues here how "it is not hard to feel that this force must outweigh other claims, including those of political liberties and civil rights".

admit that within a few decades most people over the world were going to live more or less as Western Europeans are living today.

'Developers' would bring to them the Western European 'cultural software'. Actually, Schumacher in his personal attempt to determine the best way to obtain reliable knowledge about the essentially indeterminate future argues that: "men would have to look steadily and calmly at the situation and seen it whole". Although for a long time this was not the norm, today there is growing awareness of the necessary systemic (or holistic) approach to reality and future generations' equity. In his important work *Small is Beautiful*, without a clear methodological premise, the author explains to the reader the advantages of 'creative freedom' necessary to approach the complex problem of development. In this affirmation is encompassed an entire bit of methodological foundations that surround 'sustainability' and its 'blurry' conceptual existence today.

I have not chosen Schumacher's book randomly but chose the same because of the highly inspiring approach of his work. The author devotes an entire chapter to one of the topics that is relevant for this book: Education. I believe it is necessary to analyse it briefly. The author starts his work *Small is Beautiful* by introducing the problem of production and he discusses how "one of the most fateful errors of our age is the belief that 'the problem of production' has been solved". A few lines after this assertion, there is a discussion about how this error arose, "so egregious and so firmly rooted is closely connected with the philosophical, not to say religious, changes during the last three or four centuries in man's attitude to nature". Therefore, in his view "the illusion of unlimited power, nourished by astonishing scientific and technological achievements, has produced the concurrent illusion of having solved the problem of production". He goes on to argue how we have inadequately dealt with our 'natural capital' without understanding that is not an expendable and easily replaceable commodity, as income would be and he takes the example of fossil fuels. Still, the same reasoning can be applied to all of the natural resources that our industrial system consumes. He wrote his book at the beginning of the nuclear era so he was surely trying to send a message to the world, that found had already fallen into the inability to recognise that the modern industrial system, with all its intellectual sophistication, would consume the resources on which it had been erected. Schumacher builds his whole argument, which could of course be criticised as radical or inappropriate, on his deep understanding of the failure of man to connect with nature and "cosmos", and this was and continues to be a cultural and education related problem.

Nevertheless, the way Schumacher shows "how to face the problems of our high speed industrialisation" by drawing on literature, philosophical thought, psychology, economic thought and self-intuition mixed with common sense seems the right approach to better understand the 'blurry' concept of sustainability engrained in our cultural narratives and it is of course a precedent for interdisciplinary notions of SD. Thus, I believe that an early starting point that contributes to the understanding of the multidisciplinary existence of 'sustainability' can be found in his work. He introduces the excesses of human and industrial production and the limits of the environment as necessary 'limiting principles'. He builds a discourse on the benefits of decentralisation, not command-and-control interventions, and small economic units as a specific application of the precautionary principle in the field of development to foster a notion of sustainability that resembles the legal concept embedded today within the governance mechanisms put forward by the Paris Agreement on Climate Change and the 2030 Agenda for Sustainable Development.[9]

In his "smallness", there is an attempt to guarantee that decentralised action will not generate ecological catastrophe. Schumacher's thought, emerged at a time when Western economies were just starting to struggle with the limits of their traditional production systems. This movement that started in the economic sciences, went on to permeate legal discourses by the proliferation of environmental activism which has not been happy with the UN instituted hierarchical and centralised approach to sustainability, based on the lowest 'common denominator" of environmental consensus and assuming interchangeably that sustainability is SD. The same can be said about the European Union context.

In effect as it is widely accepted today the UN transformed 'sustainability' into sustainable development despite of the fact that the former should not be confused with the latter, that is to say the normative version of sustainability: 'sustainable development'.[10] It might appear like hair-splitting semantics—Caradonna (2015) says but there have been some important differences between the concepts of sustainability and sustainable development since the beginning of their conceptual formulations. In fact, sustainable development (from now onwards SD) has been criticised for being a concept that favours classical economist thought based on growth.[11] In effect, development is seen as a synonymous with growth, and consequently sustainable development is improving (perfecting), but not challenging, continued economic growth. Under this light, it has been widely argued that the term suffers from specific conceptual pathologies: vagueness, suits pretenders and fosters misconceptions.

The truth is that a strong sustainability approach, (Bosselmann, 2008, p. 27) that often remains slightly outside the normative existence of 'sustainable development'[12] which is the one proclaimed mostly by United Nations International Agreements, has been generally claimed by those thinkers who mainstream earth systems' approach while fostering technical, programmatic, theoretical, or empirical solutions respecting the ecological limits of the planet earth; and this is so because among

[9]See resolution Adopted by the General Assembly on 25 September 2015-Transforming our World: The 2030 Agenda for Sustainable Development UN Doc GA/RES/70/1 (2015) (hereafter 2030 Agenda SD).

[10]The difference between the notions is addressed in the Third Chapter.

[11]See Worster (1994) and Victor (2008).

[12]Bosselmann (2010), p. 26, discusses that "if a worldwide awareness of environmental issues emerged in the 1970s, there was also the emergence of two directions of environmentalism that never reconciled their positions. On the one hand, the critique of the growth paradigm has inspired those who envisaged sustainability as the counter-model to economic dominance. On the other hand, connecting the 'environment' (sustainability) with 'development' (growth) found friends in all political camps".

some legal scholars' growing awareness on how environmental law and policies work, means to save some "trees", but not the "forest". The "forest" instead needs to be seen as a critical global issue including climate change and biodiversity loss provoked by our ecological footprint. Following this line of reasoning, some international lawyers (the number is growing today) make the case for a sustainability approach in law making that aims for "transformation" rather than environmental mitigation and fully embraces earth system approach (Viñuales, 2018; Kotzé & Kim, 2019).

Earth system approach offers an inclusive and deliberative scientific platform for scholars to convene around a critical global sustainability challenge (Kotzé & Kim, 2019) creating common knowledge about "organised human responses to earth system transformation, in particular the institutions and agents that cause global environmental change and the institutions, at all levels, that are created to steer human development in a way that secures a "safe" co-evolution with natural processes" (Bierman, 2007, p. 328).

Thus, "transformation" rather than "ecological damage" mitigation is the line of reasoning that should be suggested and it is part of this research plan. It is embedded in my methodological approach to analyse the 'cultural and educational challenges of the EU Sustainability Model'. A model that cannot be disconnected from the global ambitions of sustainability 'supporters' referring to those who care for a courageous 'transformation' for a sustainable future in their own spheres of action, namely theoretical, academic, domestic, activist, political, private, public, international, local, community, artistic, hidden and humble. There is space for everyone to make the case for transformation. Although I would like to say that I firmly believe that in the end, those who have the biggest responsibility today are 'educators'.

Culture and education have a vital role because they are essential instruments to empower and foster knowledge within civil society. Cultural expression, including artistic expression, is an important enabler of human development and well-being needed to fulfil the social aspects of sustainability goals. Future challenges for what it has recurrently been defined a 'successful sustainability model' (Giovanni, 2018) lie in the way we address cultural and educational issues that should help to re-connect human existence with the biosphere and the rest of humanity again.

Future laws and regulations, which should enhance our European sustainability model, must be focused on areas endorsing importance to culture and education law. For this purpose, law, like other disciplines are already doing should connect with earth system governance. Legal science role in earth system should overcome the current gap and try to understand and respond to the major implications of the transgressions of a human-dominated planet.

Therefore, lawyers should go beyond the idea of regulating individuals who act against the environment assuming that human activities will not change unless coerced by formal legal rules, and think in terms of deterrence, education and cultural shift to create a normative ground that fosters human shared responsibility for the planet earth and society. Thus, leaving aside the idealistic vision of education for the transformation of society and the world, I postulate an optimistic vision of our governance resources to build a bridge between earth system governance and all the scientific fields including the law.

We have reached the right *momentum* for disciplinary dialogues, systems thinking approach *tout court* and governance openness where the inclusion of a broad number of stakeholders gaining awareness of what each of us can do is possible by legal means. We just need more social and community engagement. Social science should be engaged with an educational transformation to help society to implement a different way of being citizens in the Anthropocene by taking up our shared social responsibilities.[13] Furthermore, we should aspire, on a political level, to drive environmental law beyond its 'coercing' role, reaffirming its value because of its broad subject (each person), broad objectives (the commons), and its wide space (global) (Bosselmann, 2010), and build a coalition between ecological policy concerns and educational and cultural issues intertwined at local and global context drawing the right balance between them and integrating the mandatory role of duties. I am not just talking about environmental and sustainability education, but referring to the necessary challenge of using legal instruments, even of a transdisciplinary nature to create the social 'consciousness' and responsibility needed to take care of the Planet on which we live. In this context, educational and cultural tools, ameliorated by legislative action, and the integration of both could foster 'transformative' action.

Turning my attention back to Schumacher's contribution, I would say that his work is useful for further understanding discussions regarding educational challenges. In Chapter 6 of *Small is Beautiful*, he speaks of what he calls and believes is the "greatest resource": education. To introduce the topic, he refers to the history of humankind who have lived and multiplied creating some form of culture and perishing.[14] He goes deep into discussing 'cultural structures' and he claims that they are just as needed as 'economic structures'. Cultural structures associated with development should necessarily be decentralised. Within such cultural structures, education is of paramount importance and becomes the most vital of all resources, arguing that "[i]f western civilisation is in state of permanent crisis, it is not farfetched to suggest that there may be something wrong with its education (. . .)".

Still lawyers who have traditionally been more focused on philosophical ideas of 'equity' and 'justiciability' and trying to grasp the slippery and blurry concept of sustainability for justiciability concerns have been incapable to address the crisis of our education and cultural institutions are going through. Legal scholarship has preferred to engage with the trend of innovating education agendas through uncritical approaches embracing the digital and technological needs of our era. However, legal scholars cannot be bystanders of educational challenges anymore, especially public lawyers. The whole value of their contribution lies in their 'functionality' as drafters of a set of rules that could foster the 'shift' that humans need to live in

[13]See further, Farrell (2011).

[14]On this line of thinking, I suggest the reading of *Collapse: How societies choose to fail or succeed*, Jared Diamond (2005).

harmony with nature and society at large, and embed a value system that does not contradict that.

Therefore, considering that my research agenda has chosen the European context to illustrate the challenges of what is widely believed to be a successful sustainability model. We must be able to read thorough the lines that 'successful' does not mean 'sufficient'. A critical overview for improvement is shown but this work needs to be continued. The work is an attempt to illustrate how to improve it by promoting changes at the foundations of its 'cultural structure' that should accordingly influence educational standards, and the chosen case studies offer faithful evidence.

The European sustainability model as it stands today is attached to a distinctive set of notions (cultural software) that can be considered intrinsic to the model. They belong to the so-called "European Cosmology" legacy (Bahro, 1994). What does this "European Cosmology legacy" include and bring to the European Sustainability Model? Bosselmann (2010) simplifies well what the German philosopher Rudolf Bahro termed the "European cosmology" including: "dualism, anthropocentrism, materialism, atomism, greed and economism". Such characteristics of modernity in Western Europe must be overcome somehow. Thus, there are of course significant cultural and educational challenges to face but there are many solutions out there too. Without a 'cultural structure' in Schumacher's sense within the context of development (in a broad sense) we cannot expect the transformation we need.[15]

Ecological considerations have invaded the economic and political scenarios easily for their transversal nature, their connection to growth and their vital connection with human life, these are all the aspects that sustainability integrates. The Earth system approach and its natural resources have added a source of a more proactive discussion about sustainability, because whilst environmentalism has triggered the defensive action of our Planet, sustainability has the mission to spell out future solutions to avoid degradation and empower every human being to find singular or cooperative solutions. That is why governance and knowledge empowerment through cultural and educational structures play an important role for systemic change.

Today with the prolific scientific contribution in the fields of climate change, technology advancements, urban studies and population and migration studies all embedded within the same paradigm shift it is impossible not to accept that we must break silos and go beyond disciplinary approaches to look for solutions. Things are changing, indicators of economic well-being that neoclassical economists have 'unthinkingly' used for decades are no longer employable.[16] It is impossible not to converge with interdisciplinary and transdisciplinary approaches to help broaden our own 'disciplinary' vision and look for solutions to urgent problems.

---

[15]Inspired by the idea developed by Göpel (2016).

[16]However, we will come to this later when we address the international scenario fostering the re-endorsement of the value of education and culture as instrumental yardsticks for a sustainable future (see Chap. 4).

2.3 Missing Narrative on the Role of Law in the Concept of SD

There is a missing narrative about the consideration of law as an additional component of SD, and this might happen because there is already a broaden assumption of 'sustainability' as a normative (not legal- emphasis added) concept after Brundtland addressing many different policy goals not necessarily caring of how law engrains there. Still, it is important to discuss the conceptual implications that this missing narrative has for the evolution of SD as it is today. I am not choosing a particular conceptual understanding of SD that can be criticised from leaving out important components if we consider the widely accepted tripartite assumption of its existence, with the addition of the 'governance' component, described above and the intrinsic cultural and educational factors.

Lawyers have been more worried with the duty to protect and restore the integrity of the Earth's ecological systems, rather than claiming a prevalent position of law in the sustainability temple considering as we have already said, that the key action principle of SD is the integrated decision making that is supported by a handful of existing legal principles. It has indeed been argued that the straightforward nature of this principle "facilitates its employment by decision makers at every level: public, private, global, national, regional or local" (Dernbach & Cheever, 2015). The integration principle has played a pivotal role in the EUSM. Some could discuss that 'integration' is not a hallmark of SD but a characteristic inherent to any development or management model dealing with environmental issues. I believe, instead, that one of the legal values of the whole paradigm lies in the way SD seeks to integrate the legal with the political, economic, ecological, and institutional arrangements to deal with the problems of the world, whichever way it is done. In this light, the legal element through the integration principle can indeed insert empowerment mechanisms that might be lacking when addressing issues of misrepresentation, marginalisation and injustice.

However, if we look at all the complexities surrounding our economic, political and social crisis, we must in the end conclude that law plays an essential role, but in reality is not sufficient even in the realm of justice if not in dialogue with culture, education policy, politics, economy, science, etc. This being the case, it is indeed crucial to understand how worrying it is that there is no real interests to tackle the challenges posed by culture and education as tools for development by legal scholarship. Nobody has dealt with the relevance of a legal reform to unbundle the potential of education and culture as transformative agents of society with important social benefits.

Still, Culture has been considered a fourth pillar of sustainability but the discussion has not found resonance in legal scholarship[17] or legal narratives. Moreover, we

[17]On this, see, "Culture: Fourth Pillar of Sustainable Development", Agenda 21, *Local Governments safeguarding culture for future generations*, retrieved from UNESCO, http://www.agenda21culture.net; and Hawkes (2001).

all know how prolific has been the field of environmental education and subsequent evolutions: Sustainable development education and education for sustainability (UN Decade for of Education for Sustainable Development). Some experts of the field have even addressed the key aspects of the insufficient approach of implanting SD education into school programs despite of its benefits (Jucker & Mathar, 2015). In this light, some authors touch upon the need for a real-world change towards sustainability and the necessary openness of educational processes that prove to be inadequate if they are not facilitated by cultural processes, economic facilities, institutional and legal reforms.

A concluding important concern concerning the legal narrative of SD has to do with definitions. Legal instruments need definitions that is why I am happy to advance the idea of 'future generations' and 'ecological integrity of planet earth'[18] as the main axes of my conceptual understanding of SD. Although I have to emphasise that the belief on perceiving environmental, economic and social aspects as equally important elements of sustainability would be an obstacle to achieving social and economic justice either at a global or local level. An ecological prevalence is always needed and it is a premise that should be advanced by our constitutional principles and embedded in the horizontal legal dimension. In fact, not by chance, the overarching importance of law and legal instruments to support the ecological prevalence has instead been addressed within Anthropocene discussions and as part of the Earth system approach in the global governance context (Kotzé & Kim, 2019).

These discussions are relevant because unsustainability and intergenerational injustice are at stake in our current liberal democracies inserting a particular model of economic growth, as an almost irrefutable fact. Actually legal systems have helped to transform natural resources and common holdings into commodities and then into capital, and our laws are still protecting (or allowing) the freedom of extraction. Therefore, if we accept this, we accept that the transforming role under sustainability premises is crucial because law is already transforming capital into social and cultural commons (Capra & Mattei, 2015) and law has a strong potential for change in connection with other systems. This is the legal element of the sustainability paradigm that cannot be understood disconnected from the social, economic and ecological. Our industrialised, globalised world has reached a level of complexity that renders it impossible to believe a unique solution as a feasible panacea for all our problems. However, an irrefutable axiom is that planet Earth needs urgent solutions and an effort on behalf of each and every one of us to establish a valid connection with it that does not undermine its protection, even if it is mainstreamed by global plans. Every one of us is essential and the legal aspects of sustainability have created the right foundations for this. The Paris Agreement is an important evidence of this passage.

[18]The draft Global Pact for the Environment embeds the ecological integrity in its Articles 2 and 18. Article 2 provides states, institutions, and individuals to take care of the environment in a way that everyone would contribute "to the conservation, protection and restoration of the integrity of the Earth's ecosystems".

Our approach to the field should look for new paths to redesign legal and institutional intervention allowing future generations 'access' to justice and building the normative basis for a major intervention in intrinsic but neglected aspects of sustainability. The cultural and educational realms empower present and future generations to re-connect with society, equity, justice and with nature. The benchmark should be "transforming" our sometimes disconnected world. A world disconnected from nature, from people, from communities, from our different realities.

This is why, if any existing and valid theoretical approach is to be suggested to help legal discourses connect better with educational and cultural ones under the premises of sustainability, this must be the 'Habermasian' theory of deliberative democracy (1996) or Sen (1999) understanding of democracy through the lens of public deliberation. However, it is outside the scope of my analyses to go in depth into Habermas' egregious and massive theoretical constructions, nor Sen's theoretical approach. It suffices to explain here that I make the case for such valid overarching theories of society and social change, combined with analyses of the problems facing late capitalist societies when trying to set SD into a theoretical panorama that can be applied to the complex process of globalisation and internationalisation,[19] and most recently to contrast the growth of 'populism' and 'radical sovereign' approaches which are enemies of the European supranational entity.

I believe that a communication-theoretical approaches can continue to lend a certain plausibility to the democratic promise of inclusion that sustainability fosters, that is to say, the participation of all citizens in the political process (whatever their reach) valid for a sustainable path. Even at a global level. In effect, the deliberative politics approach has been taken as valid to be applied in educational theoretical approaches to postulate alternative solutions through existing knowledge structures.[20] Notwithstanding, Habermas' deliberative theory has not been so far-reaching in the educational field (despite its appropriateness) because he has referred to broader social learning processes as becoming institutionalised (Habermas, 2015). Habermas' deliberative-theory is useful because within the context of SD the relationship between education, civil society, the state, culture, critical thinking and accountability all become relevant and interact.[21] This theory reinforces the integration of participatory instruments, institutional reforms seizing educational challenges, or simply strengthens equity in the education realm, access

---

[19]For a different conceptual approach within the context of overlapping legalities, see further, Palombella (2017).

[20]See further, Murphy (2010).

[21]In my opinion, Habermas (1996) provides a quite moderate theoretical view valid within the European normative context to validate a normative grounding under the paradigm of SD that embraces a social critique in which the maintenance of state political agendas, alongside the ability of capitalism to exploit new avenues for wealth creation are not valid any longer, because they have resulted in more and more decisions affecting the lives of citizens being based on the bottom line of power and capitalist instruments, and of course detrimental to nature. On a more recent discussion, see, Habermas (2015).

to justice mechanisms, information and communication processes, as well as transparency. Nonetheless, all this is arguable and open to further discussion.

2.4 Is It the End of Disciplinary Approaches? Breaking Silos into the Legal Domain

> Philosophy recovers itself when it ceases to be a device for dealing with problems of philosophers and becomes a method, cultivated by philosophers, for dealing with the problem of men.[22]

Apparently, it would seem difficult to contradict Newton's adage: "Truth is ever to be found in the simplicity, not in the multiplicity and confusion of things" (Newton, 1974). His scientific contributions, still valid and highly relevant today, would not lead anyone to doubt such an affirmation. Still, knowledge following simplification has become compartmentalised and experts are often unable to think through challenges that go beyond their area of expertise.

What has sustainability science—non-existent at the time of Newton's laws—brought to the history of thought? First, the concept of sustainability refers to a growing human awareness about the finite condition of natural resources. This 'process of awakening' (especially since 1992) has led to the creation of a naturally interdisciplinary field of research involving transdisciplinary interactions, which are commonly referred to today as 'sustainability sciences' (Fernandes & Philippi, 2017).[23] Thus, sustainability developed as a social paradigm and as field of knowledge involving diverse areas of knowledge.

The term sustainability (within this scientific field) implies the bringing together of scientific approaches coming from biology, physics, chemistry, and hydrological processes, among others, with social, political and economic problems of management at various level, including, urban and rural, as well as public and private contexts. Furthermore, beyond this diversity of themes, it simultaneously covers a global scale with a systemic focus (Fernandes & Philippi, 2017). The validity of this method lies in its cooperative model approach (leaving behind hegemonic scientific approaches), as well as in the recognition of the importance of the articulation of

[22]Dewey (1980).

[23]These authors refer to the field as 'sustainability sciences' although they argue that field emerged as sustainability science and "it was proposed by Kates et al. (2001), with a focus on the interactions between nature and society and with the aim of having integrated contributions from different disciplines to sustainability. However, the design results in a fundamental contradiction: Is it possible to outline a science of sustainability? What topics (subjects) would compose it?" There are two options: (1) designing a sustainability science to define which topics to include for its composition; or conversely (2) starting from the range of topics necessary for its analysis, considering the various science needed. The first option (1) assumes the configuration of a sustainability science. The second (2) involves a research field composes of various sciences and technologies, as well as humanities, altogether making the sustainability sciences.

non-scientific forms of knowledge applied to research problems, especially at the local level, comprising data and practice alongside a variety of issues.

Initially, sustainability offered a systemic approach based on the assumption that the knowledge that global problems in the geological era of the Anthropocene required policy intervention to sustain human and natural systems and their linkages. Now it is bringing to the fore a shift in scientific methodologies and challenging the ability of single disciplines to offer simple solutions to complex problems. Civil society itself is increasingly interacting with science and societal challenges. Thus, it would not be wrong to admit that transdisciplinary approaches, by offering the possibility of collaborative solutions from different scientific fields together with civil society stakeholders, and systemic approaches with a holistic understanding of reality, have become the instrument to foster 'mindshifts' generating changes within society in a successful manner (Göpel, 2016). Such methodological approaches, mainstreamed mostly but not only, by sustainability science, have been facilitated by the introduction of solid governance mechanisms at the policy level based on bottom-up approaches and collaborative mechanisms fostering a primary role for action for civil society.

It is not the end of disciplines at all, but it is also true that future challenges need 'a broad picture' to draft solutions. In fact, concrete environmental problems, or simply real-world problems, have been in the last decade at the centre of the integrative and collaborative research. "Transdisciplinary research is a family of concepts and approaches that aims at better fitting academic knowledge production to societal needs for solving, mitigating or preventing problems such as environmental pollutions, poverty, violence, and so on. It strives to grasp the relevant complexity of a problem, taking into account the diversity of both, every day and academic perceptions of problems, linking abstract and case-specific knowledge and developing descriptive, normative and transformative knowledge for the common interest" (Pohl, Truffer, & Hirsch-Hadorn, 2017).

The term "transdisciplinary research", already introduced a few decades ago in 1970 by a Club of Rome member, Erich Jantsch, to explain how the notion that "inherited scientific knowledge needs frequent confrontations with the 'real world' in order to test, amend and form new assumptions. Only with such an approach would science support the ability of a society to continually self-regenerate" (Göpel, 2016). Of course, this is an approach that "breaks with the dominant positivist paradigm whose goal and premise it is that universally true 'laws' governing human behaviour and natural evolution can be identified and fit into quantitative models and experiments with which future developments can be predicted and managed" (Göpel, 2016). Transdisciplinary research differs completely from the dominant positivist paradigm and follows a path to face challenges in which concepts and hypotheses at a scientific level are divided into assumptions that are epistemological, ontological, methodological and very often, in the context of social sciences axiological, embedding choices claiming to be the right solution. The definition we give to those various aspects will determine a particular outcome that could be interpreted very differently.

The Paris Agreement, as we will see, is an International agreement introducing binding and innovative (collaborative) ways to approach global problems. It is a milestone for the involvement of researchers of different disciplines, representatives of civil society and the private and public sectors involved in research and policy processes. It has introduced a governance approach outside the traditional process of drafting a "top-down" one-size-fits-all agreement. The same can be said of the 2030 Agenda for Sustainable Development.[24] After decades of seemingly ineffective efforts in climate policy and other sustainability related issues world leaders have started to think about how to proceed by going beyond traditional modes of thinking in governance and scientific approaches (transdisciplinarity). The Intergovernmental Panel on Climate Change (IPCC) had already foreseen in 2012 "the altering of fundamental attributes of a system (including value systems; regulatory, legislative, or bureaucratic regimes; financial institutions; and technological or biological systems" (IPCC, 2012, p. 5). This is at the heart of a systems thinking approach that is dominating discourses in sustainability science today (mainly). Still, not everyone within the transformation research community works with a transdisciplinary approach. Göpel argues, and rightly so, that this combination of a wide array of scientific disciplines, is still sorting out where exactly the paradigm agreement lies. The only thing that is clear is the assumption that there is a rejection of the dominant positivist epistemology and ontology which was founded in mainstream understandings of sustainability standing exclusively in contrast with economic growth.

Conventional understandings of problems have opened the door to discussions about Earth system boundaries, as well as interconnected and complex problems that should transcend the idea of reducing such problems to a single or combined domain solution (the classical economic approach has been the leading epistemological discourses). Neither regulation or environmental legislation, nor what conventional economics have to offer would provide the solution that the Earth and its citizens require. Hence, as it has already been suggested, a 'shift', especially in our 'minds', to incorporate the insights of earth systems whilst there is an increasing awareness of the risks posed by the Anthropocene, should lead to a fundamental transformation of policy discourses and their theoretical frameworks introducing a new way of thinking. Research interest in sustainability transformations is growing across a range of problem domains and (inter) disciplinary perspectives, this is, energy systems, food systems, urban systems, etc...[25] There is room for further evolution, especially in the underexplored fields of culture and education. However, it can be expected in the following years. This contribution wants to trigger further research on the field from the legal science domain. Legal scholarship should take part of this 'shift' and should take the opportunity of breaking down its own 'silos' to be part of the attempt to support a sustainable future, although it is easier said than done.

---

[24]See resolution Adopted by the General Assembly on 25 September 2015-Transforming our World: The 2030 Agenda for Sustainable Development UN Doc GA/RES/70/1 (2015) (hereafter 2030 Agenda SD).

[25]See further on this, Patterson et al. (2017).

In the field of law, things have not been different from other scientific areas. The history of Western legal thought has been deeply influenced by the fundamental transformations of science. Newton's laws of motion and his mechanistic model brought such fundamental transformation in science that influenced the whole of Western legal thought (Capra & Mattei, 2015). With Newton, in fact, the conception of the universe as and ordered, harmonious, living whole disappeared from the theoretical horizon of his time. The mechanistic approach and its notion of the laws of nature inevitably influenced Western legal thought. In fact, "the ancient holistic vision of the world *Kósmos*, of the Earth as a generous gift of God to humankind as a whole and abundant commonwealth collectively accessible by all, was replaced by humanist emphasis on the individual and human reason, which resulted in a mechanistic legal vision known as rationalist natural law" (Capra & Mattei, 2015).

Modern and postmodern legal thought are of course still influenced by scientific transformations. The complexities of today's reality have greatly increased as have the population and the risks to the planet, but the interplay between scientific domains has always followed the same pattern. This means that the most recent paradigm shift brought about by scientific contributions in the fields of physics, geology, biology, climatology, and so on, is undoubtedly influencing legal sciences thought. Capra and Mattei (2015) argue that the paradigm shift has drastically changed from the mechanistic and reductionist worldview of Descartes and Newton to a systemic and ecological worldview. This has taken place over the last three decades. This discovery has put forward that the material world, ultimately, is a network of inseparable patterns of relationships, that the planet as a whole is a living, self-regulating system. The accomplishment of the work developed by Capra & Mattei, (2015), explaining through the evolution of science how Western legal thought has been influenced, lies in advancing four main points: (1) old scientific approaches, like the mechanistic scientific approach that has been useful to humanity, can continue to serve us, for instance the principles of Newtonian physics can still be used to build a bridge, but the limitations of the approach are becoming increasingly clear, particularly in relation to social sciences, in general, and law, in particular; (2) the second valid conclusion of their theory on the 'Ecology of Law', is that assuming such a systemic, ecological Paradigm we must rethink the most intimate structure of law to reflect the basic principles of ecology and the new systemic thinking of contemporary science; (3) Why is this so relevant to legal science? The authors all assert something that is pertinent to me: "The legal order is the most important vehicle through which a worldview is enforced and transformed into social action, and thus human law is also the agency through which we may implement new ideas and values. We must rethink our human laws and their relationship with the laws governing the ecology of a living planet"; (4) Following their whole reasoning: Law is what is deemed law by civic and legal communities and it actually depends on the human interpretation of social reality (Capra & Mattei, 2015, p. 12). Therefore, the law within this paradigm should imitate natural strategies of long-term ecological survival (i.e. reduction of waste, consumption, production).

Apart from such isolated instances, legal scholarship has refrained itself from indicating theoretical roadmaps of a transdisciplinary nature according to which to operate, so through this study, I try to give an account of where we are and what we could build by breaking silos into our academic domain, by triggering transdisciplinary discussions, that every academic approach should incorporate to find applicable solutions or just by being creative as every scientist should be in concomitance with our complex realities, especially when it comes to facing challenges that concern culture and education.

The world is changing quickly. There is an increasing need to understand the complexities going beyond disciplinary boundaries to contribute to building the spectrum of solutions to face such different challenges. I believe that sustainability, education and culture are cases in which monodisciplinary study would not provide many answers for the multifaceted realities they underpin. On top of that, I believe that culture and education are major challenges beneath the necessary shift we need for a sustainable future, but policy makers should become more aware of that and react to this.

Consequently, there is of course 'not the end' of disciplines yet, but interdisciplinarity, multidisciplinarity, transdisciplinarity and the necessary bond between every science with philosophical thought outside the boundaries of theoretical problems, to say the least, is still fairly underexploited, mainly in legal sciences. Educational and cultural challenges behind our sustainability model need creative approaches and policy interventions boosting long-term solutions, initially at both normative and regulatory level. I agree with the idea that a "rapidly growing transdisciplinary transformation research community could become instrumental in helping to use such 'window' strategically".[26] It means that the methodology I will be following here will range widely across disciplines, in an attempt to consciously advocate for changes in our cultural structures and pedagogical approaches to bring to life a resilient (strong) EU Sustainability Model with robust capacities to hail future generations' and intra-generations' needs, and discuss eventual (or forgotten) transformative policy approaches. Using the term 'transformative' is a choice following the wording of our 2030 Global Agenda on Sustainable Development, I will sometimes refer to transition too, but this terminology should not be associated (even if it could be in line with the epistemological approach) with specific conceptual approaches found in social sciences.[27]

---

[26]Göpel (2016), p. 16. Maja argues the positive side of accepting such transdisciplinary approaches when analysing 'sustainable development' considering that they promise "the most telling insights into how the infamous integration of ecological, social and economic dimensions of development can be achieved in practice".

[27]See for instance the conceptual milestone work on 'International Sustainability Transitions' leaded by Grin, Rotmans, and Schot (2010). See further on this, Göpel (2016), she addresses the conceptual differences between transition and transformation approaches in a brilliant manner. Instead, for a more recent work on the notion of transformation more akin to the present work see further, Patterson et al. (2017).

References

Bahro, R. A. (1994). In P. Jenkins (Ed.), *Avoiding social and ecological disaster: The politics of World transformation: An inquiry into the foundations of spiritual and ecological politics*. Bath: Gateway. D. Translator; Translated.

Bierman, F. (2007). Earth System Governance' as a crosscutting theme of global change research. *Global Environmental Change, 17*, 326–337.

Bosselmann, K. (2008). *The principle of sustainability. Transforming law and Governance*. Farnham: Ashgate.

Bosselmann, K. (2010). Loosing the forest for the trees: Environmental reductionism in the law. *Sustainability, 2*(8), 2424–2448. Retrieved from: https://doi.org/10.3390/su2082424

Capra, F., & Mattei, U. (2015). *The ecology of law. Toward a legal system in tune with nature and community*. San Francisco: Berrett-Koehler Publishers, Inc.

Caradonna, J. L. (2015). *Sustainability. A history*. Oxford: Oxford University Press.

Dernbach, J. C., & Cheever, F. (2015). Sustainable development and its discontents. *Transnational Environmental Law, 4*(2), 247–287.

Dewey, J. (1980). The need for a recovery of philosophy. In J. A. Boydston (Ed.), *The Middle Works, 1916–197* (Vol. 10, p. 46). Carbondale: Southern Illinois UP.

Farrell, G. (2011). Towards a Europe of shared social responsibilities: Challenges and strategies. In *Trends in social cohesion, No. 23*. Strasbourg: Council of Europe Publications.

Fernandes, V., & Philippi, A. (2017). Sustainability sciences: Political and epistemological approaches. In R. Frodeman (Ed.), *The Oxford handbook of interdisciplinarity* (2nd ed.). Oxford: Oxford University Press.

Giovanni, E. (2018). Utopia Sostenibile. editoriale Laterza.

Göpel, M. (2016). *The Great Mindshift. How a new economic paradigm and sustainability transformations go hand in hand*. Cham: Springer.

Grin, J., Rotmans, J., & Schot, J. (2010). *Transitions to sustainable development: New directions in the study of long term transformative change*. Abingdon: Routledge.

Habermas, J. (1996). *Between facts and norms*. Cambridge: MIT Press. (second printing, the original was edited in 1992 by Suhrkamp Verlag).

Habermas, J. (2015). *The lure of technocracy*. Cambridge: Polity Press.

Hawkes, J. (2001). *The Fourth Pillar of Sustainability. Culture's essential role in public planning*, edited by common ground publishing Pty Ltd. in association with the Cultural Development Network (Vic).

Humphreys, M. (2017). *Sustainable development in the European Union. A general principle*. Abingdon: Routledge.

IPCC. (2012). In C. B. Field, V. Barros, T. F. Stocker, D. Quin, D. J. Dokken, K. L. Ebi, M. D. Mastrandea, K. J. Mach, G.-K. Plattner, S. K. Allen, M. Tignor, & P. M. Midgley (Eds.), *Managing the risks of extreme events and diasasters to advance climate change adaptation*. New York: Cambridge Unviersity Press.

Jucker, R., & Mathar, R. (Eds.). (2015). *Schools for sustainable development in Europe. Concepts, policies and educational experiences at the end of the UN decade of education for sustainable development*. Berlin: Springer.

Kabblers, J., & Palombella, L. (2019). *The challenge of inter-legality*. Cambridge: Cambridge University Press.

Kates, R. W., et al. (2001). Sustainability science. *Science, 29*(5517), 641–642.

Kotzé, L. J., & Kim, R. E. (2019). Earth system law: The juridical dimensions of earth system governance. *Earth System Governance, 1*, 100003.

Murphy, F. (Ed.). (2010). *Habermas critical theory and education*. Abingdon: Routledge.

Newton, I. (1974). (1687) fragment quoted from Manuel, F. E, "Fragments from a Treatise on Revelation". In *The Religion of Isaac Newton*. Oxford: Clarendon Press.

Palombella, L. (2017). *Interlegality and justice*. Available at SSRN: https://ssrn.com/abstract=3066001

Patterson, J., Schulz, V., Van der Hel, S., Widerberg, A., Hurlbert, A., & Sethi, B. (2017). Exploring the governance and politics of transformations towards sustainability. *Environmental Innovation and Societal Transitions, 24*, 1–16.
Pohl, C., Truffer, B., & Hirsch-Hadorn, G. (2017). Addressing wicked problems through transdisciplinary research. In *The Oxford handbook of interdisciplinarity* (2nd ed.). Oxford: Oxford University Press.
Pope Francis, I. (2015). *Laudato Si'. On care for Our Common Home [Encyclical].*
Schumacher, E. F. (1973). *Small is beautiful. Economics as if people mattered.* New York: Harper Collins.
Sen, A. (1999). *Development as freedom.* New York: Anchor Books.
Victor, P. (2008). *Managing without growth: Slower by design, not disaster.* Cheltenham: Edward Elgar Publishing.
Viñuales, J. E. (2018). The organisation of the anthropocene: In our hands? *Brill Research Perspectives in International Legal Theory and Practice, 1*, 1–81.
Worster, D. (1994). *Nature's economy: A history of ecological ideas* (2nd ed.). Cambridge: Cambridge University Press.

Chapter 3
The European Sustainability Model: From the Global Governance Scenario to the European Picture 'Integrating' Intergenerational Justice and Accessible Governance Mechanisms

Abstract This chapter begins by distinguishing the conceptual scope of sustainability and sustainable development that are used interchangeably. It contains a short historical overview of the notion questioning its capacity to foster social and ecological justice whilst economic growth ambitions are in general disdained. The need for a systemic ecological transition has taken International scholars most recently to make ultimate efforts to recast the importance of law in the Anthropocene by joining alternative analytical frameworks relating to the 'earth systems' approach. The analysis includes a brief account of some of those critical views contrasting normative versions of sustainability based on interdisciplinary views (see Sect. 3.2). After such global contextualisation that finds broad consensus with UN 2030 Global Agenda, the chapter presents the European Union Sustainability Model (EUSM) (see Sect. 3.3.1). This unique model is characterised by a drastic evolution of environmental protection law developing into a more emblematic multidimensional version of 'sustainable development' that is already part of the European identity despite of its social concerns weaknesses (see Sect. 3.3.2). Attention is then drawn to the education and cultural policies as key areas gaining increasing interest and defining important aspects of the social policy dimension of the EUSM that is reinforced by its emblematic constitutional framework (see Sects. 3.3.3 and 3.3.4). The chapter ends by addressing governance mechanisms and making the case for the commons supporting intergenerational justice (see Sects. 3.3.4 and 3.3.5).

3.1 A Brief History About Sustainability and Sustainable Development

In *The Ecology of Law. Toward a Legal System in Tune with Nature and Community*,[1] authors Fritjof Capra and Ugo Mattei introduce their work with a compelling story about the unfortunate consequences provoked by the Nile perch[2] to other

[1]See further, Capra and Mattei (2015).

[2]The Nile perch is among the largest of freshwater fish, capable of achieving a length of more than 6 feet and a weight of more than 400 pounds.

M. D. Sánchez Galera, *Educational and Cultural Challenges of the European Sustainability Model*, https://doi.org/10.1007/978-3-030-38716-7_3

species whenever is taken away from its native waters in the sub-Sahara to other rivers. In fact, it was introduced by humans to Lake Victoria for commercial harvest causing the disappearance of most of the endemic species in the lake.[3]

What do we actually mean when we speak of sustainability? Considering how the scientific literature in the last decades has been prolific in this topic, it would be impossible not to limit the scope of my answer to a particular field of reference. In any case the influence of the Brundtland report (1987) on the conceptual normative evolution of the term in every scientific field is undisputed.[4]

If concepts are important to understand the scope and grasp of legal regulations, the concept of sustainability should be considered within the context of environmental sustainability by no means the hard bone of the field. Not only in terms of its justiciability, also in terms of tracing an orthodox disciplinary approach to its multidimensional content. As we will see 'sustainability' and 'sustainable development' are not only important concepts *per se*, but as I will try to illustrate they have also become a 'transformative' paradigm. In the context of Europe, the sustainability paradigm has coined a (development) model introducing into the EU constitutional dimension the principle of 'intergenerational justice'.[5]

Contexts play an important role in the production of meaning. In fact, contexts are highly relevant in general, but in particular in the field of sustainability when approaching cultural and educational concerns. Having studied hundreds of scholarly works about fundamental changes in science, society and the world I have come to the conclusion that, although sometimes neglected, the paradigm shift of this century has an important cultural and educational dimension in which the legal factor plays a crucial role. This can at first be overlooked by either legal scientists or layman indistinctively. It is not by chance that we constantly neglect the invisible "laws" of nature. Perhaps this is mirrored in our limited understanding of the nature of law.

Still, going through bibliographical and legal literature I have also examine how legal instruments and legal scientist have hardly broken silos to come out from their legal domain to understand the multiple dimensions of 'Law and Sustainability' and make the attempt to craft necessary solutions through the language of a normative framework in our complex societies. On this constant and pressing search to craft new solutions there has been a recent recast of the role of law in the Anthropocene by welcoming earth systems approach and embracing the affirmation that "earth system is endowed with unique characteristics and geophysical conditions to support life" (Young & Steffen, 2009).

---

[3]Capra and Mattei (2015) in their text make reference to the excellent documentary by Hubert Sauper, *Darwin's Nightmare*. Sauper made this story known to a wide public in 2004. Another wonderful documentary by same author would come out some years later to denounce the enthralling topic of land grabbing in African countries.

[4]"*Sustainable development is development that meets the needs of the present without compromising the ability of future generations to meet their own needs*" (Brundtland, 1987).

[5]On this topic, see further Chap. 4, Sect. 4.3.1.

The lack of human awareness on how we are extracting our natural resources and the environmental impacts without considerations of 'systems limits' has leaded to unsustainable trajectories of the earth system (Randhir, 2011). Our legal and economic systems have backed up those extracting trajectories. Fortunately, some lawyers, international lawyers at first hand seem to be increasingly aware of these assertions and they have already been questioning the capacity of the concept of sustainable development to stabilise social reproduction and foster global justice (Cardesa-Salzmann & Cocciolo, 2019). Furthermore, over the past decade 'earth system governance'[6] has matured into a full-fledged and autonomous research agenda gathering together a scientific platform and convening around a complex global sustainability schedule that offers "organised human responses to earth system transformation, in particular the institutions and agents that cause global environmental change and the institutions, at all levels, that are created to steer human development in a way that secures a "safe" co-evolution with natural processes" (Biermann, 2007, p. 328).

Growing awareness on the failure of the interwoven regulatory regimes has foster the will to grasp the real meaning of the role of law in sustainability. Moreover, this has taken legal scholarship to broaden the 'theoretical' and governance narratives of law in relation to the Anthropocene, although still quite timidly. For international environmental lawyers sustainability and sustainable development have already bridged the path for discourses of planetary and interdisciplinary importance (Cardesa-Salzmann & Cocciolo, 2019). This is surely, because despite of different contextual discussions—considering the world differences—the ecological heart of the planet is also at the heart of the most relevant scientific discussions. In addition, the wellness of the planet earth has been the focus of multilateral agreements for decades, and in fact, it is the area of International law that has reached more easily global consensus, even if eventual problems of environmental relevance have a different meaning depending on the geopolitical context where they arise.

Whatever way, John Gillroy (2006) has suggested that sustainability "has emerged as the core concept of the current environmental debate within international law" and this is already a cliché. However, as we shall see further on this discussion, regardless of being the core concept of international legal debate this has not been a guarantee for a legal recognition of the term from the judiciary system *tout court*, especially considering its multidimensional aspects triggering equity and other social justice concerns. It has not even become a tool for hermeneutical interpretation in the judge's hands. Although the *momentum* for global environmental law in which sustainability occupies a chief position has arrived. Nowadays, an infinite list of regulatory topics touch upon analytical frameworks of regulatory and institutional nature engaging sustainability concerns.

The conceptual issues surrounding the sustainability paradigm and the challenges posed by the international context, the so-called global context have inevitably influenced the constitutional existence of sustainability in the EU and have spelled

---

[6]See further, Kotzé (2019).

out the basic content of its current normative reality. Specifically, global environmental law instruments, which are placed within the context of interactions between a plurality of legal orders,[7] as well as its deployed governance mechanisms, are extremely relevant today to face the cultural and educational challenges of sustainability in Anthropocene (we are assuming that we have entered a new era).[8]

In reality, a myriad of different topics that were not necessarily interrelated have come at stake under the premises of sustainability creating synergies among their different but already interconnected scientific discourses to implement laws and public policies capable of providing the right protection and implementation mechanisms towards the attainment of sustainable development in Europe as in other parts of the world. This is, climate change and the Paris Agreement, energy transition and the different multilateral agreements touching upon specific energy aspects, environmental procedural rights, economic growth in a sustainable manner and corporate social responsibility, agriculture, land management, sustainable procurement, sustainable education, urban development, cultural heritage protection, financial instruments, etc.

My attention is to give a brief account of some doctrinal discussions around the conceptual aspects of sustainability associated to the global legal order that has determined the synergies among the different sectorial political concerns and have shaped the unique sustainability model of the EU.

At first instance, it is important to draw a line of differentiation between the two concepts that, represent the core of my analysis and are usually confused or used by the public in general interchangeably: 'sustainability' and 'sustainable development' (SD).

The term 'sustainable' has indeed become ubiquitous. However, "Sustainability" precedes sustainable development and it pre-dates the late-twentieth century concept of "sustainable development".[9] Sustainability is not a trendy invention of our era, and it is not a normative framework born to hamper the bad side effects of what Rifkin (2011) calls the third Industrial revolution, the smart era. "Sustainability" focuses on the "capacity for humans to live within environmental constraints"

---

[7]Philosophical discourses about the world being a pluralist place have been discussed by different legal scholars, such as Neil Walker (2015) and Krisch (2010), with different conclusions and increasingly leaving behind strong epistemological discussions based on the search of global unity through constitutional ideals. See further the most recent theoretical discussions on this topic in, Klabbers and Palombella (2019).

[8]The contemporary debate about nature and the human influence in relation to nature has been marked by the rise of a geological hypothesis that has rapidly gained steam outside the natural sciences realm, namely, that of the Anthropocene. According to the "Anthropocene" the Earth's physical change (this is, biodiversity, climate, and so on) is mainly driven by human activity. We are, of course, the main drivers of our global-scale environmental disorder. For further analyses on this topic, see, Arias Maldonado (2015).

[9]Bosselmann (2004), pp. 62–75

(Robinson, 2004, p. 370), and the heart of the concept is the respect for ecological limits and ecological integrity.

It is important to remark that Sustainability pre-dates the normative character of "Sustainable development" whose existence belongs to our era. Concerning the historical evolution of the term "sustainability" that I will briefly address here, I must mention how indebted I am to the brilliant work of Caradonna (2014) *Sustainability. A History*. On his book, the author traces back the emergence and the existence of the concept in the Western civilisation. Thus leaving aside the intuitional historical origins of the idea of sustainability rooted in ancient civilisations seeking to live in harmony with nature.[10] It emerges that the term came out for the first time during the age of Enlightenment. This does not mean that the world did not have ecological problems before the Industrial Revolution, even if those were hardly comparable to the urgent crisis we are facing today.[11] In reality, England was hardly deforested by the thirteenth century, and deforestation was already a problem in many ancient societies, including Greece and the Roman Republic,[12] despite of the different relation that humanity and some ancient populations had with the natural world.[13]

Nevertheless, to avoid comparisons, just consider how population growth and urban concentration and sprawls have aggravated world natural problems today; without considering the problems that excessive and futile consumption together with the unlimited use of primary natural resources are causing by destroying land, flora, fauna and our oceans.

The backdrop against which the term sustainability was coined was again the experience of an ecological crisis consisting of deforestation caused by rapidly increased economic demands in Europe.[14] Not by chance, the concept was given a name in the early eighteenth century by a Saxon bureaucrat Hans Carl von Carlowitz working in the mining sector. He coined the term "*Nachhalligkeit*" to describe the practice of harvesting timber continuously from the same forest.[15] Indeed sustained yield forestry took shape at this time not only in Western Europe but also in Japan, around the other parts of Asia and on Colonial islands in both the West and East indies.[16] Thus it is among nineteenth century theorists of forest management that

---

[10]Gillroy (2006), p. 2.

[11]Although demonstrations and evidence of collapsing civilisations are given by Dimond (2005).

[12]Caradonna (2014).

[13]On this, See Bosselmann (2008).

[14]As Bosselmann explains quoting the Works of German and British naturalists, "[b]y 1650 widespread shortages of wood began to cripple the economies in European countries. At the same time, the new discipline of forest science and management emerged. Its focus was on studying the conditions for sustained forestry and sustainable yield", Bosselmann (2008), pp. 22–23; with further reference to the works of Radkau (2000), p. 245; Evelyn (1664), p. 279.

[15]Carlowitz learned about the dependence of mining on its natural resource base and a year before his death he published his work summarising this professional and lifetime experiences. See further, Carlowitz, (1713, ed. 2000).

[16]Caradonna (2014), p. 21.

'sustaining' life as a whole to provide for human life was a commonly shared view. This view was confined to scholars and forest academies in Germany, but forest academies elsewhere followed the same ecological context. Thus, during the nineteenth century the concept emerged as the central term within forest science growing broadly to include the entire spectrum of the ecosystem 'forest' comprising locations, fertility of soils, diversity of organisms, habitat for wildlife, water reservoir, protection against erosion, 'lung' function and recreational space.[17] Those were the first traces of a holistic approach of sustainability having at its core a strong 'ecological content' and giving the right working guiding tools to the forestry managers of that time. What this means is essentially that "the practice of exploiting forest sustainably was but one indication of an incipient awareness about the value of living within biophysical limits and the need to counteract resource overconsumption".[18]

Consequently, if we think on this embryonic conceptual origins, "Sustainability" goes beyond the main difficulties environmental protection has been facing up till now. Its existence focuses on action (a holistic action) as opposed to the defensive character that environmental law and environmental measures bear. In addition, this is why it is so crucial to believe that cultural and educational connotations linked to 'sustainability' are crucial to reach its fullest potential as a proactive normative instrument entrenching intergenerational justice.

So there is not such a thing as 'sustainable development' if the term is not rooted in concrete ecological boundaries with strict connotations of intergenerational justice. Therefore sustainability movements from the past to the current days did never think of sustainable development as we think of it today, but the pioneers of such a 'sustainability movement' as it is defined by Caradonna (2014, p. 138), helped developing a truly ecological thinking and ecological awareness that is more linked to educational and cultural factors and concerns than it could ever be to economic, political or development matters. In fact, some of the giants of this movement, whose works we should look at for inspiration are among others, John Evelyn, Jean Baptiste Colbert, Hans Carl von Carlowitz, Jean-Jacques Rousseau, Thomas Malthus, John Stuart Mill, Charles Darwin, John Perkins Marsh, Rachel Carson and Ernst F. Schumacher, etc. These thinkers devoted part of their writings to educational and cultural concerns, as well as to the construction of a systematised body of ecological thought.

The maturation of the field of ecology that has the greatest impact on the concept of sustainability arises from the hand of a man who was a devoted follower of Charles Darwin and his work *On the Origin of Species* from 1859.[19] Darwin's

[17]Other forest academies that followed the same German view of sustainability were Austria-Hungary, Switzerland, France, Russia, Scandinavia, the United Kingdom and with its colonies and the United States of America. Confr. Bosselmann (2008), p. 21, referring to the works of Ulrich Groeber, in his analysis of the terminological history of sustainability, Grober (2007).

[18]Caradonna (2014).

[19]Darwin's epoch-making theory of evolution.

admirer, Ernst Haeckel, coined the word "oecologie" in 1866 while he was looking for a term to encompass the study of the natural conditions of existence.[20] Still what most people remember as the breakpoint for sustainability in the world is the launching of the publication (report) in 1972 *The Limits to Growth* by the Club of Rome. It has been perceived as an idealistic and optimistic attempt to construct the theoretical basis for building awareness on the transformation of the world. 'Sustainable development' instead has achieved a normative stance in the world, putting forward an intergenerational concept of development in more recent times (Brundtland, 1987, p. 43). Before that moment, another important achievement to build on the culture of sustainability worldwide came in 1980, when the United Nations Environmental Programme (UNEP) commissioned the International Union for the Conservation of Nature (IUCN) to write a comprehensive report that would "help advance the achievement of sustainable development through the conservation of living resources".[21] The key-interpretation of today's multidimensional concept of sustainable development is inherited from the systemic approach of this incipient report of the IUCN (1980):

> For development to be sustainable it must take account of social and ecological factors, as well as economic ones, of the living and non-living resource base; and of the long term as well as the short term advantages and disadvantages of alternative actions.[22]

The first parameters of "sustainable development" were launched by the International community as a whole through this text. However, it is *Our Common Future*'s intergenerational definition of sustainable development that has adopted the leadership for international development policy and international scholarship since the end of the eighties. Our Common future text was named after Brundtland (who was the chairperson of the Committee) and it has rendered famous the following popular definition (1987):

> Humanity has the ability to make development sustainable to ensure that it meets the needs of the present without compromising the ability of future generations to meet their own needs.[23]

This is the nearest approach to a top-down definition arising from UN procedures and taking distance from more bottom-up approaches and governance models that were shaped by the theoretical approaches brought about by some of the above mentioned sustainability thinkers. This definition aims at conciliating the dominating complex systems approach not only to generate consensus but also to include the

---

[20]Caradonna (2014) refers to him through the reference to Worsters, Nature's Economy, mentioning that Haeckel's book was called, (1866) Generelle Morphologie der Organismen, Berlin: Reimer.

[21](1980) International Union for the Conservation of Nature. *World Conservation Strategy: Living Resource Conservation for Sustainable Development.* (Gland, Switzerland: IUCN), iv.

[22]International Union for the Conservation of Nature. *World Conservation Strategy: Living Resource Conservation for Sustainable Development. Ibid*, introduction.

[23](1987) World Commission on Environment and Development, *Our Common Future*: *Report of the World Commission on Environment and Development* (Oxford University Press).

protection of third generations' rights and the Earth system in the current era. Thus, this Brundtland definition, the so-called 'normative' definition of sustainable development fulfils today a chief ecological content of the UN missions that encompasses the right of future generations and social justice as having a specific and prominent role for policy guidance in every action, including justice, equity, education, poverty eradication, culture, urban development, and safety among other global values (goals).

3.2 The Global Governance Scenario: Its Normative Narrative Failing to Embrace a Multidimensional Sustainability Concept

Once we have acquired a better understanding the historical roots of the key concepts of this analysis it is important to shed light on some features of the global governance trends in the field of sustainability. This analysis is valid to acknowledge the normative narratives that influence the legal framework and the role of law in managing the education and cultural challenges of sustainability today, as well as its rule-generating potential. The progressive degeneration of our ozone layer, the greenhouse effect and climate changes and its consequences in many parts of the world, as well as the reduction of biodiversity and our natural resources, as well as other extremely serious problems,[24] have two distinctive features that are important to remark. First, they constitute global problems per se. Consequently, public policy action is elaborated in many different protection levels. Second, the problems involved are multidimensional. They are at once the product and the cause of a complex of economic and social phenomena. Consequently, national, supranational and international public policies aimed at effectively dealing with similar threats to the biosphere cannot but entail interaction involving a mix of sectors by integrating and balancing environmental protection interests with other social collective interests.

The term 'global environmental law' has increasingly been used to challenge the inter-state paradigm of international environmental law and it has determined a focus on issues of common interest to humanity as a whole,[25] such as sustainable development and intergenerational justice. According to Morgera, "[T]he concept of global environmental law assist in understanding the 'functional' role of states and the 'functionalization of national sovereignty' arising from the evolution of international environmental law in the context of the plurality of legal orders. States

[24]See the chapter entitled "Sustaining Future" contained in the so-called "Millennium Summit Report" by the Secretary General of the United Nations, We the people of the United Nations in the 21st Century, United Nations Department of Public Information, New York, 2000, p. 54 et seq.

[25]Morgera (2012), Yang and Percival (2009), Percival, Lin, J; Piermattei (2014).

exercise 'delegated powers in the interest of human kind'."[26] States under these premises are at the service of promoting intergenerational justice and well-being of individuals and certain groups within their own territory. To this end, global environmental law plays a crucial role on the implementation of the principle of common but differentiated responsibility under international law[27] that has been successfully promoted by the UN Framework Convention on Climate Change (UNFCCC) and the Kyoto Protocol, and it plays a key role in international environmental law today. Resembling the evolution of competing global powers beyond nation states (Casini, 2018) we have also witnessed the emergence of Earth systems approach to embrace the complexities of the sustainability paradigm.

Referring back to "Sustainable development" as the most trendy concept of the global political arena I should mention that is one of the three basic political objectives of UN, together with peace, international security and the protection of Human Rights.[28] It has received a reinforced protagonist role spilling over the vast area of global environmental law and it reaches its most glorious moment on 25 September 2015 with the launching of the UN 2030 Global Agenda: "Transforming our world: Agenda 2030 for Sustainable Development",[29] that will have immediate relevance at European level.

The countries of the world adopted a set of goals (17 development goals) to end poverty, protect the planet, and ensure prosperity for all humanity as part of a new sustainable development agenda. A key element of these 17 goals (SDGs) with targets to be achieved over the next 15 years is that everyone needs to do their part: governments, private sector, civil society and individuals,[30] making again a big leap towards the achievement of what the first ecology thinkers would bear in mind as a sustainable approach, a close to hand intervention accessible to everyone, rendering humanity closer to nature and its immediate benefits. These 17 objectives take inspiration from the Millennium development goals, but their most remarkable difference is that those were formulated by developed countries and had less of the current ecological and cultural content. Against this background SDGs are universal, despite of their differing applications worldwide. Nevertheless we should remember that an evident improvement of the environmental dimension of the SDGs over that of the MDGs needs to be evaluated against the long-standing shortcomings of international environmental law, consisting of strong emphasis on the sovereignty of States, lack of mechanisms to ensure compliance and certain ineffectiveness of regulatory regimes, insufficient resources, fragmentation and so forth, some of

---

[26]Morgera (2012).

[27]Hey, E., 'Global environmental Law and Global Institutions: A system lacking "Good Process", in R. Pierik and W. Werner (eds), *Cosmopolitanism in Context: Perspectives from International Law and Political Theory*, 2010, at p. 45, p. 50.

[28]See Rodrigo (2015) *El desafío del desarrollo sostenible. Los principios de Derecho internacional relativos al desarrollo sostenible*, op. cit., p. 34.

[29]UN A/RES/70/1.

[30]Available at: http://www.un.org/sustainabledevelopment/ (last time visited on 19 December 2016).

which are reflected in Resolution 70/1 itself and which together cast doubt into the possibility of a more effective systems of global environmental governance emerging from this agenda (Pavoni and Piselli, 2016). Still the Paris agreement and the current agenda are a milestone to build awareness and trust among institutions, civil society and stakeholders about the transformational change that needs to happen if we embark in the reinforcement of the role of culture and education to lead a successful social transformative action. In addition to this there are a series of developments which are crucial to mobilise stakeholders and promoting the effective monitoring of progress, this is the Addis Ababa Action Agenda on Financing for Development (United Nations, 2015c) and the Global indicator framework emerging from the work of the Inter-Agency Expert Group on SDGs (IAEG-SDGs) (United Nations, 2015e). They constitute an 'integral' part of the process to implement the Global Agenda and not something purely secondary or even hypothetical. They should enhance the global legitimacy of this non-binding instrument such as the SDGs with a comprehensive and focused action plan with the potential to induce compliance (Pavoni and Piselli, 2016).

The most recent initiative of the Global Pact for the Environment (UN Res 72/277) entitled: "Towards a Global Pact for the Environment" decides to establish an ad hoc open-ended working group to consider a technical and evidence-based report that identifies and assesses possible gaps in international environmental law and environment-related instruments with a view to strengthening their implementation and eventually launching a Global Pact to protect the Environment. The pact, as we will specify later, devotes an article to "Education" as well as the Paris Agreement does. However, this is not the first time that outside the context of UNESCO, international agreements of planetary relevance devote attention to cultural and educational factors to canalise action for transformation and change that considering the voluntary nature of the International agreements are highly pertinent. The Earth Charter is another paradigmatic instrument addressing the importance of education and culture for ecological and democratic transition in the world.

Nonetheless the present normative evolution of international instruments takes us to the (still) unresolved question of the 'multidimensionality' of the notion of 'sustainable development' that is quite important here. Most of the international community has been stuck in front of the lack of conceptual consensus around the legal notion of sustainability giving as a consequence the impossibility of its justiciability despite of being a widely accepted legal notion in principle and as a legal principle (Bosselmann, 2008).

Sustainable development can equally be understood as a political objective, a legal principle, a legal concept, a human right, or a methodological framework for the creation and application of public policies and international norms or even a hermeneutical instrument for legal interpretation. This multidimensional nature has brought confusion and it has rendered the term worthless in many instances. The social dimension of the term has particularly suffered from lack of attention by environmental lawyers. Despite of the fact that some scholarship interest points to the social dimension of sustainability as an open-wide perquisite of development accompanied by dimensions of peace, security and even culture, definitely successful in its political objective version to reach consensus (Rodrigo, 2015).

Therefore, sustainable development according to the most recent international legal scholarship could comply with a myriad of different functions and dimensions, acting as a legal principle of international law of substantial, procedural or intermediate nature, but this openness has hampered a coherent evolution in terms of justiciability and has not protected the realm form harsh criticism. Nevertheless, the vast majority of international legal scholars consider that international treaties should be interpreted under the light of the well accepted sustainability principle. However, the components are not just three (economy, ecology and equity), standing for an economic component, a social and an environmental one. On top of this tripartite classical conception that has privileged the area of environmental law and the ecological concerns, and effective governance comes out to be a key component that renders sustainable development the guidance of future evolution of democratic global governance mechanism and this has been explicitly set in recent treaties just as the Paris Agreement where governance instruments seem to be a key element to fight climate change at policy level.

Good governance, clearly established today as the fourth component of sustainability and crucial to face future challenges, includes the institutional parties, private actors, stakeholders, associations, or political components at every level of governance.[31] It was strongly proclaimed by Delhi Declaration (2002) by the International Law Association (ILA)–despite of its non-binding nature- and it has subsequently been proclaimed by the United Nations (2014).[32] This multidimensional nature of the concept has helped national and regional governments to adequate their different policies to a strong multifaceted governance model that in more regional contexts, such as the European one, can be really efficient. Moreover 'Good governance' as a political objective has also been enshrined in the Agenda 2030 for the Sustainable Development of the UN, as well as in the regional level agenda in the European Union. As it has been mentioned does not refer only to governments, it relates to every kind of civil society member action, global private actors, any kind of stakeholder, multinationals acting in the global scenario and affects our living world. The main challenge is the fragmented existence of good governance in a world aiming at not giving up sovereign control of its natural resources whatever the management should be, with major social actors of the business world just going after their own share. We are running the risk of getting into what it has been called "green developmentalism"[33] that strives for market oriented solutions and technological development that leaves untouched the current models of production and governance in the global world.

---

[31]Sachs (2015).

[32]Prototype Global Sustainable Development Report (Online unedited ed.). New *York: United Nations Department of Economic and Social Affairs, Division for Sustainable Development.* https://sustainabledevelopment.un.org/globalsdreport/.

[33]See, McAffe (1999).

The long-running dialogue on the meaning and utility of the governance[34] concept has been mirrored by a debate on the nature of European governance that I will mention below. An important advantage of employing governance perspectives—that in this discourse is given for granted as part of the sustainability narrative—is that we take the discussion around sustainability beyond stiff normative frameworks and legal rules. While legal rules refer to rules emanating from formal and traditional institutional bodies (government, parliament, etc.) typically in a hierarchical context, governance refers to the way in which political, economic and administrative power or authority is exercised at all levels, going beyond the bureaucratic state.[35]

Turning our attention back to the realm of justiciability, it becomes important to continue ascertaining the legal dimension of the concept to identify the interpretative functions of sustainable development that would seem to fit within traditional categories of normativity in the international arena.[36] The legal dimension as we will discuss later has helped the reinforcement of the notion of justice and justiciability that we need to embed in our cultural imaginary. Bosselmann indicates the validity of sustainability as a norm that "can be formulated as the obligation to promote long-term economic prosperity and social justice within the limits of ecological sustainability",[37] therefore, according to this, sustainability would slip into the lands of legal principles getting normative quality although it has not yet been recognised as such by international law.[38] This line of reasoning is also followed by more recent scholarship, considering that the normative value of sustainable development could have a myriad of expressions. Therefore, sharing the above mentioned view on the concept of sustainable development we could say along with the most authoritarian scholarship that "the concept of sustainable development is located somewhere in the spectrum of (non-legal) policies and (legal) norms" (Lowe, 1999). We can perhaps exclude two extremes. On the one hand, the concept is more than a mere political ideal as it has been referred to repeatedly in hard law (i.e., Climate Change Convention 1992, Article 3; Biodiversity Convention 1992, Articles 8, 10; Desertification Convention 1997, Articles,

[34]See for instance, the definition of governance adopted by the UN Development Programme (UNDP), "the exercise of economic, political and administrative authority to manage a country's affairs at all levels. It comprises the mechanisms, processes and institutions through which citizens and groups articulate their interests, exercise their legal rights, meet their obligations and mediate their differences" (UNDP, *Governance for Sustainable Development*, New York: UNDP, 1977). See also, the World Bank's definition of governance as the method through which power is exercised in the management of a country's political, economic and social resources for development (*Governance*, Washington, DC: World Bank, 1993).

[35]Hewson and Sinclair (1999), and Ba and Hoffmann (2005).

[36]Boyle and Freestone (1999).

[37]Bosselmann (2008), p. 53. The author that postulates for sustainability as a legal principle asserts that sustainability, "[I]s reflective of a fundamental morality (respect for ecological integrity), requires action ('protect and restore') and is, therefore, capable of causing legal effect. The standards of a legal principle are all met".

[38]On this point see also, Lowe (1999).

4, 5; Antigua Convention 1992, Article 2)[39] and, in soft law. More recently, and more related to our core discourse, SD has been described as a decision-making framework for maintaining and achieving human well-being.[40]

Nonetheless showing a critical approach and a less optimistic vision, Viñuales (2013) has spoken of the "rise and fall" of SD *momentum.* The concept is less than a rule as it lacks direct legal consequences.[41] Case law at international level have made an attempt to follow a significant flow of acceptance towards the establishment of sustainable development as a binding legal norm in the international community,[42] but more as a political objective than a legal principle.[43] The proximity of the concept to policies seems closer than to a rule, but how close? This depends on the degree of political and legal guidance the concept is capable of providing?[44]

Critical approaches to the whole normative paradigm that Brundtland and the SDG's Agenda bring about should contribute to a different appraisal concern with how this paradigm is helping or preventing from reconciling competing and conflicting interests in economic development, social welfare and environmental protection from an intra- as well as intergenerational perspective. Following these critical approaches I believe we should not be pessimistic about the eventual proactive potential of SD policies, especially if we focus attention in the cultural and educational concerns, and this is perhaps the biggest challenge. Regardless of its

---

[39]For further examples see, Cordonier Segger and Khalfan (2004).

[40]Dernbach and Cheever (2015).

[41]On this aspect, is paradigmatic for International law the case concerning the *Gabčikovo-Nagymaros Dam* Case, Hungary/Slovakia, Judgment, Merits, ICJ GL No 92, [1997] ICJ Rep 7, [1997] ICJ Rep 88, (1998) 37 ILM 162, ICGJ 66 (ICJ 1997), 25th September 1997, International Court of Justice.

[42]For a thorough overview of the concept, see Birnie and Boyle (1992), pp. 122–124, and Lowe (1999), p. 25 *et seq.*

[43]See Lowe (1999).

[44]For a good explanation about the legal guidance the concept is capable to give Bosselmann (2008), p. 54 refers to the most relevant cases: This, *Gabčikovo-Nagymaros Dam* Case, Hungary/ Slovakia, Judgment *(1997) ICJ* Reports 7, para. *140.* The case arose out of a 1977 Treaty in which Hungary and Czechoslovakia (as it then was) agreed on a joint project to build hydroelectric facilities and improve navigation and flood control on the Danube. In 1989 Hungary, suspended, and later abandoned, work on the agreed project because, it said, of serious criticisms of the environmental impact of the project. The two states concluded in 1993 a Special Agreement for the reference of the dispute to the International Court. For a thorough analyses of the case. The important thing about this judgement is that Judge Weeramantry on his judgment distinguished his conception of sustainable development from that adopted by the majority in the Court: ".....I consider it to be more than a mere concept, [it is]....a principle with normative value. For a better understanding of the case, see further Lowe (1999). In this case, the ICJ used as an argument SD on the resolution of a case, but with such "caution and delicate ambiguity in the phrasing of the passage" that there is no a well-established shift towards the belief that "SD" could become always an element of hermeneutic interpretation for the court in similar conflicts, although later interpretation of the ICJ have followed that road, see the case, *Iron Rhine Railway Arbitration* (2005) PCA, paras. 58–59; *Pulp Mills Case* (Provisional Measures) (Argentina v Uruguay) (2006) ICJ Reports, para. 80; *Pulp Mills Case* (Merits) (2010) ICJ Reports, para. 177.

debated legal character SD is helping to build a 'better world', notwithstanding that mainstream action in the field under this paradigm has been constructed in some more privileged parts of the world and spread across different geographical, economic, politic, social and cultural contexts through globalisation. The voices behind other cultural traditions interacting with the natural world according to premises different to material accumulation have been very often marginalised.[45]

In the spirit of supporting those marginalised voices emerges a legal narrative following a more critical view of traditional approaches to environmental law principles overshadowing some of the international law doctrine linked to sustainable development, and this is only positive. Indeed these emerging legal scholarship that follows interdisciplinary literature focuses on the governmentality underlying the concept of SD. Some scholars have questioned the discursive elements of SD that legitimise the present global social metabolism and modes of colonisation of nature (Cardesa-Salzmann & Cocciolo).[46] Those recent critical appraisals of the role of law for "managing" eventually the Earth system in times of the Anthropocene's ecological crisis call for a profound review of SD discourse[47] and methodologies (Parks & Morgera, 2019).

For Viñuales (2018), it is impossible to account for the development of the forces leading to the Anthropocene without a sufficient understanding of the legal dimensions, as well as non-legal ones at play. In his brilliant work "The Organisation of the Anthropocene in our Hands?"[48] He provides a useful research agenda to understand the role of law: "broadly, as a social and cultural practice reflected in institutions and texts, in prompting, sustaining and potentially managing the Anthropocene, the proposed new Epoch of the Earth system".[49] Such approach complies with the creation of a new storyline in the legal doctrine that tries to explain, first the Anthropocene, and subsequently the role of law in the Anthropocene. Thus, an approach like this urges a call upon all disciplines, the entire body of knowledge about the world to analyse what is happening and how to face it. This theoretical approach is of course valid for the analysis of the current normative narrative behind the EUSM and its cultural and educational challenges.

Once we have reached good understanding of the role of law in the Anthropocene and sustainability discussions, its potential, as well as limitations, it is important to integrate the complementary role of other disciplinary approaches to the legal narrative. Take for instance the theoretical discourse of the economic theorist Serge Latouche. He has explained in his theoretical work that we must speak of

---

[45]Gordon (2015).

[46](2019). These authors refer to some international law doctrinal narratives of interdisciplinary nature with renewed and more critical approaches. This is, Fischer-Kowalski and Haberl (1998), Hornborg, McNeill, and Martínez-Alier (2006), Hornborg (2010), Hornborg, Clark, and Hermele (2013).

[47]On this see further, Cardesa-Salzmann and Cocciolo (2019) and Viñuales (2018).

[48](2018).

[49]Viñuales (2018).

'*decroissance*' and decolonise our imagination and free ourselves from the myths of progress, global markets, science and technology that law has been regulating and deregulating for decades now under the premises of a so-called sustainable development. He refers to the contradiction of naming 'development' (as it has been forged in the North) 'sustainable development'. Certainly the author does not reject the values of science and technology, but their role should be viewed as less promethean and more respectful of nature. In his opinion, we must re-establish the economy according to the virtuous circle of the eight Rs: reassess, reframe, restructure, relocalise, redistribute, reduce, reuse and recycle. This vision could be a valid point of departure to build an effective normative framework for a valid energy package and circular economy regulation. Why not?

Still the impact of de-growth (la décroissance) on the discourse of sustainability, which has its origin in France, has had little or no impact on the policy makers responsible for developing sustainable development strategies in Europe (Slim, 2013). The intellectual origins of the de-growth discourse comes from the translation into French of the scientific writings of the Romanian economist Nicholas Georgescu-Roegen. His view is based on the rejection of the hypothesis that sustainability can be reconciled with economic growth, and indeed a strong sustainability approach embeds some of the narrative behind such discussion.

These interdisciplinary views based on global social justice are aligned with the Earth system approach and the innovative conceptual and methodological discussions of some part of international legal scholarship. Viñuales (2013) argues about the prescriptive vagueness of SD and helps us to understand that our International Law understanding of SD is part of a 'diplomatic trick' that has been effective for reaching international agreements (an it is still is, if we think of the SDG Agenda) for the growth of what Cardesa-Salzmann and Cocciolo (2019) have called "global principled agreements between the North and the South for harnessing economic, social, and environmental concerns in a wide range of issue areas".[50] So, perhaps aiming at contrasting the persuading view of development of old narratives coming from international lawyers, and economists belonging to traditional classical approaches, there has been a burst of intellectual and academic initiatives following the lines of integrated and interdisciplinary methodological approaches that illustrate better the reality that lies in front of humanity and the ecological instability of the Anthropocene with harsh consequences for humankind and the biosphere, harshening some parts of the world more than others.

These alternative theoretical narratives within the legal domain are based on interdisciplinary perspectives on global governance discussing the way in which global law fails to cope with the resonance of advanced capitalism in the world society and ecological systems. This forces us to draw our attention by all means to economic and social discourses. However, not just the ones more aligned with some

[50]Cardesa-Salzmann and Cocciolo (2019).

sort of acceptance of the 'status quo' of things,[51] but rather, with discourses that claim for a change of the 'imaginary'[52] as the already mentioned economist Sérge Latouche does. I will be drawing attention to the Elinor Ostrom's theoretical contribution (1990) indebted as I am to her theoretical approach to new conceptual lines of sustainability based on new forms of governance.

Scholarship discussions following this type of critical thinking have consequently embraced co-creation, social and ecological sustainability. They give normative shape to the social justice dimensions of the ecological transition that have been mostly neglected by the hierarchical premises of a notion of sustainability engrained in a stiff legal tradition. They help to build bridges between law, policy, culture and society. In reality, those theoretical perspectives are followed by those social actors who are taking part of the social ecological transition as main players leaving behind command and control policy frameworks, to open spaces of action to the emerging paradigm of the commons, and communities' empowerment that are increasingly spreading worldwide (i.e., Transition towns movement; Think global act local, Bristol city).[53] Even the European Parliament voted and amendment in May 2016 for the "recognition of energy as a common good" as part of a report about decentralised local production, this is the "New Deal for Energy Consumers" (2015).[54] While the amendment was voted down by 298 votes to 345 votes, this vote reflects the growing support for the change of paradigm, seeing energy as a common good, and not as an economic asset.

Another important illustrative example of a 'transformative' narrative in a social science discourse within the contours of sustainability, is offered by Göpel (2016) and I will come back to this later. She actually suggests a critical analysis of the economic dimensions of the sustainable development narrative. She tries to provide a new conceptual framework for a better understanding of the transformation challenge that we need to face today. The 'transformation' suggested by this economist, in a more sustainable direction, anchors its conceptual roots in Karl Polanyi's political economy analysis of the "Great Transformation" of the eighteenth and nineteenth century societies. An additional reference within the realm of ecological approaches related to the discourse of development meeting social and geopolitical needs is offered by Schumacher (1973). It is also important to cite his work *"Small is Beautiful"*. Such influential theoretical approaches from the vast

[51] I am referring to the global action fostered by sustainable development approaches in well-known Research Centres or Universities. See for instance, Columbia University and the Earth Institute work and network created on sustainable development, and the Earth Charter.

[52] In the sociological use of the term that captures more than ideas, including a set of values, institutions, laws and symbols with which people imagine their social existence.

[53] On this line of thinking see further, Göpel (2016).

[54] On 15 July 2015, the European Commission adopted a Communication on Delivering a New Deal for energy consumers ('New Deal'), as part of the Summer Energy Package. The New Deal is one of several consumer-related actions envisaged in the Energy Union strategy, and is designed to inform future actions in this field, including proposed legislation. See further, http://www.europarl.europa.eu/RegData/etudes/BRIE/2016/573896/EPRS_BRI(2016)573896_EN.pdf.

field of social sciences are crucial to trigger discussions on how to face future sustainability challenges breaking silos in our doctrinal approaches and place greater emphasis on education and cultural policies as crucial architects of the multidimensional sustainability action.

3.3 European Union Sustainability Model

Following the premises previously laid down concerning the global governance scenario and the doctrinal narratives behind the global scenario of sustainable development, it is important to address the fundamentals of the European model now, with all its Member States diversities but in most instances, converging ontology. I should analyse this model from the lenses of the European law doctrinal narrative to understand its weaknesses and its potential. I will start by approaching the evolution of the legal framework that has permitted the existence of such model before we go on to analyse its cultural and educational challenges.

We know now that the initial lack of uniformity in national regulations of varied nature (energy, agriculture, cultural heritage, education, environment, etc.) has not prevented Member States from reaching leadership in common policies regarding those global problems of ecological nature, such as a climate change, energy regulation, agriculture, environmental protection and regulation and, so on by conceding powers at supranational level to the EU.

The progressive broadening of competencies is distinctive to the EU. It has of course broaden its competences outside the strictly economic sphere presenting a model of integration that has embarked after Lisbon in the construction of a more 'social' Europe[55] and is trying to transpose the concept of intergenerational justice (equity) in the EU legal framework identified in the Rio Declaration as a sub-principle of the broader principle of international sustainable development.[56] Collins (2007) has suggested that the incorporation of intergenerational equity in EU policy "implicitly or explicitly" is deemed to evoke "some ambiguous notion of responsibility to future generations". He argues that there is an evidence of the EU institutions working within what Prof. Weiss (1984) referred as framework of duties

[55]The scope of the other discussion, referred to the international regime and the increasing network of international organisations endowed with international legal status and their own bureaucratic structures (secretariats), together with other transgovernmental relations Keohane and Nye (1974) Belongs to the highly analysed phenomena of global administrative law envisaging the passage from internationalisation to administrative globalisation. On this, see also Casini (2018). Closa and Casini (2016).

[56]See for instance, Commission Communication, A Sustainable Europe for a Better World: A European Union Strategy for Sustainable Development, Communication from the Commission of the European Communities to the Gothenburg European Council of 15th May 2001, COM (264) final; and Commission Communication 24th July 2009, Mainstreaming sustainable development into EU policies: 2009 Review of the EU Union Strategy for SD, COM (2009) 400 final.

associated to "intergenerational equity". He gives some examples that are useful to me in the description of the EUSM, this is, EU's Biodiversity Strategy calling for an end to the loss of biodiversity with the EU by 2010 enacting the Birds Directive and the Habitats Directive; and the EU anti-pollutions measures and the Emissions Trading Scheme (ETS) to combat climate change that I will explain later, broadening the scope of environmental protection of the atmosphere and extend protection between the current generations' limitations.

Today, at the same time, especially with the EU doctrinal, constitutional and strategical context, the 'intergenerational equity' or third generation rights are widely accepted based on the profound vulnerability of future generations to harm resulting from present environmental degradation (Collins, 2007), although from the point of view of procedural success on judicial grounds, the principle of sustainable development involving intergenerational equity is rarely recalled, it is possible within the framework of the EU Charter (Article 37), to rely upon to justify the protection of future interests and generations.

Urgenda case has shown how citizens are increasingly aware of their power to claim State action using human rights arguments (Savaresi & Auz, 2019). The evolving trend of resolving climate change litigation cases on human rights grounds does not involve real action to push the boundaries in sustainability concerns. In fact, the enforceability of Article 37, and more specifically the principle of sustainable development is undermined by Article 52 (5) of the Charter drafted to distinguish rights and principles, at a time where future generation rights where not so heavily under discussion. Christopher Stone (1972) and his work 'Do the trees have standing' have been in the past a good way to grow awareness in the European constitutional legal doctrine (echoed at global level) about the possibility to extend the application of rights to non-human living entities; and indeed, according to Kotzé (2019) while constitutions that do afford non-human entities rights entitlements still remain absolutely minimal, Stone's proposition managed to open 'the steadfast epistemological closures that have been working to safeguard the anthropocentric individualism of rights'. The same principle applies for intergenerational justice and its realisation under our current constitutional traditions challenged by what Bosselmann calls Ecological *Rechtsstaat.* Today is stronger than ever on the idea of enforcing intergenerational justice on his own right. In fact, development embedding the notion of 'intergenerational justice' with the emphasis added has progressively moved away from development as a mere present concern (according to the principles launched by the Rio Declaration) towards a conception more sensitive to temporal dimension to be regarded as "a statement of intergenerational equity" (Molinari, 2015), and this 'move' is precious to us to face the cultural challenges of the European development model. Because we must bear in mind that where the judiciary cannot yet reach, the consciousness must act.

It goes without saying that the European Sustainability Model takes its strength today from acting as a single player (representing the action of all MS) in the global administrative scenario. In many relevant instances such as climate Change protection this supranational role determines leadership and help MS to reach easier consensus and further action in topics of global relevance, such as those concerning ecological matters (e.g., energy and transport).

The EUSM has been shaped thanks to the drastic evolution of environmental law protection under strong regulatory efforts of EU law to tackle pressing problems of ecological nature.[57] This progression of regulatory nature and institutional changes parallels a progression that resembles the integration process itself, in the sense of considering how according to the principle of conferral, which governs EU action internally and on the international level, the EU has been legislating, as well as adding competencies, based not only on the explicit powers endowed by the treaties, but also on the necessities arising from geopolitical changes along the decades of its existence. I have put forward the idea that the constant and increasing evolution of the body of environmental law at first place and some other laws and doctrines subsequently, have given place to what I have decided to call the "EUSM".[58]

The more recent legal explosion aiming at integrating ecological and even social concerns into other sectorial policies has been vital to consider seriously this relevant unique model and a sort of converging ontology in the understanding the role of law in the Anthropocene, especially in the European context. Policies such as energy, climate change, public procurement, corporate social responsibility, landscape, urban management, food regulation, circular economy, cultural heritage, whose primary objective has been, first to strengthen the ecological heart of the multidimensional sustainability paradigm, and then subsequently to regulate more complex systems through a conscious political will adapting institutional intervention to a renewed trend of governance. These are the first features that illustrate this model, even if it is far from reaching Giovannini's (2018) almost *utopian* look. The EU, by regulating progressively on environmental topics, and through the "environmentalisation" of sectorial policies subsequently, has been transforming itself, as well as transforming its existential ethos in the international sphere. This process has helped the EU identity to achieve a different stage on its complex integration process, dramatically forgetting how important the education and the cultural matters are to solidify its supranational stance.

Somehow though, today the European agenda under the paradigm of sustainability is more intricate than ever; more social aspects are prompting solutions, the internal market needs a missing political 'transformative' will to lead the market into more social concerns without lessen its ecological ethos, and at the same time achieve the ambitious circular economy plans that considers the worker as part of the productive chain. Thus, the EUSM 'model' on building its *acquis communautaire* that should make the EU regional approach to development in internal and external policy highly distinctive at global level, needs to reinforce action in educational and cultural concerns making use of the strong constitutional

[57]That from its origins has had transnational consequences. See the one of the first EU directives in the environmental field, on birds, 79/409/EEC in April 1979. It was amended in 2009, it became the Directive 2009/147/EC.

[58]Sánchez Galera (2016).

implications that were set in Lisbon. Article 9 of the TFEU contains the criteria on which to mainstream strategic plans that have a direct consequence on education and culture beyond the repetitive mantra of technological innovation. In fact, the *acquis communautaire* of the EUSM has at its core a strong consensual Europeanisation of MS environmental policies broadened by the most recent European intervention on Energy, Climate change, biodiversity, farming and consumption habits and regulations, the social dimension of the model needs more political attention on the potential of a stronger coordination of educational and cultural activities based on best practices and more public financial investments.

3.3.1 An Overview of the Origins of the Current EU Sustainability Model. A Bit of History About the Origins of the Environmental Integration Principle in EU Law and the Evolution of Environmental Law Generating a Worldwide Leadership on Sustainable Development Governance

What is the EUSM? What does this model have to offer in terms of effectiveness and uniqueness at the level of intra and intergenerational justice as opposed to the global governance model?

> Europe must throw its weight onto the scales of an international level and within the UN in order to counterbalance the hegemonic unilateralism of the United States. At global economic summits and in the institutions of the WTO, the World Bank, and the International Monetary Fund, it should bring its influence to bear in shaping the design of a future global domestic politics[59]

In this paragraph authored by Jurgen Habermas, he makes the case for a European post-national order that he hopes will become the vanguard for the emergence of universal cosmopolitanism.[60] However, what is missing is a stronger European identity that has yet to be built (?).[61] Under these assumptions, I would like to

[59]Habermas (2006). On this essay, Habermas reflects on what happened on 15 February 2003 when "masses of demonstrators in London, Madrid, Rome, Barcelona, Paris and Berlin responded [to the 'coup' led by Spain's Aznar and UK's Blair, who vowed support of President Bush's war in Iraq contrary to the wishes of their EU colleagues and their electorates.] The simultaneity of these overpowering demonstrations-the largest since the end of World War II-may go down in future history books as a signal of the birth of a European public". Habermas (2006), p. 40.

[60]Miller (2019).

[61]In Habermas (2006), explains that European political unity will require overruled minorities to imagine themselves in solidarity with the majority, and he affirms "[h]owever, that presupposes a feeling of political belonging. The peoples must 'build', so to speak, a new European dimension onto their national identities. The already quite abstract civic solidarity which restricts itself to follow-nationals must in future be extended to include European citizens of other nations. This poses the question of 'European identity'".

think that the European identity does indeed exist at least in the form of what Habermas refers to "as an example of government beyond the nation-state" supporting the idea that "unlike the United States, Europe stands as a proponent of a social democracy that rejects the inevitability of gross social inequalities, like those that exist in America".[62] However, Europe cannot simply be an 'apparently good looking' example standing against an uglier one. We know that the importance of Europe today is diminishing compared to the growing economic weight of other world powers. In fact, the perception that global political power is shifting from West to East and the sense that the relationship with the United States is changing "is casting a sharp light on the synergetic benefits of European unification".[63]

One might say that this is just a positive pro Europe version, and it might well be. Still the evidence is there: we have built what I have decided to call "the European Union sustainability model" under those premises but it is always a work in progress. Considering (and wishing) that the integration process is not just exhausted in economic benefits and transactions.

When trying to offer a picture of the evolution of such model, one can choose between different instruments from the institutional history of the EU and its political evolution. However, I have chosen to start by drafting a short story about contextual events that go hand in hand with the origins of the 'integration' principle in European Union Law. It is important to say as a preliminary note that the integration principle enshrined by Article 11 of the TFEU was not part of the EU constitutional architecture since the beginning. It became later in time the heart and the main catalyst to mainstream the ecological heart of sustainability into other policy areas by introducing an instrument of integration that would give certain leadership to environmental protection criteria. This has helped to integrate environmental law concerns into every sectorial (other than environmental) policy of EU law subsequently.

I tend to affirm, as I have already mentioned, that the steady expansion and consolidation of the EU action in the field of environmental protection resembles or parallels the process of EU integration itself.[64] In fact, EU action in this field matches and reflects the evolution and impressive transformation of the Union over the last

[62]Habermas (2006), p. 47. To broaden this vision, Miller (2019) has a beautiful essay portraying a different picture of how the protagonist of McEwan's Novel *Saturday* feels the same day of the events that Habermas takes into account. Miller (2019) gives some bibliographical support to Habermas' opinion about European identity for skeptics readers: Neil Fligstein (2008), Armin von Bogdandy (2005), and Herrmann, Risse, and Brewer (2004).

[63]Habermas (2015). He argues that: "The role of Europe has changed in the postcolonial world not only when seen in the light of the dubious reputation of former imperial powers, not to mention the Holocaust. The statistical projections for the future also predict for Europe the fate of a continent with a shrinking population, decreasing economic weight and dwindling political importance", p. 17.

[64]This is obviously explained by the fact that the absence of a specific legal basis in the original Treaty establishing the EEC has not prevented EU action in fields like the environmental one to evolve over the years and override specific objectives of market integration. The body of law on environmental regulation, as well as its solid multilevel governance realm has indeed evolve through the principle of integration to foster more social concerns that have strengthen the *acquis* of what is now a unique sustainability model.

decades. A significant feature characterising the European integration process is indeed the gradual extension of EU 'material' jurisdiction in areas which fall outside the strict realm of the original economic mandate (Orlando, 2014). Nonetheless, before a specific competence on environmental law policy was introduced the EEC Treaty (1957) contained some indications that the EU's competence could possibly extend far beyond market objectives (Orlando, 2014).[65] Another important feature of the EU integration process regards the crucial role the ECJ plays generally in the development of EU law, but specifically here in the development of environmental law. We cannot say the same thing about the role played for the interpretation of sustainable development, sustainability, or the introduction of the third generation rights into the legal reasoning of the court.

Now let me now tell the story of the 'Dannish bottle' case.[66] This case was addressing the question whether a bottle recycling system introduced by the Danish government constituted a breach of what is now Article 34 of the TFEU since the Lisbon Treaty entered into force. As Prof. Jans rightly affirms the importance of this judgement is that it enabled and facilitated the integration of environmental considerations into the market freedoms of the European Community (at the time).[67] However, to me, this is essentially a case that represents how not only primary, and secondary law have been essential to the vivid evolution of the legal system of the EU and its citizens, but gives evidence on how the Court, has helped to shape EU law with equal results. Therefore, although it might be possible to trace the origins of the principle of environmental integration to the very first attempts to formulate a community environmental policy and it is more commonly associated with the Third Environmental Action Programme (EAP),[68] the legal reasoning of 'integration' of environmental consideration in favour of the population was already there.

As we know countries like Denmark, Finland, Sweden, even Germany have for a long time been more sensitive to ecological matters than other European Member States, and by the end of the eighties an important leap for the European Economic Community (EEC) would start to take shape by adopting the measures that the International Community had put forward on the Brundtland report.[69] By the eighties when this case was brought in front of the European Court of Justice (ECJ) the Danish Government had replaced the bottle recycling system with a more rigid approach; it was introduced a law stipulating that manufacturers could only use for beer and soft drinks re-usable bottles. Furthermore, the new law required

[65]Orlando (2014) cites the work of Rehbinder and Stewart (1985).

[66]C-302/86 Commission v Denmark., ECLI: EU:1988: 421.

[67]Jans (2011). Prof. Jans, dedicates this contribution to Lord Slynn of Hadley for his opinion to the famous 'Danish bottle' case. See further, Opinion of Advocate General Slynn, Commission v. Denmark, case 302/86, [1988] E.C.R.4619.

[68]OJ1983 C 46/1.

[69]See further, U.N. World Commission on Environment and Development, *Report of the European Commission on Environment and Development: Our Common Future*, at 60, The Secretary General, Development & international Economic Co-operation: Environment, Annex, U.N. Doc. A/42/427 (Aug. 4, 1987).

that returnable containers had to gain first formal approval by the National Agency for the Protection of the Environment. Only about 30 different types of container qualified under this new regulation. The reaction of foreign suppliers consequently was to argue that adapting to the new legislation's requirements would increase production costs and keep foreign suppliers out of Danish market.

It was argued that the legislation requiring the containers to be reusable was a form of discrimination against foreign manufacturing system and therefore constituted a restriction on free trade under Article 28 of the TFEU. The ECJ held that environmental protection was indeed a permissible justification for such a discrimination. The new recycling system had to be proportionate in achieving the environmental protection aim. Thus, this stricter system was held to be more eco-friendly and therefore acceptable. However the further requirement imposed by Danish law, allowing only a limited number of container shapes, was held to be disproportionate and therefore violating EC law. Curiously enough, despite of the drastic evolution of 'environmentalisation' of other sectorial (and most recent) policies, like energy, the ECJ continuous to give red light holding disproportionate certain internal (market) requirements under ecological objectives. Thus, despite the fact the first promises of integrating environmental considerations started decades ago, its precise normative character and substantive content remain unclear (Krämer, 2013). In a way, this is a common ground with other guiding principles which are meant to provide a basis for European Union action on the environment (McIntyre, 2013). However, this is also a clue aspect of EUSM that I want to illustrate by calling upon this particular case. This is, many aspects of its potential *acquis* are still in a 'switch off version' of its whole prospective power, and it could well be the EUCJ to awake it through a strong hermeneutic interpretation of the constitutional indications on sustainable development of the TFEU, or as it happened in this case, by anticipating 'virtuous' considerations integrated into the legal identity of MS.

Regardless of the end judgement, this case was a turning point for the fortunes of environmental law at EU level.[70] Fortunes that would be subsequently enshrined with stronger and broader scope every time that the European Treaties were modified, reaching its 'peak' with the Treaty of Amsterdam,[71] despite that the legal status of SD and the integration principle 'became blurred' by the time the Charter of Fundamental Rights of the EU was signed because at that time the Charter was not binding and it contained an integration principle itself.[72]

---

[70]One should bear in mind that none environmental concerns were part of the original and founding treaties, although as we know part of those treaties had at the heart of their concerns energy aspects.

[71]Jans (2011), asserts that "on each occasion that the EEC Treaty was amended, the integration principle was strengthened. Each round of revisions enhanced the profile of its impact. One could probably say that the integration principle in tis Amsterdam version was at its peak", p. 1539.

[72]Jans (2011), discusses that the "[t]he text of the Charter differs in a couple of aspects from the Amsterdam version. First, it refers only to Union policies and not "policies and activities". Second, it does not explicitly require integration as regards "the definition and implementation" of Union policies, thus rendering more uncertain its status vis-à-vis Member States", p. 1539.

Considering the evolution of the EU environmental policy, as well as the EU engagement towards the construction of a 'sustainable' Europe by integrating environmental concerns at every policy level, the implications of the integration principle have been enormous at the political, administrative and judicial level.[73] Since the adoption of the First Environmental Action Programme in 1973, EU environmental policy and legislation have expanded intensely becoming one of the main EU areas of intervention in which innovative legal tools and inclusive governance approaches[74] are more evident, as well as the process of "Europeanisation" (Orlando, 2014). Article 352 of the TFEU (formerly 235) has been crucial provision facilitating the adoption of EU legislation based on achieving the objectives of the Treaty, even in the absence of a specific treaty source.[75] Moreover, over time, the Lisbon Treaty has reaffirmed the EU commitment to environmental protection and sustainable development expressly emphasising the internal and external dimensions of EU action in this field.

The ambitious reaffirmation of the sustainable development discourse and the environmental integration approach have very much been possible thanks to the important role that the principle of subsidiarity in its double version, vertical and horizontal plays in the environmental field, where the competence for legislation is shared between the EU and the Member States. I will come to this later when I talk about governance. Although according to Krämer (2013, p. 17) this principle has often been "interpreted politically" by Member States as a way to block EU regulation in certain sensitive areas. It has definitely helped not to create extreme political fractures, considering that the progressive widening of the EU, in terms of country enlargement and policy competence (Lisbon would further introduce the vital Energy competence) has rendered difficult to maintain the relatively centralised and homogeneous decision-making paradigm that it has characterised the earlier Community.[76]

[73]Note that although there was not an environmental competence conferred by the Treaties at EU level until the Single European Act was enacted, there came about the first EU environmental measures grounded principally on former Article 100 of the Treaty Establishing the European Economic Community (EEC Treaty), enabling the Council to unanimously issue directives for the approximation of Member States laws which directly affect the establishment or functioning of the common market. the ECJ had dealt with environmental protection before, see, e.g., *Procureur de la Republique v. Association de Défense des Brûleurs d'huiles Usagées (ADBHU)*, Case 240/83, [1985] E.C.R. 531, as referred by Jans (2011).

[74]See further, Orlando (2014). She provides a brilliant illustration of EU policy evolution in the environmental field by looking at how the EEC/EU treaties have over time redefined the allocation of legislative powers among the various institutional actors and between the European Union and its Member States, from p. 3 onwards.

[75]See, *Procureur de la Republique v. Association de Défense des Brûleurs d'huiles Usagées (ADBHU)*, Case 240/83, [1985] E.C.R. 531, p. 12. In support of its reasoning, the Court held that "the principle of freedom of trade is not to be viewed in absolute terms, but is subject to certain limits justified by the objectives of general interest pursued by the Community".

[76]De Búrca and Scott (2000), p. 2.

In fact, differentiation and flexibility have been instrumental for building the most recent stronger sustainability model under some sort of acceptance of its resilient ecological heart to which Member States have joint gradually. Article 191 (3) of the TFEU clarifies that the pursuit of the twin EU objectives of environmental protection and European integration must consider the diversity of environmental, social and economic conditions of the various European regions.[77] This legal provision is of course the new legal basis for climate change, regardless of the new competence in Energy (Art. 194 TFEU) and the most recently integrated 'Winter package' for a decarbonised Europe. In the EU, the intensification of the public environmental concern has paralleled developments on the international level, including the 1972 Stockholm Declaration on the Human Environment. International declarations and international law trend have always been important catalysts for a more explicit EU role in the environmental sector. Thus upon invitation of heads of state and government, in 1973 an Environment and Consumer Protection Service was set up and the

[77]Article 191 of the TFEU defines objectives and principles of EU environmental policy, and it is the new legal basis for climate change. It reads as follows:

1. Union policy on the environment shall contribute to pursuit of the following objectives:

   – preserving, protecting and improving the quality of the environment,
   – protecting human health,
   – prudent and rational utilisation of natural resources,
   – promoting measures at international level to deal with regional or worldwide environmental problems, and in particular combating climate change.

2. Union policy on the environment shall aim at a high level of protection taking into account the diversity of situations in the various regions of the Union. It shall be based on the precautionary principle and on the principles that preventive action should be taken, that environmental damage should as a priority be rectified at source and that the polluter should pay.

   In this context, harmonisation measures answering environmental protection requirements shall include, where appropriate, a safeguard clause allowing Member States to take provisional measures, for non-economic environmental reasons, subject to a procedure of inspection by the Union.
3. In preparing its policy on the environment, the Union shall take account of:

   – available scientific and technical data,
   – environmental conditions in the various regions of the Union,
   – the potential benefits and costs of action or lack of action,
   – the economic and social development of the Union as a whole and the balanced development of its regions.

4. Within their respective spheres of competence, the Union and the Member States shall cooperate with third countries and with the competent international organisations. The arrangements for Union cooperation may be the subject of agreements between the Union and the third parties concerned.

The previous subparagraph shall be without prejudice to Member States' competence to negotiate in international bodies and to conclude international agreements.

first Environmental Action Programme (EAP) was adopted (Krämer, 2013) and EAPs have always played an important operational role at EU level.

All these emerging features although evolving in a scattered and uncoordinated group of measures (Orlando, 2014) have become incidentally the basis of the EUSM overriding objects of market integration and building a sophisticated system of regulation and multilevel governance with a robust body of environmental law protection. As an opposing tendency arises the trend towards greater decentralisation and flexibility in the EU methods of governance adopted during the nineties that have further determined the integration of environmental concerns in other policy sectors. Pollack (2000) argues that this trend is from a climate of political resistance by the Member States towards the fast expansion of centralised supranational policies touching upon topics of geopolitical importance. In terms of increased flexibility, dynamism and changes on governance, Orlando (2014) recalls the influence of the sustainable development discourses brought by the 5th EAP added to the integration approach, as well as the 'proceduralisation' of the relevant environmental obligations and greater use of framework directives and horizontal measures, which are those measures that do not focus on specific natural resources, but on cross-cutting issues such as the legislation that brings to this 'model' efficient instruments of environmental impact assessment and public access to information that render the European model quite unique on technocratic aspects.[78]

Therefore the trend of non-stopping increasing regulation in the field of environmental law, gets a less strict top-down approach and changes its governance approach with the introduction of more flexible normative elements concerning procedural measures that become crucial to define this model, such as the Integrated Pollution Prevention and Control (IPCC) Directive 1996, Air Quality Framework Directive, Water Framework Directive EU 2000. Such legislation focuses on procedural requirements such as permissions, planning and reporting obligations that have been embedded in national regulations of the MS, and at the level of individual enterprises. New Environmental Policy Instruments (NEPIs) respond to the need for more cost-effective and efficient methods of improving the implementation of environmental law (Orlando, 2014). This new instrumental legislation, which will continue to grow to include, market-based instruments, environmental impact assessment (EIA), strategic Environmental Assessment (SEA), Sustainability Appraisal (SA) and Appropriate Assessment (AA) will not replace traditional 'command and control' regulatory approaches but they will be facilitating a move towards a more 'cooperative' approach based on the involvement of multiple actors and the different levels of governance in a process of dialogue and 'mutual learning'(Lenschow, 2002; Orlando, 2014).

It is important to differentiate the unsystematic integration of environmental requirements through various administrative and more 'cooperative' arrangements (Green stars, Environmental Evaluations, Environmental Impact Assessments of new legislative proposals and the appointment of integration correspondents) from

[78]See further, Orlando (2014), Krämer (2001).

the European Council efforts to try and find a different organised strategy for environmental integration. Such policy approach was expected from the Cardiff process starting in 1998. The Cardiff European Council not only welcomed the Commission's Strategy for integrating environmental concerns, but also invited all relevant formations of the Council to establish their own strategies for giving effect to environmental integration and sustainable development, within their respective policy areas, considering transport, energy and agriculture sectors for the first wave of this process.[79] Krämer (2013) conclusions about 'the failure of the EU approach, which was linked to the so-called Cardiff process" are echoed by the Commission's own 2004 stocktaking exercise on the implementation of the principle of environmental integration, which concludes: 'However environmental integration commitments are still largely to be translated into further concrete results for the environment. To date, the Cardiff process has failed to deliver fully on expectations'.[80] It is also true that the most important environmental provision of the whole Lisbon treaty enshrined by the integration principle in Art. 11, still raises today considerable implementation problems for lawyers, policy-makers and administrations (Krämer, 2013, p. 83).

Nevertheless the evolution of environmental law either at Treaty level, by secondary law or technocratic instruments has always been drastic. Every environmental program recasts efforts to broaden the EU environmental objectives. The 6th EAP identified the objectives and priorities of the EU over the 2002–2012 and today has brought the EU protection model to a leadership in these fields. The 6th EAP came out when climate change concerns were incipient also at global level, and for that decade four thematic areas guided European regulations towards a bigger compromise to protect climate change, nature and biodiversity and nature protection and sustainable use of marine resources,[81] as well as implementing new regulation in the field of genetically modified organisms' (2003).

From Aarhus Convention to the adoption of Regulation 1907/2006 (REACH regulation) to its recent winter package, the EUSM cannot only be criticised for the lack of a stronger sense of identity of Europeans' belonging to a common 'sustainability' project and ecological transition. This is associated to a cultural and educational challenge. In terms of regulatory proliferation, the EU has reached important landmarks. Within this context the Aarhus Convention is an important instrument in citizens' hands. It was adopted on 25 June 1998, and entered into force on 30 October 2001, establishing a number of rights of individuals and associations (public in

[79]COM (98) 716 and COM (99) 640 (transport); COM (98) 571 (energy); COM (99) 22 and COM (2000) 20 (agriculture); COM (99) 263 (internal market); COM (99) 36 and COM (2000) 264 (development); COM (2001) 143 (fisheries); COM (2000) 576 (economic questions); and SEC (2002) 271 (external affairs), and on agriculture, Decision 2179/98 OJ 1998 L275/1 setting out the Community's objectives in integrating environmental requirements into the Common Agriculture Policy.

[80]Commission, Integrating Environmental Considerations Into Other Policy Areas- a Stocktaking of the Cardiff Process COM (2004) 394 final, 1 June 2004, at. P. 31.

[81]European Commission 2007, EU 2008a, 2008b.

general) with regard to the environment. The Convention provides a substantial legal framework fostering access to environmental information, public participation in environmental decision-making, and access to justice.[82] Another key landmarks concerning the most recent period of appraisal of the EUSM evolution regards the current requirements of the energy transition, the climate change policy, human rights and access to justice issues, waste management and sustainable consumption and production that is challenging already European's consumption habits.

Still, the case study of the EU's energy policy highlights the manner in which the comprehensive sustainable development paradigm has been somehow vanished by a narrow definition of sustainability, for it has too often being perceived as the dimension of the energy policy focusing on the reduction of Green House Gas (GHS) emissions to combat climate change, and not even the EU Court of Justice has tried to broaden this dimension. On the other side, it is a truism that energy policy-making process at EU level, and the significant changes introduced at constitutional level on this field,[83] have helped reinforcing the sustainability paradigm fostering a new *acquis* of communitarian origin based on a 'sustainable European making'. Unfortunately, although the energy-policy has been one of the most prominent fields embracing this new paradigm is also, in a controversial manner, the most at risk towards marginalisation by focusing on Member States interest on decarbonisation without attaining to common policies and the transfer of good practices introducing the right balance between the hegemonic position of social demands and sustainable development (Sánchez Galera, 2016). Perhaps this can be overcome thanks to the efforts put on the "recognition of energy as a common good", decentralising local production and launching an energy package that puts citizens at the core of the energy transition.

The EU is on the good track (i.e., French Energy Transition Law of July 2015, Finnish full decabornisation initiative, German phasing out nuclear power) towards the improvement of the social and environmental well-being within Member States regardless of its original functioning on market-based instruments.

The most important legal instruments of this model that have transformed the environmental *acquis* into a 'sustainability' *acquis communautaire* also relate to the most recent circular economy package and the successful European Climate and

[82]The Commission has recently launched a public consultation concerning a lack of compliance with the rights of the public that it endorses. The Aarhus Convention Compliance Committee found that the EU does not comply with the access to justice provisions of the Convention because of insufficient mechanisms to ensure review of EU acts (ACCC/C/2008/32).

[83]Note at the first place the so-called Cardiff process (regardless of its unsuccessful development), launched in 1998, which concerns the integration of the environment into sectorial policies for the sake of sustainable development. Despite several summits discussing the Cardiff Process with a view to developing a comprehensive and integrated strategy for sustainability, it still remained unclear how and to what extent the Cardiff process can be linked to the agenda of sustainability. Furthermore, the Treaty of Lisbon introduces a chapter about Energy. Energy Policy falls 'brand new' into the sovereign domain of the EU, suggesting in its wording "sustainability" with a conciliatory nature towards some ecological concerns, encapsulated in Article 194 and Article 195 of the TFEU.

Energy system. As we already mentioned, the EU is the world leader in climate policy, having already taken important steps towards a sustainable, low carbon future. The most recent Energy Roadmap 2050, calls nearly for complete elimination (80–95% reduction) of greenhouse gases by midcentury. The "Clean Energy for all Europeans' Package" has been approved and the EU is in the process of updating its energy policy framework in a way that will facilitate the clean energy transition. This is a very significant complex step towards the creation of the Energy Union and delivering on the EU's Paris agreement commitments. An important and innovative element of the new policy framework is the 'regulatory' certainty, in particular through the introduction of the first national energy and climate plans, encouraging essential investments to take place in this sector. The other essential element is the full integration and empowerment of European citizens to become fully active players in the energy transition that would have never been launched without the joint EU efforts. It also fixes two new targets for the EU for 2030: a binding renewable energy target of a least 32% and an energy efficiency target of at least 32.5%, with a possible upward revision in 2023. For the electricity market, it confirms the 2030 interconnection target of 15%, following on from the 10% target for 2020.

The previous 20/20/20 by 2020 were comprised of three key objectives: a 20% reduction in the EU GHG emissions from 1990 levels; raising share of EU energy consumption produced from renewable resources to 20%, and a 20% improvement in the EU's energy efficiency. At the level of EU as a whole, there is the EU Emissions Trading System (EU ETS) working on the 'cap and trade' principle and currently, being in its third phase (2013–2020), a single, EU-wide cap on emissions applies in place of the previous system of national caps. The Energy Union has moved from voluntary soft-objectives for decarbonisation based on the will for transition towards a sustainable Europe[84] to a system of binding targets, as well as the other way around.[85] In fact, one of the main characteristics of the EU energy policy framework lies on the prominent proliferation of soft-law instruments establishing guidelines and action plans that are a good way to react without trying to find ever-lasting political compromises. Suffices to mention the last 2015 Framework Strategy for a Resilient Energy Union with a Forward-looking Climate Change

[84]The EU strategies on Sustainability started with the Lisbon Strategy for the period 2000–2010, and followed by the Europe 2020; a 10-year strategy proposed by the European Commission on 3 March 2010 for advancement of the economy of the European Union. It aims at "smart, sustainable, inclusive growth" with greater coordination of national and European policy. It is the writer opinion that one of the strategy major achievements are the ones concerned with the Energy Union in which the wider spectrum of stakeholders is involved.

[85]Proposal for a REGULATION OF THE EUROPEAN PARLIAMENT AND OF THE COUNCIL on the Governance of the Energy Union, amending Directive 94/22/EC, Directive 98/70/EC, Directive 2009/31/EC, Regulation (EC) No 663/2009, Regulation (EC) No 715/2009, Directive 2009/73/EC, Council Directive 2009/119/EC, Directive 2010/31/EU, Directive 2012/27/EU, Directive 2013/30/EU and Council Directive (EU) 2015/652 and repealing Regulation (EU) No 525/2013.

COM/2016/0759 final - 2016/0375 (COD).

Policy that sets the basis for the EU Strategy that MS states could choose to implement immediately at whatever level of governance.

Not by chance the last package of proposed energy measures also addresses for the first time the issue of Energy Governance (being governance a crucial part of the puzzle of global climate change policy). According to the proposal "[a] resilient Energy Union with an ambitious climate policy and a fundamental transformation of our energy system can only be achieved through a combination of coordinated action – legislative and non-legislative – at EU and national level. To achieve this concrete action, the Energy Union needs strong Governance ensuring that policies and measures at various levels are coherent, complementary and sufficiently ambitious".[86]

The Energy Union project, seeks to further integrate the internal market, and to develop a more common approach to security of supply by creating a genuine solidarity basis which lies behind the climate change global dimension that integrates our energy policy and shapes European Energy Governance based on solidarity and cooperation. Unfortunately, the interaction of unexpected political, social, or economic components could create distortions that the legal framework might have not foreseen, but the new ambitious targets will stimulate Europe's industrial competitiveness, reduce energy bills, create competitive jobs and tackle energy poverty whilst improving air quality and take EU to a leadership on accomplishing the 2030 Global Agenda.

Another benchmark of the EUSM is the impact of EU legislation in the field of chemical safety (REACH regulation) in its international trade relations. REACH regulations are a first class instrument for the EU to push for compliance with its high standards and thereby indirectly export its environmental protection model (Heyvaert, 2009). The EU has also promote adherence to its environmental standards through the imposition of sustainability criteria on imported products (Kulovesi, Morgera, & Muñoz, 2011). These measures reveal EU's unique contribution to global environmental governance and can help to assist failures of international negotiations, more easily in unilateral solutions, rather than multilateral (Orlando, 2014), but can certainly make a difference in the global arena.

The EU has played a leading role in the adoption of many international environmental treaties, including the 1989 Basel Convention on the trans-boundary movement of hazardous waste, the 1992 Convention on Biological Diversity, the 2001 Stockholm Convention on Persistent Organic Pollutants and notably the 2000 Cartagena Protocol on Biosafety and the 1997 Kyoto Protocol on Climate Change (Kelemen and Vogel, 2010; Orlando, 2014), most recently the Paris Agreement 2015. On how influential its sustainability model can be to the neighbouring countries, the bilateral agreements concluded in the context of the European Neighbouring Policy (ENP), the Euro-Mediterranean partnership and the Development and Cooperation policy are important examples (Marín-Durán, and Morgera,

[86]See further, the reasons and objectives of the proposal, https://ec.europa.eu/energy/sites/ener/files/documents/1_en_act_part1_v9_759.pdf.

2012). Cremona (2008) has argued in the past that the EU has a crucial position by representing a privileged relationship on the prospect of progressive participation in the internal market and increased cooperation in sectors of justice and internal affairs facilitating gradual convergence of those countries' domestic regulatory systems with the EU regulatory framework. It means that this sustainability model is strong when facing trade with external members, bringing those states closer to sustainability requirements for the sake of international trade. Although this is not enough to face future challenges and social transformation, it is already a landmark of the EUSM.

On the other hand, from how domestic politics are evolving just now throughout Europe, important issues, including key ones such as migration and liberal democracy appear to fall apart from consensus, and the European integration dream (Rifkin, 2011) is hampered by heterogeneity of political views and withdrawal momentum. It remains to see whether the 'sustainability model' based on areas that have traditionally relied on broad consensus (i.e., climate change, agriculture, food, waste, water management, transport, chemicals), does not touch issues too much related to 'sovereignty' matters and manages to coordinate institutionally a smart program to innovate and help Member States to accelerate their societies into ecological constrains, and awareness.

The regulatory instruments and the amount of binding legislation, communication, recommendations, etc., coming from the EU Commission have rendered the whole area of environmental law, climate change, circular economy package and development and cooperation policy, extremely complicated and tremendously ambitious, but the European coordinated action has so far brought success and leadership to Europe and European Member States singularly to face the major social and economic transitions within sustainability constrains.

The Circular Economy Action Plan adopted by the European Commission in December 2015, an ambitious new Circular Economy Package launched to stimulate Europe's transition towards a circular economy which will boost global competitiveness, foster sustainable economic growth and generate new jobs.[87] The European Commission has already presented its report in which all 54 actions foreseen under the Circular Economy Action Plan have now been delivered or are being implemented paving the way towards a climate-neutral, competitive circular economy where pressure on natural and freshwater resources and ecosystems is minimised.[88] Through the Circular Economy Action Plan the Commission has mainstreamed circular principles into plastic production and consumption, water management, food systems and the management of specific waste streams. The revised waste legislation, so unique and definitely a blueprint for the EU

[87]http://Europa.eu/rapid/press-release_IP-15-6203_en.pdf.

[88]See Report from the Commission to the European Parliament, the Council, the European Economic and Social Committee and the Committee of the Regions on the implementation of the Circular Economy Action Plan, Brussels, 4.3.2019, COM (2019) 190 final.

sustainability model, includes all the revised waste legislation[89] and it requires that by 2030, 70% of all packaging waste and, by 2035, 65% of municipal waste should be recycled, while reducing landfilling of municipal waste to 10%. A five year time extension is granted to several countries.[90]

The 2030 Agenda for Sustainable Development is rooted into the international cooperation and development policy of the EU and there is a strong and renewed emphasis on the EU's global strategy. The SDGs will be a cross-cutting dimension of the implementation of the EU's global strategy. 'The European Consensus on Development' ('European Consensus on Development: our world, our dignity, our future', Official Journal of the European Union, C 210, 30 June 2017) is a plan aligning the Union's development policy with the 2030 Agenda for Sustainable Development to strengthen the EU's response to the 2030 Agenda to improve coordinated implementation and enforcement, as well as improve EU impact at international level. There are so many cross-cutting topics as part of the development and cooperation agenda in which the EU model through the regulatory and institutional action success at internal policy level could lead a way to impact the global action, this is, youth, gender equality, mobility and migration, sustainable energy and climate change, investment and trade, good governance, democracy, the rule of law and human rights, innovative engagement with more advanced developing countries, mobilising and using domestic resources. However, migration, current political changes and welfare policies are putting so much pressure on the long standing 'solidarity' realm of the EU sustainability model (that I will not discuss here).

Still, it is fair to confirm that a clearly successful new paradigm of sustainable development that is building a new body of *acquis communautaire* in all European sectorial policies is here to stay despite its complexities and uncompleted 'shape', if we considered closely the less ecological aspects, which are in any case the ethos of this model. There is an abundant and prolific set of normative components, impact data documents, performance related reports, as well as a prolific growth of bottom-up approaches that are currently gaining momentum and could lead the EU to shape the uniqueness of its growth model at international level although culture, educational, labor, and some other welfare concerns in general do not make a bigger appearance.

It suffices to say that however imperfect might be, the existence of the EUSM is undeniable, and its challenges are more related to social concerns, than to the specific value of its regulatory body integrating environmental concerns in sectorial policies in order to reach a sustainable growth.

[89]OJ, 14.62018, L 150, p 93, 100, 109, 141 Directive 2008/98/EC on waste, Directive 1999/31/EC on the landfill of waste, Directive 94/62/EC on packaging and packaging waste, Directive 2000/53/EC on end-of life vehicles, Directive 2006/66/EC on batteries and accumulators and waste batteries and accumulators, Directive 2012/19/EU on waste electrical and electronic equipment (WEEE).

[90]Greece, Croatia, Cyprus, Latvia, Lithuania, Hungary, Malta, Romania, Slovakia and Bulgaria.

3.3.2 *From the 'Environmentalisation' of EU Sectorial Policies to a More Complex Agenda Building a Strong Global Leadership of the Multidimensional EUSM*

Our next concern regards the attempt of the EU to enhance its sustainability model by adding other issues to the robust environmental protection agenda. I have referred to this attempt, somewhere else,[91] as the 'process of the EU to become a *fox* after being a *hedgehog*': "The fox knows many things, but the hedgehog knows one big thing". Such ancient Greek aphorism that, was preserved in a fragment from the poet Archilochus, helped Isaiah Berlin,[92] and later on time the same metaphor helped Dworkin[93] to describe their central thesis as it helps me to illustrate how the EU sustainability model passes from an incomplete model of sustainability exclusively based on 'environmental' concerns to integrate other policies related to social justice matters. By integrating other social, cultural and educational concerns the EU becomes a more consolidated model of SD. A major integration of social concerns becomes an instrumental cornerstone of its future strategies.

We must say that the current EU policy agenda on sustainable development is quite social already but lacks of substantial and normative efficiency. The political agenda of the current Commission is actually mainly focused on jobs, growth, fairness, and democracy, but we know Europe is still full of inequalities. In 2001, Jímenez Beltrán (2001) the Executive Director of the European Environmental Agency, recognised that "sustainability would not come directly from environmental policies, but from socio-economic policies, guided by sustainability paradigms".[94]

The political landmark of the MS towards a more social version of its sustainability policy arrived for the first time with the European Council agreement on a 'European Union Strategy for Sustainable Development' in its Laeken Declaration on the future of the EU. This declaration characterised Europe as "a power seeking to set globalisation within a moral framework, in other words to anchor it in solidarity and sustainable development".[95] This means that the social component of the EUSM

[91] See Sánchez Galera (2018).

[92] Isiah Berlin quoted such fragment to describe his central thesis on his essay on Leon Tolstoy and the philosophy of history, the subject of the epilogue to War and Peace. The subject of the essay has received many philosophical and psychological interpretations and applications. Applied to Tolstoy, the ancient aphorism sheds light on a paradox that helps explains his philosophy of history. According to Berlin, Tolstoy was a fox, but believed in being a hedgehog. See, Berlin (1953) (2009 reprinted version). As referred to by Sánchez Galera (2018).

[93] In his penultimate book Justice for Hedgehogs, Dworkin used the same metaphor made famous by Isaiah Berlin to explain his idea of justice arguing that in a coherent organisation of society, legal rules cannot be separable from moral judgments; as referred to by Sánchez Galera (2018).

[94] Speech delivered in Brussels, 9 July 2001.

[95] Under the Declaration No. 23 annexed to the Treaty of Nice, the Laeken European Council of 14 and 15 December 2001 decided to organise a Convention bringing together the main parties concerned for a debate on the future of the European Union. See, Presidency Conclusions, reference on line: http://www.consilium.europa.eu/media/20950/68827.pdf.

made its first appearance to remain within the political context of the EU. The EU Sustainable Development Strategy (SDS) should not be confused with the most ambitious plan set by the Lisbon Strategy. They are all part of the EU different phases of integration happening at the same period (Sánchez Galera, 2018).

Pallmaerts (2006), has referred to the EU and 'sustainable development' relationship as an ambiguous one in fact. However, conceptual ambivalences that were found at the back of his discourse should be forgotten based on a clear roadmap enshrined by the EU constitutional existence of SD and its full potential for policy making under more social concerns once its clear identity on the protection of environmental concerns is assumed. The renewed interest on Social rights at European level and the recently launched European Pillar of Social Rights could be an additional instrument to reinforce the EU internal agenda on SD. However, the real effect remains to be seen considering that repeats already existing EU social "acquis", but this time of non-binding legal nature.[96]

Article 9 of the TFEU, by stating that "[i]n defining and implementing its policies and activities, the Union shall take into account requirements linked to the promotion of a high level of employment, the guarantee of adequate social protection, the fight against social exclusion, and a high level of education, training and protection of human health", is defining a clear normative framework of social nature. This treaty provision, brought at constitutional level some of the substance of the social dimension of the EUSM that is also envisaged by Article 3 of the TEU that will be discussed later. Article 9 could be used as horizontal clause in sectorial policies but does not transfer any new competences to the EU, it cannot be used as a legal base for the establishment of a proactive and comprehensive EU social policy, nor as a hermeneutic tool for the CJEU, covering the domains mentioned in the text of the article. Nonetheless we can say along with Bruno De Witte (2019) that "by mainstreaming social policy into all EU policy fields, Article 9 TFEU affirms that social objectives are equivalent to economic objectives within EU primary law".

It is important to understand that excessive predominant considerations on sustainability linked to economic and environmental concerns has hampered a more substantive evolution and improvement of EU action to find solutions to other major problems threatening our societies. This approach has not helped the EU to resolve the distrust of the people of Europe towards the Union's political institutions despite of the proliferation of European strategies, and the robust EU constitutional framework. Actually more recent scholarly contributions focusing on the 'social market economy' of the EU (Ferri & Cortese, 2019) have tried to fill this

[96]The European Pillar of Social Rights was finally delivered on 26 April 2017 after presenting a first outline in in 2016 and launching a broad public consultation to gather feedback on both the content and the role of the Pillar. See further, European Commission, Launching a consultation on a European Pillar of Social rights, Strasbourg, 8.3.2016, COM (2016) 127 final; Annex- First preliminary outline of a European Pillar of Social rights, COM (2016) 127 final ANNEX 1. The Communication was accompanied by two Commission Staff Working document: the EU social *acquis*, SWD (2016) 50 final; Key economic, employment and social trends behind a European pillar of Social Rights, SWD (2016) 51 final.

gap by providing a more holistic view of the market economy and the EU, by turning attention to its 'social' components in an integrated approach that has not been done so far, if not in an isolated manner.[97] Education and cultural topics that are an essential part of the social agenda, but they are set behind labour market concerns and social justice issues associated to the energy market, are still neglected as architects of a strong sustainability model and as horizontal enablers of the systemic changes needed for the transformation of society. Cultural and education domains are still understated, on only at EU level, also in the research and policy agendas of the MS. The aim of the Lisbon Strategy launched in March 2000 by the EU heads of State and government, was to make Europe "The most competitive and dynamic knowledge-based economy in the world, capable of sustainable economic growth with more and better jobs and greater social cohesion".

The emphasis located in 'Knowledge' and 'sustainability', should have been an indicator that education, training and culture would have been placed at the forefront of political concerns for the first time, and although Europe has increasingly invested in knowledge and innovation which were part of the first priority action within the policy framework of the Lisbon Strategy, systemic institutional changes have not taken place so far. Nonetheless, the 'Education and Training 2010' work programme establishing a solid framework for European cooperation in the field of education and training in the context of the Lisbon Strategy was based on common European objectives for the first time.[98] These objectives aimed primarily at supporting the improvement of national education and training systems through the development of complementary EU level tools, mutual learning and the exchange of good practice via the open method of coordination. This work programme has been followed by the EU Council Conclusions of 12 May 2009 on a strategic framework for European Cooperation in education and training ('ET 2020').

Significantly the ET 2020[99] agrees on a range of strategic priorities for lifelong learning that go far beyond simply employment goals to include social cohesion, personal and social fulfilment and active citizenship (Downes, 2014, p. 15). Still, Downes (2014) argues that there has been a strong limitation of emphasis on the education sphere at Commission level until recently. Today, the urgent requirements of the current European 'learning society' have been translated on an emphasis placed in regulation proposals establishing the Digital European programme for the period 2021–2017 endorsing the cultural and educational reports to the Committee on Industry, Research and Energy, as the committee responsible.[100]

---

[97]See Novitz (2015).

[98]This European reinforcement of its Education policy within the policy framework of the ambitious Lisbon strategy is an answer to the international call for action in lifelong learning education launched by UNESCO, OECD to face the current demands of our 'Learning society'.

[99]Council conclusions 2009/C 119/02.

[100]See further, the proposal for a regulation of the European Parliament and of the Council establishing the Digital Europe programme for the period 2021–2027 (COM (2018) 0434-C8-0256/2018-2018/0227 (COD)); also the Tallinn Digital Summit of September 2017 and the Conclusions of the European Council of 19 October 2017 indicating the need for Europe to invest in

The other significant emphasis has been placed on the recent development of structural indicators for system level scrutiny that should be replacing the outdated outcome indicators at European Commission level in education and social inclusion (Downes, 2014). This is an ambitious instrumental approach introduced by the ET 2020 strategy at European level and its work programme, and it might turn to be very substantial. This instrumental shift, permits to examine the progress of structural funds investments in education at European level, and ultimately, considering that there are sufficient indicators it is possible to ascertain not only if change is taking place, but also why and how barriers to change may also be occurring (Downes, 2014). These structural indicators that operate at different system level such as individual institution, local, regional, national, EU and potentially UN and OECD levels, help to rely on the identification of key structural conditions for good practice, permitting system changes. The evolution of these type of indicators has been favoured by policy framework action fostered by the UN 2030 Global Agenda on SD that introduces poverty prevention indicators together with other structural indicators employed to scrutinise system changes. These new performance measurement focused on structural changes rather than on outcomes, leaves behind performance indicators that give expression to a neo-liberal agenda in education. Such agendas, unfortunately are still extended in many national policy approaches, particularly at higher education levels which are a crucial issue of the multidimensional version of sustainability. In fact, in Europe there is a broad existing gap between rhetorical engagement at political level and effective action in education policy and culture at national and European level.

Still, another important regulatory area concerned with the social dimension of sustainability that has not been overshadowed by exclusive economic interests is public procurement law. The 2014 European regulatory shift on public procurement dwells on the experience of implementing the 2004 Directives in several Member States and the judgements giving access to environmental and social considerations at the cost of the economic ones. This shift give us evidence of how "due to a more general ascension of the sustainable development concept, governments have been put in the position to lead by example and use their purchasing power in order to advance the goals of sustainable development" (Dragos & Neamtu, 2014), and there is ample room to develop further regulatory measures in this direction in Europe.

We can argue that with the new 2014 Directive the 'sustainability' paradigm is taking over the realm of public procurement and the European case law in this realm can be shown as a good example to illustrate how the EUCJ has built on the right balance between market-based economic interests and the environmental and social aspects of sustainable development.

The debate about the scope of the social elements of public procurement has always been present in European legal literature (Arrowsmith & Kunzlik, 2009;

digitising our economies and addressing the skills gap to maintain and enhance European competitiveness, our quality of life and social fabric, accessible on: https://www.eu2017.ee/news/insights/conclusions-after-tallinn-digital-summit.

Caranta & Trybus, 2010; McCrudden, 2007). Examining that literature, we notice that the European legislator has not been prone to the inclusion of clauses of social sustainability in the contracts, possibly because the issue was not mature enough at European level. Julio González (González García, 2015) argues that this opinion can still be maintained today despite the fact that Directive 2014/24 / EU of the European Parliament and Council of 26 February 2014 on public procurement and repealing Directive 2004/18 / EC has moved towards a more sustainable legal regime environmentally and socially. It is important to bear in mind that the text of the Directive is more concerned with problems of an environmental nature than with those of a social content, which are surrounded by greater difficulty at the time of their inclusion. Still, drawing on the CJEU decisions, we should note that the CJEU has constantly stressed as a matter of principle that the main objective of the EU law on public procurement is the opening up to competition of the public markets in the Member States and ensuring the free movement of goods and services throughout the territory of the EU (González, 2015). However, in a series of decisions, the Court has stated that other objectives than the pure economical or Internal Market ones may be pursued by contracting authorities (Sánchez Galera, 2018).

Hopefully, there should be an intensification of social and legal science literature building on new scholarly approaches that turn their focus on the understanding of new ways of broadening institutional commitments towards the social aspects of sustainable development at EU level. These analytical interventions could be extended to the policy level to irradiate MS policy action.[101] It is important that the CJEU also starts to be more prolific on this.[102] The idea behind those analytical approaches is to strengthen EU social action to reinforce its sustainability model as an integrated body of action useful to face topics that need to go beyond market mechanisms' interests.

In fact, Novitz (2011, Novitz, 2015) has contributed to the scholarly debate that builds on more social aspects of sustainability. She has been invoking the involvement of the sustainability paradigm with a forward looking policy, as it corresponds to the current external and internal commitment to comply with the UN Agenda on SDGs. She argues indeed that "sustainable development cannot be understood as a static endpoint ascertained through expert advice. Rather, it is a dynamic process with a future orientation looking towards improved economic, social and environmental conditions. Further, it is a participatory process, for we cannot have sustainability (or its synonym, durability) without social engagement and commitment to the conditions we seek to achieve and the means of their realization" (Novitz, 2011). In fact, her proposal is concerned with the invigoration of democratic participatory processes which go beyond that reduced interest base (Novitz, 2015) and beyond the

[101]See Sjåfjell (2009), Novitz (2015).

[102]See further on this, Novitz (2015). She illustrates the limited approach of the CJEU through the analysis of its legal reasoning precluding workers that had suffered after 'austerity' policies. The approach of the CJEU in, precludes workers affected by those policies from being consulted over the future development of key workplace matters which affects their livelihoods and their communities. The CJEU not only does not aid sustainability concerns, but it is actually overlooked.

economic dynamics of the market. Under this light, she claims for trade unions to play a more significant role through the "legal recognition that *future interests* come within the sphere of their legitimate concerns" (Novitz, 2015). On her reasoning she mentions some European trade union experiences who have assisted in enabling environmental change in the workplace (Norwegian LO, The Danish Confederation of Trade Unions and the British Trades Union Congress (TUC)). She gives a picture of the difficulties for trade unions to represent citizens for sustainable development purposes when there are clashes between short term interests of trade union members (e.g., retention of jobs in a particular industry) and the longer terms interests of a wider range of society in environmental protection from pollutants emanating from that industry (Novitz, 2015). Under the 'intergenerational' component of the EU constitutional claim for sustainable development, legal recognition under EU law based on sustainability would be a corollary for trade union entitlement to voice concerns "not only relating to present current worker's immediate needs, but those of the future worker we envisage and their needs-our younger colleagues, our future colleagues and indeed, our children and those not yet born" (Novitz, 2015).

To me, however how crude this statement might sound, a multidimensional Europe is only half way to achieve a suitable role model on the sustainability governance scenario. The idea of a 'social Europe' broadening support under market law, or even human rights law (as it has been argued)[103] is still far from representing a potential future to contrast the unidirectional and damaging neoliberal picture of a market that cannot longer ignore its social compromise with the peoples of Europe. Yet, the EU's growing role on coordinating the sustainability strategy has been growing over time and the complexity of its economic governance that this process implies needs to be discussed elsewhere. "Europe 2020" promoting "smart, sustainable and inclusive growth" implies an important refit for the governance structure, but much falls into the existing gap between inertia and effective action. The introduction of the European Semester in 2011, combining governance instruments in economic and social governance of the EU within one single annual policy coordination cycle was also a way to introduce an improved economic policy coordination in the Union and 'push towards implementation of the EU's economic rules' (Gornitzka, 2018, p. 14), stealing leading role from social policies' concerns.

Another important aspect of the multidimensional EUSM regards the current role of communities leading social transformation. Legal scholarly research is also missing in this instance. The 'Bristol accord' and later the 'Leipzig Charter on Sustainable European Cities'[104] detail a common European approach to 'sustainable communities' concerned with social issues signed up to by EU MS, which build on previous EU initiatives including the Aalborg Charter and Agenda 21. This charter has been a yardstick instrument for 'European Urban Development' together with the local climate Change initiative raised in Europe by the Covenant of Mayors and has influenced the growth of cultural and education activities promoted at urban

[103]Novitz (2015).

[104]http://ec.europa.eu/regional_policy/archive/themes/urban/leipzig_charter.pdf.

level. The EU climate change and energy policy, provides compelling evidence that unprecedented institutional, cultural and socio-technological transformations are required to address the challenges that underpin a sustainable transition in our cities, and not only we regards to regulation concerning climate change and the energy transition, but with the regards to the most social aspects of citizenship. Those social aspects, should become a point of departure in a looking-forward policy building a strong sustainability model with an ecological heart. Not by chance, even the transition towards a new way of consumption and production (circular economy policy) and towards a new energy model in the EU (which was already established in 2011), constrains the EU to the challenging objective of moving beyond metrics and progress assessment based on indicators concerned with material self-sufficiency and recycling. The energy and the circular economy package are the best policy areas to test future challenges and eventual opportunities of the unique EU social market economy. Mete & Heffron (2019) have discussed the challenge of reconciling economic and social concerns in the EU energy law. The authors show how the continuing imbalances and injustices could be addressed in the realm of the EU social market economy. Their focus addresses social and economic rights regulated within the sphere of EU energy law despite of the tensions that neoliberal market interest bring to the fore in a sector that is highly associated with strong competitiveness. Heffron and McCauley (2017) have worked on the idea of providing a core concept model of energy justice to develop a knowledge based instead of challenging other core concepts neglecting social justice in the energy realm. This conceptual approach is useful and if extended can grow as part of the EU energy governance which is one of the most relevant pillar of the EUSM. It presupposes a wider approach to the energy life cycle building on a common knowledge based approach with its own conceptual model based on the idea of energy justice integrating social justice concerns and broadening the energy life cycle including notions of restorative justice and education. This approach revisits the whole body of energy law to facilitate social and democratic aspects of energy consumption, production and transmission.

Economists have been working for a longer time on the need to discuss new conceptualisations in the different sustainability related policies to foster systemic changes (Göpel, 2016). Legal scholars need more encouragement to engage with this sort of analysis that needs new conceptual frameworks and common based knowledge to further develop and strengthen the multidimensional EUSM. A crucial sector in which systemic changes are urgent regards the whole circular economy plan of the EU which will be a key instrument for further evolution of the EUSM. The Circular economy plan is very ambitious and a whole integrated regulatory regime is not enough. This action plan of the EU regards a wide variety of policy issues (production, consumption, market, culture, agriculture, food, etc.) and it has become increasingly important component of the EU's development strategy. Economists have been drawing our attention to the lack of critical studies on the socio-economic implications of the shift towards a circular economy system. They argue that behind the selection and interpretation of the metrics proposed by the Commission there is a weak political will to rightly address deficiencies of the policy instruments of such circular economy plan. In addition there is a lack of critical studies on the socio-economic implications of the shift towards circular Economy promoting the diffusion of 'non-conflict' scenarios (Llorente-González and Vence, 2019). They suggest the development of a monitoring framework for the transition towards circular economy representing a "unique opportunity to reinforce the most comprehensive and systemic meaning of the concept, in order to assess its real contribution to sustainability", for this purpose they recommend to incorporate the indicators on energy, land and water use, and emissions which are already included in other European policy areas; as well as indicators to track the average durability of products, together with its main determinants linked to eco-design, repair, reuse and collaborative consumption activities (Llorente-González and Vence, 2019). The systemic approach they suggest should in turn demand the development of new metrics and incorporation of dimensions, such as the institutional drivers required for an ecological transition of the EU. Applied to the context of circular economy action plan, it involves, among other things, "an assessment of the evolution of legal and fiscal enablers and barriers to circular economy-related innovation, together with the resources and actions put in motion by UE innovation system to that end" (Llorente-González and Vence, 2019, p. 18).

The same can be done in every single policy sector under the light of social justice premises shaping a better sustainability model, but although legal scholarship engagement has grown in this realm, the highest interest is still focused on the legal consequences of the digital burst of our societies.

3.3.3 Education and Culture as Emergent Social Policies Defining the Unique EUSM

Two crucial aspects should be discussed under this heading: (1) the first one regards the timid emerging initiatives building the governance identity of sustainable development related to more social issues in Europe. These initiatives are proliferating striving for a smart, inclusive and sustainable growth and policy strategies in the central fields of education and culture have been increasingly proclaimed. However, it still emerges an existing gap between pretentious policy arrangements and soft normative instruments. Actually, Europe has a big potential for subsidiary and coordinating action in these areas according to its Constitutional foundations but they are not used at their fullest capacities. (2) The second crucial aspect concerns social policies of the EUSM associated to the Open Method of Coordination (OMC), it enables policy cooperation in those areas where the EU has only limited legislative powers.

It has been affirmed that the development strategies include a strong contribution of the cultural sector, with creative industries and education as main factors supporting European economic improvement (Jagielska-Burduk, 2019). However, the opposite is also true. In reality, because of the ongoing political strains undermining the European integration process, and the boost of populisms and anti-European movements, building society's awareness on the importance of cultural heritage, as well as supporting European citizenship values and tolerance for cultural diversity are more important than ever. They are crucial. Nonetheless cultural heritage policy has been neglected for decades. Still the fact that the EU has limited powers in respect of cultural heritage has not prevented the EU and its institutional body from having a leading role for financial support, coordination of joint projects, efforts and sharing of knowledge in this area. In fact, early discussions on the design and structure of cultural OMC were characterised by the absence of pre-existing coordination processes operating in the framework of the EU's cultural policy (Psychogiopoulou, 2018).

Article 167 of the TFEU does not elaborate on any coordination mechanism and only refers to incentive measures and recommendations on legal instruments available for the objectives that this legal provision enumerates. The cultural OMC has suffered a drastic evolution since its first cycle. The main challenges have been addressed modifying its structure and operation, involving the implementation of the strategic objectives and priority areas, and introducing a close coordinated action between the Council and the Commission keeping informed the EU Parliament, the European Economic and Social Committee of the Regions. Triennial working plans and specialised working groups linked to a revised set of policy priorities have been introduced. The major improvement has been noticeable by introducing the possibility of consultation mechanisms available for the different stakeholders and the participation of civil society in the working groups' activities. However, the OMC does not involve any particular guidelines with goals to be attained within a detailed time schedule, even if the process is performed under the overarching framework of the Agenda for Culture[105] and other priorities set under EU 2020 Strategy (Psychogiopoulou, 2018). In addition it also lacks any concrete institutionalised follow-up mechanism which would be more valuable than any eventual enhancement of policy instruments to reach convergence as opposed to 'coordination'.[106]

However it is important to highlight the EU international expertise in the field of cultural heritage and cultural heritage preservation as a focal cultural asset of the EUSM. According to the 2014 Communication, Europe shall be 'a laboratory for heritage-based innovation',[107] it mentions many forms of cooperation and cooperative activities to enhance further European integration through cultural heritage based initiatives. These cooperation processes are based on different methods and tools involving activities at different administration levels. Integrated policy approaches like this particular EU initiative hail openness to face current social problems that build a sustainable Europe through education and cultural heritage

[105]Communication COM(2007) 242 final of 10 May 2007 from the Commission on a European agenda for culture in a globalising world.

[106]Coordination that has been envisaged by MS as policy 'cooperation' (Psychogiopoulou, 2015, p. 39).

[107]COM (2014) 477 final (n60) para 4.

issues. They are occurring in multiple interrelated fields.[108] It has to be noted that 'the interaction of policies in both the areas of culture and education is also determined by other policies in the areas of regional development, social cohesion, agriculture, maritime affairs, environment, tourism, education, the digital agenda, research and innovation' (Jagielka-Burduk, 2019) and this collaboration helps facing education and cultural sustainability defies in a more systemic way with eventual long lasting consequences for the EUSM.

The role of culture with a cross-sectorial relevance is actually gaining policy interest from European expertise on the cultural sector worldwide. Besides the ability of culture to provide answers to wider economic and social concerns in the EU has been resolutely advanced by the European Institutions and culture has gained recognition as an area of broad policy relevance (Psychogiopoulou, 2018).[109] This has been evidenced by strong pro-cultural policies for institutional capacity building, more financing on cultural initiatives, marketing, tourism, and protection of Intellectual Property Rights (IPRs). Under sustainability premises the most immediate challenge is the urgent requirement of valuing culture for enhancing awareness on the linkage between culture and development of ecological consciousness, and the well-being of society. Cultural activities in the EU have become in the last decades an integral part of preservation and social cohesion activities.

When drawing attention to the education things are slightly different. It emerges with stronger emphasis in the last European communications and strategies concerning SD. However, after an overview of the field, it emerges that vocational training has been the most important component of community education and training policy. In reality it was the only education-related field in which the original Treaty of Rome had endowed the Community with formal competences. It is still central to the policies of the union because of its strong connection with employment policy. Thus, school policy, which can be considered a different subsystem of the overall education policy, is a relatively recent component of community education policies (Halász, 2013, p. 271).[110] The trend towards certain transforming engagement at EU institutional level to enhance action in a wider spectrum of public policies, and other education subsystems outside market interests started with the changes introduced by the Maastricht Treaty and should not stop after subsequent constitutional developments that have helped integrating sustainability premises in every EU policy. Those normative developments have fostered the proliferation of political-administrative organisation at the European supranational level and this has been a catalyst for promoting interest for the study of emerging institutions and soft

[108]CEU 'Conclusions on Cultural heritage as a strategic resource for a sustainable Europe Education, Youth, Culture and Sport Council meeting' Brussels, 20 May 2014.

[109]The author stresses that this call for a holistic approach going beyond cultural policy, finds support in the opportunities offered by Art. 167 para. 4, TFEU for synergies between culture and other policies.

[110]See further for an overview of the EU education policy plan, European Agenda for European Cooperation in Schools, European Commission (2008).

law instruments shaping the unique EU development model. This is specially the case with European agencies as newcomers in the EU regulatory space.[111]

Different forms of coordination are materialised in fields such as social and economic policy, employment, culture, education and research and they have been proliferating since the emergence of the OMC. The OMC has become a central feature among the new forms of soft governance that are part of the emblematic multidimensional nature of the EUSM and its most recent normative developments associated to neglected social policies. The OMC plays an important role within the domains of education and increasingly in the cultural domain too but these areas are not deemed to be harmonised according to the EU constitutional basis.

The OMC is an EU policy-making process, formally initiated by the Lisbon European Council in 2000. Its main feature is that the OMC does not result in EU legislation but it constitutes a flexible and valuable method of soft governance which aims to spread best practices and achieve convergence towards EU goals in those policy areas which fall under the partial or full competence of the MS. Thus, where binding EU rules cannot be used as the means to achieve convergence among MS OMC relies on other mechanisms. These mechanisms involve establishing guidelines, quantitative and qualitative indicators and benchmarks, and national and regional targets, backed by periodic evaluations and peer reviews.[112] Cultural policy indeed needs more quality and quantity evidence to support the economic and social benefits of its achievements. The lack of evidence has often resulted in an undervaluing of cultural instruments and cultural institutions.

Nowadays the idea of culture and education as precious instruments to advance systemic changes through compelling guidelines pursuing the ecological transition in Europe is more widely accepted, but the EU package of policy measures of the European Green Deal has not advanced a specific roadmap for cultural and educational matters that should be considered transversal to the green transition Europe ambitions to achieve by reviewing each existing law on its climate change policy, circular economy, building renovation, biodiversity, farming and innovation, technology and research. The plan was put ahead on the 13th of December 2019, with an opt-out for Poland. The Europeanisation of policy fields related to climate change issues has been evident since Lisbon onwards, but we have to wait and see what happens with an eventual green Europeanisation of the cultural and education field turning more attention to the European institutional mechanisms for social policy intervention such as the OMC.

According to the Lisbon European Council the OMC has four elements as its main characteristics: (1) identifying and defining common goals for the Union with specific timetables for achieving them; (2) establishing indicators and benchmarks for assessing progress towards the goals; (3) translating common objectives to national and regional policies taking into account national and regional differences;

---

[111] Vos (2000).

[112] See further, *The open method of coordination at a Glance*. European Parliament, 2014. http://www.europarl.europa.eu/EPRS/EPRS-AaG-542142-Open-Method-of-Coordination-FINAL.pdf.

and (4) engaging in periodic monitoring, evaluation and peer review organised as mutual learning processes.[113] The potential that this system has for the current educational and cultural challenges at EU level is enormous. Gornitzka (2018) asserts, indeed, that the Lisbon strategy in 2000 is a landmark for European Education policy, since the moment EU heads of state policy stated the EU's ambition to become the most competitive knowledge-based economy in the world, in the sense, that this political declaration positioned education in the interface with the EU's economic and social policy. In fact, Education received attention in Lisbon as part of a much larger agenda and political project, and although it has never been at the forefront of the EUSM is gaining attention, and not only at governmental level.[114]

The novelty introduced by the Lisbon strategy was the definition of the whole knowledge and skills area as a necessary component of an economic and social reform strategy. The Commission's Directorate General Education and Culture (DG EAC) pushed the education sector's contribution to this strategy and the visibility of the education sector as a whole.[115] In addition to this, the reference the Lisbon Spring Council in 2000 made to the OMC with regard to education and culture opened a procedural way forward for how the education sector could be organised in a different way. A good example of this is offered by a new governance template to match the new ideas about the EU's transition to the knowledge economy.[116] The Lisbon summit sought to address challenges of globalisation and the new knowledge-driven economy, but the goals addressed in the education sector were presented in such a broad manner that, according to Gornitzka (2018), they left the entire policy domain open. Other intergovernmental process (considering the lack of direct EU competence on such sensitive sector despite of its important relation to the job market sector and social integration domain)[117] towards establishing the European Higher Education Area ("The Bologna Process") and the EU's "Copenhagen Process" for vocational education and training were subsequently added to include the whole range and forms of education subsystems. In fact, from then onwards the OMC process in education was referred to as "Education and Training 2010".[118]

---

[113]European Council Conclusions of 23-24 March 2000.

[114]See last Pope Francis I declarations on the Global Compact on Education the 14th May 2020, http://www.unitedworldproject.org/en/workshop/pope-francis-a-global-pact-for-education/. In line with Francesco (2015).

[115]In fact, Gornitzka (2018) argues that the Commission's DG EAC was central in the process of setting up the OMC. Without DG EAC's organisational capacity and attention attached to the OMC this organisational innovation would not have been included in the governance arrangements of EU Education policy.

[116]Gornitzka (2018).

[117]See further Garben (2011).

[118]Gornitzka (2018). The author refers to the Communication COM (2003) 685 final of 11 November 2003 from the Commission, "Education and Training 2010": The success of the Lisbon Strategy hinges on urgent reforms (Draft joint interim report on the implementation of the detailed work programme on the follow-up of the objectives of education and training systems in Europe).

The TFEU does not mention OMC as such specifically, but it does introduce its characteristic elements in specific Treaty provisions (De la Porte, 2002). Several provisions in the TFEU refer to it in substance, without naming it as such: Articles 149 on employment; Article 153 (2) (a) and Article 156 on social policy; Article 168 (2) on public health; Article 173 (2) on industry; Article 181 (2) on research and development; in addition, there is an OMC in education that is unhelpfully not mentioned in the Treaty (Garben, 2015). It is evidently a way to further integrate nationally sensitive policy areas where legal competence is lacking but coordination on the European level is necessary. The OMC's application in the field of culture was first suggested by the European Commission in the strategic policy document titled 'A European agenda for culture in a globalizing world', which was issued in 2007.[119]

Nevertheless, some doctrinal discussions argue rightly that this method, underestimates the OMC's tangible effects in opening up sensitive national sectors, consequently misjudging the way such mechanisms respect national autonomy. In fact, this sort of non-judicialised policy areas have challenged some of the traditional ideals of EU law, suggesting that soft norms and coordination may provide a viable alternative to hard norms and the Community method (Garben, 2015). This is true concerning social challenges of sustainability at EU level. Gornitzka (2018) argues how Member State's response to the "Education and Training 2010" agenda and OMC template was controversial because of the challenge of coordinating employment policies. In fact, before the Lisbon European Council, the European Employment Strategy had already included lifelong learning as an area of cooperation, so that National Ministers of Education were nudged towards defending the educational domain (Gornitzka, 2018, p. 12).[120] Since then, the evolution of the OMC mechanism and the institutional evolution of the EU has been more relevant. The quantified aspects of the OMC process have been institutionalised, such as the role of the Standing group on Indicators and Benchmarks. A specific Centre for Research on Education and Lifelong Learning (CRELL) was established as part of the Commission's Joint Research Centre. To this day, CRELL continues to monitor the EU 2020 targets fostering a new strategy for creating jobs and promoting "smart, sustainable and inclusive growth". CRELL monitors development in education and training and conducts analysis to feed policy decisions at the EU level.[121]

The relevance of the OMC for the EUSM lies on its validity as a coordinating policy instrument in multiple problematic areas of European law with relevant social implications, but it is outside the scope of this analysis to define further its impact on social policies and its contradictory governance effects.[122] Giubboni (2015) argues how Eastern Enlargement and the Great political-financial crisis of the Eurozone

[119]Communication from the Commission to the European Parliament, the Council, the European Economic and Social Committee and the Committee of the Regions on a European agenda for culture in a globalizing world, COM(2007) 242 final.

[120]Gornitzka explains how the OMC process became a way of reclaiming European cooperation in the area of lifelong learning from the EES and fending off the invasion of the labour market/employment perspective of the educational policy turf.

[121]Gornitzka (2018).

[122]On this topic see further, Zeitlin (2005, 2009); and Psychogiopoulou (2017).

"have totally altered the political economy of the European integration" and as such its ambitious social goals that need enhanced action through flexible instruments, considering how some judicial decisions might show retrenchment in the discourse on EU citizenship as a source for transnational social solidarity (Giubboni, 2015). This observation is also applicable to any other social or cultural matter aiming at closer integration and social enhancement as part of EU objectives. As a matter of fact, the OMC, has been surpassed for harder versions during the last financial crisis with the stability and growth path; also the governance structure of the energy governance surpass the method of open coordination, and has been perceived as case of "harder" soft governance in conflict with Article 194 (2) of the TFEU that lacks specific energy competences with respect to the national energy mix (Ringel & Knodt, 2018). The OMC can be used as a conciliatory strategy policy tool, prioritising emerging needs and goals, especially where competences at EU level is limited but needed for common European targets and further coordination. Still, the direct consequence of the European Semester introduced by the European "Strategy 2020"[123] and the stronger role in policy coordination given to the Commission has of course represented a severe transformation of the OMC, and the whole context in which the main operating mechanisms for the coordination of the education and cultural field operate, but national sensitivity on matters of educational nature and culture will continue to help these sector's specific work programme to privilege and defend the OMC as coordination and policy action method at EU level.

The current "Education and Training 2020" strategy proposed by the European Commission was adopted by the ministers of education in 2009, that is, before the overall "big" growth strategy (Halász, 2013, p. 269). This is supposed to be an important fact "because it shows that the education sector is not simply implementing the "big" strategy, but it also plays a kind of forerunner role" (Halász, 2013, p. 269) in the EU strategic future plans. This is also an indication of the prominent role of the education sector in the Europe 2020 growth strategy, which is further evidenced by the fact that from eight measurable key policy targets ("headline targets") approved by the heads of states in summer 2010, two are directly related with education (early school leaving and tertiary graduation), and three others (employment rate R&D and poverty reduction) are strongly, although indirectly linked with the performance of the education sector (Halász, 2013, p. 269). Still, it has been argued that,[124] beyond the programmatic role this strategy might have for key policy initiatives, the policy plan that might have the soundest influence on the development of the education systems in the Member States is the reform of national qualifications systems triggered by the adoption of the European Qualifications Framework (EQF).[125] This voluntary harmonising shift linking the level of each

[123]Communication COM (2010) 2020 final of 3 March 2010 from the Commission, Europe 2020: A Strategy for Smart, Sustainable and Inclusive Growth.

[124]See further Halász (2013).

[125]Recommendation of the European Parliament and of the Council of 23 April 2008 on the establishment of the European Qualifications Framework for lifelong learning (Official Journal C 111, 6 May 2008). It is also called the *meta-framework* which aims at orienting national qualifications reforms within the member countries.

national qualification to the European standards and describing specific qualifications in terms of learning outcomes defined as knowledge, skills and competences is a strong measure with important consequences for the European labour market and social sustainability, but is based on fully voluntary basis. It shows how in certain sectors, compelling regulations might not be the finest path. In fact, in this light, Halász (2013) argues that while "harmonising the structure of educational system of its member countries is formally excluded by the EU Treaty, this is something that can be done and is being done on a voluntary basis".

Currently the existing political agenda is mainly focused in social concerns: jobs, growth, fairness and democratic change. The commission's higher education policy is mainly related with funding and governance which are not part, and have a different scope from, the intergovernmental decision (so-called Bologna process) creating a *European Area of Higher Education* harmonising higher education systems. Today's political agenda following discussions with the European Parliament and inspired by the European Council's "Strategic Agenda for the Union in Times of Change"[126] follows the guideline action of the 2030 Agenda for SD and its 17 Sustainable Development Goals, adopted by the UN in September 2015 giving a new impetus to global efforts for achieving sustainable development in a more consensual atmosphere towards its social components, and not only.

The UN Global Agenda 2030, reflected for the first time an international consensus that peace, security, justice for all, and social inclusion were not only to be pursued on their own but they reinforced each other. The same spirit prevails at the level of EU Governance architecture and its ecological protection standards. European standards are a good start for global leadership in ecological action and coordinated action of MS. In fact, as an immediate reaction the European action for sustainability (2016) put forward ten priorities.[127] The ten priorities touch upon key European challenges of social nature. Many of these challenges are deeply intertwined with those of the Sustainable Development Goals. Accordingly the Commission's objectives set in these ten priorities focus mainly on: jobs, growth, education; including topics such as life-long learning, education and training. An investment plan for Europe concerning circular economy is intertwined with more than one goal at the crossroads with educational and cultural concerns and it has to be highlighted as a hallmark of the EU sustainability and new economy model. It means that there is finally some room for devoting importance to more social concerns related to culture and education even as part of highly related economic topics to pursue the systemic changes that any ecological transition needs. The consensus reached with this agenda, its new targets and its monitoring mechanisms at a top-down administrative level are the basic support for a coordinated action that will be bottom-up based with initiatives addressing systemic changes with alternative governance mechanisms and initiatives. The most recently developed initiative of the European Year of Cultural Heritage 2018 (EYCH) gives evidence of this.

[126]Agreed on 26, 27 June 2014. See further; https://www.consilium.europa.eu/uedocs/cms_data/docs/pressdata/en/ec/143477.pdf.

[127]See further, European action for sustainability, COM (2016) 739 final, Strasbourg, 22.11.2016.

The EYCH brings a wide array of opportunities to develop educational measures and boost cultural initiatives at urban level within the scope of enhancing Europe's ecological transition. Notwithstanding that the Work Plan for Culture 2011–2014 presented already a strong link between educational and cultural activities, especially in relation to cultural diversity, intercultural dialogue, and accessible and inclusive culture.[128] According to the European constitutional mandate (Art. 2 TEU),[129] all actions of the EU concerning culture should be in line with the values declared in the EU's founding treaties. According to Article 3 (3) paragraph 4 of the TEU, asserts that the Union "shall respect its rich cultural and linguistic diversity (....)".

Within the European continent context, although outside of the EU institutional body, the role of the Council of Europe with its 47 European member countries, has been crucial to enlarge its original mission focused on human rights and the rule of law and democracy, to a subsequent inclusion of culture and cultural heritage as elements of democratic governance. The EU commission also supports some of the CoE cultural initiatives, they have several joint programmes.[130] The European Landscape Convention of the Council of Europe 2000[131] that will discuss later has been a landmark worldwide for integrating early sustainability concerns into natural resources and landscape protection, and has helped to enlarge the governance mechanism for landscape protection and its cultural enhancement taking into account 'locality' and the need to avoid standardised assumptions.

Still cultural policy is the sole responsibility of the Member States without forgetting that Article 3 (3) of the TEU states that the Union shall 'ensure that Europe's cultural heritage is safeguarded and enhanced'. The substance of this policy area and its legal basis are enshrined in Article 167 of the TFEU, the EU's

---

[128]CEU 'Conclusions of the Council and the Representatives of the Governments of Member States, meeting within the Council, on the Work Plan for Culture 2011-14' [2010] OJC325/1, Annex 1.

[129]Article 2 of the TEU states that "the Union is founded on the values of respect for human dignity, freedom, democracy, equality, the rule of law and respect for human rights, including the rights of persons belonging to minorities. These values are common to the Member States in a society in which pluralism, non-discrimination, tolerance, justice, solidarity and equality between women and men prevail'.

[130]See further, https://www.coe.int/en/web/cultural-routes/eu-joint-programme. Two important initiatives in the field of culture and education are: the joint programme with the CoE of the cultural routes; and DISCO. It is he Joint Programme "Democratic and Inclusive School Culture in Operation". It was launched in May 2013 under the name "Human Rights and Democracy in Action" by the Council of Europe and the European Commission. It provides funding to enable at least three States party to the European Cultural Convention to cooperate on projects of common interest within the field of education for democratic citizenship and human rights education (EDC/HRE). At least one of the states should be a member of the European Union.

[131]European Landscape Convention adopted by the Committee of Ministers of the Council of Europe on 19 July 2000 and opened for signature by its Member States in Florence on 20 October 2000. Followed by, Recommendation CM/Rec (2008)3 of the Committee of Ministers to Member States on the guidelines for the implementation of the European Landscape Convention, adopted on 6 February 2008; Resolution CM/Res(2008)3 on the rules governing the Landscape Award of the Council of Europe, adopted by the Committee of Ministers of the Council of Europe on 20 February 2008.

role in this domain is limited to encouraging cooperation between MS and supporting the improvement of the 'Knowledge and dissemination of the culture and history of the European peoples' and the 'conservation and safeguarding of cultural heritage of European significance'. Article 167 of the TFEU also defines the role of the EU Parliament in this context as one involving the adoption of incentive measures together with the Council. Article 107 of the TFEU completes the picture of EU cultural heritage legal basis. It declares that state aid for the promotion of cultural heritage conservation shall be compatible with internal market rules if it does not affect trading conditions and competition.[132] The most relevant issue related to this specific dimension of the EUSM relates to the European MS shared responsibility with regard to the legacy of previous generations, our efforts to pass it onto the next generations, and our creative contribution to the future embedding ecological principles, and the duty of care. The EUSM entrenches a 'European Framework for Action on Cultural Heritage' (EFACH)[133] that reflects the common set-up for heritage-related activities at European level, primarily in EU policies and programmes that should boost action for heritage protection and promotion in view of third generation interests. The framework has also established a Cultural Heritage Forum, which will act as a platform for consultation and exchange of best practices for sustainable and participatory cultural heritage policies in Europe.[134]

The fact that the Global Agenda on SD has not placed specific emphasis on culture despite of the transversal and overarching dimension of culture and cultural heritage in the different goals, offers the EUSM the chance to be at the forefront with regards to the erogation of public policies at EU regional level and eventual political efforts for policy development in cooperative basis in such field at global level.

3.3.4 *Constitutional Existence of the EU Model of SD*

The EU institutions have recognised sustainable development as a primary objective of the EU and both the TEU and TFEU include specific references to sustainable development as a guiding theme for the EU (Humphreys, 2018). The treaties in their

[132]See further, *Cultural Heritage in EU policies*, http://www.europarl.europa.eu/RegData/etudes/BRIE/2018/621876/EPRS_BRI(2018)621876_EN.pdf.

[133]SWD (2018) 491 final, Brussels, 5.12.2018. Commission staff working document on European Framework for action on cultural heritage. The framework was prepared through regular exchanges with EU MS, EU Council Presidencies, the European Parliament, civil society organisations, cultural operators and international organisations such as the Council of Europe and UNESCO. It also builds on lessons learned from ten long-term projects entitled "European initiatives" carried out by the European Commission as part of the policy input to the European Year of Cultural Heritage.

[134]To achieve this, there are four principles for action within the framework: (1) a holistic approach, looking cultural heritage as a resource for the future and putting people at its heart; (2) mainstreaming and integrated approach across different EU policies; (3) Evidence-based policy making, including through cultural statistics; (4) Multi-stakeholder cooperation; encouraging the dialogue and exchange among a wide range of actors when designing and implementing cultural heritage policies and programmes.

consolidated version clearly indicate that a principle of sustainable development may emerge in EU law. The internal commitment of the EU to sustainability is enshrined in Article 3 (3) of the TEU.

Article 3 (3) reads as follows:

> The Union shall establish an internal market. It shall work for the sustainable development of Europe based on balanced economic growth and price stability, a highly competitive social market economy, aiming at full employment and social progress, and a high level of protection and improvement of the quality of the environment. It shall promote scientific and technological advance.
>
> It shall combat social exclusion and discrimination, and shall promote social justice and protection, equality between women and men, solidarity between generations and protection of the rights of the child.
>
> It shall promote economic, social and territorial cohesion, and solidarity among Member States.
>
> It shall respect its rich cultural and linguistic diversity, and shall ensure that Europe's cultural heritage is safeguarded and enhanced".[135]

Article 3 (5) read as follows:

> In its relations with the wider world, the Union shall uphold and promote its values and interests and contribute to the protection of its citizens. It shall contribute to peace, security, the sustainable development of the Earth, solidarity and mutual respect among peoples, free and fair trade, eradication of poverty and the protection of human rights, in particular the rights of the child, as well as to the strict observance and the development of international law, including respect for the principles of the United Nations Charter.

As we can see from these selected sections of the text of Article 3 of the TEU SD integrating economic growth, a highly competitive social market economy, and a high level of protection and improvement of the quality of the environment become pivotal objectives of the EU. This constitutional provision lays down the basis for a proactive and integrated action under a sustainability paradigm for its future advance in its internal and external action.

After Lisbon, as I noted before, the social components of the EUSM become more evident and the pressing demands for political action on this sphere added to the growing attention to legal narratives on the social pillar of sustainability should force future research agendas to build a common conceptual approach to address culture and education as neglected elements of such storyline. In any case, Art. 3 (3) of the TEU is rarely mentioned by the legislator or the EUCJ and even if it could be a key interpretative instrument to contrast the neoliberal picture of our economic constitutional reality still needs an enhanced comprehension of its further potential on social rights, welfare and social concerns for the present and future of a sustainable Europe. In addition an improved understanding and proactive use of Article 3 (3) would help to gain an increasing trust on European institutions that it is missing as part of our current European citizenship identity.

---

[135]Valuable insights about the expression "highly competitive social market economy" is given by Ferri and Cortese (2019). Explaining that while Article 3 of the TEU leaves the expression formally undefined, is undoubtedly borrowed from the German ordoliberalism of the Freiburg School that advocated in favour of a form of market freedoms that can achieve social justice.

Maastricht introduced for the first time a specific reference to environmental protection among the objectives of the European Union. The Amsterdam Treaty complemented this by adding a reference to sustainable development' among the Union's objectives and moved up the principle of environmental integration from the specific Environmental title to former Article 6 in the section outlining the general principles of EU policy (Orlando, 2014). The well-established constitutional framework that has evolved substantially from its original economics concerns to more social ones, offers a satisfactory standpoint for the model (EUSM) we are describing. Not by chance this contribution seeks to show how the EU vision of 'sustainability' inherited partially from the global scenario that we have described operates in the current EU legal framework fitting in within traditional categories of normativity that have been changing and boosting a multidimensional version of sustainability that is still under-operationalised.

A reasonable first premise describing the strong constitutional basis of the EUSM should start by ascertaining how the EU is quite a unique successful experiment in regional (strong) environmental governance, especially after having seen the lack of such legally binding operational governance at international and global level. This is widely accepted considering how states have incrementally transferred sovereign rights to a supranational level (Bosselmann, 2008, p. 187), of course the obvious advantage of this is that Member States coordinate their efforts, through binding (at different levels) legislation and centralised decision-making. Therefore to this end the EU provides an exemplary model of governance for sustainability.

The second premise that should be immediately considered is that the EU had an immediate recognition of the call for sustainability launched by the international scenario and it quickly added notions of sustainability into its constitutional framework. The two first steps of this adoption of sustainability norms into the EU as an incipient form of what they are today were introduced by the fifth Environment Action Programme (EAP) and the Amsterdam Treaty on the European Union (TEU). The first EAP takes up the definition of sustainable development proposed by the Brundtland Commission with the objective to transform patterns of growth within the EU community in a manner that promotes sustainability (5th European Community Environment Programme: Toward Sustainability). The Treaty of Amsterdam amending the Treaty on European Union embraced the international accepted definition of sustainable development proclaiming that "The Community shall have as its task promoting a harmonious, balance and sustainable development of economic activities". The Treaty of Amsterdam also established a horizontal provision linked to sustainable development introducing the principle of integration of environmental concerns into other EU policies with a view to promoting sustainable development.[136] Therefore, within the EU Constitutional setting sustainable development was initially deployed through the "integration principle" as we discussed in

[136]Article 6 of the Treaty of Amsterdam Amending the Treaty on the European Union, the Treaties Establishing the European Communities and Related Acts [1997] OJ C340, reads as follows: "Environmental protection requirements must be integrated into the definition and implementation of the Community policies and activities referred to in Article 3, in particular with a view to promoting sustainable development".

the previous section. However, 'sustainability' in its multidimensional ethos came prominently into life subsequently with the Lisbon Treaty, at least potentially.

Article 11 of the TFEU and Article 37 of the European Convention of Fundamental Rights (EUCFR) are crucial to find the foundational constitutional framework of sustainability outside the realm of internal market interests. The definitions that are enshrined in these two provisions represent the primary law of the EUSM and frame together the constitutional scenario of the EU not referring exclusively to the development of MS economic activities. Article 11 of the TFEU re-proposes the integration principle, it provides that: "Environmental protection requirements must be integrated into the definition and implementation of the Union Policies and activities, in particular with a view to promoting sustainable development", not so different from this formulation, Article 37 of the EUCFR reads: "A high level of environmental protection and the improvement of the quality of the environment must be integrated into the policies of the Union and ensured in accordance with the principle of sustainable development".

However it is important to understand that sustainable development, as well as the evolution we have traced back associated with environmental protection cannot be detached from internal market concerns, regardless of the progression of the concept towards a conciliatory nature by balancing environmental issues with economic and social concerns.[137] This should be understood when reading Article 3 (3) that simply starts by committing the EU to the creation of an internal market (however social market). It is the secondary part of Article 3 (3) and the international commitment of the EU to the principles of International law, not only relevant for the external EU policy which should act as guidance of the strong EU constitutional SD mandate. Such requirement is also reflected in thousands of secondary law instruments striving to create a consistent and separated area of *acquis communautaire* in SD not yet openly recognised.[138] Notwithstanding that the obligation to take into

[137]The original appearance of such conciliatory nature was offered by a court decision by the ECJ, *First Corporate Shipping*, a case on development taking place in protected bird habitats, is testament to a conciliatory approach. Case C-371/98, *First Corporate Shippping*, [2000] E.C.R. I-9235, par. 54 (opinion AG Léger).

[138]It is possible to identify these aspects of the sustainability discourse in the EU through the initiatives of the EU's Environmental Action Programmes (EAP), the first of which was adopted in 1972 (First Environmental Action Programme (1972–1977), followed by others 1977–1982, 1982–1987, 1987–1992, 1992–2002, and 2002–2012, 2013–2020. The approach of the first EAP was to advocate the development of command and control initiatives designed to resolve specific pollution control problems, such as acid rain. This reflected the discourse of the period and demonstrated an approach which was unlikely to lead to an effective and comprehensive sustainable development strategy. However, it was evident by the time the EU adopted the Fifth EAP (1992–2000) that the approach had become closer to the 'strong sustainability' position. The changing nature of the commitment to a strategy for sustainable development was shown in the use, for the first time, of a specific title for the Action Programme 'Towards Sustainability'. The initiatives proposed in the Fifth EAP concentrated on measures targeting specific sectoral policies and priorities to achieve the sustainable development objectives. The discourse had shifted from its origins as action on pollution control to a model based on ecological modernisation as the dominant ideology. See Chapters 2 and 13 of Barnes and Hoerber (2013) on this point. The seventh EP

consideration sustainable development in the EU international relations is of remarkable importance (Marín-Durán & Morgera, 2012). In fact, the establishment of sustainable development as an objective, in its different forms by the constitutional framework of the EU means a step forward when considering environmental matters of transnational character, and nature preservation mandates regardless of its fragmented approach in secondary legislation (i.e., agriculture, technology, transport, Hazardous waste, Energy, renewable energy resources, etc.). Besides the clear and strong 'recognition' of the social aspects of the internal market (Article 3(3)) is of decisive importance for the validity of the multidimensional nature of the EUSM.

In the AGET *Iraklis* decision[139] regardless of its outcome, where the CJEU referred directly to Article 3(3) of the TEU, the Court in its reasoning recalled that "The European Union is not only to establish an internal market but is also to work for the sustainable development of Europe, which is based, in particular, on a highly competitive social market economy aiming at full employment and social progress, and it is to promote, inter alia, social protection". The Court stressed that one important element for the sustainable development of Europe was a 'highly competitive social market', stressing that 'the European Union thus has not only economic but also a social purpose' (Ferri & Cortese, 2019). This important Court decision is decisive to enshrine the fact that sustainable development is condensed in these different provisions placed at the top of the hierarchical pyramid of the EU legal order to protect and promote its significant legal status that needs to be further developed by further secondary law provisions. This also means that its legal status is not vanished by disputes. Still, as Sadeleer puts it, sustainable development has a "status dogged by controversies" (Sadeleer, 2015) causing some problems perhaps regarding conceptual and status interpretation that of course might lead to a reluctance by the European Union Institutions (specially the CJEU) to develop and to stick to a firm interpretation of sustainability[140] as an hermeneutic instrument for case-law resolutions. Court decisions preserving its interpretative value are not very numerous in fact. There is of course an absence of cases decided based on sustainable development, despite the existence of recent crucial cases where the court has

---

"Living well within the limits of our planet", shows an even further commitment to sustainability approaching all the aspects that constitute the challenges of our present time, fostering a holistic vision of sustainability that goes beyond an anthropocentric approach to build on a more eco-centric approach, that by enlarge brings about social justice and good governance.

[139]Case C-201/15, AGET Iraklis, EU:C:2016:972.

[140]See the interpretation given by AG Léger to sustainable development in its opinion in *First Corporate Shipping*, a case on development taking place in protected birds habitats, is testament to a conciliatory approach. Case C-371/98, *First Corporate Shippping*, [2000] E.C.R. I-9235, par. 54 (opinion AG Léger).

tackled on its definition in certain aspects of the EU Union cooperation policy after Lisbon,[141] and on the interpretative features of its sectorial legislation.[142]

From this, could sustainability really become a normative concept within EU law according to its constitutional setting? Authors like Sadeleer (2015) have no problem affirming that "combined with the requirements of integration, a high level of protection, and the different principles of environmental law (prevention, precaution, polluter-pays, etc.) sustainable development had become a normative concept".[143] It is undoubtedly a binding constitutional objective. Therefore, rather than being skeptical about the possibility of sustainability to represent a primary legal source and paradigm of the numerous secondary law provisions and EU policies, we should look at its quick evolution and the crucial role of the EU trying to coordinate its Member States to fight for ecological problems, energy supply, technological development and local initiatives for the development of good governance mechanisms following the action plan of the "Covenant of Majors" and other relevant initiatives.

In this light it is possible to affirm that at the EU level the *acquis communautaire* on sustainability, has four main challenges at the forefront: first, the implementation of an ambitious agenda to combat climate change and create the basis for an energy transition and low carbon economy; second, the circular economy package should be implemented and somehow culturally embedded and promoted in Member States production and consumption habits; on top of that every social policy is, or rather should be, related to the European Sustainability Model that European Institutional bodies should support and promote; last but not least, at judicial level 'sustainable development' should be invoked as a legal principle, or normative paradigm and interpretation tool in its most broad and inclusive sense with the obligation of compliance.

EU legislation in the field of "sustainability" can only be understood in light of the parallel effort of the international agreements towards the determination of concepts, categories and basic principles developed for the sake of the development of a principle of intergenerational justice. Among these legal categories, "sustainability" should be remarked without giving up a dynamic speech challenging its substance. In fact, regardless of the hegemonic character of "sustainability" the global legal order in which different levels of governance interact modifying and developing the protection keys aiming at compliance with a supranational criteria have focused their attention on climate change talks. As a consequence the challenges that sustainable development and sustainability have posed to public policy have often dwarfed in economic speeches. The freshly launched new European Green deal which should be considered the landmark of the EUSM and it has been brought forward as a set of initiatives by the European Commission has indeed as an overarching aim the transition to a climate neutral Europe. Still, nowadays there is a

[141]C-377/12 *European Commission v Council of European Union* (Philippines PCFA) EU: C:2014:1903, Judgement of the Court Grand Chamber.

[142]C-461/13, *Bund v Germany*, ECLI:EU:C:2014:2324 (opinion AG Jääskinen). See further, Palonitty (2016). Aloniitty (2016), pp. 151–158.

[143]Sadeleer (2015), p. 19.

strong global effort by public institutions and a myriad of stakeholders worldwide to put at the forefront many of the social ambitions put forward by the UN Global Agenda and the Sustainable Development Goals that the EU has incorporated to its political mandate. The Agenda is bringing cultural and educational concerns into the fore for the first time. Still, most of our constitutional traditions are not ready to include the notion of 'sustainable development' in association with the idea of future entrenched in the concept of 'future generations' (Zagrebelsky, 2013). It is not easy to allocate primacy to an intergenerational defensive approach that would need to be embedded in cultural and educational policy instruments as a future action strategy of the EU. Unfortunately the complex regulatory body of SD especially related to social concerns appears to be still weak and fragmented despite of its strong constitutional mandate.

3.3.5 A Note on European Governance Under the Sustainability Paradigm as a Yardstick for Bottom-Up Approaches in EUSM

The topic of governance under sustainability premises is vital in this research agenda. The meaning and definition of Governance has been for a long time now contested regardless of its long history in the political science literature. It is out of the scope of this study to examine its meaning. On this topic, I do not want to be exhaustive, my intention is to provide an instrumental overview on EU governance mechanisms following the analytical lines that have preceded this paragraph, this is presenting the different governance approaches that are re-shaping public policy intervention in present times and could guide future plans of the EUSM.

When referred to the EUSM we should consider the basic role of first, the primary role of subsidiarity to regulate governance at EU level; second, the evolution of environmental governance at EU level from top-down approaches and command-control mechanisms to more participatory, technical, collaborative and localised action.

So, in the first place, good governance being a key element of sustainable development arises from the necessity to deal with transboundary issues that are best approached at EU level, often through subsidiary mechanisms. Currently the principle of subsidiarity and its rules of application can be found in Article 5 of the TEU and in Protocol 2 respectively. It plays a crucial role in the field of environmental law, social and economic policies and it is of course an important legal provision (generally speaking) of the constitutional traditions of the MS.[144]

Second, the legal bases of the EUSM governance are instead enshrined in the following treaty provisions: Art. 15 (1) of the TFEU, to promote good governance and ensure the participation of civil society, 'the Union's institutions, bodies, offices and agencies shall conduct their work as openly as possible'; and Art. 21 (2) of the TEU: the Union shall define and pursue common policies and actions, and shall

[144]See further Sadeleer (2012).

work for a high degree of cooperation in all fields of international relations, to: (. . . .) (h) promote an international system based on stronger multilateral cooperation and good global governance. Previous to the enactment of this constitutional provision different top-down initiatives of soft nature but highly influential had been introduced. The Commission's 2001 White Paper on European Governance was the principal policy document specifically setting out the Commission's vision of European governance before Lisbon. The Commission defined governance in the EU context as "rules, processes and behaviour that affect the way in which powers are exercised at European level, particularly as regards openness, participation, accountability, effectiveness and coherence".[145] As opposed to some instances of global governance the EU by focusing on the question of how the EU uses the powers given to it by its citizens' the White Paper placed the EU institutions at the heart of the European Governance debate and focused on those five principles: participation, accountability, effectiveness; and coherence.[146]

The Lisbon Treaty constitutionalised them in some instances for the first time, in some others many of the Articles contained in the TEU reinforce the White Paper's approach (e.g., Article 10 (2) on democratic accountability of national Heads of State or government; Article 10 (3) on open decision-making; Article 11 (2) on open and transparent dialogue with representative associations and civil society, and open and transparent dialogue with representative association and civil society; Article 11 (3) on consultations with parties concerned; etc.). They are organised under a new title heading: 'Provisions on Democratic Principles'. The goal of the White Paper at the time was to make policy making more inclusive and accountable to increase legitimacy, and reduce distances between EU institutions and its citizens.[147] Lisbon reinforced and elevated those five principles of good governance in constitutional instances and obligations to which the EU's action would have to comply. Accordingly, Article 11 of the TEU[148] integrates participation broadly understood as the possibility for non-institutional actors to take part in decision-making. From a legal stand point it is important to discuss that although this has been a constitutive

[145]White Paper on European Governance COM (2001) 428 final, at p. 8.

[146]Kingston (2013), p. 6.

[147]Kingston (2013), p. 7.

[148]Article 11 of the TEU reads as follows:

1. The institutions shall, by appropriate means give citizens and representative associations the opportunity to make known and publicly exchange their views in all areas of Union action.
2. The institutions shall maintain an open transparent and regular dialogue with representative associations and civil society.
3. The European Commission shall carry out broad consultations with parties concerned in order to ensure that the Union's actions are coherent and transparent.
4. Not less than one million citizens who are nationals of a significant number of Member States may take the initiative of inviting the European Commission, within the framework of its powers, to submit any appropriate proposal on matters where citizens consider that a legal act of the Union is required for the purpose of implementing the Treaties.

The procedures and conditions required for such a citizens' initiatives shall be determined in accordance with the first paragraph of Article 24 of the Treaty on the Functioning of the EU.

feature of the European administration and polity since the beginning of the integration process some authors[149] have argued that law had been left largely outside the political and institutional developments that had concretised participation as a principle of EU governance and that ultimately led to the insertion of Article 11 in the Treaty. This means that legal rights of participation in particular have been kept within rather strict limits. Except where otherwise provided by law, they are limited to the right to be heard in adjudicatory procedures leading to the adoption of individual decisions. Beyond such cases, there are no legal mechanisms to ensure voice to citizens or persons affected in decision making procedures of the EU institutions and bodies. This has been the position tenaciously adopted by the Luxembourg Courts on participation rights (Mendes, 2011). The author argues that this *status quo* may change because of the Lisbon Treaty from the fact that Article 11 of the TEU postulates a transition from the instrumental usages of participatory governance to participation conceived as a basis of participatory democracy. However, Mendes (2011, p. 11) goes on to argue that while equality is essential to the idea of democracy, participatory governance as it has been fostered so far at the EU level has largely excluded considerations of equality whilst equality of citizens is now a democratic principle of the EU by force of Article 9 of the TEU and, arguably, ought to be extended to participation exercised under Article 11 of the TEU. This requires that the Union's institutions, bodies, offices and agencies also treat legal persons participating in EU decision-making procedures equally (Mendes, 2011, p. 11).

So, despite of a wider proliferation of strategies and venues for citizen involvement in the governance of life at the EU level as part of the evolution of the EU integration process which are relevant part of the flesh of the EUSM. For instance, the European Citizen's initiative.[150] established by Art. 11(4) of the TEU and Art. 24 (1) of the TFEU is described as the first transnational instrument of participatory democracy in world history, but such legal foundations have been reinforced by the Aarhus Convention.[151] The Convention does not codify substantive standards of environmental protection, but provides for an ecological transformation by enlarging and improving access to information, public participation, and justice in environmental matters. The procedural mechanisms and arrangements refer primarily to implementation by national authorities, a specific monitoring system as international level has been established. Still, the Aarhus Convention in Europe[152] remains one of the hard bones of the European environmental governance (reflexive or

[149]Mendes (2011).

[150]www.citizens-initiative.eu/?page_id=2.

[151]UN Economic Commission for Europe, Aarhus Convention on Access to information, Public Participation in Decision-making and Access to Justice in Environmental Matters (adopted on 25 June 1988, entered into force on 30 October 2001) 2161 UNTS 447.

[152]The EU became a party through Decision 2005/370/EC on the conclusion, on behalf of the European Community, of the Convention on access to information, public participation in decision-making and access to justice in environmental matters.

non-reflexive)[153] but it is an example successful regional arrangement of the EUSM providing for a closer, systemic cooperation in the enforcement of recognised global principles of environmental governance.

The European Territorial Agenda (European Commission, 2007) whose focal point is territorial cohesion, a less clear concept than that of its predecessor the European Territorial Strategy of 1999 aimed at a balanced and sustainable development of the territory and incorporated for the first time the concept of territorial governance understood as a permanent cooperative process, involving all agents, which mainly derives in two processes: public-private partnerships for the execution of policies and transparency (and publicity) of responsibilities of government, as well as the policies approved, in this case, within the European Union.

Other instruments in territorial matters, such as the European Landscape Convention (also known as the Florence Convention, 20th October 2000), is the first international treaty to be exclusively devoted to all aspects of European landscape and it incorporates a myriad of governance instruments. In effect, it incorporates the landscape as a challenge and an opportunity in terms of governance at European level. Its internal complexity arising from the articulation of natural and social processes inevitably leads to the coordination of sectoral policies of landscape incidence, and of the different scales of government of the territory, to the cooperation between the public and the private sector (Mata, 2008).

The need to improve the EU's legitimacy, and with this more democratic governance has been gradually increasing driven by the gradual broadening of the EU's aims far beyond the economic goal of achieving the internal market. The principle of environmental integration enshrined by Article 11 of the TFEU adds emphasis on this gradual broadening of policy goals integrated into an ecological dialogue. Thus, departing from this, I make the case for a multidimensional and dynamic concept of sustainability containing ecology, equity, economy and governance with the same level of importance and fundamental implications for the governance trends of European modern societies. The paradigm of action that sustainability brings into life has at its roots at the governance principles of the European environmental sphere such as openness and participation so long well-established in the instruments of environmental impact assessment and access to environmental information. Unfortunately, the broad and overreaching content that the Treaty of Lisbon and the Aarhus Convention bring to the already existing mechanisms do not mean that the field is free from controversies. However, not only the constitutional support is valuable, the institutional support to the broadening of governance premises is strongly assisted at EU institutional level, not only by the EUCJ but by other institutions less engaged with the legal and procedural aspects of governance.

On 27 June, 2019 European Committee of the Regions and Congress of Local and Regional Authorities of the Council of Europe celebrated their 25 anniversary as a landmark for the achievements on the field of open governance. The theme of the joint anniversary event was "The Added Value of Local and Regional Authorities in

[153]Voss, Bauknecht, and Kemp (2006).

the Unification of Europe". Both institutions have been providing grounds for development of local and regional democracy in Europe with synergies between the work of the two institutions to further strengthen local self-government and regional democracy emphasising the importance of decentralisation as an indispensable requirement of modern democracy, noting that local and regional governments are essential to tackle local, regional, national and global challenges. In one of the most critical moments in the History of European the integration of local and regional authorities are instrumental in the delivery of policies that meet people's needs and channels citizens' voices.

On the whole the EUSM is characterised by a strong European concept of environmental governance emerging with the potential to capture the increasingly multi-level, networked nature of decision-making affecting the environment, and the broad range of actors implicated in such decision-making.[154] Within this context, there are of course less virtuous types of governance interventions leaded by the use of market-based instruments (such in the case of Climate protection policies) or the educational field, and this is of course part of the trend of an increasing importance of profit-motivated actors (such as corporations) as players under the EU paradigm of sustainability these days. Still, the increasing role given to 'open government' mechanisms supported by important institutions such as the Congress of Local and Regional activities and the European Committee of Regions is going to be fundamental in the next years. The common definitions of open government tend to include three key principles: transparency, participation and accountability that. In the context of Environmental law these three principles, have long been proved to be the most valid instrument for a sustainable development that incorporates important social and territorial aspects, as well as other procedural tools of relevant value for policy decision that still need to be further develop in the next coming years. Open governance in the policy-making and implementation will be strengthened through the sound application of the principles of subsidiarity and multi-level governance. It is all about reinvigorating democracy and will be vital to the recovery of trust in public institutions.

In the education realm the importance of open government mechanism facilitating grass-root solutions and bottom-up approaches has been discussed within the context of the promotion of greater social equity and equality in public education. In fact, the Global Agenda on Sustainable Development brings to the scene local and national civil society, understood as all non-state actors acting otherwise than for profit as opposed to for profit actors. This bottom up approaches that have been increasingly fostered by international agreements and are a crucial part of EUSM embed in their consultation processes all types of stakeholders in important decision processes as part of a strong sustainability model. In the education sector it means to integrate the "needs, motivations and opinions of grass-roots stakeholders such as learners, teachers, and parents of school going children. Parity of esteem is needed

---

[154] Kingston (2013), p. 7.

between those who develop education policy and those who implement it" (Roche, 2017).

It has been argued that it is questionable that the European environmental governance mechanism could have been truly effective, in particular, existing access to justice mechanisms for private parties in direct action before the EU courts (Kingston, 2013, p. 11). It remains to see if the multidimensional and broaden concept of sustainability improves past experiences of restrictiveness for interests being pursued for purely environmental sake, and opens-up bottom-up participation to 'democratised' social realities. Especially when directly related to the management of common resources that we will discuss later.

A bibliographical review on the topic of governance mechanisms gives evidence of how the current sustainability discourse in Europe is, at least, a unifying one where potential conflicts between economic growth and environmental protection appear to be surmounted or even erased for the sake of conciliating and integrating environmental, economic and equity concerns under Article 3(3) of the TEU. This does not mean that in practice governance for environmental sustainability does not fail to overcome tensions and dilemmas in the EU. Still even the new body of energy regulation has a section devoted to 'governance'. Thus, the newly enacted 'Winter package' in the Energy field might bring further evidence of how governance at EU level under the premises of sustainability has a crucial role to play in areas where hegemonic top-down discourses have been traditionally leading national and supranational scenarios. Nonetheless, since the hegemonic emergence of climate change as an emblematic issue structuring the energy governance system and the market discourses, bottom-up approaches have a legitimate place in many varied policy aspects, for example important social aspects on access to energy and energy justice issues (Mete & Heffron, 2019). Suffices to say here -because I will come to this later- that the suggestive context of 'sustainability', systems thinking and earth system approaches and the study of global changes affecting national and local rulers, as well as the government of the city and the urban context have opened a rich debate about improved governance in many different contexts, even at global level.

Under European Governance mechanisms we must absolutely discuss the trend of "making communities sovereign", innovative institutional solutions, such as the jury of the commons deciding on the use of blighted property are emerging to face the crisis-induced housing emergency in some local Italian municipalities (Capra and Mattei, 2015). Such participatory governance approach is drawing attention back to the 'enclosure' period and have also taken lawyers, private, as well as public lawyers, to talk of a new phase, based upon a new pluralist humanist paradigm which stands in contrast to the traditional "bipolar paradigm" (public and private law division) according to the classic scheme of administration that realises the public interest by availing itself of the instruments typical of administrative law (Arena, 2003).

The topic of the 'commons' is widely discussed at theoretical and juridical level. Political economists have dealt with it extensively, and I am indebted to the work of Ostrom (1990) for the inspirational tools she provides for a scientific discourse with specific legal resonance at European level. In a closer to home context there are some legal scholars whose work has also inspired some radical changes in my way of thinking about governance and common interests (Ugo Mattei, Stefano Rodotà, Gregorio Arena, and Sheila Foster and Christian Iaone).

Hess (2008), offers a comprehensive map to move around this complex academic territory that has most recently had a successful application in the Italian urban context, finding a legal basis on the principle of horizontal subsidiarity introduced by the Constitutional law no 3/2001, which is the main constitutional revision approved to date, extensively revising the Fifth Title of the Constitution (on regional and local authorities). The horizontal version of the principle of subsidiarity approaches—in its horizontal version (introduced by Article 118 (4) of the Italian Constitution)—public responsibilities to the ordinary citizens. These experiences have developed a broader idea of civic participation inducing many municipalities in the last years to adopt some original models of urban management of public spaces. Within Europe, even if the phenomena in places like Spain, Greece, Belgium or the Netherlands have not an institutionalised arrangement (yet), we come across the Italian context where the experience is drastically extended thanks to this constitutional reform and developed among private and public law scholarship alike, institutionalised rapidly by regulations adopting sharing agreements between citizens and the municipalities (*patto di condivisione*) to take care of urban spaces such as empty buildings, urban gardens, schools, etc.

So departing from urban laboratories and experimentation, specifically within the Italian context[155] there is a global movement of transition versus citizen administration of public spaces. Mattei and Quarta (2015) argue that this trend could be embedded into the 'right to the city' movement theorised by Lefebvre (1968) and reactivated by Castells (1977), a decade later. The truth is that particularly after 2008 when the economic and financial crisis exploded, citizens and communities have claimed the public use of urban spaces and demanded more participation in the decision-making processes that concern city planning (Mattei and Quarta, 2015). This drift, at practical and theoretical level goes in stark contrast against the influential public law scholarship (Cassese, 1991; Oliver, Dawn, & Prosser, 2010) that legitimised the dissolution of the public sector through privatisation, and reducing the role of the State to a regulatory State, a mere controller (through independent authorities) of the game of private market actors.

What can be learned from these realities is the normative dimension in the re-definition of a new European governance under the paradigm of sustainability and intergenerational practice that combines protection and accessible management at the same time for the sake of future generation's interests. Still the dominant European policy priorities, generally speaking, are in stark contrast with the commons perspective that considers people as main players embedded in strong social

[155]In Italy the Italian Senate installed a commons commission led by Stefano Rodotà, a well-known lawyer to explore the legal definition of the commons and what it implies. The suggested reform of the Italian civil code never took place, but the work of the Commission has been followed by prolific success for water battles in Naples, and the Venice lagoon. The Italian initiative has been echoed through Europe, see further, https://www.epsu.org/article/european-parliaments-intergroup-commons-kicks. Of drastic importance are the prolific work of labsus accessible at https://www.labsus.org/ and also the work of city labgob with international resonance and accessible at https://labgov.city/about-people/.

ties, communities, relationships and ecosystems. On this task strong cultural and educational interventions should be engaged.

3.3.6 Future Challenges of the Emerging 'Sustainability' Model in Europe. From 'Protection' and 'Merchandising' to 'Access' and 'Protection of Common Interest of Human Kind': The 'Commons'

There is a single argument that I want to tackle under this paragraph considering its sounded relevance on the emerging governance models proliferating in Europe under sustainability action and 'transformation' premises: 'the commons'. Across Europe, more and more people are co-governing and co-creating the way to manage and to preserve cultural heritage and (natural) resources in an alternative way. It has been suggested that the 'commons' could revitalise Europe. The European Parliament has a "Commons Intergroup" since 2015. Whether in small contexts, or larger networks, new civic and economic structures are moving beyond rigid dichotomies under the capitalist logic, commercial and non-commercial, state and market, public and private law domain. The relevance for the legal doctrine is obvious, but most important than that, it is the relevance of the commons for transforming EU institutions by taking a more holistic ecosystem approach. This is favouring social cohesion and ecological objectives entrenched in governance mechanisms based on collaboration, public participation and egalitarian principles and concrete action at localised level that nowadays is essential for education and cultural policies.

The topic is of vital importance for the EUSM, it has been quickly mentioned under the previous paragraph. My argument will be substantially compressed on three important ideas: (1) 'access', (2) 'protection of common interest for humankind', and (3) 'management' of resources for the common interest which is particularly relevant for future challenges concerning cultural and natural heritage preservation and management. I will deal with the three of them to understand their importance to be integrated in the governance model of the EUSM and its future opportunities and challenges.

(1) Access considered from 'an intergenerational perspective' as it has been discussed somewhere else before[156] introduces us to the topic of the 'commons'. The paradigm of the common appears to be having an increasingly strong influence on rethinking the issue of access to nature. Of course, it is not possible to talk of a full acceptance of the commons as the legal regime of choice, but some aspects of the debate on the commons are pertinent to the discussion on how the access to nature can be framed as an alternative to protection and merchandising spaces, especially in a view of protecting intergenerational rights. A good example is found when we examine the profound changes which have

[156] See Valguarnera (2013).

occurred in the way national parks are conceived all over the world and how the legislator has been recently reacting to what we consider 'outdoors'. Valguarnera (2013) picks the example of "the old open-air museum" model that has been ousted in favour of co-management systems that considers human as an integral part of the environment, but this development is not homogenous across the different legal systems, taking natural heritage law and cultural heritage management to explore the importance of local communities and local identities for monitoring landscape protection, access, and enjoyment. This fields cannot be standardised at the regulatory level, but public policies for institutional change are needed. An interesting example is probably in England recognising the 'right to roam' in later years; and Sweden where it has never been lost the historical institution of the "*allemansrätt*" by which passers-by have the right to roam on already existing ways and paths even if they are part of private property or belong to the surrounding areas or private property.

Valguarnera (2013, 2017), has devoted extensive attention to this topic. In one of his essays touching upon the aspects that interest me most, he explains quite well what happens in many parts of Europe when trying to take a walk: "It can be a complicated enterprise, at least if the walker does not stick to public roads and lacks the audacity to violate the law. The walker would be soon confronted with a fence and 'no trespassing' signs, clearly signalling that the landscape that he would like to access is not something he or she should be concerned about. It belongs to someone else, someone who claims to own it" (Valguarnera, 2013). Unfortunately the drastic disconnection between man and nature has taken, especially kids to suffer from the lack of the most simple 'access to nature' and alarming messages are all over the place. We are all almost aware (even if we unconsciously neglect it) of today's lack of contact with green areas put the physical and psychological health of children at risk. This is not only related to physical well-being in terms of the effect of toxins in the air of our cities, to which children are particularly susceptible, but also to other aspects of their well-being such as cognitive functioning, emotional health, obesity, capacity to concentrate, academic performance and aggression levels. All these aspects of well-being are impacted positively by experiencing access to nature' (Valguarnera, 2013, referring to the studies of Strife & Downey, 2009).

If we want to continue expanding the current governance parameters of the EUSM we get the possibility of going beyond the 'bipolar paradigm' and get practical answers about how to allocate a place for the 'commons' here (e.g., natural spaces, and natural resources in particular areas and contexts). If we do not try to open a discussion about how to allocate in our current governance mechanisms access to nature beyond the traditional divide, public and private we will not have exhausted a coherent and courageous discourse about the EUSM governance model, considering that expanding access to nature leads to a more equal distribution of wealth, especially considering many of the suburbs of big European capitals where access to natural resources is costly and difficult. Some commons would help to naturally integrate nature into our daily routine, especially important for the well-being of kids and elderly people. Thus some commons will consist of reducing the costs of leisure for many segments of society that cannot allow an easy access to nature. Those commons would consist of "making areas for walking, bathing or camping much more easily accessible to people of low income".[157]

This argument will assist me to provide the right argument to foster a discourse about the challenges that lie at the doorsteps of our ambitious global Agenda on SD. We have built so far the analytical parameters of a model that gives European citizens answers and political action plans on almost every concern under the premises of 'sustainability'. However, is the component of intergenerational justice really there?

The normative parameters of the EUSM—needless to say—still need institutional changes and renewed action on cultural and educational systemic interventions missing at the heart of the model. A lot of attention has been placed on workers, and technology and other equally important concerns, but little attention has been placed on institutional changes that would also have resonance on the field of education and cultural heritage management in particular. Especially if we refer to outdoors education in the public school context. Moreover, the Constitutional dimension of the EUSM still needs to face the challenge of broadening its vision to include an overlooked dimension: time and the rights of future generations by fighting the battle in the name of 'duties' towards future generations, instead of fighting the battle for the sake of adjudicating rights to the current ones.

(2) On the issue of 'protection of the common interest of humankind' instead, Europe is quite well equipped already, and the EU conservation law covers both terrestrial and marine environments and has been highly influenced by International law in the last decades. In 1997, UNESCO adopted a specific Declaration on the Responsibilities of the Present Generations towards Future Generations.[158] There is concern about the fate of future generations in the face of the vital challenges of the next millennium. The International legal scholar, Edith Brown Weiss (1988), in her book *In Fairness to Future Generations* developed the legal concept of planetary trust whereby: "all generations are partners caring for and using the Earth. Every generation needs to pass the Earth and our natural and cultural resource on in at least as good condition as we received them, [according to a principle of] equity between ourselves and future generations and among communities in the present and the future".

Equally, more recently, within the context of climate change discussion, some scholars are referring to the atmosphere as a global commons and common good (Bosselmann, 2015; Edenhofer, Flachsland, & Jakob, 2013). The European conservation sites and species fall under the legislation of two main European Conservation Directives: The 1992 Habitats Directive and the most recently codified (amended version) the 2009 Wild Birds Directive. In addition to this the EU has made significant progress towards globally agreed targets for

[157] Valguarnera (2013).

[158] http://portal.unesco.org/en/ev.php-URL_ID=13178&URL_DO=DO_TOPIC&URL_SECTION=201.html.

establishing marine protected areas. Goal 14 "Life below water" as part of the UN Global Agenda 2030 is concerned with conservation and sustainable use of the oceans, seas and marine resources, and its point of the departure is a very solid body and complex protection system under international law. Furthermore, in 1999 the General Assembly decided to establish the United Nations Open-ended Informal Consultative Process on Oceans and the Law of the Sea (the Consultative Process) to facilitate the annual review by the General Assembly in an effective and constructive manner of developments in ocean affairs and the law of the sea by considering the report of the Secretary-General on oceans and the law of the sea, and by suggesting particular issues to be considered by it with an emphasis on identifying areas where coordination and cooperation at the intergovernmental and inter-agency levels should be enhanced (resolution 54/33). The integration of more participatory mechanisms is more recent, and it has become a binding mechanism after the Paris agreement (2015). In Europe, the 7th Environment Action Program (7th EAP) "Living within the limits of our planet" has well embedded (in theory) all the substantial aspects that Europe needs under the 'sustainability' paradigm to avoid lagging behind on protecting habitats and species generally speaking. The 7th EAP includes the objective of halting biodiversity loss and the degradation of ecosystems services by 2020. The European Environmental Agency most recent assessments have foreseen the need for larger protected marine sites to supplement European marine protected areas networks, because the European sites might be too small to sustain ecosystem resilience and hence, they do not fully deliver ecosystem's services.

My question is, would a specific protocol on sustainable development further clarify the nature of actions that the EU would need to undertake to accomplish current and future generation's protection needs and reinforce fairer and accessible effective governance mechanisms?, and then, would the logic of the market disappear at some point considering that seems to be not sufficient for the protection of the biosphere, our societies, our public education systems, our welfare systems in general, our living habits and the sustainability of our cultural heritage?, and last, but not least, Would this specific protocol resolve the problem of justiciability of intergenerational equity?

The answer is not easy. However, I definitely want to give my contribution by providing new analytical tools based on an interdisciplinary approach, going beyond reviewing just legal frameworks, bibliography or policy plans. There is a need to opening new discussions and breaking silos into the current legal domain to see how other disciplines are reacting to face the challenge of what the political economist Giovannini has called "*utopia sostenibile*" (sustainable utopia), in contrast to the 'retrotopian trend' described so brilliantly by the renowned sociologist Zygmunt Bauman.

As I learned,[159] Bauman a few weeks before his death on 9 January 2017 sent a short text to Italian journalist Francesco Antonioli as a contribution to an edited book on Pope Francis. In the text, published with the meaningful title: '*il dono'* ('the gift'), the sociologist of Jewish background described Pope Francis as 'the most precious gift offered by the Roman Catholic Church to our world'.[160] On his note, the sociologist is compelled by admiration to describe how in today's world, among world-wide authorities, only Jorge Mario Bergoglio, Pope Francis has understood and defined clearly which priorities the world must face. The priorities that Bauman describes are: "1. The art of dialogue (as a way of developing a *modus convivendi* among people for our time), 2. Inequality (attention for poverty and suffering caused by a social and economic inequality empowered by widespread indifference), and 3. School curricula (the need to resurrect the lost moral standards and restore spiritual values in the young; the spiritual values to resist the erosion of values caused by materialism, consumerism and profiteering)".

The art of dialogue is crucial in Bauman's latest contributions where he talked of the importance of 'civility' which he explained as 'the ability to interact with strangers', 'the ability to live with differences and 'the art of negotiating common interests and shared destiny' (Bauman, 2000). For Bauman the art of dialogue is of course a crucial tool that humanity is missing. In fact in his book '*Retrotopia*' Bauman (2017) discusses the growing tendency of running away from the idea of building a better future and instead there is a search for returning to an ideal past.

The need for dialogue in Bauman recalls the 'deliberative narratives' of Habermas that urges to be discussed on the ambit of the above mentioned commons' sites to consider the question of participation in protected areas governance from a normative perspective. Those deliberative narratives have been applied to the 'educational' context (Murphy 2016); and need to be included in natural resources integrating the questions of access, participation and third generation rights to surpass these neglected aspects embedded in environmental management practices which have long been individual protection centred (Pieraccini, 2015). The need to include third generation considerations correlates to the collective dimension of environmental protection and participatory governance processes, and here is where the 'intellectual shadow of Habermas' deliberative democracy' could work for new conceptual frameworks. For those who are not familiar with Habermas' deliberative theory and communication processes applied to law and governance, in a nutshell: Habermas utilises 'deliberation' to shape his perspective of law. For him, the laws can only be promulgated via deliberation, whereby, the members of the society actively take part in the varied sorts of debates and ponderations that

[159]See review on Bauman's Retrotopia by Polhuijs (2017) https://www.theoryculturesociety.org/review-zygmunt-bauman-retrotopia/.

[160]Bauman (2017) contribution to Antonioli (2017) Francesco e noi. Milano: Piemme, 25–27.

arise from the public sphere. Aarhus Convention is of course an important achievement versus 'participatory democracy', still insufficient despite of the important steps taken at international level. Nonetheless, most recently the trendy argument around improved governance of global commons focusing in the atmosphere have triggered discussion in three areas: carbon pricing and taxation, global cooperation, and national and sub-national action. The argument around this trend is moulded by the idea that the atmosphere has degenerated from a global commons to a mere commodity, so, it has been suggested an earth-centred governance providing grounds for an increased sense of global commons governance as an adequate solution (Bosselmann, 2015).

In this disruptive legal science discourse about the protection of common interests we come across to the already mentioned debate of the commons that pose a challenge to the increasing commodification of current and future generations' lives. The emerging commons have pose a challenge to the law which is now requested to provide legal tools to resist the dispossession of the common wealth (Marella, 2017) and formalised the judicial recognition of collective interest and collective action. According to Marella (2017), two judicial decisions are particularly relevant to offer a first formal recognition of the category of common goods that is a clue instrument when approaching third generation rights justiciability[161]: (1) "the first decision refers to political corruption case involving the transfer from the local government to a private developer of an area located in a village in the State of Punjab, which included a pond that was crucial for local inhabitants as a source of water for drinking, washing and watering cattle. The Court condemned this widespread practice of the public administration and declared the need to protect common rights in order to defend the lives of communities; (2) The Italian decision is relevant because it offered a first formal recognition of the category of common goods. Examining the claim of private fishery to an area of the Venice Lagoon, the Court maintained that state properties had to be considered common goods when they were devoted to the fulfilment of people's fundamental rights (in this case, the right to enjoy the environment)".[162] In both cases, the commons have acquired legal status.

As, it has been indicated the approaches to the topic are many, but the important element for us here is "the protection of the common interest of the human kind" as it is extrapolated from the above court decisions. This is so much associated to natural resources, knowledge and culture. At the private law level, Mattei (2013) draws attention to the power of generations in collective action. Collective action is an extremely important concept for the sake of challenging legal formalism and traditional institutions. He insists on the idea of recuperating all the potential legal wealth stemming from a transgenerational approach by getting rid of the individual-centred scheme imbedded in our law of property.

[161](1) Supreme Court of India, Civil Appeal No. 1132/2011 @SLP© No. 3109/2011, 28 January 2011; (2) *Cass. Civ. Sez. Unite*. Sent., 14 February 2011, n. 3665.

[162]Marella (2017).

Thus, generations should be seen as collective entities even if they lack recognised legal standing. His discourse emanates from a holistic vision of reality and therefore a new 'common sense' based on the centrality of the commons and the collective rather than of the individual (Mattei, 2013). His discourse is quite pertinent in the context of this legal analyses that attempts to 'open' the 'window' of cultural and methodological 'transformation'. On his introductory essay to the book *Protecting future generations through commons* he speaks of some European realities, such as Alpine villages, where the connection between age groups is still very strong and in certain areas they develop as commons organisations, which are involved in fulfilling crucial social needs in the direct management of irrigation and drinking water. The sophisticated commons organisations recalled by Mattei, the *Nus* in the Aosta Valley, at the foot of Mont Blanc, or the Alpine common of Premiata Comunità di Fiemme in the Trentino region, are another example to add to the communities' case studies analysed by Ostrom (1990) explaining the essence of a sustainable way of life under the premises of solidarity between generations.

Mattei's (2011) view of the commons is a sample discourse of a whole trend of theoretical insights on the commons that has invaded the social science literature in a varied number of heterogeneous set of studies, concerned with a variety of topics, such as knowledge commons (Hess & Ostrom, 2007); global environmental commons (Bosselmann, 2015; Stern, 2011), and cultural shared resources (Bertacchini, Bravo, Marrelli, & Santagata, 2012). Mattei's approach gives a flavour of the 'transformative' trend taking place in Europe, whereby communities of citizens can organise themselves by entering pacts to share the care of the commons with municipal authorities. A European network of resisting local communities has developed to link together the commons movement in Spain, Italy, Greece, Germany, France, and many other places and the willingness to engage with representative politics has determined a new phase in the European movements (Capra & Mattei, 2015).

Legal scholarship approaches are still insufficient, and the normative discourse of the analyses is highly relevant. There is perhaps a lack of creative imagination among those who are more closely related to 'institutions', lawyers and politicians. However, the truth is that this "model of participatory government" (Mattei, 2011) is already part of the EUSM, and the ever-growing diffusion of the discourse on the commons is just a symptom of an institutional crisis, not only to face recognition of the rights of future generations, but to take (finally) seriously access and equal protection of natural and cultural resources and by imposing concrete "duties" on humankind (Fracchia, 2005) which should complement the vision of future generations embedded in our European constitutional traditions (EU Constitutional Treaty, Germany, Norway, France, Poland, Italy, Netherlands, etc...). Fracchia, suggest that our legal anthropological approach must change when dealing with vested rights on humans to live in a certain environment that must be protected. Environmental law should embrace an area of provisions devoted to setting and disciplining human actions under an obligation to respect and protect nature by using the concepts of duty, solidarity and responsibility towards nature itself and third generation rights that are the essence of sustainable development. The EUSM must embed such normative ethos.

The Brazilian-American Scholar Roberto Unger (1996) in his book *What Should Legal Analyses Become?* Offers a theoretical account of what the duty of scholarship should ideally be that I fully share. For those who are not familiar with his theoretical approach I would just say that his thoughts and his contribution helps the scholar to understand the importance of questioning accepted norms and standards in legal theory and practice.

He talks of the 'limits of contemporary legal thought' by referring to them as a 'ridle' that if unresolved would consequently provoke the failure to turn legal analyses into institutional imagination. He defines this as the major consequence of the arrested development of legal thought today, and goes along his discourse introducing as an example of such arrest of development the 'American traditional style of adjudication', with its emphasis upon the structure-preserving assignment of rights among individual litigants. On re-defining possible paths to solve the 'ridle' he first tries to shed light on one of the most important reasons for the arrested development of legal thought: the history of modern politics (Unger, 1996). In his opinion the same period that saw the development of legal thought arrested also witnessed a connected series of radical reforms in the institutional and ideological context of political and economic life: the reforms labelled in Europe as social democracy and described in the United States as the New Deal. These changes had one of their points of focus and support in Keynesianism: a connected series of institutional and ideological innovations, freeing national governments from sound-finance doctrine and thus diminishing the dependence of public policy upon the level of business confidence (Unger, 1996). Those changes, he describes, helped set the boundary conditions within which individuals and organised groups would, in the succeeding period, understand and defend their interest.

His key message goes hand in hand with the supposed mission of the legal thinker today, especially the legal thinker engaged with sustainability matters. In his opinion the task of the legal thinker would be to develop a theory of law that, freer of the nineteenth-century devotion to a predetermined private-law system, would do justice to social-democratic commitments. Further on his arguments, almost by the end of his book, he refers to legal analyses and political imagination as the twin disciplines of the institutional imagination—It is in fact under the premises of the message contained in Unger's resolution of the 'ridle' that I want to proceed when seizing EUSM challenges.

Our first challenge then, as I understand it, is to take part on the immediate legal 'narrative' that we have been analysing during all its evolution process and try to contribute in a creative way. We cannot be bystanders any longer.

(3) What about the issue of management behind this 'paradigmatic' move Europe is witnessing under its sustainability model to approach active civil participation in relation to the 'commons'? European cities are an important laboratory for this. Cities in Europe, as in the rest of the world, are changing, in the next years more

billions of people will be living in cities. Migration floods are constantly challenging size, services, and everyday life everywhere in Europe. People are changing too and we need solutions for cities that need to create resilience and sustainable solutions for the increasing urban spaces. People are not aware yet of their own transformative power through collective action. However, the limits of the economic growth (and linked to this, of the welfare state) equal to the new technological opportunities have forced us to reconsider the governance model both for goods and services that, within the European welfare state, we have long considered as "public". The concept of collaborative city and sharing economy are also well-established and strategies to help local governments across Europe and worldwide are growing. Accepting citizens collectives as a third provider of public goods and services minimises the risk of failure and enhances resilience in worldwide societies.

Academics, scientists (not so much legal academics) have recently engaged on the institutionalisation of such urban movements in which real transdisciplinary solutions[163] are at hand, so academics, city council and citizens work hand in hand to develop 'sustainable' solutions and build the pathway to sharing experiences and create resilient institutions run by citizens where there is no more space for the old dichotomy of Public and Private (*labgov/urbancommons; labsus, transition towns movement*). Those approaches and actions often try to give evidence that co-operation through institutions for collective action can be sufficiently robust to survive economic crisis (social, political, economic or natural resources crisis) depending on the institution, the context and the circumstances, and create a resilient society and follow, as we mentioned before, the revival of the 'right to the city' approach.

Examples, of this new bottom-up movement are plenty as we have seen, and I would say that the education and cultural sector need even more engagement considering the efficiency of those solutions at local level: childcare centres run by parents, co-operatives from neighbours who create and utilise their own energy, cultural centres, community gardens, public libraries run by neighbourhoods, city-gardens, and numerous collectives providing care for specific social groups, the list is not exhaustive. What is important to us is to acknowledge that these movement is taking place and legal scientist have an important role to play.

At the basis of this intergenerational sensibility, which should emerge more than ever in every political imperative, lies the heart of the "commons" theoretical discussion: Commons thinking takes a community and ecosystem perspective, placing issues of care, solidarity, ecology, social equity and long-term stability at the forefront of policy. With the 'commons' paradigm, we can go beyond a purely individual rights and market-oriented restricted worldwide vision to enlarge legal instruments. Within the European context is needed a

[163]For a clear and concise introduction to transdisciplinary methodology used by a political economist to build a theory of 'transformation' read, Göpel (2016).

closer look at the 'normative' aspect of the 'commons'. Considering the importance is gaining in urban contexts.

On the issue of management of the commons, generally the point departure for an analytic of the commons is Elinor Ostrom's eight general design principles from her foundational book *Governing the Commons* (1990) and her latter essays on the Institutional Analyses and Development Approach (IAD) which address relevant contextual factors previously overlooked by the eight design principles such as: political rule, legal polity, geography and the historical dimension of resources. IAD was a breakthrough in its heightened flexibility in studying very diverse commons regimes and its most useful analytical tool was its differentiation of rule-making into three layers: (1) operational day-to-day rules (2) collective-choice rules which involve decisions about how operational rules can be changed, and (3) constitutional rule which determine how collective-choice rules may be changed. However, as Bailey (2013) asserts, while this analyses provided a better understanding of the interplay of the normative values (such as participation and co-operation that are merely procedural) of these communities underlying—and even driving-these processes, it completely ignored the values themselves, such as participation and co-operation.

The central question in this study is how groups of principals who are in an interdependent situation can organise and govern themselves to obtain continuing joint-benefits when all face temptations to free-ride, shirk, or otherwise act opportunistically. Before this carefully designed endogenous institutions and theoretical discussions based on empirical research, Hardin's Tragedy of the Commons (1968) was the reference analytical point for open access resources. This antagonist classic example with actually made famous the dogma: "the tragedy of the commons" was about a shared pasture upon which many herders can graze their cattle. Hardins' Tragedy of the commons consisted on the impossibility of the herder to have a rational incentive to hold back, and so they will put as many cattle on the commons as possible, taking as much as he could for himself. The pasture in this case (or so called "tragedy") will inevitably be over-exploited and ruined.

In Ostrom's analytical approach (1990) the term open access resource is transformed in the term commons. It identifies the auto-government microsystems of local territorial resources: reservoirs, fishing and grazing areas, forests. Documented and well delimited empirical cases: irrigation systems in Spanish *huertas*, fishing areas in Canada, Sri Lanka and Turkey, Grazing areas in Swiss Alps.

In defining the institutions responsible for governing common goods, Ostrom gives us the key for a new 'imaginary' in what concerns legal tools. She states, when defining institutions (working rules of the 'commons'), that "working rules are those actually used, monitored and enforced when individuals make choices about the actions they will take" (Ostrom, 1990, p. 51). A crucial point on this theoretical approach is that institutional intermediation under pre-established rules giving voice to our needs that is the mode of functioning of current representative democracies, is not valid anymore on the face of deterioration of the economy, ecology and social cohesion. What it is suggested here is "collective modes of production and solutions, creating and changing rules via exchange and discussion (*lexis*), while the common practice (*praxis*) concurrently proves its value" (Farrell, 2013).

Thus, departing from the contextual background of the commons discourse we build upon a different conception of society. Our societies cannot be any longer a mere collection of atomised individuals principally living as consumers and extractors of natural resources. We need to integrate the intergenerational factor that our constitutions are missing today as we have already mentioned. Intergenerational justice and third generation rights are at the heart of our discourse considering that most of the resources needed for satisfaction are not created but extracted (food, soil, water, energy). The logic of the market seems not to be sufficient for our societies, our welfare systems, our living habits and the problem of intergenerational justice.

Commons thinking points to the reality of people's lives as deeply embedded in social relationships, communities, histories and traditions. Challenging the dominant ideas of ownership and governance, the commons approach enables policy to assess the collective interests of citizens as a whole.[164] The commons demolish the premise of the rule of law embedded within the dualisms: Private property v State Sovereignty that has impoverished the possibilities of modern political life. Urban assets and resources or the city as a whole can be transformed into collaborative ecosystems that enable collective action for the urban commons, and partakes the road to consider 'services of general interest', such as water, education, electricity, universities, etc. (market and non-market oriented) that are considered of central interest for the collectivity as commons. In addition, this is of course the most controversial aspect of this proposal. Particularly in the context of 'traditional public services' or more akin to our European administrative scholarship, 'services of general interest'. 'Commonification' of those services would mean managing the resources to which the services if connected separately from market and profit logic, as a commons to which everyone must be able to have fair access, including even rights of future generations. However, what about the infrastructural costs of many of these services? Sometimes this question is put forward as a hampering levy in commons discourse, but forgetting the crucial aspect of the necessary of self-governance associated with commons management. Commoners do not own but govern collective goods and use them collectively in a socially fair and sustainable manner.

Regardless of the craving for solutions towards 'commons' approaches, especially in urban contexts already mentioned, only a minority of legal scholars have displayed interest for the commons outside the context of intellectual property in Europe. In Italy, Arena, Mattei, Lucarelli, Rodotà (well-known

[164]Mattei (2011), Foster and Iaone (2016), Capra and Mattei (2015).

Italian scholars)[165] the list is not exhausted of course, have worked at the practical as much theoretical and even political level on the issue of commons, although their notions of the 'commons' can differ slightly (if we think of the way Mattei or Arena theorise 'the commons') have completely changed the civil participation *panorama* in the urban contexts. For Mattei (Capra & Mattei, 2015) in "the ecology of law", law itself is a 'commons' in which law is part of the solution to our problems requiring us to imagine an eco-design approach to law. For Arena, the departing point is the administrative setting in the urban context completely modified by horizontal subsidiarity and the disruptive scenario provoked by the passage of passive citizenship to active citizenship in the public law domain, which has proved to be effective in the Italian administrative domain by the proliferation of the *patti di amministrazione condivisa* as opposed to the traditional *remunicipalización* practice (Tornos Mas, 2016). The Italian movement has had a particular success at the municipal level, and the 'institutionalisation' at local administrative level is drastic through the *patti di collaborazione.*[166]

What is of interest to us is their proposed change of paradigm. Valguarnera (2017) argues that "regardless of the importance of these exceptions, it is difficult to deny that the average Western legal scholar is unaware of, or at least not interested in, the rich debate about the commons that in the last decades has been so crucial to other social sciences".

As Capra & Mattei (2015) remind us in "The Ecology of Law", whereas most communing practices are local, some needs, such as those satisfied by culture and knowledge, share an important global dimension. Knowledge that is capable of facing current challenges cannot afford to be parochial, and thus social networks, powerfully facilitated by the internet, are extremely important. Within such context the European Union therefore is facing an urgent challenge: How to manage common knowledge and common resources in a way that is socially and ecologically sustainable? How can it candidly acknowledge epochal shifts in education and how can devise policies appropriate to the current age? Policy structures would need to enable ordinary people, ordinary citizens to freely access, share and manage knowledge, natural and cultural resources acquiring the benefits of collaborative resources, access to nature, spaces, heritage and technologies.

---

[165] In June 2007 was appointed a Commission in Italy set up by the Prodi Government, best known as the Rodotà Commission after its president, for reforming Article II of the Book III of the Civil Code. The Commons received the first technical-legislative definition by the bill of the Rodotà Commission. To date the bill of the Rodotà Commission has not been discussed in Parliament, but the work of this Commission helped to reach a positive result for achieving a positive result in the Italian referendum on Water challenging the laws to privatise water. An English versión of the Rodotà Commission Bill is available online at: http://iuccommonsproject.wikispaces.com/file/view/Rodotà+Commission+Bill_+EN.pdf.

[166] https://www.labsus.org/patti-di-collaborazione/.

References

Aloniitty, T. (2016). The Weser Case: Case 461/13 Bun v Germany. *Journal of Environmental Law, 28*(1), 151–158.

Antonioli, F. (2017). *Francesco e noi*. Milano: Piemme.

Arena, G. (2003). Users, customers, allies: new perspectives in relations between citizens and public administrations. In G. Arena & M. Chiti (Eds.), *Public Administration, competitiveness and sustainable development* (p. 9 et seg). Firenze University Press.

Arias Maldonado, M. (2015). *Environment and society: Socionatural relations in the Anthropocene*, Springer.

Arrowsmith, S., & Kunzlik, P. (Eds.). (2009). *Social and environmental policies in EC procurement law*. Cambridge University Press.

Ba, A., & Hoffmann, M. J. (Eds.). (2005). *Contending perspectives on global governance: Coherence, contestation and World Order*. Routledge.

Bailey, S. (2013). The architecture of commons legal institutions for future generations. In S. Bailey, G. Farrell, & U. Mattei (Eds.), *"Protecting future generations through commons", in Trends in social Cohesion* (Vol. 26, p. 107). Council of Europe Publishing.

Barnes, P., & Hoerber, T. (Eds.). (2013). *Sustainable development and governance in Europe*. Routledge.

Bauman, Z. (2000). *Liquid modernity*. Cambridge: Polity Press.

Bauman, Z. (2017). *Retrotopia*. Cambridge: Polity Press.

Bertacchini, E. E., Bravo, G., Marrelli, M., & Santagata, W. (Eds.). (2012). *Cultural commons: A new perspective on the production and evolution of cultures*. Chelthenham: Edward Elgar.

Biermann, F. (2007). Earth System Governance' as a crosscutting theme of global change research. *Global Environmental Change, 17*, 326–337.

Birnie, P. W., & Boyle, A. E. (1992). *International law and the environment*. Oxford: Oxford University Press.

Bosselmann, K. (2004). In search of global law: The significance of the Earth Charter. *Worldviews: Environment, Culture, Religion*, 8(1), 62–75.

Bosselmann, K. (2008). *The principle of Sustainability*. Ashgate.

Bosselmann, K. (2015). Germany's 'Energiewende': What can environmental law scholarship learn from it? In J. Jaria I Manzano, N. Chalifour, & L. Kotzé (Eds.), *Energy, governance and sustainability*. Elgar.

Boyle, A., & Freestone, D. (Eds.). (1999). *International law and sustainable development. past achievements and future challenges*. Oxford: Oxford University Press.

Brown Weiss, E. (1988). *In fairness to future generations: International law, common patrimony, and intergenerational equity*. New York: Dobbs, Ferry.

Brundtland Report. (1987). *World Commission on Environment and Development, Our common future: Report of the World Commission on Environment and Development*. Oxford University Press.

Capra, F., & Mattei, U., (2015). The *Ecology of law. Toward a legal system in tune with nature and community*, Berrett and Koehler.

Caradonna, J. L. (2014). *Sustainability. A History*. Oxford: Oxford University Press.

Caranta, R., & Trybus, M. (Eds.). (2010). *The law of green and social procurement in Europe*. DJOF.

Cardesa-Salzmann, A., & Cocciolo, E. (2019). Global governance, sustainability and the earth system: Critical reflections on the role of global law. *Transnational Environmental Law*, Symposium Article, pp. 1–25.

Casini, L. (2018). "The future of (international) cultural heritage law", guest editorial. *International Journal of Constitutional Law, 16*(1), 1–10.

Cassese, S. (1991). *Le Basi del Diritto Amministrativo*. Torino: Einaudi.

Castells, M (1977). *The Urban question. A Marxist approach*. From original work *La question urbaine* (1972, 1976). (Trans: Alan Sheridan). London: Edward Arnold.

CEU. (2014). *Conclusions on Cultural heritage as a strategic resource for a sustainable Europe Education, Youth, Culture and Sport Council meeting*. Brussels, 20 May 2014.

CEU. 'Conclusions of the Council and the Representatives of the Governments of Member States, meeting within the Council, on the Work Plan for Culture 2011-14' [2010] OJC325/1, Annex 1.

Closa, C., & Casini, L. (2016). *Comparative regional intregration. governance and legal models*. Cambridge: Cambridge University Press.

Collins. (2007). Environmental rights for the future? Intergenerational equity in the EU. *RECEIL, 16*(3), 325.

Cordonier Segger, M. C., & Khalfan, A. (2004). *Sustainable development law: Principles, practices and prospects* (p. 95). Oxford University Press.

Cremona, M. (2008). The European neighbourhood policy: More than a partnership? In M. Cremona (Ed.), *Developments in EU External Relations Law* (pp. 244–300). Oxford/New York: Oxford University Press.

De Búrca, G., & Scott, J. (2000). Introduction. In G. de Búrca & J. Scott (Eds.), *Constitutional change in the EU external relations law* (pp. 244–300). Oxford and New York: Oxford University Press.

De la Porte, C. (2002). Is the open method of coordination appropriate for organising activities at European level in sensitive policy areas? *European Law Journal, 38*(8).

De Witte, B. (2019). Foreword. In C. Ferri (Ed.), *The EU social market economy and the law. Theoretical perspectives and practical challenges for the EU*. Routledge.

Dernbach, J. C., & Cheever, F. (2015). Sustainable development and its discontents. *Transnational Environmental Law, 4*(2), 247–287.

Dimond, J. (2005). *Collapse: How societies choose to fail or succeed*. Viking Press.

Downes, P. (2014). *Access to Education in Europe: A framework and Agenda for system change*. Dordrecht: Springer Netherlands.

Dragos, D.-C., & Neamtu, B. (2014). Sustainable Public Procurement in the EU: Experiences and Prospects (April 27, 2014). In The collective works of Lichere, F. Caranta, & R. Treumer (Eds.), *Novelties in the 2014 Directive on Public Procurement*. DJØF Publishing. Available at SSRN: http://ssrn.com/abstract=2488047

Edenhofer, O., Flachsland, C., & Jakob, L. (2013). *The atmosphere as global commons: Challenges for international cooperation and governance*. Harvard Project on Climate Agreements, Harvard Kennedy School of Governement.

European Commission. (2007). Conclusions from the Consultation on a European Maritime Policy (COM (2007) 574 final), Retrieved October 10, from http://eurlex.europa.eu/LexUriServ/LexUriServ.do?uri=celex:52007dc0574:en:not

Evelyn, J. (1664). *Sylva or a Discourse of Forest-Trees and the Propagation of Timber in His Majesties Dominions, London,* 1664, p. 279.

Farrell, G. (2013). Common goods in urbanised societies. In S. Bailey, G. Farrell, & U. Mattei (Eds.), *"Protecting future generations through commons", in Trends in Social Cohesion, no. 26*. Council of Europe Publishing.

Ferri, D., & Cortese, F. (Eds.). (2019). *The EU social market economy and the law. Theoretical perspectives and practical challenges for the EU*. Routledge.

Fischer-Kowalski, M., & Haberl, H. (1998). Sustainable development: Socio-economic metabolism and colonization of nature. *International Social Science Journal, 50*(158), 573–587.

Fligstein, N. (2008). *Euroclash: The EU, European identity, and the future of Europe*. Oxford University Press.

Foster, S., & Iaone, C. (2016) "The City as commons". *Yale Law and Policy Review, 34*(281).

Fracchia, F. (2005). "The Legal definition of environment: From rights to duties", in Bocconi legal studies research paper, No. 06–09.

Francesco. (2015). Laudato Si'. Sulla cura della casa comune. Lettera encíclica, EDB.

Garben, S. (2011). *EU higher education law*. Kluwer Law International: *The Bologna Process and Harmonization by Stealth*.

Garben, S. (2015). Confronting the competence conundrum: Democratising the European Union through an expansion of its legislative powers. *Oxford Journal of Legal Studies, 35*(1), 55–89.

Gillroy, J. M. (2006). Adjudication norms, dispute settlement regimes and international tribunals: The status of "environmental sustainability" in international jurisprudence. *Stanford Journal of International Law, 42*, 1, 2.

Giubboni, S. (2015) Free movement of persons and European solidarity revisited. *Perspectives on Federalism, 7*(3).

González García, J. V. (2015). Sostenibilidad Social y ambiental en la Directive 2014/24/UE de Contratación pública. *Revista Española de Derecho Europeo, Dic*, 13–42.

Göpel, M. (2016). The great mindshift. How a new economic paradigm and sustainability transformations go hand in hand. Springer Open.

Gordon, R. (2015). Unsustainable development. In S. Alam et al. (Eds.), *International environmental law and the global South* (pp. 50–73). Cambridge University Press, 55.

Gornitzka, A. (2018). Organising soft governance in hard times. The unlikely survival of the open method of coordination in the EU Education policy. *European Papers, 3*(1), 235–255.

Grober, U. (2007). Deep roots. A conceptual history of "sustainable development" (Nachhaltigkeit), Wissenschaftszentrum Berlin für Sozialforschung (WZB), Berlin.

Habermas, J. (2006). *February 15, or: What Binds Europeans*, in the Divided West 39 (Ciaran Cronin translation).

Habermas, J. (2015). *The lure of technocracy* (p. 17). Polity.

Halász, G. (2013). European Union: The strive for smart, sustainable and inclusive growth. In Y. Wang (Ed.), *Education Policy Reform Trends in G20 Members* (pp. 267–288). Springer.

Heffron, R. J., & McCauley, D. (2017). The concept of energy justice across the disciplines. *Energy Policy, 105*, 658–667.

Herrmann, R. K., Risse, T., & Brewer, M. (Eds.). (2004). *Transnational identities: Becoming European in the EU*. Lanham MD: Rowman and Littlefield.

Hess, C. (2008). *Mapping the new commons*. In Conference governing shared resources: connecting local experience to global challenges, the Twelfth Biennial Conference of the International Association for the Study of Commons, Chelthenham. Available at: http://dlc.dlib.indiana.edu/dlc/handle/10535/304

Hess, C., & Ostrom, E. (Eds.). (2007). *Understanding knowledge as a commons: From theory to practice*. Cambridge, MA: MIT Press.

Hewson, M., & Sinclair, T. J. (Eds.). (1999). *Approaches to global governance theory*. Albany: SUNY Press.

Heyvaert, V. (2009). Globalizing regulation: Reaching beyond the borders of chemical safety. *Journal of Law and Society, 36*(1), 110–128.

Hornborg, A. (2010). *International Trade and environmental justice: Toward a global political ecology*. Nova Science.

Hornborg, A., Clark, B., & Hermele, K. (2013). *Ecology and power: Struggles over land and material resources in the past, present and future*. Routledge.

Hornborg, A., McNeill, J. R., & Martínez-Alier, J. (Eds.). (2006). *Rethinking environmental history: World-system history and global environmental change*. AltaMira.

Humphreys, M. (2018). *Sustainable development in the European Union. A general principle*. Routledge.

International Union for the Conservation of Nature. (1980). *World conservation strategy: Living resource conservation for sustainable development* (p. iv). Gland, Switzerland: IUCN.

Jagielska-Burduk, A. (2019). "Cultural heritage, education and research in the European Union". In Jakubowski, Hausler & Fiorentini (Eds.), cultural heritage in the European Union. A critical enquiry into law and policy, Nijhoff, Leiden: Brill.

Jans, H. J. (2011). Stop the integration principle? *Fordham International Law Journal, 33*(5)., Article 8.

Jimenez-Beltrán, D. (2001). (Executive director, European environment agency), 'Making sustainability accountable: The role and flexibility of indicators. From Gothenburg to Barcelona',

Speech delivered in Brussels, Retrieved July 9, 2001, from https://www.eea.europa.eu/media/speeches/Speech%20Brussels20%July209%2C%202001
Kelemen, R., & Vogel, D. (2010). Trading places: The role of the United States and the European Union in international environmental politics. *Comparative Political Studies, 43*(4), 427–456.
Keohane, R., & Nye, J. (1974, October). Transgovernmental relations and international organizations. *World Politics, 27*, 39 and following.
Kingston, S. (2013). *European perspectives on environmental law and governance*. London: Routledge.
Klabbers, J., & Palombella, G. (2019). *The challenge of interlegality*. Cambridge University Press.
Kotzè, L. (2019). Global environmental constitutionalism in the anthropocene, Bloomsbury.
Krämer, L. (2001). Differentiation in EU environmental policy. In B. De Witte, D. Hanf, & E. Vos (Eds.), *The many faces of differentiation in EU law* (pp. 83–100). Antwerpen: Intersentia.
Krämer, L. (2013). Environmental governance in the EU. In M. Alberton & F. Palermo (Eds.), *Environmental protection in multi-layered systems. Comparative lessons from the water sector* (pp. 11–30). Leiden: Nijhoff.
Krisch, N. (2010). *Beyond constitutionalism: The pluralist structure of postnational law*. Oxford University Press.
Kulovesi, K., Morgera, E., & Muñoz, M. (2011, June 9). Environmental Integration and multifaceted international dimensions of EU law: Unpacking the EU's 2009 climate and energy package. *Common Market Law Review, 48*(3), 829–891.
Lefebvre, H. (1968). *Le droit à la ville*. Paris: Anthropos.
Lenschow, A. (2002). New regulatory approaches in 'greening' EU policies. *European Law Journal, 8*(1), 19–37.
Llorente-González, L., & Vence, X. (2019). Decoupling or 'decaffing'? the underliying conceptualisation of circular economy in the European Union monitoring framework. *Sustainability, 11*(18), 4898.
Lowe, V. (1999). Sustainable development and unsustainable arguments. In A. Boyle & D. Freestone (Eds.), *International law and sustainable development. Past achievements and future challenges* (p. 19 et seg). Oxford University Press.
Marella, M. R. (2017). "The Commons as a legal concept", in Law Critique, Springer pub.
Marín-Durán, G., & Morgera, E. (2012). *Environmental integration in the EU's external relations, modern studies in European law* (Vol. 29). UK: Hart.
Mata, R. (2008). "Acercamiento al paisaje'en Sostenibilidad local". *Observatorio de la Sostenibilidad en España*. Informe inédito.
Mattei, U. (2011). *Bene Comuni*. Laterza: Un Manifesto.
Mattei, U. (2013). Future generations now! A commons-based analysis. In S. Bailei, G. Farell, & U. Mattei (Eds.), *Protecting future generations through commons, Trends in social Cohesion, no. 26*. The Council of Europe Publishing.
Mattei, U., & Quarta, A. (2015). Right to the City or urban commoning? thoughts on the generative transformation of property law. *The Italian Law Journal, 01*(02).
McAffe, K. (1999). "Selling nature to save it? biodiversity and the rise of green developmentalism" in Environment and Planning, vol. 17, nº 2, pp. 133-154.
McCrudden, C. (2007). *Buying social justice. Equality, government procurement, & legal change*. Oxford University Press.
McIntyre, O. (2013). Environmental protection of international watercourses under international law, Ashgate
Mendes, J. (2011). Participation and the role of law after Lisbon: A legal view on Article 11 TEU. *Common Market Law Review, 48*(6), 1849–1878.
Mete, G., & Heffron, R. (2019). The social dimension of EU energy law. In D. Ferri & F. Cortese (Eds.), *The EU social market economy and the law. Theoretical perspectives and practical challenges for the EU*. Routledge.

Miller, R. A. (2019). The day the earth stood still?-Reading Jürgen Habermas' Essay "February 15" Against Ian McEwan's Novel Saturday. *German Law Journal, 10*(1)., (Special Issue: The Kantian Project of International Law).
Molinari, C. (2015). From a right to development to intergenerational equity. In J. E. Viñuelas (Ed.), *Rio declaration on environment and development: A commentary* (p. 141). Oxford University Press.
Morgera, E. (2012). Bilateralism at the service of community interests? Non-judicial enforcement of global public goods in the context of global environmental law. *European Journal of International Law, 23*(3), 743–767.
Novitz, T. (2011). "Big unions and big business: Can international framework agreements promote sustainable development at a local level?, in T. Novitz & D. Mangan. *The Role of Labour Standards in Development*, British Academy.
Novitz, T. A. (2015). The paradigm of sustainability in a European social context: Collective participation in protection of future interests? *International Journal of Comparative Labour Law, 31*(3), 243–262.
Oliver, A., Dawn, H., & Prosser, T. (2010). *The Regulatory state: Constitutional implications*. Oxford University Press.
Orlando, E. (2014). "The Evolution of EU policy and law in the environmental field: Achievements and current changes", In C. Bakker & F. Francioni (Eds.), The *EU, The USA and Global Climate Governance*, Routledge.
Ostrom, E. (1990). *Governing the commons: The evolution of institutions for collective action*. Cambridge University Press.
Pallmaerts, M. (2006). The EU and sustainable development: An ambiguous relationship. In M. Pallmaerts & A. Azmanova (Eds.), *The European Union and sustainable development: Internal and external dimensions*. Brussels University Press.
Palonitty, T. (2016). The Weser Case: Case 461/13 Bun v Germany. *Journal of Environmental Law, 28*(1), 151–158.
Parks, L., & Morgera, E. (2019). Reflections on Methods from an Interdisciplinary Research Project in Global Environmental Law. *BENELEX Working Paper* No. 20.
Pavoni, R., & Piselli, D. (2016). "The sustainable development goals and international environmental law: normative values and challenges for implementation", in *Veredas do Direito. Belo Horizonte, 13*(26), 13–60.
Pieraccini, M. (2015). Democratic legitimacy and new commons: Examples from English protected areas. *International Journal of the Commons, 9*(2), 552–572.
Piermattei, M. (2014) "The Union's political parties: historical evolution and research" In M. Mascia (Ed.), Towards a European Transnational Party System, Associazione Universitaria di Studi Europei, pp. 35–44.
Pollack, M. (2000). The end of creeping competence? EU policy‐making since Maastricht. *Journal of Common Market Studies*, 38(3), 519–538.
Psychogiopoulou, E. (2015). The cultural open method of coordination. In E. Psychogiopoulou (Ed.), *Cultural governance and the European Union: Protecting and promoting cultural diversity in Europe* (p. 39 et seg). Basingstoke: Palgrave Macmillan.
Psychogiopoulou, E. (2017). The cultural open method of coordination: A new boost for cultural policies in Europe? *Maastricht Journal of European and Comparative Law, 24*(2), 264–288.
Psychogiopoulou, E. (2018). The cultural open method of coordination: A new but different OMC? *European Papers, 3*(1), 257–279.
Radkau, J. (2000). *Natur und Macht. Eine Weltgeschichte der Umwelt* (p. 245). Munich: Beck.
Randhir, T. (2011). Towards sustainability of the earth system. *Journal of Earth Science and Climate Change, 2*(2), e101.
Rehbinder, E., & Stewart, R. (1985). *Environmental protection policy*. Berlin: DeGruyter.
Rifkin, J. (2011). *The third industrial revolution*. St. Martin's Press.
Ringel, M., & Knodt, M. (2018). The governance of the European Energy Union: Efficiency, effectiveness and acceptance of the Winter Package 2016. *Energy Policy, 112*, 209–2020.

Robinson, J. (2004). "Squaring the circle? some thoughts on the idea of sustainable development" in *Ecological Economics*, vol. 48, nº 4, pp. 369–384.
Roche, S. (2017). Listening to the grassroots. Bottom-up approaches to lifelong learning. *International Review of Education, 63*, 145–152.
Rodrigo, Ángel J. (2015). *El desafío del desarrollo sostenible. Los principios de Derecho internacional relativos al desarrollo sostenible*, Centro de Estudios Internacionales, Madrid: Marcial Pons.
Sachs, J. D. (2015). *The age of sustainable development*. Nueva York: Columbia University Press.
Sadeleer, N. (2012). Principle of subsidiarity and the EU environmental policy. *Journal for European Environmental Planning Law, 9*(1), 64–65.
Sadeleer, N. (2015). Trade v environmental law-the fable of the earthen pot and the iron pot. *Environmental Policy and Law, 45*(1), 23–27.
Sánchez Galera, M. D. (2016). "A European vision of "sustainability" and what it entails in a global legal system", Revista relaciones internacionales, UAM.
Sánchez Galera, M. D. (2018). "Sustainable Development: The "hedgehog" or the fox of the European integration dream? a closer look to its social dimension". In P. Masala (Ed.). *La Europa Social: Alcances, retrocesos y desafíos para la construcción de un espacio jurídico de solidaridad*, CEPC.
Savaresi, A, & Auz, J. (2019) Climate change litigation and human rights: Pushing the boundaries. *Climate Law*. Available at SSRN: https://ssrn.com/abstract=3374730
Schumacher, E. F. (1973). *Small is Beautiful. Economics as if People Mattered*. New York: HarperCollins.
Sjåfjell, B. (2009). T*owards a sustainable European Company Law. A normative analyses of the objectives of EU Law, with the takeover directive as atTest case*, Kluwer Law International, European Company Law Series, vol. 3.
Slim, A. (2013). The impact of de-growth (la décroissance) on the discourse of sustainability. In P. M. Barnes & C. H. Thomas (Eds.), *Sustainable development and governance in Europe. The evolution of the discourse on sustainability*. Routledge.
Stern, P. C. (2011). Design principles for global commons: Natural resources and emerging technologies. *International Journal of the Commons, 5*(2), 213–232.
Strife, S., & Downey, L. (2009). Childhood development and access to nature: A new direction for environmental inequality research. *Organization and Environment, 22*(1), 105.
Tornos Mas, J. (2016). Servicios Públicos y Remunicipalización. *PUCP*, 76. Accessible on line: http://revistas.pucp.edu.pe/index.php/derechopucp/article/view/14848/15390
Unger, R. (1996). What should legal analyses should become?, 1st edition, Verso Books.
United Nations. (2015c). *Addis ababa action agenda financing development*.
United Nations. (2015e). *Work from the Inter-Agency Expert Group on SDGs* (IAEG-SDGs).
Valguarnera, F. (2013). Access to Nature and intergenerational justice. In S. Bailei, G. Farell, & U. Mattei (Eds.), *Protecting future generations through commons*, Trends in social Cohesion, no. 26. The Council of Europe Publishing.
Valguarnera, F. (2017). Legal ideology and the commons: Why are jurists falling behind? *Philosophy and Society, 29*(2), 153–316.
Viñuales, J. E. (2013). The rise and fall of sustainable development. *Review of European Comparative and International Environmental Law, 22*(3), 3–13, p. 4.
Viñuales, J. E. (2018). The organisation of the anthropocene: In our hands? *Brill Research Perspectives in International Legal Theory and Practice, 1*, 1–81.
von Bogdandy, A. (2005). The European Constitution and European identity: Text and subtext of the treaty establishing a constitution for Europe. *International Journal of Constitutional Law, 3*, 295.
Vos, E. (2000). Reforming the European Commission: What role to play for EU agencies? *Common Market Law Review*, 113 et seg.
Voss, J.-P., Bauknecht, D., & Kemp, R. (Eds.). (2006). *Reflexive governance for sustainable development*. Cheltenham: Elgar.

Walker, N. (2015). *Intimations of global law*. Cambridge University Press.

Weiss, B. (1984). The Planetary trust: Conservation and intergenerational equity. *Ecology Law Quaterly*, 495.

World Commission on Environment and Development (UNWCED). (1987). *Our common future, 'Brundtland Report'* (p. 43). Oxford: Oxford University Press.

Yang, T., & Percival, R. V. (2009). The emergence of global environmental law. *Ecology Law Quartely*, 36, 615–664.

Young, O. R., & Steffen, W. (2009). In C. Floke, G. P. Kofinas, & F. S. Chapin III (Eds.), *The earth system: Sustaining planetary life-support systems. Principles of ecosystem stewardship* (pp. 295–315). New York: Springer.

Zagrebelsky, G. (2013). "In the name of children: If the law had the duty to think of the future", in *Protecting future generations through commons* , Council of Europe publishing, Trends in Social Cohesion, No.26

Zeitlin, J. (2005). Conclusion: The open method of coordination in action. Theoretical promise, empirical realities, reform strategy. In J. Zeitlin, P. Pochet, & L. Magnusson (Eds.), *The open method of co-ordination in Action: The European employment and social inclusion strategies* (p. 447). P.I.E.-Peter Lang.

Zeitlin, J. (2009). The open method of coordination and reform of national social and employment policies: Influences, mechanisms, effects. In M. Heidenreich & J. Zeitlin (Eds.), *Changing European employment and welfare regimes: The influence of the open method of coordination on national reforms* (p. 214). Routledge.

Chapter 4
Conceptualising and Understanding Education and Cultural Challenges for Sustainability Transformation. Raising Awareness on the Big Picture

Abstract The aim of this chapter is to claim for a fresh view on the way we should think about education and culture as horizontal enablers of a strong sustainability model. It starts with a new conceptual approach that would enable us to understand the main challenges of both education and culture: new working definitions under SD premises are suggested, with the goal of laying out a new research agenda for an effective transformation process (see Sect. 4.1). Section 4.2 starts with the assumption that the importance of culture for economic growth has not been addressed adequately. Consequently, the preeminent role of education has also been ignored. The section continues with an analysis of the reasons behind the necessity to grow awareness among legal scholarship on transformation through education and culture. Section 4.3 tries to present the legislation potential for educational change, grounded on basic international agreements, which give support to educational and cultural instruments to face the challenges posed by the Anthropocene. Emphasis is made on the transforming capacities of these international treaties and principles. Finally, the global scenario is described as a possible trigger to reframe the EU current roadmap for sustainability (Sect. 4.4).

4.1 Unexplored Conceptual Frameworks of Education and Culture for Sustainability Transformation in Legal Scholarship

Until now, the legal discourses on sustainability have not adequately addressed the relevance of culture and education as main builders of SD. However, this is not a surprise. Culture and education are enablers of a more 'empathic'[1] relationship with our planet Earth in the Anthropocene but outside philosophical discussions, the trend is to ignore the legal and policy means needed for a substantial reform in these neglected sectors. Nevertheless, the broadly referred Earth governance phenomena may help the increasing presence of horizontal links between law, sustainability,

[1]Rifkin (2011), Papa Francesco (2015) and Morin (1999).

M. D. Sánchez Galera, *Educational and Cultural Challenges of the European Sustainability Model*, https://doi.org/10.1007/978-3-030-38716-7_4

Anthropocene and other social actors that might have a strong relevance within the context of education and culture. Still, the preeminent role of culture and education as sustainability builders has not been theoretically analysed referred to the powers and goals of the public administration.

Today when sustainability concerns are introduced into the field of culture they mostly relate to cultural heritage (the trend is growing), particularly in managerial terms. The risk is that public cultural heritage is suddenly exclusively perceived as an economic resource to make profit, whilst preservation, public access, and enjoyment of cultural heritage should be placed at centre of today's social policies in Europe to foster community ties, and engage civil society at large in its care, management and development.

In 1976, the Italian Jurist, who is considered the father of environmental law and built the inextricable tie between cultural and natural resources, Massimo Severo Giannini[2] conceptualised the essence of the cultural resources by affirming that although cultural properties were associated to one thing, they would not necessarily identify with it. Why? For Giannini, the thing is a material element representing (or supporting interests) "of an immaterial and public nature". The public component involves the competences of the public domain over it, thus, the public administrative body has powers over the cultural heritage. Still, those powers would not concern the patrimonial enjoyment of the thing, but "[t]he conservation of the cultural value and its enjoyment as part of the cultural universe" (Giannini, 1976).[3] This is, the public function mission would consist of facilitating the public enjoyment of cultural goods (detached from any property law concerns) that must deploy the principle of effective legal protection in administrative law with all its procedural and regulatory consequences involving public administration innovation processes (Parejo Alfonso, 2016).

If we look at official documents providing the roadmap for a sustainable Europe launched by the European Commission, we will notice how culture has been completely ignored, as much as the enjoyment of the "cultural universe" that would represent its intergenerational dimension already embedded in environmental protection regulations. In agenda for sustainability transformation, culture should trigger issues that go beyond heritage, nature conservation and environmental concerns: the anthropological and social settings of the three aspects are vital.

Paradoxically Education, training and life-long learning are presented as horizontal enablers of sustainability and are highlighted as indispensable tools to create a sustainability culture.[4] Therefore, the question I want to formulate is: how can the missing cultural component be introduced into our current education systems,

---

[2]Giannini (1976).

[3]Giannini (1976) personal translation from the original text: *"[L]a cosa è elemento materiale d'interessi di natura immateriale e pubblica (...) como tale è bene culturale, su cui lo Stato-Amministrazione dei beni culturali ha delle potestà che non riguardano l'utilizzabilità patrimoniale della cos, bensì la conservazione alla cultura e la fruibilità nell'universo culturale"*, p. *5 et seg.*

[4]See further, Reflection Paper towards a Sustainable Europe by 2030, COM (2019) 22 Final, Brussels, 30.1.2019.

consumption, production, waste, transport, and working patterns? Apparently, there is no answer to the question. However, considering how imminent the requirements of our energy transition and our circular economy plans are, the pressure of changing our cultural patterns becomes mandatory, to avoid the proliferation of regulation in a cultural *vacuum*. In addition, we urgently need to react to the merchandising trend affecting the cultural heritage sector. Another reaction should consist, when making the laws regulating natural heritage, in avoiding excessive focus on an anthropocentric view, because this might wrongly affect public action under strong sustainability premises.

In addition to this, we need to have a look on how cultural patterns shape our lifestyles. Culture is crucial for social transformations (even if it has also been neglected by the UN SDGs) where education plays a more preeminent role. Although cultural and education cannot be separated from each other, especially in this context of transformation where they become strategically interdependent. Education in fact has a double function when building a sustainable future: (1) modification or renewal of culture patterns and empowerment through educational practice; (2) conservation and awareness of our cultural heritage and identities. These two aspects are fundamental for the understanding of current cultural and educational challenges of the EUSM.

Once said that, we must admit that there is hardly any legal-based literature in the educational and cultural challenges of sustainability. Neither there is enough legal scholarship data about their transformation potential under sustainability requirements. On top of that, we should always bear in mind one important thing that is the result of our complex times: economy, politics, social relations and consumer habits (to name a few) have become globalised. This trend is fluctuating towards the opposite direction when we refer to the issues of culture and education. Education in this complexity needs to go through a process of 'deculturisation' from the global tendencies of standardisation following exclusively technological and industrial requirements. The 'deculturisation' of education should contrast the detrimental effects of international intervention introducing homogeneous parameters of acceleration to reach higher technological commands and innovation based on standards, tests and marketisation of education. Unfortunately, the homogenising policies do not differ much from country to country. Our task should be to open the path of public administration concerns on this field and find specific solutions to specific (meaning local) cases with the available resources.[5]

Within the European context, EU primary law should re-emerge as the constitutional reference point for a stronger and more enriching solidarity dialogue highly 'underused'[6] to reawaken European values in the educational context. This would push Member States to reform their education systems based on sustainability needs, which would strengthen its most social aspects. Thus, at supranational level, EU

[5]A shift on the inertia of public administration education in Europe is unfolded by a niche of law-based literature. See further, Hajnal (2015).

[6]Grimonprez (2014).

should show more ambitious concerns acting as guiding force towards an ecological educational transition—at the same rhythm as it is guiding the energy transition—despite of the subsidiary competence of the EU in Education issues (notwithstanding the non-indifferent jurisdiction[7] and increased importance of soft law and the OMC, that for education is unhelpfully not mentioned in the TFEU[8]). Education should be re-conceptualised based on Europeans' sustainability ambitions and should integrate cultural concerns on it.

A call for awareness and more participatory research coming from education policy academics and legal scholarship can provide the adequate knowledge platform to guide transformation by gathering teachers, educators, researchers, and leaders engaged with different competencies and "listening to the grass roots bottom-up approaches" that are already enriching communities and proving to be more transformative than legal innovation movements (Roche, 2017). It is mandatory to focus on the idea of providing a new conceptual content to a public service that should run outside the logics of the market, and should enable 'quality' outside private profit perspective, this is, everywhere and to everyone according to the requirements framed by SDG 4, "to ensure inclusive and equitable quality education and promote lifelong learning opportunities"[9] addressing human development to its fullest capacities in relation with his or her natural (consequently cultural) context at first instance.

Leaving aside for a moment the challenges education poses to public administration concerns, especially those related to the cultural aspects considering the mixed multicultural society in which we live and the ways society increasingly oblige us to change organisation and the ways and means of teaching, we urgently need to find conceptual approaches that foster the necessity to integrate culture and education policy at the top of economic concerns that should be at their service. The fact that cultural heritage could be considered an economic asset does not help to think

[7]See, Case 293/83, Gravier v City of Liège [1985] ECR 73; Case 242/87, Commission of the European Communities v Council of the European Communities [1989] ECR 1425.

[8]See further Garben (2015). Garben, argues, how through the OMC, which is commonly perceived as a 'soft' policy instrument, with a focus on cooperation, leaving considerable discretion to the Member States. Member States executives agree on certain objectives, but remain free to implement them in the way they see fit, taking into account their system differences. This however, underestimates the OMC's tangible effects in opening up sensitive national sectors, and overestimates the way it respects national autonomy. On the Open Method of Coordination see further, de la Porte (2002); on the most concrete relevance of the OMC and the Bologna process and harmonisation process of European Higher Education, see further Garben (2011, 2015).

[9]Current progress reports already refer to the necessity of addressing Education from top-level political and legal intervention to create the right learning environments. Despite the considerable progress on education access and participation over the past years, 262 million children and youth, aged 6 to 17 were still out of school in 2017, and more than a half of children and adolescents are not meeting minimum proficiency standards in reading and mathematics. Marginalised people in vulnerable settings and teacher's training continue to present the biggest challenge. See further, Goal 4: Sustainable Development Knowledge Platform, retrieved from http://sustainabledevelopment.un.org.

beyond economic interests, but should instead foster new legal research agenda promoting new governance mechanisms for the preservation, promotion and knowledge awareness of our cultural heritage accessible to present and future generations in a sustainable way.

It is detrimental to oversimplify or take broad views in anything but in cultural and education issues we must avoid this for the sake of tracing a valid research agenda for future discussion on the topic of transformation within the axis of sustainability and human development matters. Thus, conceptualisation for a research agenda addressing cultural and educational challenges is mandatory but difficult if we were to approach this task without going beyond disciplinary boundaries. If we take as a start the cultural field, we will see how lawyers are increasingly joining the quest to find a (legally) suitable definition, and already the amount of official documents that could be a source of reference for a legal concept is confusing. In any case, even after some accomplishments in the field of cultural law grasping working definitions (Becerril Atienza, 2015; Prieto de Pedro, 1995), the notion is still quite unclear and perhaps we can talk more of fragmentariness. The field is huge and overarching, and it is impossible to discuss here all its singular aspects. However, it is risky to fall (by contrast) in a holistic understanding of culture that could lead us to overgeneralisation.

To understand the challenges that give title to this monographic work, I believe it is indispensable to address at first instance the following query: how does the concept of culture and culture in relation to education become relevant within the context of sustainability in its multidimensional form?

I have assumed as a truism that culture generally speaking, and cultural heritage can contribute towards well-being and quality of life of communities. It can also help to mitigate the negative homogenisation process of cultural globalisation. In effect, as it has already been mentioned, the EUSM entrenches a European Framework for Action on Cultural Heritage (EFACH) that reflects the common set-up for heritage-related activities under sustainability premises at European level, primarily in EU policies and programmes. The main challenge of the EFACH is the putting into (effective) practice the principle of mainstreaming of cultural heritage in different EU policies, which renders the scope of culture within the context of European policy-making overarching as much as sustainability itself. Empowering local communities for an effective promotion, preservation and enjoyment of culture is not at the forefront of such frameworks. However, local, both public and private, which try to compensate for this lack of empowerment command are growing all over Europe.[10]

I have no intention to get (in depth) into the definition of culture for other purpose than designing a path for transformation towards sustainability through collective tools. The same reasoning should be applied to the notion of education. It would be a highly ambitious endeavour to do otherwise, and it would be out of place here. This chapter is an attempt to present a narrative setting an action-oriented vision of the

[10]See further, http://commonstransition.org/how-the-commons-can-revitalize-europe/.

concept of culture and education that play an important role as a starting point for further (hopefully) academic research and action sprawl.

In fact, the present conceptual framework should be used to inform further multidisciplinary research in the field of education, culture and sustainability. To this end, I am taking up some of the most important traits of the complex notion of culture that can potentially engender a shift toward socially and ecologically sustainable cultural practice and influence educational systems. I am overall presenting an action-oriented vision of these concepts making assumptions and trying to avoid ineffective conceptual disquisitions necessarily required for command and control approaches, but unnecessary for more creative environments and alternative narratives that have proven to be more adequate for these specific sectors in relation to sustainability practices.

4.1.1 Culture

Culture in the context of sustainability is "(...) what enables sustainability as a source of strength of values and social cohesion, self-esteem and participation". It frames people's relationship to others in a specific social context and the world around them, including the natural environment. The impact of cultural process for shaping, influencing and transforming behaviours is infinite but is neglected. Culture is and should be "our most powerful force for creativity and renewal" (Parker, 2014). This quote from Jenneth Parker gives us the flesh to start with the added value of the conceptual approach that I am providing. The purpose of making available an unorthodox view of culture lies in its instrumental significance for a better understanding of future challenges associated with the sustainability paradigm.

A broad definition of culture is available in the preamble to the Universal Declaration on Cultural Diversity (2001) where culture is defined as: "(...) the set of distinctive spiritual, material, intellectual and emotional features of society or a social group, and that it encompasses, in addition to art and literature, lifestyles, ways of living together, value systems, traditions and beliefs". Still, it is important to understand and acknowledge that culture, as well as education, has been the centre of growing attention since the nineteenth century, and their definitions are still highly contested today in the different scientific fields. This contribution makes the case for a less controversial conceptual approach of culture by narrowing down the theoretical scope to the context of sustainability.

The essential arguments of such conceptual approach touch upon two crucial interrelated aspects: (1) its policy and regulation level, and consequently (2) the issues associated to the whole process of social patterns transformations under sustainability premises.

The analysed[11] legal literature does not address concepts that can fill the gap missing between culture as a passive (and neglected) field within the context of sustainability, and culture as promoter and main instrument for change. The risk is that the lack of consensus in conceptual approaches, especially referred to the notion of cultural heritage could compromise an effective engagement of law making powers to provide concrete solutions using culture as a tool for sustainability promotion and intergenerational responsibility towards cultural heritage. The legal doctrine refers mostly to the notions provided by anthropological studies applied to the legal science field, and they refer to the notion of culture according to its uses.[12] The numerous and diverse notions of culture offered by anthropologists such as Kroeber and Kluchon already in 1952 (they offered more than 164 definitions) are too wide, much alike to the ones advanced by the anthropological approaches of Tylor (1871)[13] and have been widely analysed by legal and sociological doctrine. The concept is often defined in very broad terms and this renders the notion useless because it is identified with society as a whole, blurring any distinction between culture, institutions or social structures (Polavieja, 2015, p. 167). The truth is that the notion of 'culture' is a complex and polysemic concept that is difficult to understand (Prieto de Pedro, 2007), but from the standpoint of a multidisciplinary setting[14] culture can and must boost transformation in the Anthropocene and European future action and legal scholarship should not undermine this when defining action plans.

Actually my focus here is not concerned with all the possible dimensions of the concept of culture, but only with those that directly lead to the construction of a collective identity (including natural heritage), which in turn result in a socio-political inclination embracing ecology and diversity within solidarity constrains. Let us say that this is my own instrumental definition and should be helpful for the conceptual context of education and sustainability and it will become evident with the case studies that I have chosen. Notwithstanding, the most recent initiatives and attention focused on the cultural field at European level (i.e., EYCH 2018) go in this direction too. It is important to highlight what recitals 11, 12 and 13 of the Decision (EU) 2017/864 EYCH state:

(11)	Cultural heritage plays an important role for community cohesion at a time when cultural diversity is increasing in European societies. Sites that have been awarded the European Heritage Label have a strong European dimension, as they have been selected for their role in European history.

[11]Prieto de Pedro (2007), Becerril Atienza (2015), Bekemans (1990), Craufud (2004) and Polavieja (2015).

[12]On this, see further Bekemans (1990).

[13]See for further reference, Becerril Atienza (2015).

[14]Sacco (2011), and the works of this author in (2008), (2009), help to understand the need for such a disciplinary setting.

(12)	The role of cultural heritage is also recognised in the UN 2030 Agenda for Sustainable Development ('2030 Agenda'), which acknowledges global citizenship, cultural diversity and intercultural dialogue as overarching principles of sustainable development.

(13)	The increased recognition at international level of the need to put people and human values at the centre of an enlarged and cross-disciplinary concept of cultural heritage reinforces the need to foster wider access to cultural heritage, inter alia, in light of its positive effects on the quality of life.[15]

One may think that defining culture as heritage might be easier, because a considerable amount of legal documents have been dealing with this. In reality, the truth is that a problem arises as well when we intend to put forward a definition of culture heritage. Casini (2018) argues that "the oldest legal dilemma in the cultural heritage field is the complexity of the very notion of cultural heritage and cultural property and the wide range of their definitions". The same extent of problems associated with culture as social patterns becomes evident in cultural heritage with regard to its constant change.[16] Therefore, it becomes unavoidable making reference to culture by tracking its etymology. Etymologically, culture is rooted in the Latin verb *colere*, emphasising the process of cultivation, so nature[17] could be well considered conceptually opposite to culture. However, this dichotomy is widely overcome today.

Why is culture so relevant in the context of sustainability? In the legal field, the link between culture and environmental sustainability in conceptual terms lies in the fact that cultural heritage resources are contained in the legal definition of environment worldwide in the version of 'natural heritage' and in a more autonomous conceptual setting in the notion of landscape (European Landscape Convention).[18] In fact, landscape finds its most refine expression as part of cultural heritage that can be misguiding when associated to natural resources which should remain disentangled from omnipotent and damaging anthropocentric approaches.

[15]Decision (EU) 2017/864 of the EU Parliament and of the Council of 17 May 2017 on a European Year of Cultural Heritage.

[16]See for instance how recent documents shed new light on cultural heritage shaping its constant evolution and application: FARO Convention on the Value of Cultural Heritage (2005); The Bruges Declaration on Cultural Heritage: A resource for Europe stressing the benefits of interaction (2010); The Namur Declaration (2015) considering the cultural heritage is "a necessary response to the current challenges" (I, Art. 3); The European Cultural Heritage Strategy for the twenty-first century further referred to as Strategy 21 focusing on the three main components of cultural heritage: social, economic and territorial, and knowledge and education.

[17]Nature takes its root from the Latin verb *nascere,* which means to be born.

[18]Also Known as the Florence Convention, promotes the protection, management and planning of European landscapes and organises European Co-operation on landscape issues. The Convention was adopted on 20 October 2000 in Florence (Italy) and came into force on 1 March 2004 (Council of Europe Treaty Series No. 176). It is the first international treaty to be exclusively concerned with all dimensions of European landscape. https://www.coe.int/en/web/landscape.

Another important landmark for the association of sustainability and culture can be found within the context of the Council of Europe the 2005 Framework Convention on the Value of Cultural Heritage for Society. Such Convention (the Faro Convention) highlighted the social and economic benefits of preserving cultural heritage as a perquisite for achieving sustainable development for the first time.[19] In this regard, Europe has a unique approach and public administration in MS have dealt with these issues broadly (Becerril Atienza, 2015). The same is true within the urban development context.[20] Europeans have been more concerned and more prolific about such cultural issues, concerning heritage, and property issues,[21] than about deep changes in the educational systems, or culture-value systems to include other relevant issues. The Council of Europe with a different role with respect to the EU, but with shared values, has prolifically contributed to the evolution of the notion of culture associated with sustainability and prevailing within the confines of cultural cooperation (European Cultural Convention)[22] and landscape inclusion with certain ecological distinctiveness as part of a unique European identity.

In any case, the social and economic value of culture at global level has also increasingly grown and this trend definitely helps to conceptualise culture within the context of sustainability transformation influencing policy developments worldwide. Within the European law context, despite of direct legal competencies, the latest policy and legislative initiatives have boosted awareness about the importance of sustainable cultural development and the enhancement of human capabilities (in Amartya Sen's sense). For instance, the already mentioned European Year of Cultural Heritage (2018 EYCH)[23] involves crucial activities at the Union, national, regional and local level and it was launched to "[...] encourage the sharing and appreciation of Europe's cultural heritage as a shared resource, to raise awareness of common history and values, and to reinforce a sense of belonging to a common European space".[24] According to Psychogiopoulou the EYCH could actually play an

---

[19]Council of Europe Framework Convention on the Value of Cultural Heritage for Society- CETS-Treaty No. 199. Faro, 27/10/2005. In line with the Faro Convention principles and criteria, civic initiatives enable institutions and communities to develop decision-making capacities and to manage their development processes, ensuring that heritage contributes to the social, cultural and economic dynamics of the communities.

[20]Moreno Molina (2010).

[21]See Becerril Atienza (2015).

[22]The European Cultural Convention was adopted on 19 December 1954 in Paris (France) and came into force on 5 May 1955 (Council of Europe Treaty Series No. 018). The purpose of this Convention is to develop mutual understanding among the peoples of Europe and reciprocal appreciation of their cultural diversity, to safeguard European culture, to promote national contributions to Europe's common cultural heritage respecting the same fundamental values and to encourage in particular the study of the languages, history and civilisation of the Parties to the Convention. It can be retrieved from http://coe.int.

[23]Decision (EU) 2017/864 of the European Parliament and of the Council of 17 May 2017 on a European Year of Cultural Heritage (2018) *OJ L 131, 20.5.2017, pp. 1–9.*

[24]Art. 1, para. 2, of Decision 2017/864/EU of the European Parliament and of the Council of 17 May 2017 on a EYCH (2018).

important role "in the development of standards, which is a perquisite for policy coordination through benchmarking and the use of common indicators, in addition to ongoing efforts in the field of culture statistics, to produce comparable data across the EU and overcome differences in Member State's statistical approaches" (Psychogiopoulou, 2018).

Still, it might be argued that this euro-centred approach does not help to hail the universal and intergenerational value of cultural heritage that should prevail and should guide any sustainability consideration as much as it accessibility and its localised management outside the capitalist logics of the market.

In effect, the logics of the market emerge even in soft law documents at European level where some decisions are following the logic of a wrong conceptualisation of cultural heritage, in which landscape and nature and their immaterial value do not emerge as much as its property law components. Besides, when the immaterial value of nature emerges this should be free from cultural property law views. However, in fact this has not necessarily been the truth. According to Casini (2010, 2018) in the past few decades, cultural property has been increasing in economic and political relevance worldwide, and for that reason, its global dimension and interest with the complexities derived from it, have been constantly emerging, and the same reasoning has to be applied to the European level. This phenomena has immediate relevance for the protection parameters provided by its sustainable dimension, not only referred to natural heritage sites, but also to all the possible dimensions comprehended by cultural heritage law, considering the many challenges posed by access to nature, access to cultural sites, tourism, as well as the respect for environmental parameters impressively put at the same level of other property concerns. This logic is also applied to the most liminal expression of culture as a system embracing ideas, language, values, education, actions, etc. However, the relevance of culture in all these versions is vital to promote sustainability, especially within the European urban hubs.

The urban context, in addition to the natural one, should be increasingly part of the conceptualisation of culture under sustainability premises. This is because urban spaces hail the creative context where most of our cultural interactions take place in Europe today. On top of that, for the sake of a broad and proactive conceptualisation of culture in the highly crucial urban contexts we also need to bear in mind the growing role of cities and municipalities encouraging more sustainable practices of cultural activities. Cities contribute to the widening of environmental awareness when they engage, and are engaged by, citizens and other different stakeholders in improving urban performances towards sustainability. Culture has a primary role within these contexts,[25] and the intertwined role of culture and urban contexts is vital for a sustainable future. Current EU policy acknowledges this, and the EFACH provides the right framework for integration of cultural heritage in every policy field. Thus, European Urban contexts and communities are key elements for future successful policy action.

---

[25] See further on this argument, Concilio and Rausell (2019).

What happens is that we tend to forget the socio-cultural dimension of communities and integration and we translate 'integration' under the parameters of our democratic societies with limited attention to the fate of minorities.[26] We tend to homogenise. Nowadays, this has also become a hot topic within the context of Europe, so broad and so complex considering the variety of situations that may affect minorities.[27] The lack of legally binding definition of culture renders difficult to agree as to the identification of the potential minorities and the implantation of protection measures when they are needed (Ruiz Vieytez, 2016). I believe that there is a growing need to devote more attention to this in the future and forge transdisciplinary solutions to avoid leaving anyone behind in what our sustainability model is building as welfare.[28]

Conceptual evolution takes place according to universal paradigms according to what history teaches us.[29] In Europe, the topic of cultural integration and minorities should regain importance under social sustainability premises. It is essential because different cultural identities merge, the paradigm of sustainability might rule as an overarching principle in our legal orders (national and supranational) embracing these aspects embedded in peace, democracy, rule of law and sustainable development, etc. Still, our legal systems might fail at the moment of providing faithful recognition of minority rights in some cultural contexts such as education

---

[26]Explains this well. He argues that managing cultural diversity is recognised as a horizontal task that involves a variety of players and contexts and includes both legal standards (human rights law) and policy measures. Indeed, the relevance of this dimension is that the cultural elements that shape collective identities determine the ownership and enjoyment of human rights in democratic societies. In this regard, what happens is that a nation-state has been a powerful factor in cultural and identity homogenisation based on those democratic traits, without considering that, here, democracy is understood solely as a rule of majorities not resolving issues related to respecting the identity of minorities. See further, how Amartya Sen (1999), in Chapter 6, when he speaks about the importance of 'Democracy' explains this principle in a brilliant manner and applied to a much global context. He explains, taking the example of the honey collectors of the Sundarbans that risk their lives every day in the land of the Bengal tiger to collect some honey, how those people might not be concerned about their civil or political rights at all. On balancing the problems of economic needs and political freedoms, we might find the key to understand minority rights.

[27]See further on this Palermo and Woelk (2008), p. 16.

[28]On this topic concerning the European cultural challenge associated to cultural diversity and multiculturalism, Costa-Lascoux (1995), makes an interesting point on the ambivalent role of legal instruments in relation to this issues. For her, the law is a reflection of the political philosophy of integration and underlines its coherence, but also reveals its limitations and contradictions, because through definitions and criteria defined by law and institutional intervention there should be discriminatory actions towards category of persons concerned. On her discussion, the role of education and associations is essential in defence of those who feel trapped by bureaucratic machinery whose purpose and working cannot reach every person, nor every concern.

[29]This approach is associated to the theories that have prevailed throughout the history of Europe, particularly in the eighteenth, nineteenth and twentieth centuries: Universalism and relativism. A certain concept of culture corresponds to each theory. Attached to universalism is a notion that claims to transcend cultural particularities. On the other hand, relativism is linked to a notion that respects cultural differences and rejects all federative or totalitarian points of view. Reference taken from "Otherness and cultural differences" by Oriol and Affergan (1995).

institutions.[30] Articles 2 and 3 of the TEU provide for the highest standards of recognition of cultural diversity but if we do not consider the cultural identity of individuals and groups, especially if they are a minority in their respective policy fields it is not possible to build the right legal framework fostering human rights protection that characterise our democratic identities,[31] and this is not an easy task. Perhaps, within the realm of culture, this is one of the biggest challenges Europe and the world are experiencing today.

Coming back to the already mentioned EU Decision 2017/864/EU of the EU Parliament and the Council of 17 May 2017 on EYCH (2018) in its Article 2, the decision triggers most of the challenges associated to sustainability concerns and enshrines the potential of culture as crosscutting sector when it announces the fourteen general objectives of the European Year of culture. In fact, the first objective gives some clues about a conceptual approach appropriate for the analyses of the challenges of the EUSM. According to it, Europe should 'encourage approaches to cultural heritage that are people-centred, inclusive, forward-looking, more integrated, sustainable and cross-sectoral'. Education should be entrenched in such conceptual framework because another one of the EU main challenges is the integration of education and the promotion and protection of our heritage, therefore the EYCH brings about the opportunity of "raising awareness of the importance of Europe's cultural heritage through education and lifelong learning, in particular by focusing on children, young and elderly people, local communities and hard-to-reach groups".[32]

Beyond legal sciences approaches, in anthropology and philosophy, we find conceptual approaches that study the intersection of cultural theory and sustainability education that we do not find in legal sciences approaches yet. In fact, in those fields, it is possible to find interesting and very valid critical approaches advancing the required transdisciplinary solutions[33] that current challenges need. Haraway (2004), for instance argues that the modern idea of culture is not only constructed or discovered (this is, inherited), it is also a projected truth-making process created within the history of science, politics, education and elsewhere.

We take the works of Haraway as an example because he explains how we, as a form of "technoscientific culture", have attempted to extend beyond "normal" human limitations and, in turn, have become obliged participatory actors in producing a culture that separates human and nature, and not only, a culture that places humans above and beyond nature; and it has been argued that trying to change that cultural approach by intervening at the level of culture in sustainability education research can be deeply political, because it complies an excavation of all that is taken for granted as legitimate in our collective experience (Anderson, Datta, Dyck, Kayira, & Mcvittie, 2016). This is because it is assumed a concept of culture as a

[30]The case of the Romani people, colloquially known as gypsies, is paradigmatic of this affirmation.

[31]See further, UNESCO Declaration on Cultural Diversity of 3 March 2001, Article 4.

[32]Article 2 para 2 (j) of Decision 2017/864/EU of the European Parliament and of the Council of 17 May 2017 on EYCH (2018).

[33]On this, see further Parker (2014).

"living practice suffused within our policies and governance, our education and communications, and our sensibilities and desires alike".[34] However, these notions of culture are not easily accepted by legal scientists. Nonetheless, it is also true that if we were to circumscribe our understanding of culture to our own disciplines we would not travel far.

Today there are successful examples of culture-led local and regional development activities across Europe and elsewhere that I could use as patterns to illustrate a valid concept of culture in a sustainability setting. These patterns representing culture are not recent phenomena,[35] still there is a widespread perception that the role and potential of culture in the sustainability strategy is seriously under-recognised,[36] consequently a conceptualisation of culture under strong sustainability premises has not developed as much as it seems looking at recent International agreements and European strategies. This is a consequence of the persisting gap in the conceptualisation of the role of culture in an advanced, knowledge based economy, as it is the European one nowadays that is at the forefront of its sustainability strategies (Sacco, 2011).[37] Such tendency has impeded culture from gaining attention for more prolific legal, economic and political engagement. Things are slightly changing, but cultural activities even when they are designed to create ecological and social awareness are short of financial resources and lack adequate public support. Still, there is much more engagement for cultural issues in public administration research and cultural assumptions in multidisciplinary approaches than there is concerning Education related issues.

Education (outside the scope of the language of rights), even for public lawyers, has been a bit more neglected than culture, and this is because of the consideration of culture and cultural heritage as economic assets. However, contrasting this tendency most recently, education has become instrumental to promote, create knowledge and engage European citizens on the management of cultural heritage. The Europe 2020 Strategy does not mention at all culture and boost a preeminent role to education.[38] However, the growing proliferation of strategies, communications, document, action frameworks and so on at EU level in those fields have become complex and misguiding to understand effective intervention in both fields.

---

[34] Anderson et al. (2016), citing an extensive literature on the same conceptual assumption, see further, Duncombe (2002), Kapoor (2008) and McKenzie (2009).

[35] Sacco, Ferilli, and Pedrini (2008) and Sacco (2009).

[36] Ibid. Sacco (2011) argue that this reflects in the difficulty to bring cultural policy issues at the top ranks of the broader policy agenda, and consequently explains why the share of structural funds devoted to culture badly fails to match the share of cultural and creative sectors in the total EU value added.

[37] Sacco argues that the direct consequence of this lack of conceptualising the importance of culture in the economic activity that is extended to the neglected role of culture boosting sustainability and sustainable places, has also contributed to funding cuts during phases of economic crisis (Sacco, 2011).

[38] Education has a primary role in the Europe 2020 Strategy, emphasising its pre-eminence for a smart, sustainable and inclusive growth as a way to overcome the structural weaknesses in Europe's economy, improve its competitiveness and productivity and underpin a sustainable social market economy.

Culture should be examined in as much as it is apprehended in terms of its interactions among its many parts, its people, places, ideas, actions and inactions, as well its multiple pasts, presents and futures. The concept should not be covered in its whole spectrum but only the scope of its characterisation and usefulness to integrate nature and strong sustainability concerns spilling over ecological, social, community and solidarity, and educational aspects.[39] Our education systems have a primary role on this, but our cultural heritage, our cultural production and other materialisations of culture today should play a significant role too. In view of this, it is important to bear in mind the importance of promoting future integration of education and culture, and cultural heritage related initiatives.

A critical aspect of the notion of culture that Europe is embracing under sustainability premises regards the inclusion of "knowledge-based economy" is an element that brings our world cultures to what Haraway (2004) has identified as a 'technoscientific' notion of culture that cannot longer be detached from its conceptual evolution. All these passages give evidence of the dynamism of the notion under the framework of international law agreements even if those agreements do not deal with every current and future challenge sustainability must face yet. Digitalisation is profoundly changing our cultural experience, not only in terms of (passive) acceptance of new technology-based, but also in terms of participation, creation and learning in the so-called knowledge society. We are shifting culture to respond to the changes imposed by the digital age. This is one of the cultural challenges that the Council of Europe has faced more promptly lately: Recommendation CM/Rec (2018) on culture's contribution to strengthening the internet as an emancipatory force; Recommendation CM/Rec (2017) 8 on Big Data for culture, literacy and democracy, and in 2016 there was a Recommendation CM/Rec (2016) on the internet of citizens. It shows the dynamism and flexibility of culture as opposed to education issues. Erlewin (2017) asserts that "Culture is increasingly understood as both exclusive and dynamic as well as dialectic, as unique and simultaneously open for development and as such as prone to processes of globalization, assimilation and change".

These different definitions show that we can *operationalise*[40] a concept of culture whose essence is the understanding of culture as a 'process',[41] and this is only positive considering the issues that this concept can leave behind under the parameters of a certain set of values determined by every specific period of time. The flexibility of this notion is at odds with what the notion of education and its different institutional subsystems have become.

[39]It is outside the scope of this study to address anthropological disputes concerned with the meaning of culture. The bibliography is broad.

[40]I add emphasis on this point.

[41]Here its liminal (definition) nature provoking concerns at legal and judicial level would not be a problem anymore.

4.1.2 Education

If we trace the notion of education in the legal literature we are directly connected with the language of rights and policymaking resolutions mostly found in roadmaps, international conventions and agreements, etc., but there is little interest for conceptualising education as the social experience of learning that essentially is (Dewey, 2007). Moreover, 'creativity', collaboration, and innovation in the emotional aspects of education are ignored by the legal doctrine. What is indispensable for our conceptualisation of education is the generational aspect. It is crucial generally speaking, but it is essential within the context of understanding the challenges of a sustainability model: education is one of the things that corresponds to the care that people must have of the generation that follows, and it is inseparable from the concern to preserve society itself, and culture. Actually, education is perceived not only as a human right but also as a force for social change, it is described as the single most vital element in combating poverty, exploitation, and promoting democracy and human rights (UNICEF, 1999). Today, sustainability is equally important to the promotion of peace, the rule of law, democracy and human rights, thus, important changes in education should not be left to shortsighted political whims.

What in education is done or ceases to be done in families, schools, businesses, homes or wherever educational task affects not only the children, youth or adults with whom it is directly acted, indirectly the influence also reaches the communities to which they belong, and their future. The 'community' aspect is relevant in our complex societies today and it is vital under sustainability premises. To translate it into the language of legal intervention is complex and challenging.

The core of the generational aspect and the community are the basic cornerstones of our conceptual approach to education. Considering the challenges we are facing, education is presented here as a key driver of socio-cultural transformation.[42] In fact, it embraces some of the 'emancipation tool' features that were part of Freire's pedagogical theory. This conceptual approach is also following the most critical education tendencies advanced by Henry A. Giroux falling into a positive hope for change through education. In the light of this approach, "critical pedagogy needs to be grounded in a keen sense of the importance of constructing a political vision from which to develop an education project as part of a wider discourse for revitalising democratic public life" (Giroux, p. 219), and not only through digital means, but through 'knowledgeable' means assuring equal access to all.

Therefore, if we just follow International agreements, judicial decisions, or International Resolutions that we cannot ignore will be hard to find a path for building a theoretical framework for transformations. Nevertheless, considering that we should always bear in mind that we must work out solutions establishing

[42]This book presents a modest contribution to the conceptual axis needed for starting to build a research agenda to face educational challenges, and trigger future research and policy engagement in the field.

links with well-established international cooperation agreements—considering how difficult it is at first instance to get out from the logics of the system, even if we make the case for transformation (Göpel, 2016)—we need to stick to those available instruments. Still, the reader must acknowledge that the transforming learning approach we are advancing here is rarely found in current legal instruments or court decisions. This concept is unavoidably associated to the educational and cultural challenges that our sustainability model is facing in our complex societies.

To achieve transformation we need to go far beyond the traditional notion of education, this is, "[Education is] the whole process, in any society, adults endeavour to transmit their beliefs, culture and other values to the young, whereas teaching or instruction refers in particular to the transmission of knowledge and to intellectual development".[43] The Education concept should also include all upbringing and socialisation aspects of the young, as well as adults (Janna, 1972), although more commonly now is associated with teaching and learning in schools and universities. Education should be seen as having social aims allowing individuals and societies to 'better themselves' (Dewey, 2007). Inculcating desirable qualities' in someone could be the key aim of education for modern pedagogical tendencies that go through a revival time today (see Marina, 2017).

An important desirable premise under sustainability grounds is that public law intervention at State level in Europe should aim at providing education and vocational training as a public service that should not be compromised by the needs of the market.[44] The State cannot delegate to private institutions or individuals its obligations to secure the right to education for all. Still, this does not preclude that there remains space for local, individual and community initiatives. Actually, many aspects of literacy, in its widest context today (this referred to the use of internet, information technology (IT) instruments in general or any communication medium) need to be addressed by not formal education systems. Thus, the potential for local initiatives is infinite. Hawkes (2001) refers to some of them that are useful here, cultural programs in child-care facilities, the opening up of school resources to communities, the advocating of increased interaction between school children and specialist cultural workers (in the arts, media, design, etc.), the integration of post-secondary institutions with their surrounding communities, etc.

Local governance can fill vacuums and stimulate partnerships between private parties, third sector organisations and public institutions. Such initiatives have proved to be adequately suited to face present and future sustainability challenges in our learning society where education includes all the human development and integrates all the human capabilities (Sen, 1999). The recently deceased internationally known Psychiatrist Claudio Naranjo (2016) made the case for "an educational

[43] *Campbel and Cosans v The United Kingdom*, ECHR judgment Series A No 48 (1982). The Court took a broad view of education: "The use of corporal punishment may, in a sense, be said to belong to the internal administration of a school, but at the same time it is, when used, an integral part of the process whereby a school seeks to achieve the object for which it was established, including the development and moulding of the character and metal powers of its pupils".

[44] Leading to the privatisation of education.

change to change the world". He would speak of optimising resources involving all the stakeholders (government, local administration, religious entities, enterprises, etc.). However, he would argue that the wellness of society being not cost-effective at public expenditure level would always make difficult to have humanist leaders (Naranjo, 2016).

It is quite helpful in this context to mention the spiritual concerns needed to foster a strong relationship with nature and community. Such concerns are at the core of the most enlightening holistic discourses about this matter.[45] In effect, environmental education and sustainability education are paradigmatic within the context of defining an action-oriented notion of education but they are insufficient under a completely transforming notion of education. The conceptual approach would be quite poor if we were going to fill the notion just with these two approaches to education. In fact, even if it has proved to be useful, education should not be considered "an area of spillover from Environmental policy" (Sarti & St. John, 2019).

We need to fill the normative conceptual gap in education by focusing on building transforming legislative frameworks based on individual needs within our complex societies.[46] This is it, because one of the most important challenges Europe faces today regards the education systems of its Member States to find strong foundations for sustainability concerns that go beyond informing people of their impact of their everyday actions with regard to the environment. Education, generally speaking, is one of the domains that evolved less since the nineteenth century. Rethinking the educational system breaking down institutional inertia to adapt to the changing word, but preserving the essential value of education for human development that should be provided at first instance by the State tends to be underrepresented in political agendas, if not to modify formal or superficial arrangements.

However, a key element, such as the school curricula still remain too centred on key subjects with little connection between one another. Following such view, the conceptual lines of this study embrace the broad sense of construction of opportunities that the EUSM has at hand, with the potential to provide the economic, institutional and human resources to enable people to develop skills and ways of action that prepare them, not just for market-led activities, but trains them to become responsible and active citizens in a constantly changing world.

The static situation and lack of political agenda tackling upon such concerns has taken to well-recognised advocates of environmental and (post) sustainability education, and some pedagogical theorists, to consider, not without certain concerns, that larger institutional structures of education, such as schools, colleges, universities, research institutions, etc. have grown according to a certain logic of command and control mastery and, it is difficult to come out from this logic. This, they argue, imply toleration only for incremental changes at the margin (unfortunately), as long

[45]Morin (1999), Papa Francesco (2015) and Naranjo (2016).

[46]See Pope Francis (2015, paragraph 211).

as they do not threaten the existing structures of power and reputation,[47] without considering structural changes. Following this reasoning a conceptual view of education that needs to be underlined for the value of its contribution to the politics of making and un-making (sustainable) futures, regards the conceptual approach of education tied to the 'degrowth' movement.[48]

The principles of degrowth theoretical constructions[49] are of course valid to build a new pedagogical theory of education from a degrowth perspective[50]; nonetheless, such theoretical constructions are still work in progress, although Illich, one of the original theorist of the movement provides radical solutions against the whole education system by suggesting the alternative: "deschooling".[51] On Illich's view, schooling was incompatible with the idea of universal citizens. Such view goes hand in hand with the attempt to problematise the sustainable development paradigm and its most contemporary reincarnation in the concept of a "green economy". Today degrowth theorists demolish the idea of conciliating economic growth with ecological preservation as we mentioned in the previous chapter. The theoretical paradigm emphasises that there is a contradiction between sustainability and economic growth (Asara, Otero, Demaria, & Corbera, 2015). When taken to the educational context, the consequences are not far from a conceptual framework that claims for an education system fostering substantial political action to transform public education services by freeing them from the market boundaries. Nonetheless, regardless of its validity within the context of degrowth theory, I would find more helpful to emphasise the contribution to the *Laudato si'*[52] conceptual reference to education and institutional needs involved in its core message without demolishing completely the idea of schooling. The *Laudato si'* is a call for action and (change) against the capitalist sovereignty over the world more akin to these conceptual lines. The *Laudato si'* claims for big transformations and it should not be ignored in this research agenda. The 'degrowth' theories instead, consider education in the context of making and unmaking sustainable futures (repoliticising sustainability)[53] and a growing relevance is attributed to the role of shared beliefs or mental infrastructures that shape the way people perceive crises and solutions.[54]

---

[47]See further, Jickling and Sterling (2017).

[48](From the French *décroissance*), one of the current theoretical authorities of such movement is the French economist, Serge Latouche. However, the concept of "degrowth" appeared during the 1970, proposed by André Gorz (1972) and other intellectuals such as Georgescu-Roegen, E.F. Schumacher, and Ivan Illich. It is a political, economic and social movement based on ecological economics, anti-consumerist and anti-capitalist ideas. It is also considered an essential economic strategy responding to the limits-to-growth dilemma. See further, D'Alisa et al. (2015).

[49]Asara et al. (2015).

[50]See further, Kaufmann, Sanders, and Wortmann (2019).

[51]Illich (1971).

[52]Pope Francis (2015) devotes Chapter 6 to "Education and Ecological Spirituality".

[53]Asara et al. (2015).

[54]See further, Kaufmann et al. (2019).

I share most of the concerns of the degrowth movement but I should take distance from a radical view that does not reconcile with certain achievements of the global picture underpinned by the language of rights, international agreements, intergovernmental action and institutional arrangements in which the main players of the education field, teachers, learners, families, societies and communities at large, have little by little gained recognition within the context of our complex societies.

The 'universal' principles directly relating to education are set out in the Universal Declaration of Human Rights, particularly Article 26:

> (1) Everyone has the right to education. Education shall be free, at least in the elementary and fundamental stages. Elementary education shall be compulsory. Technical and professional education shall be made generally available and higher education shall be equally accessible to all on the basis of merit. (2) Education shall be directed towards the full development of the human personality and to the strengthening of respect for human rights and fundamental freedoms. It shall promote understanding, tolerance and friendship among all nations, racial or religious groups, and shall further the activities of the United Nations for the maintenance of peace. (3) Parents have a prior right to choose the kind of education that shall be given to their children.

All international agreements concerning education adopted since the Universal Declaration owe part of their content to this article, whether or not the agreement has been specifically focused on human rights or on related questions of international concern such as peace and development. The agreements fall under two different categories: those that deal with education along with several other fields that broadly correspond to the international agreements adopted under the auspices of the United Nations, and those that are confined to education adopted under the auspices of UNESCO.

Two different Covenants followed the Universal Declaration of Human Rights resulting from the prevailing view by which two separate treaties or covenants were needed after the Universal Declaration.[55] Education was included among economic, social and cultural rights; and the rationale behind was that civil and political rights could, in principle, be secured immediately, whereas economic, social and cultural rights could be achieved only progressively, according to each state's available resources.[56] This is highly significant, because as we know, even within the context of the EU there are significant differences as the expenditure on education among

[55]Other important declarations adopted by the UN containing provisions concerning education are the Declaration of the Rights of the Child (1959); the Declaration on the Promotion among Youth of the Ideals of Peace, Mutual Respect and Understanding between Peoples (1965); The Declaration on the Elimination of Discrimination against Women (1967); the Declaration on Social Progress and Development (1969); the Declaration on the Rights of Mentally Retarded Persons (1971); the Declaration on the Rights of Disabled Persons (1975); the Declaration on the Rights of Persons Belonging to National or Ethnic, Religious and Linguistic Minorities (1992); The Declaration and Program of Action on a Culture of Peace (1999); and the Millennium Declaration (2000).

[56]Thus, education was placed under the 1966 International Covenant on Economic, Social and Cultural rights.

Member States.[57] In fact, the narrative of the right to education at European level is essential to understand challenges. Article 2 of Protocol No. 1 to the European Convention on Human Rights-right to education reads: "No person shall be denied the right to education. In the exercise of any functions which it assumes in relation to education and to teaching, the State shall respect the right of parents to ensure such education and teaching in conformity with their own religious and philosophical convictions". The first sentence of Article 2 of Protocol No. 1 guarantees an individual right to education. The second guarantees the right of parents to have their children educated in conformity with their religious and philosophical convictions. Notwithstanding that holders of the right to education are children, but also adults, or indeed any person wishing to benefit from the right to education (*Velyo Velev v Bulgaria*).[58]

If we turn our attention to the International Agreements adopted under UNESCO's auspices, for the sake of finding a valid action-oriented vision of education we find two valid definitions: (1) in 1960, UNESCO adopted the Convention against Discrimination in Education,[59] which acknowledges the crucial role of education in ensuring equality of opportunity for members of all racial, national or ethnic groups. It was the very first time that a binding instrument in the United Nations system contained a detailed definition of the term 'discrimination'. The Convention qualifies it as *"Any distinction, exclusion, limitation or preference based on race, color, sex, language, religion or political or other opinion, national or social origin, economic condition or birth"*. The Convention calls on States to adopt immediate measures in favour of equality in education and links the concept of Education directly to Human Rights. (2) The second valid definition that UNESCO provides under general guideline premises is the notion provided under the mandate of the 'role of education' in society today. Such definition is straightforward enough for our discussion and, on top of that is operational. "Education should be a means to empower children and adults alike to become active participants in the transformation of their societies. Learning should also focus on the values, attitudes and behaviours which enable individuals to learn to live together in a world characterized by diversity and pluralism".[60]

UNESCO has been promoting Education for Sustainable Development (ESD) since 1992. From 2005 to 2015, it led the UN Decade for ESD and has launched its

[57]See the most recent data available accessible here: https://ec.europa.eu/eurostat/statistics-explained/index.php/Government_expenditure_on_education.

[58]*Velyo Velev v Bulgaria* ECHR (16032/07-Chamber Judgement, Bailii, [2014] ECHR 527).

[59]Paris, 14 December 1960 The General Conference of the UNESCO, meeting in Paris from 14 November to 15 December, at its eleventh session adopted the Convention against Discrimination in Education; available at http://portal.unesco.org/en/ev.php-URL_ID=12949&URL_DO=DO_TOPIC&URL_SECTION=201.html; see also, http://www.unesco.org/new/en/social-and-human-sciences/themes/fight-against-discrimination/role-of-education/.

[60]Retrieved from UNESCO's official website: http://www.unesco.org/new/en/social-and-human-sciences/themes/fight-against-discrimination/role-of-education/.

follow up now, the Global Action Program (GAP) on ESD that should have a crucial role defining action for the 2030 Agenda.

The idea of governments adopting agreements concerning education "emerged from the broader movement of opinion among the leaders of the major industrial countries after World War I in favor of new approaches to the challenge of fostering international understanding and peace".[61] In fact, the League of Nations, which is the immediate precedent to the current UN system, was conceived in such spirit to avoid disagreements to develop into armed conflicts. Education was not a specific concern of the League of Nations. It has traditionally been felt mainly as an internal matter. Nevertheless, in 1921, the League established an International Commission on 'Intellectual Co-operation'[62] and further on, the French government (without the financial support of the League's) had set up a body, which we could recall as the immediate precedent of UNESCO: the International Institute of Intellectual Co-operation.[63] Much of its work has been taken up later in time by UNESCO.

The League of Nation members' interest on education took them to take action on educational matters despite of the absence of specific mandate, showing that educational matters have always been at the heart of international concerns somehow. They created another framework for cooperation provided by the International Bureau for Education (IBE).[64] In 1999, the IBE became the UNESCO Institute responsible for educational content, methods and teaching/learning strategies through curriculum development. Still, over the years the core mandate of the IBE has changed, reaching an apex in 2011 when the 36th session of the UNESCO General Conference declared the IBE a Global Centre of Excellence in curriculum and related matters.

Therefore, today's mandate is to strengthen the capacities of Member States to design, develop and implement curricula that ensure 'equity, quality,

---

[61]International Education Agreements - International Agreements in General, The Years between the Wars (1918–1939): International Education Agreements - International Agreements in General, The Years between the Wars (1918–1939) - Rights, Nations, United, and Adopted - StateUniversity.com http://education.stateuniversity.com/pages/2121/International-Education-Agreements.html#ixzz5LzpJu3TD.

[62]It was composed of eminent personalities in the sciences and humanities from different countries and charged with advising the council on measures that governments could take with a view to stimulating international cooperation among scientists, artist, philosophers, writers, and other groups of intellectuals to enhance the League's objectives. For further reference, see previous note.

[63]It was created to carry out operational activities in the areas of concern of the Commission on 'Intellectual Co-operation'. Such Commission and International Institute, of course, indirectly had an educational dimension. The Institute became active in promoting exchanges between researchers in different countries, in both the sciences and humanities and in promoting international cooperation between universities in what regards teacher and student exchanges and the mutual recognition of degrees and diplomas.

[64]It was established in Geneva in 1926 as an offshoot of the University of Geneva's School of Education (Institute Jean-Jacques Rousseau). In 1929, the International Bureau for Education open its membership to other countries and became the first intergovernmental organisation in the field of education.

development-relevance, and resource-efficiency of education and learning systems'. Such mandate is relevant to us to seize future challenges under the paradigm of sustainability when approaching the topic from the legal standpoint.

At EU level, education is considered by the new European Strategy a horizontal enabler of sustainable development. Furthermore, the Global Agenda calls for joining efforts to implement Sustainable Development Goal 4 by "ensuring inclusive and equitable quality education and promoting lifelong learning opportunities for all". The Council of the European Union on acknowledging the 21st challenges included in the text of its current Sustainability Strategy, is assuming that European citizens should be equipped with the necessary knowledge, skills and attitudes to understand and tackle the challenges we are facing as a learning society. Still, the EU has not provided a clear roadmap of the means for a transforming educational guiding policy, not even in the form of soft legal instruments given the lack of legal competence on the education policy for enhancement or far reaching consequences of the current Europe of knowledge Agenda.[65]

On the other side, the governance arrangements of the OMC in the education field that seem to have been constantly legitimised even in political hard times[66] considering MS' sensitivity in education matters could still proof valid to coordinate action and re-gain institutional legitimacy for future arrangements. On top of that, the emblematic task of education to create awareness on biodiversity protection and on the wealth of European cultural heritage needs concrete Sate action to favor tailor-made initiatives, and forge the interaction between cultural expressions of the various MS and advance the understanding of the importance of the protection and promotion of the diversity of cultural expressions for the sake of future generations.

4.2 Raising Awareness About the Neglected Role of Education and Culture at the Level of Policymaking. The Big Picture

Cultural and educational issues were formerly bonded and helped to build nation states. Today, complex bureaucratic procedures, institutional and public administration management commands, as well as financial protocols have tended to separate them at central administration level and little by little neglect their preeminent role as drivers of socioecological transformation.[67]

[65]COM (COM) 12 Nov 1997: Towards a Europe of knowledge has been followed by COM (2018) 306 final, Brussels, 15.5.2018, a renewed European Agenda for Research and Innovation. Europe's chance to shape its future.

[66]Gornitzka (2018).

[67]Only Austria, Slovakia, the Netherlands, Cyprus, Faroe Islands, Greece, Spain, Sweden and Romania within the Europe have kept the joint functions of cultural and education in their education ministries, the rest of European countries have evolved separating the functionalities and devoting

If it was not for the commercial interest tied to the promotion, creation, management and enjoyment of cultural heritage; or for how instrumental education has become at the service of innovation and smart technologies to face the job market requirements of the future, the interest of research and policymaking would have been less significant. In fact, interests on both sectors have often been exclusively linked to merchandising and profit values. I am taking distance from such reductionist approaches. I suggest that despite of these fair motivations fulfilling society and job market needs, education and culture should stand as a crucial yardstick to build a successful European sustainability model.

Some models of political, economic and socio-cultural organisations have suffered from detachment from their cultural belonging to communities and have created absolute dependency on and servitude to the strongest economic and political forces. These old, and "new forms of economical control and ways to dominate people are developed worldwide, planned by large multinational corporations, the most powerful nations of the world" (Naranjo, 2016), and certain international organisms have contributed to this dynamics.[68]

Other disciplinary sectors have been more prolific than legal scholarship to understand and react to the challenge of strengthening culture and education institutions to foster change and embrace an 'ecological' transition.[69] In the legal field, the main concern is still the ponderation of the existence of the sustainability principle to transform law and governance in the sectors more closely related to growth and innovation.

What happens is that the importance of cultural diversity issues, education and ecological values (towards humankind and nature) have been greatly underplayed in sustainability discourses at the intergovernmental level, and they are also underplayed in the 2030 Agenda for SD. Cultural and educational policy issues are not at the top ranks of the broader policy agenda. At the top level of the political agenda, crucial links between culture, sustainability and equity are neither worked out, nor recognised. This is actually reflected in our central administration regulation.

Europe is facing major cultural changes, but education is one of the domains that public administration has most widely ignored. The increasing Europeanisation largely triggered by the Bologna process,[70] although mostly referred to higher education, has of course radiated consequences on the teaching of certain subjects that might have an influential factor at other levels of education (such as teacher's training) and the formerly more entrenched national fields opening up as a result.[71]

---

different ministerial functions to education, research, training and youth (and sometimes even sport) as part of the same umbrella, and in a different instance, culture.

[68]See further, Stiglitz (2002).

[69]See further some of the most recent economist's approaches on the matter, Latouche (2009) and Rifkin (2011).

[70]On this topic, see Garben (2011).

[71]See further, Hajnal (2015).

However, cultural patterns where education plays a leading role have been totally neglected by public lawyers as a crucial factor of change, address society targets to reach human wellness and tackle the most instant problems of multiculturalism, ecological overexploitation, social collaboration, solidarity, etc. Perhaps, this sort of reasoning has been left to other scientific fields, and lawyers have not found the drive to address the main challenges linked to their institutional and cultural inertia. This inertia should be all at once broken in legal science, by looking beyond legal boundaries. However, this still seems to be a difficult path. This is one of the main reasons for the proliferation of (so-called) radical alternatives for human well-being triggering changes in cultural patterns, such as '*buen vivir*', ecological *Swaraj* (RED) and 'degrowth' movement that we mentioned before. It is under these instances that some timid fruitful educational and cultural debates have emerged despite of their debatable validity to address institutional changes within the European policy context.

I must take some time to refer to these approaches for the simple reason that they give a preeminent position to the issue of culture; more than any other current theoretical approach. Thus, considering the dominant role assigned to culture, and arising from different cultural and social contexts, such theoretical approaches sometimes "differ upon the prognosis (what shall be done to achieve transformations in society); but they share the main characteristics of the diagnosis (what is the problem and who is responsible for it), as well as possessing the a similar or equivalent *Weltanschauungen* (worldview)" (Kothari, Demaria, & Acosta, 2014). They are substantially a critique of the current development hegemony based on the homogenisation of cultures and they focus on new appraisals based on human resources and local circumstances looking for the so much needed socio-ecological transformations taking distance from the widespread adoption of technologies in every field, and consumption and production models experienced in the so-called Global North.[72] The most sounded examples include: the *Buen vivir*, a culture of life with different names and varieties in various regions of South America; *Ubuntu*, with an emphasis on human mutuality and cooperation in South Africa, with several equivalents in other parts of the African continent, with a strong connection with the cultural roots of the populations; and *Swaraj*, with a focus on local knowledge, self-reliance and self-governance in India.[73] They are born for radical change, addressing a critique from local to global; and what is remarkable and a common denominator of these alternative proposals, is that they often arise from traditionally marginalised groups.

They oppose their views to those followed by mainstream debates on sustainable development and the Green Economy, because they seek to envision and achieve more radical transformations than those ones proposed by SD approaches. They believe that SD is a concept based on false consensus (Hornbog, 2009), and from the importance they give to the cultural component of development they argue in favor

[72]See further on this, Latouche (2009) and Kothari et al. (2014).

[73]Kothari et al. (2014).

of the '2015 post-development agenda' instead of the 2030 Global Agenda (or post-2015 development agenda).[74] Their concerns, even if they are not completely shared by the public, at least should be well acknowledged. More and more social scientists raise public awareness about them, and about available alternative global instruments for measurement of economic performance and social progress.

Unfortunately, the SDGs only list the development of GDP-complementing measurements for progress as the very final target (17.19) under SDG 17 on means of implementation and global partnerships. Göpel[75] argues that this gives it much less prominence than the multifarious targets on GDP growth scattered across the other 16 goals (UN 2015), and this can be considered a critical aspect. Nonetheless, reports like that of the Stiglitz-Sen-Fitoussi Commission on the Measurement of Economic Performance and Social Progress in 2009 have shown a growing consensus on the idea that a small dashboard of lead indicators that are easy to understand by all would be most helpful.[76] Still, the critical alternative approaches attack globalised standards and measuring mechanism such as Gross Development Product (GDP) for homogenising and leaving behind cultural, societal and environmental concerns. Those alternative measurement instruments stand for a new economic paradigm introducing other indicator system. The leading example here is the Gross National Happiness Index (GNH) from Bhutan.[77] Those alternative indicators, have five overarching goals: human development, culture and cultural heritage, a balanced societal development benefiting everyone, good governance and protection of the environment.[78] It is out the scope of this study to refer to a whole mapping

---

[74]See further, Kothari et al. (2014).

[75]Göpel and Maja (2016), pp. 131–132.

[76]This assertion is based on the assumption that it is only possible to understand a system and actor motivations if you ask people about their experienced reality (Stiglitz et al., 2009). Göpel (2016) brings to this argument an astonishing example supporting such assumption: The OECD's 2013 Report on Health at a Glance in which a question about whether respondents felt healthy was answered positively by 89.5% of Americans but only 30% of Japanese. According to the objective data, Japan has the second highest life expectancy figures in the world and very high scores in terms of the number of hospital beds, health equipment in hospitals etc., the length of stay in hospital and the number of times people go to the doctor. In the United States life expectancy is four years shorter and rising much more slowly than in other OECD countries. Its obesity rate is twice that of others and 15% of the population live without health coverage, despite of the world's highest per capita expenditure on health care (OECD, 2013; as quoted from Göpel, 2016), what Göpel, and anyone can conclude from this example, is that, without talking to people directly, much insight about experienced well-being and need satisfaction may be missed.

[77]The development aim of GNH was already set out in 1972 by Bhutan's fourth King, Jigme Singye Wangchuck. He presented happiness as the logical outcome of the legal code which sealed the unification of Bhutan in 1729, and stated that, "if the government cannot create happiness ('dedidk') for its people, there is no purpose for the government to exist" (see further, Ura & Zangmo, 2012, p. 6). Bhutan has made of this 'obligation' a societal endeavour, as opposed to the individualised attempt leading to high economic growth (note that US Constitution of 1776 declares "life, freedom and the pursuit of happiness" to be the basic rights of each individual and their protection the duty of the state).

[78]See further Göpel (2016), pp. 131–135, and Bertelsmann Stiftung (2013), p. 70.

of progress in Bhutan according to the governmental duties to create happiness. It suffices to say that these are valid instruments in creating awareness and breaking up with the existing invalid theoretical models based on unlimited economic growth. In effect, the GNH Index is meant to orient the people towards happiness, primarily by improving the conditions of non-yet happy people. The GNH Index enables the government and others to increase the GNH in two ways: (1) it can either increase percentage of people who are happy or, (2) decrease the insufficient conditions of people who are not-yet-happy and this can be done by mitigating the many areas of insufficiencies around the not-yet-happy people. Those not-yet-happy people in Bhutan (rural and urban) according to a broad range of research evidence, in rural areas tend to be those who attain less in education, living standards (depending on atmospheric conditions for agriculture activities, etc.) and balanced used of time. In urban Bhutan, not-yet-happy people are insufficient in non-material domains such as community vitality, culture and psychological well-being.[79]

GNH survey taken with alternative economic models and measurement instruments has been applied to some education leading initiatives in countries experiencing structural problems in fields such as education.[80] Those alternative research agendas are concerned with the fact that people educated abroad come back to India and become highly critical to the lack of mainstream global culture. Consumerism and tourism-based exposure to the conventional global culture are seem to increase local problems. This is why the promotion of GNH values and ideas in educational institutions has become crucial and it is seem as strategic goal at global level. Some of those theoretical discussions could be helpful within the EU context too.

In our current paradigm of 'sustainable development' and 'transformative resilience', the human and social capital are as crucial as economic and natural capital, so many of our definitions, classifications, economic measures used by the current National Financial System should be reviewed based on this, or at least, as it has been already suggested in doctrinal economic analyses, alternative 'satellite accounting' measures need to define new fundamental parameters for a European fiscal policy that manages to promote material and immaterial investments in essential social sectors such as education, inside of a shared "golden rule" (Giovanni, 2016). This is still 'utopic'. However, if we do not address alternative ways of economic measurement an ecological transition that just looks at the production of green energy and green consumption products, and waste systems is bound to fail.

Little attention has been placed to these topics by legal scholarship at International level, especially outside the margins of the analytical approaches of human rights, or outside the protection of cultural heritage and cultural diversity. There has been little consideration as to the real relevance of education and culture outside development or economic terms. The same reasoning must be extended to the EU level despite of the increasing attention given to the education and cultural policy framework for future coordinated policy development at higher education level

[79]See further, Ura and Zangmo (2012).

[80]See further Manish (2008).

because of its consequential relationship with the job market. The other significant deficiency at international policy level regards cultural issues related to education in sustainable development law discourses. On top of that, an integrated approach of both issues in the light of sustainability is essentially inexistent.

One symptomatic aspect of this sparse attention to these issues is that social issues related to law within the domain of 'Sustainable Development' have not proliferated at all outside market integration interests. Thus, we might point to the integrated decision making—incorporating environmental considerations and goals into economic and social development decisions—as the most relevant achievement. It seems as if we had lost interest for education *per se* without introducing digital agenda concerns. The integration of both policies has been insufficient and has not gained enough scholarship attention despite of the distinctive role of the EU Directorate mainstreaming both mandates and framing action for both tenures under the same command.

Surely, a better understanding of the social pillar of SD incorporating international and intergenerational dimensions is needed to understand that although specific cultural goal is not included in the UN 2030 SD Agenda, if not through mentions in other goals, culture underpins every other substantive goal content. Furthermore, the EUSM is missing a cultural and educational identity despite of EU constitutional framework fostering sustainable development.

The theoretical approach of this contribution lies on the assumption that the EUSM should host a sociocultural system in which its legal and economic systems are subordinated means in successfully structuring nature-human relations. This is radically different from the view of the mainstream economic paradigm that pursues the ongoing integration of social and environmental concerns into global and European economic governance logics by 'valuing' them.

Under this line of reasoning, we need to organise knowledge again by adjusting our way of thinking when facing the 'complexities' that our responsibility for future generations generate. At the heart of these complexities, there is 'the common good' that is not only material wealth for the present generation, but it embeds the interest of future generations, this is the Earth that nurtures us and should nourish our children. In this light cultural heritage, and education should be viewed as a "common good" in Europe, as well as in the rest of the world.

This approach is also an attempt to re-endorse education and culture the preponderant role they merit in the European institutional and policy domain by: (1) assuming the complexities of the Anthropocene and keeping sight of the long term responsibility for future generations and, (2) conceiving new ways to reconnect and redesign our knowledge to join efforts and call upon a EUSM that successfully embeds a new sociocultural model through significant reforms of national educational and cultural policies and programs more highly integrated.[81] In such model,

[81]See further the report that was prepared by the German Federation for Arts Education and Cultural Learning (BKJ) and the international foundation Creativity Culture and Education (CCE) and was supported by the German Foundation *Stiftung Mercator*. It explores how the reach and impact of

every involved sector should have a voice. This is also applicable to the global policy level. Education in the broadest sense plays a preponderant role boosting fundamental changes in our ways of living and behaving. This cannot be only the view of radical transformation movements; otherwise, our discourses must become radical to be finally heard.

Most recent doctrinal discussions in International law seem to give recognition to the importance of cultural diversity and local understanding of resources for SD. Those doctrinal approaches are swamped by the Earth system line of thinking that is actually akin to my ethical perspective. However, they not address with due attention cultural and educational issues. A new ethical perspective validating the importance of education and culture and a major integration of both is needed to influence decision makers. Our governmental 'nudges' if any, should be focused on driving people to build solidarity and solid communities helping them to connect with nature, their cultural heritage, and local knowledge in Europe.

Still, the difficulties are many, because although the trend on sustainability science has been to embrace systems theory or holistic endeavours, the technical approach of separating cultural and education as every other field of our social lives has also been at the forefront of political and legal action for many years now, and it is not aleatory, particularly in the European context.

The technical and financial involvement needed for political and legislative intervention in education and culture has so far determined the separation of the two fields. In fact, government distribution of technical ministries in its most simplistic version has always contained under the same umbrella education and culture, although the trend has been to separate them in later times. We should not forget that United Nations Education Science Culture Organization (UNESCO)'s original existence had both mandates and its existence was instrumental for a worldwide contribution and common mandate to reach peace and security in the world by promoting collaboration among nations through education, culture, science and communication to further universal respect for justice, the rule of law and for human rights.

Legislation on education and culture deal with issues where the state desires to penetrate into the educational and cultural institutions characterised by closure, by lack of openness, by resistance to any influence from outside. Studies on European law and policy on these topics have mostly addressed in a descriptive manner the institutional framework of such EU competences, without moving forward from there. A valuable critical and functional approach should start by shedding light not only on ecological concerns, but also on the multicultural needs of our societies.

In fact, in intercultural and multicultural education research emerge strong gaps surrounding the intercultural policy approaches, both as public policy and as a

---

creative and cultural education in Europe can be improved, how creative and cultural education can strengthen our understanding of the value of Europe and how we can improve capacity in Europe for working collaborative Collard and Witte (2015) On line access at: https://www.creativitycultureeducation.org//wp-content/uploads/2018/10/NAE-Final-Report.pdf.

school practice, these profound gaps reveal the conventional value of the existing policy lines and undermine substantially their educative effectiveness and their political coherence. Tozzi (2012) has identified two fundamental gaps: (1) the first one is between EU institutions approach and national policies. Despite the attempts of many European institutions to define and to promote a common policy and shared practices that after Lisbon have been facilitated by the OMC; (2) the second important gap, can be found between the official education policies and what really happens within the classrooms, and the intercultural education approach does seem to caught on. In this second aspect, it is important a thorough look at the research data, to see how integration in the classroom based on these policy approaches becomes difficult.[82]

Despite of the gaps, it is important to understand how there has been a drastic evolution in the educational field in the last fifteen years. This evolution has helped to challenge the nation-state as the dominant level of governance in European education. In this sector, as in other public sectors, the development have been moving from State dominance to an organised multi-level system and on top of that it has been argued that "[E]ducation has also proven itself as least nationally sensitive in its economic rationale compared to when it is culturally and to some extent socially argued" (Gornitzka, 2006). In fact, not by chance, there is further internationalisation and cooperation in vocational training and higher education than in other education stages. Within the European Union context, the EU has a stronger legal foundation in the area of vocational training when compared to other areas of education because of its direct relation to the job market sphere. The same argument should be applied to higher education issues that in terms of economic integration play a crucial role. Still, European education programmes have rested on a cultural rationale and even if they have been often pointed to strengthening "the European dimension",[83] the topic seems to be quite irrelevant for major legal scholarship engagement. When it comes to analyse this topic under the light of integrating sustainability concerns, the legal scholarship *vacuum* is still bigger.

However, the increasing role of European Agencies to define the roadmaps of national policy intervention should not be neglected in the cultural and education policy. Moreover, the growing global trend on interregional integration and international institutions cooperation on cultural and educational issues under the sustainability paradigm will increasingly give support to multi-level governance initiatives that may prove to be valid instruments for the transformation of our educational systems (at first instance) and address cultural challenges.

Under this reasoning, we should tackle the following questions:

---

[82]See further the research data provided on this aspect by Tozzi (2012) on the second part of his contribution, where he makes a comparative study of public policies and school models and then, refers to some research data to see if multicultural education catches on effectively. See also, Faas, Hajisoteriou, and Angelides (2014).

[83]See Corbett (2005).

(1) How has the international scenario dealt with the issues of cultural and education under the paradigm of sustainability to embed a holistic and cooperative vision of intervention (even if localised) to protect the planet Earth?
(2) Where does Europe stand trying to follow an ambitious global agenda defining 'standards' in the educational and cultural areas whilst these topics remain part of the national identity of the Member States?
(3) How such neglected architects of our Sustainability model (education and culture) could gain predominance at the forefront of policy and financial domains*?*

Our sustainability model has been wrongly based on economic market considerations and market unification criteria for so long (!) at international and regional level. Environmental aspects embedded in the transnational cooperation entered the International and European arena and the language of 'cost' and 'value' entered too. Little attention has been devoted to landscape, images, beauty, or the ambit of cultural heritage standing as a roof for our sustainability model. Migration flows (legal and illegal) which are an increasing challenge for our welfare system with direct consequences for the public education sector have been ignored as part of sustainability discussions too. However, migration will continue to be a central societal issue at global, European and local level, and this issue should be at the heart of educational and cultural policy discourses, and should be embedded as much as possible in the 'new biosphere consciousness'. This problem, as many others related to the ecological transition of European MS do not relate to a single phenomenon, but to multiple social challenges, starting by the socio-political and legal failures to face the complexities, such as migration, wealth very unevenly distributed, world population growth, the aging of our developed societies, climate change disasters, and the lack of skilled labour for increasingly complex, internationally and tightly interconnected "knowledge societies".

Rifkin (2004), once talked of the 'European dream' referring to our supranational system, and leading role of Europe focusing on SD, quality of life and interdependence, while the 'American Dream' was lagging behind putting an emphasis on economic growth, personal wealth and independence. This must be today our 'cultural' truism. Article 3 of the TEU may help MS to coherently converge towards a EUSM depicted by strong cultural principles to protect the wealth of our identity, unity in diversity, solidarity, social market, and sustainable development. Nonetheless, concrete action and the enhancement of awareness about the need to turn our attention to educational and cultural requirements of our current and future society are still missing. Thus, we have to wait and see if the most disruptive doctrinal approaches that are based on Earth system approaches, 'Earth identity, Earth awareness',[84] could help to integrate such consciousness into cultural

[84]In the sense referred by Edgar Morin (1999), in Chapter IV, he digs into the concept of Earth identity that humans should acquire to "understand the *human condition* in the world, and the condition of the human world, which in the course of modern history has become the condition of the *planetary era*" (The Italics are Morin's).

issues concerned with educational policies and the integration of ecological values, and the other way around. My approach is an attempt to build the right analytical path in this direction.

4.3 The Global Scenario

4.3.1 Culture and Education Issues Entrenched in International Agreements: Creating Global Awareness on the Necessity of Transformation

The debates that surrounded the post-2015 development agenda took place within a paradigmatic shift for the whole aid and development world characterised by the realisation that the challenges are complex and interconnected, and cannot be solved in isolation or fragmented manner. The New Global Agenda and the Paris Agreement signed in the same year, 2015, are already settled into an international (global) context of growing awareness on the need for a more holistic and integrated approaches to sustainable development. Consequently, this has been followed by sectorial regulation under the premises of ecological preservation, but not every sector has been influenced in the same manner.

Fortunately, the pioneering and disrupting ideas advanced by economists like Schumacher on his book *Small is Beautiful*, are today abundant. Further, examples of the banker of the people and transformative approaches have generated awareness and they can be taken to policy levels pushing also for a radical transformation of our educational interventions. Thus, the measurement of development, which was traditionally theorised from an economic growth perspective, has definitely been expanded today to include other significant aspects of our societies and the ground-breaking role of education and culture is not completely new. Social scientists have been testing other measurement of economic performance and social progress (CMEPSP)[85] not only in recent times. When tackling intergenerational discourses, scholars have addressed the topic of a different value system implicitly. In fact, the first systematic discussions on intergenerational justice attributed to Rawls (Meyer, 2012) touched upon the value and relevance of these issues. Rawls' work was originally developed to consider accumulation of capital (economic and social) to offer an alternative to the unsustainable paradigm of economic growth for its own sake (Taylor, 2013).

[85]The Commission on the Measurement of Economic Performance and Social Progress, generally referred to as the Stiglitz-Sen-Fitoussi Commission after the surnames of its leaders, is a commission of inquiry created by the French Government in 2008. The inquiry examined how the wealth and social progress of a nation could be measured, without relying on the uni-dimensional gross domestic product (GDP) measure. See further; http://www.communityindicators.net/system/publication_pdfs/9/orginal/Stiglitz_Sen_Fitoussi_2009.pdf?132396102.

Simplifying Rawls egregious contribution to the theory of law for the sake of mentioning his impact on the international theory of 'justice between generations' and the substantial role of culture and educational institutions can be a useful research instrument. Rawls illustrates a clear idea of fair equality of opportunity helping to define the obligations of current generations to future ones and to provide an overarching framework introducing the term 'just saving' from which actions can be derived and assessed in political economy context (Rawls, 1971). 'Just savings' for Rawls include: 'preserving the gains of culture and civilisation'; His theory of justice contains in fact, when dealing with distributive shares, a specific discussion about intergenerational justice (Rawls, 1999, p. 251). On explaining 'just savings' he argues: "[T]he appropriate expectation in applying the difference principle is that of the long-term prospects of the least favoured extending over future generations. Each generation must not only preserve the gains of culture and civilization, and maintain intact those 'just institutions' that have been established, but it must also put aside in each period of time a suitable amount of real capital accumulation. This saving may take various forms from net investment in machinery and other means of production to investment in learning and education" (Rawls, 1999, p. 251).

Thus, some long term investments as 'just contributions' for third generations' wealth are associated with industrial machinery as well as cultural capital, knowledge and skills. His famous 'veil of ignorance' is also introduced in his discussion about justice between generations in addition to the constraints on one generation to distribute wealth for the future ones, "to ensure that any one generation looks out for all" (Rawls, 1999, p. 252). Still, his theoretical discussion in my opinion is too much limited to the theoretical constrains of economic benefits, but it can be revisited based on 'transformation' economic theory (Göpel, 2016). Still, it has been pointed that his ideas were appropriate to consider the issues of sustainability by the Brundtland report. The Brundtland definition of sustainable development "development that meets the needs of the present without compromising the needs of the future" (WCED 1987, 2.1), is based on intergenerational equity put forward by Rawls.[86]

In addition, international law scholars like Weiss (2010) anchored their discussions about equity between generations looking at Rawls' theory of law. Weiss, in particular, asserts that "every generation receives a natural and cultural legacy in trust from its ancestors and holds it in trust for descendants" introducing a more legally focused institutional approach using the concept of 'trust' to mainstream an institutionalised 'fairness' towards future generations.[87] The use of 'trust' to mainstream access and protection of the natural and cultural world for future generations have recently re-emerged in the context of 'commons' theoretical approaches. Bollier and Weston (2013) essay on "*Establishing commons trusts to manage common assets for future generations*" is a good starting point for a discussion on 'trust' as an institutional form to safeguard long-term interests structurally.

---

[86]See further on this, Taylor (2013).

[87]See further Weiss (2010).

Nonetheless, the absence of more recent theoretical discussions on the topic of cultural and educational issues as essential instruments to mainstream sustainability parameters, give us the flavour of how lawyers have been neglecting today's advanced notions of justice and rule of law under the sustainability paradigm. Consequently, following a systemic approach by which we cannot longer separate natural resources and Earth decline from our scientific clusters,[88] we find transformative processes without alienating law from the cultural, economic, social and political huddles. In fact, such transformative processes are successful if they are governed by our legal systems when there is not an alienation of law from other systemic approaches (Capra & Mattei, 2015). This takes me to the affirmation that we need more legal approaches focusing on cultural and educational aspects taking on a transdisciplinary analytical approaches. Nonetheless, even if this is not frequent yet, the content and meaning of sustainable development has witnessed a paradigm shift with significant focus on the different social dimensions of human development. Culture is central to this process because through the growing empowerment of people and local identities and communities there is a hidden recognition of culture central to the process of finding solutions to global problems that are interconnected.

Sen (1999) suggests the characterisation of development as "human capacity expansion,"[89] explaining that human capacity expansion is the enhancement of a person's capacity to lead the kind of life he or she ambitions, including access to cultural resources and cultural participation that has become a crucial empowerment element at international level (disregarding the economic value of the cultural diversity context). Thus, if people have to take charge of their own development, they need to be supported to fully develop their capacities, not only by respecting the intrinsic cultural diversity of communities but also through instrumental education tools and transformation, understanding people as a 'primary resource' (Schumacher, 1979). Still, it has taken time to reach to this assertion to render it a 'truism' at international level and provide the right legal framework. It was not until the Human Development Report published by the United Nations Development Programme (UNDP) in 1990 introduced an annual report on the human dimension of development.[90]

Today, this line of thinking seems to be more settled into the development models with the result of a proliferation of proposals for the inclusion of culture as a key element for the full development of people and communities, but we seem to have forgotten that in our national cultural policies. Actually, the focus on human development is promoted on an international scale by the United Nations outside

[88]See, Göpel (2016).

[89]Sen (1999) "Development as Capacity Expansion" 41–58.

[90]The central message of this Human Development report is that while growth in national production (GDP) is absolutely necessary to meet all essential human objectives, what is important is to study how this growth translates-or fails to translate-into human development in various societies (UNDP, 1990, p. iii). Among the consultants for this report, there was Amartya Sen, guided by Mahbub ul Haq.

the scope of UNESCO by the UNDP. The 1990 report starts shaping the 'human development' concept that would foster awareness on 'human capabilities' worldwide.[91] Chapter 1 is devoted to 'Defining and measuring human development', and it opens the chapter:

> People are the real wealth of a nation. The basic objective of development is to create an enabling environment for people to enjoy long, healthy and creative lives. This may appear to be a simple truth. But it is often forgotten in the immediate concern with the accumulation of commodities and financial wealth.[92]

Those reports analyse a range of issues that have a significant impact on human development like human security, mobility, global warming and cultural freedom, etc.[93] It is in this context that "culture" began to be depicted as a very prominent dimension of human development (Owosuyi, 2015). Furthermore, in 1998, the International Conference on Cultural policies for Development held in Stockholm proposed that governments should recognised culture in such way that cultural policies become "one of the key components of endogenous and sustainable development". However, the most significant role for the enhancement of cultural diversity as a key issue for sustainability and development is held by the International Convention on the Protection of Diversity of Cultural Expressions (2005), also known as the Convention on the Diversity of Cultural Expressions. It enshrined an important premise: "culture shapes the ideology of development and conditions how people interact with the environment". Article 13 of the Convention (that I will discuss further on its 2015 edited version) encourages Member States to integrate culture in their development policies at all levels for the creation of the right conditions for sustainable development.

It is for this reason that it seems a drawback in the international sphere the lack of a formalised recognition of culture as part of the UN SDGs. There is not a recognition of culture as an expressive and dynamic force for development at every level and in every context in the most sounded international cooperation engagement for sustainable development in defence of our 'Planet'. Therefore, the direct consequence of this is clear, there will be no culture-focused programming followed by evaluations and reports that is mandatory within the context of international cooperation even if the Agenda itself is not a binding instrument. Still, this is a challenge

---

[91] Sen (1995), UNDP (1990) and Nussbaum (2002).

[92] It continues by adding considerations on technical development, "technical considerations of the means to achieve human development-and the use of statistical aggregates to measure national income and its growth-have at times obscured the fact that the primary objective of development is to benefit people". Further on in the report, there already emerge critics on the 'measuring' mechanism, by arguing that "excessive preoccupation with GNP growth and national income accounts has obscured that powerful perspective, supplanting a focus on ends by an obsession with merely the means" (UNDP, 1990, p. 10).

[93] UNDP 1994 http://hdr.undp.org/en/content/human-development-report-1994; UNDP 2009 http://hdr.undp.org/en/content/human-development-report-2009; UNDP 2007 http://hdr.undp.org/en/content/human-development-report-2007; UNDP 2004 http://hdr.undp.org/en/content/human-development-report-2004.

that needs to be solved. A closer look to the agenda and their detailed targets shows important mentions to the cultural component although in the education goal, a reference to safeguarding cultural heritage in cities and human settlements as part of sustainable cities, food security, the environment, economic growth, and it is also featured twice with reference to tourism as part of sustainable economic development, production and consumption. These references, plus increasing local awareness, the governance mechanisms available and research and policy development on the strategic role of culture for sustainable development worldwide at local and national level open the door for new conceptual frameworks and systemic approaches in which culture interacts with other systems interconnecting parts that create a whole. Such conceptual frameworks not only recognise the prides of the Agenda on the many venues of implication of different stakeholders, especially civil society, but also on identifying art, creativity, education as 'tools' to integrate science, technology, philosophy, emotions, and include the local, regional, national and international sphere. From this achievement, a big educational reform that has not taken place yet should come about.

In fact, if one goes through the literature of the history of education, education policy according to some scholars has gone through two main necessary reforms that reflect the cultural and socio-political momentum (Lundgren, 1982). The first one would follow the course of the development of the industrial society and fitted into the context of post-war consensus, from 1940 onwards.[94] They arose in response to changes in population structure, within the context of a labour market that would demand more and better educational and professional qualifications. These reforms were open to change and were sustained by commitments towards social change to contrast fascism or oppression (Freire, 1971, 1990). They were reforms that were sustained by commitments in favour of democratic education, open to new ideas in terms of personal development (Zufiaurre, 2010). After this first generation of reforms, in the middle of a period of economic crisis, events developed toward second generation reforms[95] whose competency-based curriculum organisation pattern mostly remains today. Through these second reforms support was given to features such as integration, decentralisation, participation and educational dialogue while minimising the demands of curricular integration; but gradually the reforms moved towards models of competency-based curriculum organisation not easily fitting the supposed democratic and egalitarian effects, by introducing pressure of qualifications, control and delegation of autonomy (Zufiaurre, 2010).[96] Taking the story from here, considering that it would be impossible to address every particularity of subsequent reforms and modernisation of the education system since the 1970s, as well as it would be impossible to address the different education systems;

---

[94]See further on this Jones (1983).

[95]During this second period of education reforms is quite well known the case of the Finnish system of Education that hailed a complete reform based on a major State investment on the teaching body.

[96]Under these second wave of reforms the proposals of educational progressivism, described once by J. Dewey (1916) were gone. Those would have fitted the first momentum of educational reforms, when the whole school system was on the making.

we must say that subsequent reforms in Europe take with them as a fixed pattern of competencies-curriculum design and an increasing amount of bureaucratisation in terms of teaching and public administration management.

Oversimplifying the picture we could say that since these two big passages took place leading our systems to the place they are now there has not been another paradigmatic transformation, if not superficial innovations, but none of them has brought a culture passage. Recent legal interventions have mostly helped central states to adjust their systems to international standards.[97] Thus the Global Agenda should lead, not just to a curriculum integration of SDGs (according to what target 4.7. commands),[98] but to a more substantial structural reform that could lead our education system to embrace the epochal change of fostering biosphere consciousness, in which the human race is fully aware of being part of an indivisible community part of the Earth where each one of us needs to take on responsibilities as stewards of the planetary ecosystems that sustain all of life.[99]

Some International law agreements and some scholarship discussions provide some of the instrumental component that cultural and educational institutions need to gain a more substantial role in the development picture for a paradigm change. In this spirit, perhaps the Earth Charter's approach is the most relevant one.

[97]Some of the most debated issues in school education, i.e., increased wage claims made through the union corporations without counterproposals in terms of 'educational' content improvement or change; the role of (the Catholic) religion in public schools; the right to be taught in minority languages; demands for more focus on one subject or another, according to which corporate sector is demanding (science, technology, engineering and mathematics (STEM), and English language, to name a few, taken from the education policy studies literature), would need some drastic changes introduced by central administration with the courage of investing financial resources and boost forward-looking programs of change at every education level. Otherwise the inequality gap will keep growing and private schooling would always go ahead of times and central administration school policy changes.

[98]Target 7, of the SDG 4 on 'quality education' establishes that "by 2030, ensure that all learners acquire the knowledge and skills needed to promote sustainable development, including, among others, through education for sustainable development and sustainable lifestyles, human rights, gender equality, promotion of a culture of peace and non-violence, global citizenship and appreciation of cultural diversity and of culture's contribution to sustainable development"; this can be reached through the means provided by the indicators (4.7.1): Extent to which (i) global citizenship education and (ii) education for sustainable development, including gender equality and human rights, are mainstreamed at all levels in: (a) national education policies, (b) curricula, (c) teacher education and (d) student assessment.

[99]See further on this, Rifkin (2011); on the topic of creating an intimate relationship with the biosphere that should not be considered utopic any longer, see the works of the biologist, Wilson (1993).

4.3.2 *International Instruments That Hail Education and Culture as Horizontal Enablers of Sustainability*

There are some international instruments with different degrees of policy relevance that favour the importance of education and culture as empowerment tools for change and transformation under the premises of a shared-responsibility for the whole humanity, planet Earth, and future generations. I will draw attention to the different international policy instruments of different legal or political nature containing the 'formal' nucleus that provides the basis for empowering people through governance mechanisms that are deployed at different policy level. Those international agreements foster legitimised action eventually needed to endorse education and culture an instrumental value to become providers of the basic foundations of our social systems' transformation to live in harmony with 'planetary existence'[100] today: (1) The Earth Charter; (2) Landmark declarations and conferences and UNESCO's Cultural Conventions intended to safeguard and nurture some aspects of culture and creativity, from tangible and intangible heritage, the diversity of cultural expressions and creative industries, to the fight against the illicit trafficking of cultural goods; (3) The UN 2030 Agenda on Sustainable Development, (4) The Paris Agreement on Climate Change; and (5) the most recent General Assembly resolution on the Global Pact for the Environment.

4.3.2.1 The Earth Charter

The first and most relevant International agreement for its underpinning ambition as global *Grundnorm* mainstreaming Earth systems approach is the Earth Charter.[101] The Earth Charter is an ethical framework for building a just, sustainable, and peaceful global society in the twenty-first century, seeking to inspire in all people a new sense of global interdependence and shared responsibility towards a greater community of life and future generations.[102] When approaching the Earth Charter,

---

[100]Indebted to Morin (1999) for this reference.

[101]The Earth Charter was finalised and then launched at The Hague (29 June 2000) as a people's charter by the Earth Charter Commission in a ceremony at the Peace Palace, in The Hague. The Earth Charter commission was an independent international entity.

The drafting of the Earth Charter involved the most inclusive and participatory process ever associated with the creation of an international declaration. This process is the primary source of its legitimacy as a guiding ethical framework. The legitimacy of the document has been further enhanced by its endorsement by over 6000 organisations, including many governments and international organisations. In light of this legitimacy, an increasing number of international lawyers recognise that the Earth Charter is acquiring the status of a soft law document. Soft law documents like the Universal Declaration of Human Rights are considered to be morally, but not legally, binding on state governments that agree to endorse and adopt them, and they often form the basis for the development of hard law (earthcharter.org).

[102]See further, http://earthcharter.org.

Professor Bosselmann (2004) provides good analytical lenses to understand its relevance for a discourse that promote the necessary role of education and culture for the change of paradigm, especially among legal scholars.[103] Bosselmann[104] has indicated that as a defining feature of modernity, the law mirrors its ecological ignorance, this of course is because in social sciences, nature is "externalised" and not accounted for in social modelling. Thus, Economics and jurisprudence have no comprehension of nature other than referring to the anthropocentric (or instrumental) term "natural resources", reinforcing the exploitative behaviour of economic and legal decision-making (Bosselmann, 1995). In legal scholarship, it is difficult to go beyond certain theoretical assumptions, and modern legal traditions have favoured the freedom of *homo eoconomicus occidentalis*, who is not only the *fulcrum* of institutional development, but also the object of rights and freedoms. As opposed to him, Bosselmann (2004)[105] introduces the figure of an enlightened *homo ecologicus universalis* who asserts a connection with its global and natural environment and it becomes a useful and helpful image in explaining the growing number of people who see themselves not in competition, but solidarity with each other. According to this trend, we find the Earth Charter's Preamble providing the basis for a paradigm shift where there is room for the *homo ecologicus universalis:* "We are at once citizens of different nations and of one world in which the local and global are linked" (Earth Charter 2002, Preamble). The notion of the *homo ecologicus universalis* is echoed throughout the entire Earth Charter means that this document is an attempt "to revolutionise humanity's relationship with nature" (Taylor, 1999, p. 326). In fact, the importance of the Charter lies precisely on this paradigm shift, especially concerning ethical values[106] and enhanced relationship with nature and the humankind. The Earth Charter initiative, at global level, has built the path on this direction, although it has not been enough to spill out in the international community the necessary ambition to convert versus placing more attention into the educational and cultural needs of the sustainable development parameters. However, what is the Earth Charter?—Bosselmann (2010) believes that the Earth Charter would represent the basis for an ecological *grundnorm.* He notices that the Charter has diverse impacts on the society as an educational tool, a system of values, and as draft ambitious covenant on ecological grounds. It is an international (*sui generis*) legal document of soft law, combining features of legal, ethical and moral norms. It is not well known even in the international arena, if not by international environmental lawyers and believers of a 'strong' sustainability approach, in need of transformation

---

[103]He is one of the legal scholars providing the most complete insights and account of the Earth Charter in a global perspective.

[104](1995).

[105]Bosselmann cites the work of Peter Häberle (1988) suggesting that 'recent events' call for a more ecological reflection of human existence: "humans consider the previously merely used world as their environment and 'with'-world (*Um- und Mitwelt*)….struggling for 'peace with nature'….and asking for rights of nature" (Häberle, 1988, p. 20).

[106]The Earth Charter is in fact also mentioned by Papa Francesco as a crucial instrument to build a universal consciousness and awareness.

of civil society engagement in search of a strong sustainability way of life opposed to the current ethical values of our industrial society. It is indeed, the first international document with educational concerns under the paradigm of sustainability. It has been described by the 'Earth Charter Initiative' as a "product of a decade-long, worldwide, cross cultural dialogue on common goals and shared values".[107] Its drafting period started 10 years before it was launched in 2000. It remains a leading broad and inclusive document of ethical principles, which inspire individuals and institutions from all regions and many spheres of action and knowledge, this is civil societies, academia, governments and other entities in their development towards a sustainable future, (Bosselmann, 2010) and continuous to work for the transformation of teaching within the ethical framework promoted by the Charter. According to Bosselmann (2004, p. 67) the Charter takes a systemic view of peace, security, social and ecological justice, human rights and democracy embedding the Charter's idea of sustainable development launched by Brundtland (WCSD 1987, 43), but introducing a major standing to the role of law for the attainment of sustainable development and boosting a different ethical approach towards the Earth system; thus, claiming for the full integrity of the planetary ecosystem for future generations that goes beyond 'the business-as-usual' approach commonly known as 'weak sustainability' (Bosselmann 2002, p. 90) whilst preserving the integrity of the planetary ecosystem as the only reliable alternative and desirable goal mainstreaming a passage from 'weak' sustainability to 'strong' one.

The integrity of the planetary ecosystem is reflected in the first set of principles of the Earth Charter: (I:1 to 4 on "respect and care for the community of life") and principles II: 5 to 8 ("ecological integrity"). They describe the environmental ethic that has been missing the states' discourses on SD. Only subsequently, the principles, which describe the social ethics behind governments and stakeholders interpretation of the SD by the Brundtland definition, are introduced by principles III: 9 to 12 ("social and economic justice") and IV: 13 to 16 ("democracy, non-violence, and peace"). As Bosselmann (2004), puts it in short: "in the centre of concern about sustainable development is not 'human beings' as Principle 1 of the Rio Declaration proclaimed, but the 'community of life' as Principle I of the Earth Charter states". He highlights the three key aspects of distributive justice contained by the notion of SD introduced by the Earth Charter: "intragenerational, intergenerational and interspecies justice". From a legal and economic perspective, this shift of paradigm is much more complex than for natural sciences or ethical discourses surrounding "interspecies justice".

At this stage, is important to mention Rawls' answer about 'interspecies justice': "(the) status of the natural world and our proper relation to it is not a constitutional essential or a basic question of justice" (Rawls, 1993, p. 246). For Rawls, in this regard there exist duties "duties of compassion and humanity" rather than duties related to justice matters on which a civil judge could decide. If one needs to see how the constitutional reality worldwide has changed substantially on this matter, good

[107] https://earthcharter.org/.

examples are brought by the lawsuit on defence of *Río Atrato* (Atrato River). In early 2015, the Colombian group *Tierra Digna* began a litigation process to defend the *Atrato* River and the rights of the communities inhabiting its basin. The lawsuit was brought in collaboration with the *Foro Interétnico Solidaridad Chocó* and different *Afro-Colombian Community Councils* located in the river basin. In a landmark verdict reached in November 2016, but only announced in May 2017, Colombia's Constitutional Court has recognised the *Río Atrato* basin as having rights to "protection, conservation, maintenance and restoration."[108] The High Court in Colombia recognised for the first time in its jurisprudence that a natural resource, in this case a river and its watershed, are subjects and holders of rights alone, and it is the State's responsibility to protect it.[109] Transforming nature to be considered as *rights-bearing*—and thus in possession of legally enforceable rights—is part of the growing "Rights of Nature" movement. The Community Environmental Legal Defense Fund (CELDF) has been at the forefront of this movement, collaborating with communities and governments in developing the world's first Rights of Nature Laws. The November decision in Colombia comes ahead of a March 2017 decision in India, where a state High Court found that the Ganges River and other ecosystems were "legal persons" with certain rights. In addition—as the Colombia Court refers to in its decision—it comes as a settlement between the Maori people and the government of New Zealand. In that settlement, the *Whanganui* River, the third largest river in New Zealand, is recognised as having personhood rights.

Turning back to the Earth Charter and its resonance for the International community engagement on a holistic and proactive approach in creating a strong sustainable development, the final provisions of the Charter under the epigraph "the Way Forward" are important when requiring the process of building sustainability by the international community: (1) renew their commitments to the UN (UN), (2) fulfil existing international obligations, and (3) implement legally binding instruments on sustainability and development. The Charter is a boost to the type of justice and legal adjudication shown at the above-referred judicial decisions concerning the *Atrato* and the *Whanganui* Rivers. Bosselmann (2018) has argued that the Earth Charter draws the vision of not just three pillars but the 'temple of life', being ecological integrity the fundamental of the temple, and the roof of the cultural identity. Under this light, the Earth Charter qualifies as a founding document for global law; it gives to global law a solid foundation for worldwide consensus (Bosselmann, 2003). Its preamble states: "...that we, the peoples of the Earth, declare our responsibility to one another, to the greater community of life, and to future generations". Such a solid foundation on a particular action path is indeed fostered at the international normative level through soft law instruments like this one, or the new UN Agenda 2030. This, is because 'soft law' has become an

[108] *República de Colombia, Corte Constitucional, Sala Sexta*, T-622 de 2016. Text retrieved from: http://cr00.epimg.net/descargables/2017/05/02/14037e7b5712106cd88b687525dfeb4b.pdf.

[109] https://intercontinentalcry.org/colombia-constitutional-court-finds-atrato-river-possesses-rights-protection-conservation-maintenance-restoration/.

important source of international law (Kiss & Shelton, 2000, p. 46). In contrast to 'hard law' (treaties, custom, general principles of law), 'soft law' although not legally binding and lacking direct legal effect, has a strong political strength that cannot be underestimated in terms of reaching broad consensus. A successful example on the promotion of sustainable development through a soft law instrument has also been given by 'Agenda 21' with its bottom-up initiatives that gained immediate recognition and acceptance by wide sectors of civil society all around the world. In the particular case of the Earth Charter, its virtue stands on having initiated a global dialogue definitely shifting an anthropocentric and short-sited vision of sustainable development as well as environmental protection worldwide.

4.3.2.2 UNESCO Conventions and Declarations

When we turn our attention to UNESCO's policy framework, we can identify several Conventions with different ambitions, normative relevance and scope of action relevant to us. There are 4 UNESCO's Cultural Conventions and the 2001 Declaration on Cultural Diversity, intended to safeguard and nurture some aspect of culture and creativity, from tangible and intangible heritage and the promotion and protection of the diversity of cultural expressions and creative industries. They all have implications for development both in terms of how they can contribute to it and in the impact that development has on culture, as well as some relevance for the educational sphere:

1. The Convention for the Protection of the World Cultural and Natural Heritage (1972);
2. The Convention on the Protection of the Underwater Cultural Heritage (2001);
3. The Universal Declaration on Cultural Diversity (2001);
4. The Convention for the Safeguarding of the Intangible Cultural Heritage (2003);
5. The Convention on the Protection and Promotion of the Diversity of Cultural Expressions (2005).

But there are also other selected milestones within the international policy framework in which culture is advocated as an explicit (or implicit) aspect of sustainability, some important examples are[110]: (1) United cities and Local adoption of 'Agenda 21 for Culture (2004); (2) UN Declaration on the rights of indigenous people (2007); (3) Fribourg Declaration on Cultural Rights (2007); (4) UN Human Rights Council established a post of independent Expert in the field of cultural rights for a 3 year-period (Extended); (5) Policy Statement on 'Culture: Fourth Pillar of Sustainable Development' by the United Cities and Local Governments (UCLG) (2010); (6) Adoption of new UNESCO Recommendation on the Historic Urban Landscape (2011); (7) Outcome Document on the UN Conference on Sustainable

[110]For a more detailed list of international policy instruments setting the framework for culture as a part of sustainable development see further, Dessein, Soini, Fairclough, and Horlings (2015), p. 15.

Development, endorsed by UN General Assembly/High-Level (2012); (8) UNESCO International Congress 'Culture: Key to Sustainable Development': Placing Culture at the Heart of Sustainable Development Policies, The Hangzhou Declaration (2013); (9) The role of culture for sustainable development is also advocated by the 'Creative Economy Report 3: Special edition-Widening Local Development Pathways; (10) UN General Assembly Resolution on Culture and Sustainable Development A/RES/68/223; (11) The 3rd UNESCO World Forum on Culture and the Cultural Industries: 'Culture, Creativity and Sustainable Development' concluded with the adoption of the 'Florence Declaration'[111]; (12) 'Culture 21 Actions: Commitments on the role of culture in sustainable cities', approved in Bilbao by the First culture Summit organised by UCLG.

The concepts and approaches of these international instruments, policy frameworks, may help to integrate culture more explicitly into sustainable development frameworks, even if it has not been done comprehensively,[112] there is now ample room for a more far-reaching action on this regard.

A landmark declaration for the instrumental introduction of the definition of cultural diversity is the UNESCO Universal Declaration on Cultural Diversity adopted by the 31st Session of the General Conference of UNESCO.[113] This 'wide-ranging' instrument for the International community reaffirms "that cultural should be regarded as the set of distinctive spiritual, material, intellectual and emotional features of society or a social group, and that it encompasses, in addition to art and literature, lifestyles, ways of living together, value systems, traditions and beliefs".[114] However, the most relevant one to my discourse here is the UNESCO International Convention on the Protection and Promotion of the Diversity of Cultural Expressions 2005 advocating for the recognition of culture as an autonomous dimension in sustainable development rather as part of the social dimension of development (Owosuyi, 2015). At international level, the special organisation of the United Nations for cultural and educational matters, the United Nations Educational Social and Cultural Organization (UNESCO), is my point of departure before dealing with the 2005 Convention on Cultural Diversity. It has of course been the object of attention of international lawyers for decades now because of its successful

[111]Recommendations on maximising the role of culture to achieve sustainable development and effective ways of integrating culture in the Post-2015 Development Agenda.

[112]See further, Dessein et al. (2015).

[113]Paris, 2 November 2001. This UNESCO Declaration was adopted unanimously in a most unusual context. It came in the wake of the events of 11 September 2001, (After the terroristic attack to the twin towers hosting the World Trade Centre at the heart of Manhattan) and the UNESCO General Conference, which was meeting for its 31st session, was the first ministerial-level meeting to be held after those terrible events. It was an opportunity for States to reaffirm their conviction that intercultural dialogue is the best guarantee of peace and to reject outright the theory of the inevitable clash of cultures and civilisations.

[114]This definition is in line with the conclusions of the World Conference on Cultural Politics (MONDIACULT, México City 1982), of the World Commission on Culture and Development (Our Creative Diversity, 1995) and of the Intergovernmental Conference on Cultural Policies for Development (Stockholm, 1998).

role in international treaty making. Still, it was only in the 1990s that UNESCO took a concrete interest in protecting cultural diversity from the undesirable effects of economic globalisation. Such specific action starts with the *World Decade for Cultural Development* (1988–1997) and UNESCO's role substantially expanded thereafter with the objective to acknowledge the cultural dimension of development, affirm and enrich cultural identities, broaden participation in culture and promote international cultural co-operation.[115] As a principle, the concern for cultural diversity has always been at the forefront of UNESCO's concerns; still, the idea of a legally binding instrument on cultural diversity was also only a second thought in UNESCO (Burri, 2014). The process originally started outside the UN agency framework and it was leaded by the International Network of Cultural Policy (INCP) and the International Network for Cultural Diversity (INCD).[116] It was only later on time that UNESCO took part, to enhance efforts to protect cultural diversity through international instruments in 2003.[117] Thereafter, the *Convention on the Protection and Promotion of the Diversity of Cultural Expressions* was adopted by the 33rd UNESCO General Conference in 2005. Through this historic agreement, the global community formally recognised the dual nature, both cultural and economic of contemporary cultural expressions produced by artist and cultural professionals. It is for this reason that the Convention has been the focus of legal and economic scientist alike, without endorsing importance to the binding nature of the respect for cultural diversity in a non-stopping globalised economy that has tended to bypass the respect (*strictu sensu*) for local and indigenous cultures for the sake of economic development. Still, this landmark Convention over its first decade has been ratified by 140 parties, including the EU and thanks to the UN SD Agenda for 2030 has received a renewed focus of attention reinforcing the message that "an investment in culture and creativity is an investment in SD". In fact, in 2015 there was launched a new edition of the Basic Text of the 2005 Convention on the Protection and Promotion of the Diversity of Cultural Expressions as a practical tool to continue moving forward on the light of the proclamation of the UN SD Agenda 2030. Therefore, there has been a recent re-indorsement of the importance of culture for sustainable development by UNESCO. Further than that, UNESCO has also made a declaration about the eventual preparation of new guidelines that respect the Convention's principle of technological neutrality while reaffirming the sovereign right of the Parties to introduce policies to promote the diversity of cultural expressions in the digital era.

---

[115]UNESCO, *UNESCO and the issue of Cultural Diversity: Review and Strategy, 1946–2004*, Paris: UNESCO, revised version 2004, p. 16. See also Resolution adopted by the General Assembly of the United Nations, World Commission on Culture and Development, *Our Creative Diversity*, 2nd ed., Paris: UNESCO, 1996; UNESCO *World Culture Report 1998: Culture, Creativity and Markets*, Paris: UNESCO, 1998; UNESCO, *World Culture Report 2000: Cultural Diversity, Conflict and Pluralism*, Paris: UNESCO, 2000.

[116]On this topic see, Acheson and Maule (2004).

[117]See further, UNESCO 32 C/Resolution 34, Desirability of Drawing up an International Standard Setting instrument on Cultural Diversity, 17 October 2003.

The 2015 edition includes revised Guidelines for Article 9 on "Information sharing and transparency" and the Framework for Quadrennial Periodic Reports that were approved by the fifth ordinary session of the Conference of the Parties in June 2015.[118] This edition is designed as a practical tool to continue moving forward, providing a roadmap rather than a recipe for action.[119] Bruner (2008) has argued that within the context of trade versus cultural discourse which is of crucial relevance for us, the Convention was intended to take up a critical role and counterbalance the highly institutionalised economic rules of the World Trade Organisation, as well as ensure the attainment of non-economic, in particular cultural objectives at the global level; Nonetheless, it is questionable whether the Convention or further instruments are sufficient to combat unsustainable practices and counterbalance economic interests that are adverse for cultural contexts in line with a sustainable future. There is in fact a substantive critique of the Convention (Burri, 2009; Craufurd Smith, 2007; Hah, 2006) and despite the limited obligations on the Parties to protect and promote cultural diversity considering that the Convention formulates an extensive block of rights to that end, the critiques relate to the vague definition of 'cultural diversity'[120] and the lack of proportionality or efficiency tests that open the door to state activism in a wide range of economic sectors that affect culture in one way or another (Burri, 2004).[121] This discussion triggers a different issue concerning the economic value assigned to cultural and creative industries today. We should not confuse the renewed interest on cultural topics due to this value following the old sustainable economic paradigm with the re-endorsement of interest focused in cultural matters for their intrinsic human value to build sustainability and generate development respecting future generation's rights and natural resources. Legal scholarship has drawn attention to these issues within the context of the economic system measuring value and impact of cultural diversity under economic premises and not for the sake of paradigmatic change of our social system. Thus, what is clear is that legal scholarship has analysed the document with the intention of showing counterbalance between culture and sovereign economic interests that have always been at stake since cultural and creative industries are among the fastest growing sectors in the world. Indeed, the culture sector now accounts for 6.1% of the global economy.[122] It remains to see if the cultural endeavor with regard

[118]See further, 2015 UNESCO edition of the Basic Texts of the 2005 Convention on the Protection and Promotion of the Diversity of Cultural Expressions, retrieved from: http://en.unesco.org.

[119]Foreword to the 2015 UNESCO edition of the Basic Texts of the 2005 Convention on the Protection and Promotion of the Diversity of Cultural Expressions, retrieved from: http://en.unesco.org.

[120]Article 4 (1) defines 'cultural diversity' as referring to the manifold ways in which the cultures of groups and societies find expression. These expressions are passed on within and among groups and societies'.

[121]See Article 6 (2) (a)-(h) of the UNESCO Convention on Cultural Diversity 2003.

[122]Culture Creative Industries revenues worldwide exceed those of telecom services (US$1570b globally), and surpass India's GDP (US$1900b). Within the total, the top three earners are television (US$477b), visual arts (US$391b), and newspapers and magazines (US$354b). With

to sustainable development will be further devoid to economic interests and attempts of sustainable growth without going beyond the contours of strengthening the economic system itself, or rather, cultural endeavor will create the basis for planetary cooperation and preservation mainstreaming action for the respect and the preservation of wealth of local and indigenous cultures, as well as for the creation of awareness and the promotion of cultural through educational activities worldwide. Following this trend in fact, cultural and creative industries have become essential for inclusive economic growth, reducing inequalities and achieving the goals set out in the 2030 SD Agenda in a varied array of approaches that we can discuss related to the EU SM further. However, most of all, cultural and creative industries should be endorsed the potential of creating human awareness on global needs and risks, as well as transmitting emotions.

The fact that the Convention (UNESCO, 2005) has been revised under the auspices of a renovated engagement of international cooperation of planetary importance with 2030 UN Agenda is not of little relevance. The importance of the inclusion of an article devoted to 'Education and Public Awareness', is a meaningful departing point for my analyses in this second part of the study. Article 10 of the Convention reads as follow:

> Parties shall: (a) encourage and promote understanding of the importance of the protection and promotion of the diversity of cultural expressions, inter alia, through educational and greater public awareness programmes; (b) cooperate with other Parties and international and regional organisations in achieving the purpose of this Article; (c) endeavor to encourage creativity and strengthen production capacities by setting up educational, training and exchange programmes in the field of cultural industries. These measures should be implemented in a manner which does not have a negative impact on traditional forms of production.[123]

Concerning Article 10, in the new operational guidelines, we find measures that are devised to forge a roadmap by which educational tools and programmes are at service of sustainable development and the strengthening of the ties between cultural and education at the policy, and institutional levels.[124] Following these guidelines, schools are considered important platforms for transmitting information and knowledge on the importance of protecting and promoting the diversity of cultural expressions to young people. In this context there is call for action for bottom up intervention of every actor involved in the promotion, access and production of culture together with the educational actors (i.e., teachers, parents, community) and the main aims suggested by the guidelines are quite exhaustive: (a) including the

29.5 million jobs, CCI employ 1% of the world's active population. The top three employers are visual arts (6.73m), books (3.67m) and music (3.98m). See further, the first global map of cultural and creative industries (2015), retrieved from: https://en.unesco.org/creativity/sites/creativity/files/cultural_times._the_first_global_map_of_cultural_and_creative_industries.pdf.

[123]UNESCO (2015).

[124]Operational guidelines approved by the Conference of Parties at its second session (Paris, 15–16 June 2009), third session (Paris, 14–15 June 2011), fourth session (Paris, 11–13 June 2013) and fifth session (Paris, 10–12 June 2015).

diversity of cultural expression in school curricula adapted to local contexts and cultures; (b) developing educational and training materials in multiple formats, including those online, such as books, CDs, videos, documentaries, manuals or brochures, interactive games, etc.; (c) inviting artists and cultural professionals in the development of such materials and to participate in the activities of schools and other educational institutions; (d) enhancing the capacities of teachers to raise students' awareness about the diversity of cultural expressions and use, wherever available, guides and manuals to this end; (e) involving adults and parent associations to suggest themes and modules for teaching expressions in their communities; (f) transmitting acquired experiences through the promotion of participatory educational methodologies, mentoring activities and apprenticeships.

International legal scholars have not turned their attention to the 'instrumental role of education, training and research in synergy with culture if mainstreamed with national action and financial plans to achieve a substantive part of the targets belonging to the SDGs. There is no need to consider culture the fourth pillar of sustainable development to reach far-reaching results on embedding culture on sustainable development frameworks, but we will come back to this later, concretely to the public planning aspects to endorse cultural pre-eminence in our societies (Hawkes, 2001). Just now, suffices to emphasise the necessity to perceive the importance of the normative dimension in cultural and educational factors to mainstream and organise action to preserve the planet and provide the right ways for empowerment of youth as the key 'actors' and 'recipients' for SD.

4.3.2.3 The 2030 Agenda for Sustainable Development

SD has become even more prolific at the level of governance and organised action at International, regional, national and local level thanks to the action framework provided by the 2030 Agenda for SD.[125] This Agenda is a "plan of action for people, planet and prosperity" and it "seeks to strengthen universal peace in larger freedom". "All countries and all stakeholders, acting in collaborative partnership, will implement this plan. Today it includes substantially the main traditional mandates of UN by integrating in a balanced manner all the concrete needs of the world (Planet) in the different speeds of development. Moreover, the 2030 Agenda[126] integrates the three traditional dimensions of sustainable development—economic, social and environmental—but reflects for the first time an international consensus that peace, security, justice for all, and social inclusion are not only to be pursued on their own but should reinforce each other. This is the most ambitious cooperation agreement of the international sphere, and its lack of binding nature in the legal sense, has surely

[125] See Resolution Adopted by the General Assembly on 25 September 2015-Transforming our World: The 2030 Agenda for Sustainable Development UN Doc GA/RES/70/1 (2015) (hereafter 2030 Agenda).

[126] UNGA Resolution A/RES/70/1 (21 October 2015).

helped to integrate flexibility as one of its main features, helping to reach consensus in a wide range of topics and include bottom up approaches coming from all kind of different actors and stakeholders. Thus, different goals, with a variety of targets to be achieved at different stages. Beyond that, it leaves behind Agenda 21 with a strong focus on environmental aspects, without leaving them behind but reaching international consensus to achieve goals of social nature, equity and justice, which are also contained in the Paris Agreement (of binding nature). The principle of systematic integration of Article (31) (3) (c) of the Vienna Convention on the Law of the Treaties gathers together the ambitions of these agreements to shape the systemic coherence of international law towards SD, and this should give us hope for further development on the attainment of the planet and the world we want.

Education cuts across the entire sustainable development agenda and it plays a crucial role in the implementation of the sustainable development goals (SDGs). It should be identified as a primary instrument of development and as a yardstick for social and economic growth having a transformational role in addressing all development challenges of the present and the future (Sánchez Galera, 2019). The SDGs were formed to build on the accomplishments of the Millennium Development Goals (MDGs) but, there are some difficulties to ensure equitable quality education in some parts of the world despite of the strong consensus built about the foundational role of education worldwide, and this is understandable also under the light of educational action with a westernised imprinting not respecting the necessary local contextualisation.[127] It is true that in the early twenty-first century the great majority of the world's young people go to school, with nearly half of them enrolled in formal education beyond the elementary and fundamental stages. The more that such agreements have been affirming one or another aspect of the right to education, then the more difficult it becomes for countries to disregard this right. However, unsatisfactory results of the index performance show that there is a lot of work to be done to reach a satisfactory level for this challenge.[128] The former UN Agenda for Development, the UN Millennium Declaration (2000) expected universal primary education to be achieved in all countries by the year 2015, although the World Declaration on Education for All (1990) had earlier targeted the year 2000. Thus, although there is significant progress, how should we monitor the effectiveness of the existing monitoring mechanisms? With the growing number of international agreements in education and other fields, there are signs of a reporting overload on

[127]On this, see further Manish et al. (2008) retrieved from: www.swaraj.org/shikshantar.

[128]2018 SDG Index and Dashboards. Available at: http://www.sdgindex.org/assets/files/2018/01%20SDGS%20GLOBAL%20EDITION%20WEB%20V9%20180718.pdf. It is also useful to read the last GEM Report. According the Report, "children cannot read after several years of school in sub-Saharan Africa (Africa Progress Panel, 2012); examination pressure is having an impact on gender gaps in China (Yangcheng Evening News, 2016); the excess focus in education on employability is being questioned in Germany (SWR, 2017); decentralization is posing challenges for underfunded rural schools in Pakistan (Dawn, 2011); refugee children have severely constrained education chances, especially those fleeing was in the Syrian Arab Republic (Reliefweb, 2016)" (Highlights of the GEM Report, UNESCO 2018/2019).

governments without providing effective solutions for improvement (Sánchez Galera, 2019), I should emphasise that the wording of the Agenda is courageous and its vision is featured as "supremely ambitious and transformational". It definitely reinforces and re-endorses at the forefront of development the preeminent human side and the crucial role of education by 'envisaging': "[a] world free of poverty, hunger, disease and want, where all life can thrive". Further, "[a] world with equitable and universal access to quality education at all levels, to health care and social protection, where physical, mental and social well-being are assured", Education and human needs have a preeminent position and the empowerment of youth action by UN has given proof of such preeminent role and the need to create awareness and diffusion among the youth of the planet.[129]

With regard to culture, even if it seems that the 2030 Agenda has made a step backwards in the international sphere the lack of a formalised recognition of culture as part of the UN SDGs. It is the first time that there is an explicit mention to the "appreciation of cultural diversity and of culture's contribution to sustainable development" in the Goal 4.7 of the 2030 Agenda devoted to Education. Target 7 of this, goal 4 on equality education aims at ensuring by 2030 that all learners acquire the knowledge and skills needed to promote SD, including, among others, through education for sustainable development and sustainable lifestyles, human rights, gender equality, promotion of a culture of peace and non-violence, global citizenship and appreciation of cultural diversity and of culture's contribution to sustainable development.

The agenda sets the key guiding tools that policymakers need to integrate cultural and education in the multidimensional version of SD. Their role is actually endorsed by the 2030 Agenda when stressing the importance of global citizenship, cultural diversity, sustainable lifestyles, human rights, gender equality, promotion of a culture of peace and non-violence, and reinforcing culture's contribution to sustainable development (SDG 4.7).

Over the years, the importance of the key role of advancing sustainable development at local level through education has been quite underdeveloped. Still, the academic interest in the interconnection of sustainability and education at local level seems to increase considerably based on the attention that higher education is getting as a stakeholder to build knowledge within the context where is located (Gunasekara, 2004; Lang & Oppong, 2018). Higher Education institutions (HEI) are helping to reinforce the primary role of knowledge building (especially at local level) and to appraise the links with the various stakeholders and communities (Jongbloed et al., 2008). The fact that evidence has been provided as to their role on developing the skill needs of the locality within which they are established (Oppong, 2018) has strengthened their renewed leading role in the education sector in the global agenda.[130] As I have argued elsewhere, there is broad evidence of a groundbreaking

[129]See further, Youth and the 2030 Agenda for Sustainable Development. United Nations for Youth, as part of the Department of Economic and Social Affairs.

[130]See further, the report 'Getting started with SDGs in Universities' (2018).

achievement in education and research at Higher Education level under the premises of the 2030 Agenda. Universities are going through the process of recognising the need for shifting and transforming established structures and practices in research, teaching, and operations to meet the sustainability challenges of the twenty-first century (Ferrer-Balas et al., 2008; Gough et al., 2017; Lang & Wiek, 2012; Molthan-Hill, 2015; Whitmer et al., 2010; Wiek et al., 2011). The most relevant aspect of this transformation is the growing emergence of international educational programs in sustainability; and this trend shows how HEI are more prompt for change and innovation than Primary and Secondary School Institutions. Still, the focus on HEIS is insufficient to mainstream all the desired efforts for committed educational models needed to achieve sustainable development at every governance level.

The agenda has helped the world community to understand better, what Education for sustainability mission at UN framework has been claiming for some decades now. There is an urgent need to train students to be capable of working across national, geographical, and cultural boundaries, and to adapt those capabilities to any given local context. To achieve this process the internationalisation of HEI should be more imminent than ever before. In Europe, this goes beyond the Bologna process ambitions. Capabilities trained and endorsed at Higher education level should allow students to recognise the cultural, historical, epistemological and ethical context of perceiving sustainability problems and developing solution options at every action level.

Another major achievement today linked to the context of education, regards the recognition of the traditional approach of learning through community. Nowadays, it is recognised globally as excellent approach for conserving biodiversity and maintaining ecosystems processes. Thus, traditional, especially indigenous knowledge in areas such as agriculture, food production and natural resources conservation that have played an important role in environmental sustainability for centuries, today after decades of neglected attention, has been recognised.[131] The Agenda promotes the enhancement of such approach by emphasising the importance of (1) lifelong learning (SDG 4.3, SDG 4.4) and; (2) and integrated policy approaches (SDG 13.2).

This means that, beyond formal education, government agencies, religious organisations, non-profit and community groups, labour organisations and the private sector can all help individual and collective behaviour at local level rising awareness and launching education initiatives that benefit from public funds or private-public partnerships launched at the local administration level.

4.3.2.4 The Paris Agreement

It has already been proved that broadening access to education is more effective against climate change effects than the investment in infrastructures such as sea

[131]See further, *Global Education Monitoring Report*, UNESCO (2016).

walls and irrigation systems (UNESCO, 2016, pp. 29–35). The importance of knowledge building and capacity building is more evident now than it was ever before. The Paris Agreement, as an international law binding instrument contributes to a potential change of scenario by introducing the topic of education as a cooperative action measure within the context of a bottom up governance oriented approach in Article 12 of the Agreement:

> Parties shall cooperate in taking measures, as appropriate, to enhance climate change education, training, public awareness, public participation and public access to information, recognising the importance of these steps with respect to enhancing actions under this a Agreement.

Cooperation and open-governance approaches in line with a decentralised and bottom-up participation that influences the instrumental role of education (introduced by Article 12) are covered by Article 6. Article 6 (1) covers the general concept that Parties may choose, on voluntary basis, to cooperate in the implementation of their nationally determined contributions (NDCs). Section 8 Article 6 of the Paris Agreement reinforces the autonomy of the parties to develop their own ambitions or goals in the form of their NDCs defined and required by Article 3 of the Paris Agreement recognising the importance of integrated, holistic and balanced non-market approaches. Article 4 (9) establishes that "Each Party shall communicate a nationally determined contribution every five years in accordance with decision 1/CP.21 and any relevant decisions of the Conference of the Parties serving as the meeting of the Parties to this Agreement and be informed by the outcomes of the global stocktake referred to in Article 14".

It is of course outside the scope of this contribution further analyse the Paris Agreement, but explicit mention to the binding legal instruments and governance mechanisms introduced by the agreement are necessary for the sake of assessing its innovative approach to build on human capital, knowledge, communication and integrated approaches that foster coherence for sustainable development transformations at every action level. The Paris agreement has demonstrated to be highly relevant for capacity building and education and training related relevance (Molthan-Hill, Worsfold, Nagy, Leal Filho, & Mifsud, 2019). It suffices to say that education emerged for the first time as a crucial issue for Action for Climate Empowerment (ACE) that was also included in Article 6 of the United Nations Framework Convention on Climate Change (the parent Treaty of the Paris Agreement) covering education, training, public awareness, public participation, public access to information and international cooperation. Each country was encouraged to name an ACE focal point and prepare an ACE national strategy. The Paris agreement also calls for the creation of new academic programmes across a diverse range of disciplines, to ensure our future professionals have a better understanding of both, challenges posed by climate change and of the tools to be used for mitigation and adaptation (UNESCO, 2017). It is widely accepted that education and training are the driving forces of sustainability but we have neglected the importance of introducing compulsory curricula changes by law to foster action and awareness for sustainable development.[132]

The Paris Agreement requires all Parties to put forward their best efforts through "nationally determined contributions" (NDCs) and to strengthen these efforts in the years ahead. This includes requirements that all Parties report regularly on their emissions and on their implementation efforts. There will also be a global stocktake every 5 years to assess the collective progress towards achieving the purpose of the agreement and to inform further individual actions by Parties.

Despite of the recognition of climate change education and public awareness at international policy level, there is a gap, not only on public compliance, but also on the legally binding instruments emanated to give compliance to such command. The gap identified between such policy commands and implementation compliance today—that was also mentioned concerning multicultural education—has been suggested it could be filled by Higher Education Institutions (HEI) action and research.[133] It has been argued that despite of the importance of climate change education at all levels, it is the higher education sector that is most in need of developing a systemic approach (Leal-Filho et al., 2018). The literature review on law-based documents on the topic shows evidence of how distant the issue of education and empowerment through education for sake of combatting climate change is from the legal standpoint. Therefore, if the Earth Charter might have certainly included the need to address the challenge of launching training programs on the Earth Charter and its contents at higher education level, the same sort of initiative has not been considered even in an uncoordinated version by the IPCC, nor by the SDGs coordination networks. Although in a fragmented and isolated manner at Higher education level a substantial amount of initiatives have echoed the paradigm shift.[134] In fact, the role of universities in climate change education (CCE) has increasingly gained importance to face scientific, social, environmental and political challenges, even it may still be insufficient.[135] Therefore, not only CCE has become crucial, also the role that Higher Education institutions can play by implementing different strategies that could help the different stakeholders to find the right instruments to address the challenges climate change poses. This binding requirement[136] has activated a prolific amount of scientific work to design teaching

[132] According to the formal requirements of SDG 4.7, and its indicator 4.7.1.

[133] See Molthan-Hill et al. (2019).

[134] See further, Filho (2010) and Leal-Filho et al. (2018).

[135] See further Molthan-Hill et al. (2019). When conceptualising climate change education, note that that Climate Change education has been an under-research topic, and they include their conceptual existence into the field of education for sustainable development (ESD). Within this context, CCE bears the risk that institutions and academics prefer to focus on other less complex issues of ESD framework than the teaching task of climate change, which might be considered a "super wicked problem".

[136] Although before the Paris agreement, there were already active an extensive variety of climate change education research and training activities, not only at Higher education level, but also at other education levels. See further Molthan-Hill et al. (2019) and Filho (2010).

and training programs on climate change. Still, it emerges that most of the research on CCE was embedded on education for sustainable development.[137] Of course, embedding CCE in sustainability education and implementing undergraduate specialised subjects or postgraduate programmes on both fields, climate change or other sustainability topics seems to be the easiest approach to spill out educational and cultural concerns on sustainability (generally speaking) considering how difficult it is to change educational structures.[138]

4.3.2.5 The Global Pact for the Environment

The last international policy instrument that we want to address here to understand how education becomes a horizontal enabler of sustainability, and in this particular case environmental protection awareness, is the Global Pact for the Environment (UNGA 2018). It is important to note that the Earth Charter has been an inspirational starting point for it. Some of the people involved in the drafting process of the Global Pact were also part of the drafting of the Earth Charter, professors such as Nicholas Robinson, Judge Antonio Herman Benjamin, and Dr. Parvez Hassan. Robinson mentions that the French government's proposal for the Global Pact is rooted in the French domestic Charter for the Environment and is of course an ambitious attempt to overcome fragmentation of international environmental law by a unique binding global instrument protecting the 'Earth'.[139] The process, which may ultimately lead to the negotiation of a legally binding Global Pact for the environment, formally commenced under the auspices of the United Nations General Assembly in 2018. It is an ambitious Pact hailing big expectations evidenced in particular by its multiple and overlapping objectives: "to serve as a generic binding instrument of international environmental law principles; to integrate, consolidate, unify and ultimately entrench many of the fragmented principles of International Environmental law; and to constitute the first global environmental human rights instrument" (Kotzé & French, 2018).[140] The lack of an environmental *grundnorm* in

[137]Molthan-Hill et al. (2019) argue that recent research indicates that if at all, CCE is addressed within ESD; and there has been no research on implementation strategies specifically for CEE. They indicate in their study, an excellent example identified to show how to implement successfully climate change topics in teaching and learning practices. The example comes from the University of Dar es Salaam in Tanzania. Their curriculum aims to allow every university student to obtain at least a basic understanding of climate change studies and sustainable development. Because of this work, the University of Dar es Salaam has become a reference centre for climate change studies.

[138]See further, UN *Decade for Education on Sustainable Development*, Johannesburg Summit, 2002.

[139]See further Kotzé and French (2018).

[140]Kotzé and French have argued the importance and relevance of the Global Pact in the Anthropocene. They have analysed it within the theoretical construction of the Earth System approach, and their assessment aims at addressing if the Global Pact was to provide normative provisions to strengthen those public and private global governance efforts that aim to halt the deterioration of Earth system integrity, as well as to maintain and even improve integrity, to be able

international law and the current fragmentation led to such initiative.[141] The World Commission on Environmental Law is leading the International Union for the Conservation of Nature's (IUCN) contribution towards establishing a Global Pact for the Environment. It was presented to the world in Paris by the French think tank, *Le Club de Juristes*, which also coordinated its drafting process (together with the World Commission on Environmental Law). The final outcome of a relatively swift process that consisted of five consultations, the Pact was drafted by a Group of Experts.[142] The United Nations General Assembly adopted Resolution 72/277 "Towards a Global Pact for the Environment" on 10 May 2018.

Following the two international Covenants adopted in 1966 by the United Nations General Assembly, one related to civil and political rights and the other to economic, social, and cultural rights, the Global Pact for the Environment will strongly establish a third generation of fundamental rights: the rights associated with the protection of the environment, the Global Pact would aim at reaffirming environmental rights and not only, it would reaffirm the Declaration of the United Nations Conference on the Human Environment, adopted in Stockholm on 16 June 1972, the World Charter for Nature adopted on 28 October 1982 and the Declaration of the United Nations Conference on Environment and Development, adopted in Rio on 14 June 1992; and it would recall their commitment to the Sustainable Development Goals adopted by the General Assembly of the United Nations on 25 September 2015, Considering in particular the urgency to tackle climate change and recalling the objectives set by the United Nations Framework Convention on Climate Change adopted in New York on 9 May 1992 and the Paris Agreement of 12 December 2015, the Global Pact would be the environmental milestone the world needs to operationalise at its fullest capacity the entire body of international environmental law and global environmental governance, focusing on the extent to which the draft Pact accommodates both existing and more recent rules and principles for environmental protection that are crystallising in treaty law, soft law and jurisprudence.

Still the Pact has been criticised for its singular "environmental" focus and its failure to embrace an Earth system approach to international environmental law and global environmental governance, and its anthropocentric ontology. These critics are contextualised on the belief of the Anthropocene's potentially far-reaching normative consequences. Kotzé and French agree with Dalby that "[t]he future configuration of the Earth System is now the key matter of geopolitics, of how the world is

---

to offer a firm foundation of the type of Anthropocene Law, termed in their study as the *Lex Anthropocenae*, required to confront head-on the deep socio-ecological crisis of the Anthropocene (Kotzé & French, 2018).

[141]The lack of such *grundnorm* has created a vacuum that is filled with utilitarian, state-centred and other traditional considerations that undermine environmental concerns in many instances worldwide.

[142]A network of over 100 lawyers representing almost 40 nationalities and chaired by Laurent Fabius, the president of Climate Change COP21, the current President of the French Constitutional Council, and recently appointed United Nations (UN) Environment Patron on Environmental Governance.

known, reorganized and rebuilt in the struggles for economic and political mastery in rapidly changing circumstances" (Dalby, 2016, p. 34). Thus, Kotzé and French believe that a globally binding instrument such as the Pact might play a potentially significant normative and immense governance role, on the navigating humanity through the Anthropocene (Kotzé & French, 2018). Still, it is my opinion that Article 2 of the Global Pact by claiming a 'duty to take care of the environment': "Every State or international institution, every person, natural or legal, public or private, has the duty to take care of the environment. To this end, everyone contributes at their own levels to the conservation, protection and restoration of the integrity of the Earth's ecosystem". The wording of this article seems to be in line with the Earth system approach, although the wording corresponds to a diplomatic and political instrument using a less academic terminology.

In fact, with a less critical view, there have been welcoming perspectives for the Pact within the context of the Sustainable Development Agenda and the relevance within the context of the implementation of the ambitious global environmental concerns.[143] What should be mentioned here for its significant role towards building our conceptual framework are Articles 12 and 1 of the Global Pact.

Article 12 aims at presenting education as a horizontal enabler of sustainable development based on environmental protection. In fact, the Global Pact devotes one specific article to education and training, by focusing excessively on environmental education:

> The Parties shall ensure that environmental education, to the greatest possible extent, is taught to members of the younger generation as well as to adults, in order to inspire in everyone a responsible conduct in protecting and improving the environment. The Parties shall ensure the protection of freedom of expression and information in environmental matters. They support the dissemination by mass media of information of an educational nature on ecosystems and on the need to protect and preserve the environment.

It is my opinion that the article, considering its potential could have focused far beyond environmental education and environmental matters concerns going beyond such reductive wording taking into account more advanced doctrinal approaches of global environmental law today. Despite the fact that this version of education and training, within the context of environmental issues, is improved with regard to the wording of Article 12 of the Paris Agreement in which the role of education and training for combatting climate change is endorsed together with equal significance to public awareness, and public participation, by integrating all these horizontal enablers under one article. The only critic that could be made to Article 12 of the Global Pact is that its wording could have gone beyond 'environmental' issues to embrace sustainability concerns, or as it has been argued,[144] an Earth System approach, more adequate to a multidimensional vision of sustainable development that renders environmental issues instrumental to a more coherent global framework

[143] See further, Parejo Navajas (2018).

[144] See Kotzé and French (2018).

aiming at environmental protection in its most advanced version. This project is timidly favoured by the wording of Article 1 of the Pact:

> Every person has the right to live in an ecologically sound environment adequate for their health, well-being, dignity, culture and fulfilment.

The resonance given to culture in this article is not indifferent, and gives voice to one of the challenges any sustainability model has, an adequate level of environmental preservation adequate for any specific cultural context and the fulfilment of human cultural needs.[145]

4.4 The Drivers of Transformation: The Impossibility to Find a Unique Successful Formula

The promising role of education (and culture) for nation-building identity and for a successful establishment of the rule of law made education policy compulsory education and, consequently compulsory schooling has proved repeatedly to be key device for the development and transmission of a sense of different values, such as 'nationhood' (Lowe, 1999, p. 231). Not by chance, the legal mandate of establishing compulsory education, despite of its international acceptance, is bounded to the national legal sphere; and it is the central government that establishes the National Curriculum. The 'National Curriculum' sets out the content matter, which must be taught in the different subjects in public authority-supported schools worldwide. At international level, the prominent role of education for the reconstruction of peace and the transmission of global values has been endorsed since the Second World War. Thus, the importance of this policy area has been increasingly supported by the growing number of International Governmental Organisations actively engaged with education and cultural concerns. Among the first organisations engaged with educational and cultural matters after 1945 were UNESCO, The Council of Europe, the Treaty of Brussels and its successor,[146] and the Western European Union (WEU), until its termination in 2010.[147] A common feature to all of them is their united founding mission to deal with education and cultural matters all together aligned in importance with security, peace and economic prosperity. The

[145]However, this is of course, open to further interpretation.

[146]The Treaty was signed on 17 March 1948 by Belgium, France, Luxembourg, the Netherlands and the United Kingdom, the members of the Western Union, as an expansion to the Treaty of Dunkirk, signed between Britain and France the previous year to guard against possible German or Soviet aggression after the end of the Second World War.

[147]When the EU gained its own mutual defence clause upon the entry into force of the Treaty of Lisbon in 2009, the members of the WEU, who were also EU Member States regarded the WEU as redundant. Consequently, the modified Treaty of Brussels was terminated on 31 March 2010, followed by the closure of WEU bodies on 30 June 2011.

European Communities[148] and the Organisation for Economic Co-operation and Development (OECD) would follow.[149] Nevertheless, the education and cultural policies of the Nation States members to these different organisations have developed in a highly uncoordinated manner subsequently.

The European Communities (EU today) history on involvement on education as policy area has been often described as a leitmotif for national defence of the systemic borders and the sovereignty of Nation State systemic control (Corbett, 2006; Gornitzka, 2006; Murphey, 2003), and political competence on education issues, not even in subsidiary manner were originally an interest of the European Communities founding treaties, but the same cannot be said with regard to culture.

Still, the most recent global trend has been to claim the establishment of educational concerns and political activity on this field beyond the nation state, and the same concern, in a more prolific manner has been applied to the cultural field. The millennium played a decisive role for this trend launching overarching strategies worldwide. The period 2005–2014 has been declared as the UN Decade of Education for SD[150] with the goal of integrating the principles, values, and practices of sustainable development into all aspects of education and learning. An urgently needed integration of SD principles into educational and cultural needs was boosted upon the recognition of facing the challenge of poverty eradication, changing consumption and production patterns and protecting and managing the natural resources of our planet that are our children's and future generations patrimony.

During the summit opening the UN Decade for SD, different stakeholders, and the government expressed the desire for Higher Education Institutions to expand their activity in response to sustainable development.[151] Considering the proactive component of SD policies this is key for the crucial role that has been assigned to Higher Education Institutions to expand their activity in response to SD most recently. Within the European context, this has been clearly pointed through the Bologna process (Garben, 2011). The contribution of universities to the sustainability agenda is expressed in the growing activity and the importance given to transdisciplinary research and knowledge exchange activity. Today, transdisciplinary methodology has been embedded within teaching and learning provisions aligned with achieving sustainable environmental, social and economic development. Research and collaboration initiatives under this light, have helped to reaffirm the vital role of the indigenous peoples in SD, and pay special attention to the developmental needs of Small Island Developing States and the Least Developed

[148]Treaty establishing the European Economic Community, Rome, 25 March 1957; Treaty establishing the European Atomic Energy Community, Rome 25 March 1957.

[149]Convention on the Organisation for Economic Co-operation and Development, Paris 14 December 1960.

[150]UNDSD, Johannesburg Summit, 4 September 2002.

[151]The results in Higher Education are more evident than at other learning stages, see for instance, Molthan-Hill et al. (2015); and the work of the Pedagogical Research in the Responsible and Sustainable Research Lab, available at: https://www.ntu.ac.uk/research/groups-and-centres/groups/responsible-and-sustainable-business-lab-rsb-lab-research-group.

Countries.[152] Initiatives such as Education for Sustainable Human Development give evidence of these significant developments, especially at higher education level.[153]

Actually, I would dare to say that the most constructive partnership for change and for achievement of common global goals, which are part of a multi-layered system of governance that is the new shape of our international relations, is brought by universities partnerships and research endeavours helping to face the most important sustainability challenges of the twenty-first century.[154] The UN Decade on Education for SD enhanced new approaches and marked a new culture of education and a new direction in teaching and learning of content and methods. On an international level it is increasingly acknowledged that Education for SD (ESD) represents a main element of high-quality education (Dannenberg & Grapentin, 2016, p. 7), this is confirmed by the inclusion of ESD in a growing variety of International documents, agreements and roadmaps for global action, being the landmark of all, the 2030 Agenda for SD.[155]

This is why a unique solution on the best driver for transformation would not be possible, but in 're-visioning education and learning for the future' it is important to build upon the legacy of past analyses.[156] Thus, two landmark UNESCO publications, *Learning to Be: The World of education today and tomorrow* (1972), the 'Faure Report'; and *Learning: The Treasure within* (1996), the 'Delors Report', help us to rethink the end scope of education today and the re-organisation of learning. The 'Faure report' (1972), established the two interrelated notions of the 'learning society' and 'lifelong learning' at a time when traditional education systems were being challenged. The paradigm shift started already in the seventies. As technological progress and social change accelerated, the report said, no one could expect that a person's initial education would serve them throughout their life. The already established institutions (i.e., schools) would be supplemented by other aspects of social life where learning contexts could develop, this is, social institutions, the work environment, leisure and the media. It affirmed lifelong education as the keystone of educational policies in both developing and developed countries (UNESCO, 2015).[157] The 'Delors report' introduced seven different tensions generated by technological, economic and social change that are still applicable today in front of the most challenging social changes. They include tensions between (1) the global and the local; (2) the universal and the particular; (3) tradition and modernity; (4) the spiritual and the material; (5) long term and short-term considerations; (6) the need for competition and the ideal of equality of opportunity; (7) and the expansion of

[152]See further, UNDSD Johannesburg Summit, 2002.

[153]See further, Landorf et al. (2008).

[154]See further on this topic, Caniglia et al. (2017), Molthan-Hill et al. (2015) and Gough et al. (2017).

[155]See further, UNESCO (2014a) Shaping the Future we want; UNESCO (2014b) Roadmap for Implementing the Global Action Programme on ESD; UNESCO (2014c) The Muscat Agreement.

[156]See UNESCO (2015) Rethinking Education.

[157]See further, Medel-Añonuevo, Oshako, and Mauch (2001).

knowledge and our capacity to assimilate it. As the UNESCO report (UNESCO, 2015) remarks itself, these seven tensions remain useful perspectives from which to view the current dynamics of social transformation.

UNESCO report remain a valid reference point because they have always presented analyses and recommendations that were more humanistic and people centred than other market-driven studies that are increasingly part of the reform movements of the time. The reform movements and the critical approaches are part of the idiosyncrasy of education and its challenges. Education, considering its recognition and importance today at every level of human development and in every ambit, covers 'life-long learning' and today we can actually say along with Murdoch and Miller (2011) that we are going through a 'learning explosion' boosted by all the digital innovations of our time an apparently accessible to everyone. This opens the door to the risk of transforming education in another big business of our time considering how much global education industry is growing the, very much well-established and visible at higher education level.

I believe that a stronger legal recognition of the educational challenges should be built in connection with cultural problems and cultural solutions at once, including life-long learning and non-formal education initiatives as well. The whole sector (from public administration level view) formal and informal, has been very much influenced by addressing the idea that educational systems today contribute to social inequalities, consequently ignoring educational needs of students in disadvantaged areas or, students living in poor countries has drastic consequences for a successful sustainable future. At the same time, educational opportunities are highly concentrated among the most prosperous, thus turning training and education opportunities very exclusive. The public sector policy addresses minimum standards and does not integrate cultural heritage concerns that are relevant for life long preservation and quality of life. This is a basic challenge that goes hand in hand today with the challenges posed by: (1) the lack of recognitions of cultural diversity that is inherent to nation-states, and today it is the result of greater migration and mobility; (2) Current patterns of consumption and economic growth. Such patterns of consumption have helped to merchandise educational goods (languages, music, sport), and the lack of coordinated policy approaches that integrate the need for certain pedagogical programs with neuroscience studies[158] is boosting a system in which technology has basically occupied all the room for innovation, and the rest is left to private opportunities.

The report launched by UNESCO (2015) builds on its preceding work and 'rethinks education following the idea of 'a global common good' and places sustainable development as a central concern, by addressing such challenges that our poly interventions would have to boost through legal constrains and structural changes involving institutional change.

[158]Considering the introduction of school curricula activities based on the well-being of the child and the detrimental influence of digital devices at an early age. See further, Spitzer (2013).

International Conventions call for interdisciplinary action and collaboration mechanisms as the most urgent and valid solutions. In 2003, when UNESCO adopted the Convention for the Safeguarding of the Intangible Cultural Heritage acknowledging and including traditions or living expressions inherited from our ancestors and passed to our descendants, such as oral traditions, performing arts, social practices, rituals, festive events, knowledge and practices concerning nature and the universe, or the knowledge and skills to produce traditional crafts, was also claiming for the need to raise awareness about its importance for future generations which is the essence of sustainable development (according to the World Commission on Environment and Development 1987). This cultural concern today should go along with a growing recognition of cultural diversity considering "the dramatic increase in cultural and religious chauvinism and in identity-based political mobilization and violence. Terrorism, drug related violence, wars and internal conflicts and internal conflicts [...] raise questions for education in its capacity to shape values and attitudes for living together" (UNESCO, 2015).[159]

What is undeniable is the driving role for transformation that has been recently transferred to cultural and education matters. This is timidly endorsed by different soft law instruments and policy agendas at EU level that enshrine for the first time, not only the necessary joint action of education for the preservation of cultural heritage and common EU identities, but the necessary crosscutting action and the bottom up approaches in which action from different stakeholders becomes crucial.[160]

The growing awareness that culture and education play a crucial role in sustainability is already an extension of the role that culture and education play in development. For decades, Scientist and international UN agencies like UNESCO have been focusing on the role of culture and cultural diversity in the overall societal development and political agendas. There is a long list of UNESCO documents, programmes and conventions underlining the interrelation of culture and sustainability. Somehow, along those lines the process of mainstreaming environmental values in the context of liberal democracies has shaped modern ideas about sustainability. Caradonna (2015, p. 90) suggests that the most significant achievement of the environmental movement in the 1960s was establishing "the environment" as a conceptual prism through which to view the world and humanity's place in it. Today, what it has been called postenvironmentalism follows two principal directions: (1) the realist trend, which claims that solutions to environmental problems can be provided by the advancement of scientific knowledge and technical measures (most notably regulatory norms or market-based instruments); and the (2) constructivist trend, based on the idea that appropriate solutions to environmental problems require

[159]The Report provides data concerning the amount of children, 30 million, who are deprived of their right to a basic education because of the violence patterns. The consequence of this deprivation is the generation of uneducated adults who are often ignored in development policies (UNESCO, 2015, pp. 16–17).

[160]See further EYCH (2018).

a radical change in cultural attitudes and behaviours (e.g., the Agenda 21 provisions provided by UN Summit in Rio de Janeiro in 1992) (Certomà, 2016, p. 113). This is to say that since Agenda 21 there has been a radical change worldwide. When referred to the European context, the changes have been mainly brought to local administrative level. The way local administration acts. It has increasingly focused its action towards favouring social change and governmental policies that favour the environment within specific social and economic conditions favouring public procurement contracts involvement of the third sector, and organised civic action. The theoretical orientation of this study is aligned with the constructivist trend of the postenvironmentalism era (Certomà, 2016), and I believe that there is a global momentum for culture and education coming from the global consensus on sustainability action having at its core global ecological concerns but local action. Our current governance structures have open the path for mainstreaming possible transformations through many different ways.

The founding roles of education and culture that can be easily validated by active political action following the path of implementing our Global Agenda[161] should be taken by our governments as a departing framework of action to be worked out to increasingly hail organised civil society movements, people, and community action to attain the goals that refer to the horizontal enablers of sustainable development. We should not only "ensure that all learners acquire the knowledge and skills needed to promote sustainable development, including among others through education for sustainable development sustainable lifestyles, human rights, gender equality, promotion of a culture of peace and non-violence, global citizenship and appreciation of cultural diversity and of culture's contribution to sustainable development" (SDG 4.7), we should render those requirements part of our constitutional interpretations. It is not by chance that there is for the first time in such an ambitious and unparalleled global agenda on development an explicit mention to culture embedded into educational aims. It means many things. Culture, integrated within the right policy framework can surely gain power in policy-making mechanisms and related processes, but we need further action for this with an immediate reform of financial budgets at national and local level for culture accessibility and management and also for a major integration of culture into educational policy, as well as major attention to the legal means needed for a structural reform on both sectors.

Hawkes (2001) suggests that for public planning to be more effective under the sustainability paradigm, its methodology should include an integrated framework of cultural evaluation along similar lines to those being developed for social, environmental and economic impact assessment. Innumerable meetings and documents regarding education build up the resources of a rich governance framework that should develop further. The Incheon Declaration for Education 2030 (May 2015) has been instrumental to shape the Sustainable Development Goal on Education to "Ensure inclusive and equitable quality education and promote lifelong learning opportunities for all". It entrusted UNESCO with the leadership, coordination and

[161]UN 2030 Agenda for Sustainable Development.

monitoring of the Education 2030 agenda, and it calls upon the Global Education Monitoring (GEM) Report to provide independent monitoring and reporting of the Sustainable Development Goal on education (SDG4), and on education in the other SDGs, until 2030.

The World Conference on Education for Sustainable Development (ESD) (Aichi-Nagoya, Japan, 2014) focused on generating and scaling up ESD action at all levels and in all areas of education, and in all sustainable developments sectors. UNESCO's Global Action Programme (GAP) was launched at the Conference but it had already been endorsed by UNESCO's 37th General Conference (November 2013) and acknowledged by UN General Assembly Resolution A/RES/69/2011 as official follow-up to the UN Decade of Education for SD (2005–2014), led by UNESCO (2005). The mission of the Global Action Programme relates to a vision of the world "where everybody has the opportunity to benefit from education and learn the values, behaviour and lifestyles required for a sustainable future and for positive societal transformation". The following Action areas will be furthered by maintaining a global network of ESD partners that have committed to promoting ESD action: (1) Advancing policy; (2) Transforming learning and training environments; (3) Building capacities of educators and trainers; (4) Empowering and mobilizing youth; (5) Accelerating sustainable solutions at local level.

Under this light, Education for sustainable development goes beyond environmental education approaches, it has to do more with an ecological transformation that embraces every aspect of humanity, and it is much related with creating awareness and progress of social knowledge. Definitions are not free from controversy, as much as the concept itself. However, Chapter 36 of Agenda 21 at the Earth Summit in Rio de Janeiro in 1992 is the landmark Declaration for a first conceptual grasp of ESD. It was at a later stage defined by UNESCO as: "Education for SD is an emerging but dynamic concept that encompasses a new vision of education that seeks to empower people of all ages to assume responsibility for creating a sustainable future" (UNESCO, 20002: I). Yet, despite the fact that education has been seen for decades (in the public policy rhetoric) as a key transformative factor in the improvement of the environment and our future sustainability, very few countries and communities have moved to integrate ESD into their educational curriculum, let alone implemented it as the basis of a reorienting or transforming education (Landorf, Doscher, & Rocco, 2008), and when ESD, EfS or EE has been implements has proved to be not sufficient. Outside HE solutions, in Europe, schooling for SD counts on some successful experiences, introducing SD in school curricula following the commands of the UN Decade of Education for SD trying to move schools towards a different Education philosophy (Jucker & Mathar, 2015). These experiences are very much based on enhancing environmental education, without bringing into the fore a real institutional engagement with the complex interactions that should take place between people and their environments.

This role assigned to education I am claiming it should be echoed into the realm of culture and aim at assisting a paradigm change. It is the "European Cultural Convention of the Council of Europe" (1954) insisting on the role of culture "in the progress of social knowledge, the understanding of others and the transmission of values" that advocates for culture's transformation role. In this only in this spirit that the content and meaning of sustainable development can witness a paradigm shift with significant focus on the different social dimensions of human development, which include education and culture (as discussed above) in joint venture to develop community's ability to improve economy, environment and social concerns.

In 2001, UNESCO's Universal Declaration on Cultural Diversity launched a process that has never stopped (although the UN 2030 Agenda on SD proclaims cultural concerns in a very timid wording) aimed to add culture as the fourth dimension of sustainability. During this process within the context of Europe that will be analysed further below, an important contribution for the sustainability of culture was also made by the Council of European Union through the Digital Agenda for Europe and in particular through the European digital library, *Europeana*. Behind this contribution, there was the understanding that cultural heritage was one of the best solutions to preserve social, and collective memory and of course extend public access, which is indispensable for heritage preservation and access for current and future generations. Considering the mission of the museums to preserve cultural heritage and foster their sustainability is also crucially important, the International Council of Museums (ICOM) latest initiatives have pursued the promotion of cultural sustainability at global level.

International, supranational, regional, national, local objectives with regard to sustainability will continue to evolve, but the basic understanding of the interdependence of the world in front of the most urgent problems of humanity today in the Anthropocene, such as climate change, global migrations fluxes, armed conflicts and excessive use of natural resources have proved to need universal solutions that are useful if guided by solidarity concerns and deploy creative and democratic solutions, even if they should be implemented locally. However, we are still concerned with our political instability, especially within the European context without giving support to integral national reforms of education and cultural institutions. The humanist approach of legal and economic science should come out in this context, to avoid isolated realities of transformation, instead of a whole movement of structural changes into our institutional and legal systems, especially at public administration level. For, this, an improved focus on how to institutionalised education initiatives that bring benefits to communities at local level should help, and we need partnerships, comparative approaches and new conceptual frameworks to improve the possibilities of structural changes, even in the current epistemology of our legal systems (Capra & Mattei, 2015). In fact, community developments in educational projects have shown all over the world to be an effective solution to devote investment in semi-public goods, or public-private partnerships.

The initiatives leaded by the Association for Development of Education in Africa (ADEA) in local communities (that is sometimes the only way to approach schooling and alphabetisation in a continent suffering from despair and drastic public corruption, still in so much need on development assistance from third countries) show evidence of the importance of organising policy dialogue between policymakers, donors and local actors to elaborate strategic medium-term plans, which could be more helpful and realistic in terms of achieving immediate objectives of alphabetisation (enshrined today by SDG 4). In Africa, this tailor made approaches have helped to extend basic education from six to nine years in many African countries. Instead, increasing internal capabilities (especially through higher education) could proof to be dangerous in the sense of destroying the sense of belonging to a specific local community that does not offer clear professional career paths once capabilities have been improved at higher education level.[162] This commonly happens in many parts of the world as part of the globalisation trends that have of course homogenised our cultural patterns and job market expectations with some detrimental consequences. The topic is complex, but fascinating.[163]

Two initiatives that are part of the economic approach of degrowth,[164] referring to the educational foundations of this movement and the need for contrasting economic, social and cultural globalisation, to come back to the wealth of our local cultural contexts, are worth mentioning here. These initiatives emerge with the spirit to avoid destructive dynamics of natural wealth and human resources: *Navdanya* International and the *Swaraj* University. They are both settled in India. Both institutional initiatives invest on natural resources from the local land and on human resources as the custodians of the natural resources from the local land and on human resources as the custodians of the available natural resources. *Navdanya* International promotes a new agricultural and economic paradigm, a culture of food for health, where ecological responsibility and economic justice replace the present greed, consumerism and competition that have become dominant in society. It aims at regaining the common good as a foundation for a renewed sense of community, solidarity and culture of peace by investing on education and research.[165] *Swaraj* University is another informal (in the sense of being outside of the formal institutionalised Central State education structure) and significant example of local development empowering youth through education in India. It was born in 2010 as a two-year learning programme for youth. The focus of the programme is on self-designed learning and on ecological sustainability and social justice. The programme is as much about developing the capacities and confidence we need to create and pursue our unique learning paths as it is about strengthening the leadership capacity and right livelihood opportunities in communities that are far from being located in big cities in the India of our times.[166] The programme takes inspiration from the spirit extended to all of the activities of Udaipur as a Learning City. Many 'private' spaces, services and goods have been brought back into the service of the public/community goods. Udaipur locals have hosted workshops in their homes; they have opened their art galleries, offices, kitchens and farms to visitors; they have brought

---

[162]See further on this topic, Oppong (2018).

[163]See further, Reyes (2018), Gunasekara (2004), Jain (2010) and Jain and Jain (2008).

[164]Also associated to the global movement of the "Economic of happiness", rooting its theoretical foundations on Sérge Latouche works on degrowth.

[165]See further info accessing to their website: https://www.navdanyainternational.it/en/about-us-navdanya-international.

[166]See further info accessing to their website: http://www.swarajuniversity.org.

their knowledge and talents to participate in new collective experiments in rooftop farming, rainwater harvesting, mural-making; they have freecycled their leftover waste materials (scraps of wood, rubber tire tubes, cloth scraps, old wedding cards, etc.) for workshops with kids—all without one rupee being exchanged or demands for self-promotion in the media. This kind of volunteer spirit has enabled Shikshantar's budget to go down every year, while the movement expands into new individuals, families, neighbourhoods, organisations and places (Jain & Jain, 2008).

This inspiring 'tale' from Udaipur where local economy has probably suffered a drastic hijacking from the global market economy seems to have no correlation to any given European reality where the global market culture seems to be more embedded, and where sustainability principles embedded into educational practices should take other shape, nonetheless these experiences should be of great inspiration for European law makers too considering the drastic effects of cultural homogenisation and the rapid losses experienced by local knowledge.

In Europe is also difficult to break up with traditional law making in the education and cultural field. There is little communication between those who develop education and cultural policy and those who implement it. It is important to note that some researchers have even argued that there is little use to attribute UNESCO programs such as "Education for All" to issues of sustainable development in countries like Germany where basic education is realised (Dannenberg & Grapentin, 2016) based on applying ESD from a national perspective, without necessarily associating such national approach to the sovereignty of States, but with other specific issues, such as social structures and existing expertise and professionalism (Dannenberg & Grapentin, 2016). Those examples and contrasting ideas taken from the global arena, enshrining opposing realities show us clearly how a valid unique solution is not possible but give us the key information needed: Community action for sustainable change based on the best available local knowledge and experiences is the most suitable solution for a paradigm change that would affect as many levels of the education and cultural systems as possible.

The need to provide the basic learning instrument for transforming our current social structures and the existing expertise and professionalism to face sustainability and improve our sustainability models are urgent. Integration of culture and education should be mainstreamed by a structural legal reform applied to the education and the cultural sector for a real transformation of our current societies under the light of sustainability. However, in a time when "[t]here is more public spending on education than ever before (though spending as a proportion of GDP has remained static at around 5 per cent in most of the wealthier countries since the 1960s and has even clipped slightly in recent years) yet social inequality has persist" (Roche, 2017) the local context seems to be the right place to start fighting inequalities and deficiencies whilst the global scenario is also endorsing the importance of local action even if cooperation mechanisms (often) are better designed at other governance level.

Today it is possible to affirm that education, long-life learning issues are somehow part of all the institutional structures, and even if education "*ni le problème ni la solution*",[167] the paradox lives with us and it has been the motto of many distinctive political discourses, in which the priorities of political intervention when formulated at the public level seem to be 'education, education, education',[168] but at the practical level, implementation has been limited to a curricular activity on SD education at school level. An important example of how a successful program on ESD introducing curricula-based lessons can work can be found in Germany[169]; but the real challenge of our century involves a bigger transformation of educational and cultural institutions, to be leaded by legal empowerment to respond to real human needs for participation, sociability and ecological shared responsibility.

References

Acheson, K., & Maule, C. (2004). Convention on cultural diversity. *Journal of Cultural Economics, 28*, 243–256.

Anderson, V., Datta, R., Dyck, S., Kayira, J., & Mcvittie, J. (2016). Meaning and implications of culture in sustainability education research. *Journal of Environmental Education, 47*(1), 1–18.

Asara, V., Otero, I., Demaria, F., & Corbera, E. (2015). Socially sustainable degrowth as a social-ecological transformation: Repoliticizing sustainability. *Sustainability Science, 10*(3), 375–384. Retrieved from https://link.springer.com/article/10.1007/s11625-015-0321-9

Becerril Atienza, B. (2015). *Hacía una Política Cultural de la Unión Europea*. Aranzadi.

Bekemans, L. (1990). "European integration and cultural policies. Analysis of a dialectic polarity", in European University Institute Working Papers, (ECS n. 90/1), Florence.

Bertelsmann Stiftung. (2013). *Winning strategies for a sustainable future*. Reinhard Mohn Prize 2013. Gütersloh, Germany: Bertelsmann Stiftung. http://proxy.library.oregonstate.edu/

Bollier, D., & Weston, B. (2013). Establishing commons trusts to manage common assets for future generations. In Bailey, Farrell, & Mattei (Eds.), *Protecting future generations through commons* (Trends in Social Cohesion, No. 26). Council of Europe Publishing.

Bosselmann, K. (2010). Outlook: The Earth Charter- A model constitution for the world? In K. Bosselmann & J. R. Engel (Eds.), *The Earth Charter: A framework for global governance* (pp. 239–255). Amsterdam, the Netherlands: KIT Publishers.

Bruner, C. M. (2008). Culture, sovereignty, and Hollywood: UNESCO and the future of trade in cultural products. *International Law and Politics, 40*, 351–436.

Burri, M. (2009). Trade versus culture in the digital environment: An old conflict in need of a new definition. *Journal of International Economic Law, 12*, 17–62.

Burri, M. (2014). The trade versus culture discourse: Tracing its evolution in global law. In V. Vadi & B. De Witte (Eds.), *Culture and international economic law*. Routledge.

[167]This is the title of a popular journal contribution to *Le Monde diplomatique*, by Renaud Lambert and Allan Popelard (October 2013); where they argue about the success of the idea that 'the education system could be the remedy for the ills of society', still there is no solution for education, nor for the ills of society.

[168]Lambert and Popelard (2013) *Ibid supra note*; give account of the public speech of British Prime Minister Anthony Blair (October 1997) in which he states: "*Ask me what the three priorities of my government will be and I will answer you: education, education, education*".

[169]See further, Mathar (2015).

Caniglia, G., Luederitz, C., Groβ, M., Muhr, M., John, B., Keeler, L. W., et al. (2017). Transnational Collaboration for sustainability in higher educaiton: lessons from a systematic review. *Journal of Cleaner Production, 168*, 764–779.
Capra, F., & Mattei, U. (2015). *The ecology of law. Toward a legal system in tune with nature and community*. Berrett and Koehler.
Casini, L. (2010). "Italian Hours": The globalization of cultural property law. *Jean Monnet working paper* 11/10.
Casini, L. (2018). "The future of (international) cultural heritage law", Guest Editorial. *International Journal of Constitutional Law, 16*(1), 1–10.
Collard, P., & Witte, R. (2015). *Creative alliances for Europe*. Report prepared by the BKJ (Germany) and CEE (England) funded by Stiftung Mercator.
Concilio, L., & Rausell, T. (2019). Cities as enablers of innovation. In G. Concilio & I. Tosoni (Eds.), *Innovation capacity and the city. The enabling role of design*. Springer Open.
Corbett, A. (2005). *Universities and the Europe of knowledge. Ideas, institutions and policy entrepreneurship in European Union Higher Education Policy, 1955–2005*. Houndmills: Palgrave Macmillan.
Costa-Lascoux. (1995). Cultural diversity or multiculturalism? In C. Camilleri (Ed.), *Difference and cultures in Europe*. Council of Europe Press.
Council of Europe Framework Convention on the Value of Cultural Heritage for Society- CETS-Treaty No. 199. Faro, 27/10/2005. https://www.coe.int/en/web/conventions/full-list/-/conventions/treaty/199
Craufurd Smith, R. (2007). The UNESCO Convention on the protection and promotion of cultural expressions: Building a new world information and communication order? *International Journal of Communication, 1*, 24–55.
D'Alisa, G., Demaria, F., & Kallis, G. (2015). *Degrowth: A vocabulary for a new era*. London: Routledge.
Dalby, S. (2016). Framing the anthropocene: The good, the bad and the ugly. *The Anthropocene Review, 3*(1), 33–51.
Dannenberg, S., & Grapentin, T. (2016). Education for sustainable development-learning for transformation. The example of Germany. *Journal of Future Studies, 20*(3), 7–20.
Decision 2017/864/EU of the EU Parliament and of the Council of 17 May 2017 on European Year of Cultural Heritage (2018).
Dessein, J., Soini, K., Fairclough, G., & Horlings, L. (Eds.). (2015). *Culture in, for and as Sustainable Development*. Conclusions from the COST Action IS1007 Investigating Cultural Sustainability. Published by University of Jyväskylä.
Dewey, J. (2007). *Experience and education*. New York: Simon and Schuster.
Erlewin, S. (2017). Culture, development and sustainability: The cultural impact of development and culture's role in sustainability. In Albert, Bandarin, & Pereira (Eds.), *Going beyond perceptions in sustainability in heritage studies* (n. 2). Springer.
Faas, D., Hajisoteriou, C., & Angelides, P. (2014). Intercultural education in Europe: Policies, practices and trends. *British Educational Research Journal, 40*(2).
Filho, L. (2010). Climate change at universities. Results of a world survey. In W. Leal-Filho (Ed.), *Universities and climate change: Introducing climate change to university* (pp. 1–19). Springer. Retrieved from http://www.springer.com/de/book/9783642107504
Garben, S. (2011). *EU higher education law. The Bologna process and harmonisation by Stealth*. Kluwer Law International.
Garben, S. (2015). Confronting the competence conundrum: Democratising the EU through an expansion of its legislative powers. *Oxford Journal of Legal Studies, 35*(1), 55–89.
Göpel, M. (2016). *The great mindshift. How a new economic paradigm and sustainability transformations go hand in hand*. Springer Open.
Gornitzka, A. (2006). The open method of coordination as practice-A watershed in European Education Policy? *Working Paper*, No. 16, ARENA project. Retrieved from http://www.arena.uio.no

Gornitzka, A. (2018). Organising soft governance in hard times. The unlikely survival of the open method of coordination in the EU Education Policy. *European Studies, 3*(1), 235–255.

Gunasekara, C. (2004). The third role of Australian universities in human capital formation. *Higher Education Policy Management, 26*(3), 329–343.

Hah, M. (2006). "A clash of cultures?" The UNESCO Diversity Convention and international trade law. *Journal of International Economic Law, 9*, 515–552.

Hajnal, G. (2015). Public administration education in Europe: Continuity or reorientation. *Teaching Public Administration, 33*(2), 95–114.

Haraway, D. (2004). *The Haraway reader*. New York: Routledge.

Hawkes, J. (2001). *The fourth pillar of sustainability. Culture's essential role in public planning*. Edited by common ground publishing Pty Ltd. in association with the Cultural Development Network (Vic).

Illich, I. (1971). *Deschooling society*. Retrieved from http://ournature.org/

Jain, M., & Jain, S. (Eds.). (2008). Reclaiming the gift culture. *Artwork: Sunny Gandhrva Shikshantar*. The Peoples' Institute for Rethinking Education and Development. Retrieved from www.swaraj.org/shikshantar

Janna, H. (1972). Future policy. *Education and Culture, 19*, 14.

Jickling, B., & Sterling, S. (Eds.). (2017). *Post-sustainability and environmental education. Remaking education for the future*. Palgrave Macmillan.

Jucker, R., & Mathar, R. (Eds.). (2015). *Schools for sustainable development in Europe. Concepts, policies and educational experiences at the end of the UN Decade of Education for Sustainable Development*. Springer.

Kaufmann, N., Sanders, C., & Wortmann, J. (2019). Building new foundations: The future of education from a degrowth perspective. *Sustainability Science, 14*, 931–941.

Kothari, A., Demaria, F., & Acosta, A. (2014). Buen vivir, degrowth and ecological Swaraj: Alternatives to development and the green economy. *Development*, Springer.

Kotzé, L. J., & French, D. (2018). A critique of the Global Pact for the environment: A stillborn initiative or the foundation for *Lex Anthropocenae*? *International Environmental Agreements, 18*, 811. https://doi.org/10.1007/s10784-018-9417-x

Kroeber, A. L., & Kluckhohn, C. (1952). Culture: A critical review of concepts and definitions. *Papers of the Peabody Museum of American Archeology and Ethnology, Harvard University* (Vol. 47, p. 18).

Landorf, H., Doscher, S., & Rocco, T. (2008). Education for sustainable human development. Towards a definition. *Theory and Research in Education, 6*(2), 221–236.

Latouche, S. (2009). *Farewell to growth*. Cambridge: Polity.

Leal-Filho, W., Morgan, E., Godoy, E., Azeiteiro, U. M., Bacelar-Nicolau, P., Ávila, L. V., et al. (2018). Implementing climate change research at universities: Barriers, potential and actions. *Journal of Cleaner production, 170*, 269–270.

Lowe, R. (1999). Education and national identity. *History of Education, 28*(3), 231–233.

Mathar, R. (2015). Project variety and established structures: Development and actual practice of ESD in Germany. In R. Jucker & R. Mathar (Eds.), *Schooling for Sustainable Development in Europe. Concepts, policies and educational experiences at the end of the UN Decade of Education for Sustainable Development*. Springer.

Medel-Añonuevo, C., Oshako, T., & Mauch, W. (2001). *Revisiting lifelong learning for the 21st century*. Hamburg: UNESCO Institute for Education.

Meyer, L. H., (2012). Introduction. In L. H. Meyer (Ed.), *Intergenerational justice* (pp. xi–xxiv). Farnham: Ashgate.

Molthan-Hill, P. (2015). Making the business care? Intercultural differences in framing economic rationality related to environmental issues. *Critical Perspectives on International Business, 11* (1), 72–91.

Molthan-Hill, P., Worsfold, N., Nagy, G., Leal Filho, W., & Mifsud, M. (2019). Climate Change education for universities: A conceptual framework from an international study. *Journal of Cleaner Production, 226*, 1092–1101.

Moreno Molina, Á. M. (2010). *Urbanismo y Medio Ambiente. Las claves jurídicas del planteamiento urbanístico sostenible*. Tirant Lo Blanch.

Morin, E. (1999). *Seven complex lessons in education for the future*. Retrieved from https://unesdoc.unesco.org/ark:/48223/pf0000117740
Murdoch, M., & Miller, T. (2011). *The learning explosion*. RosettaBooks.
Naranjo, C. (2016). *Changing education to change the world. A new vision of schooling*. Gateways Books & Tapes.
OECD. (2013). *A "Health at a Glance" 2013: OECD Indicators*. Paris: Organisation for Economic Co-operation and Development. http://www.oecd.org/els/health-systems/Health-at-a-Glance-2013.pdf
Oppong, K. C. (2018). The nexus between universities and local development. *Current Research Journal of Social Science, 9*(2), 21–27.
Oriol, M., & Affergan, F. (1995). *Differences and cultures in Europe*. Council of Europe Press.
Palermo, F., & Woelk, J. (2008). *Diritto Costituzionale comparator dei gruppi e delle minoranze*. Padova: Cedam.
Papa Francesco. (2015). *Laudato Si'. Sulla cura della casa comunes*. Lettera encíclica, EDB.
Parejo Alfonso, L. (2016). *Estado y Derecho en proceso de cambios. Las nuevas funciones de regulación y garantía del Estado social de soberanía limitada*. Valéncia: Tirant lo Blanch.
Parejo Navajas, T. (2018). The proposed global pact for the environment: A framework for consistent realisation of the sustainable development goals. *Environmental Policy and Law, 48*(5), 256–262.
Parker, J. (2014). *Critiquing sustainability. Changing philosophy*. Routledge.
Prieto de Pedro, J. (1995). *Cultura, Culturas y Constitución*. Madrid: Editorial Centro de Estudios Culturales.
Prieto de Pedro, J. (2007). Cooperación en la educación, la ciencia y la cultura. In E. Bustamante (Ed.), *La Cooperación Cultura-Comuniación en Iberoamérica*. Madrid: Editoria AECI.
Psychogiopoulou, E. (2018). The cultural open method of coordination: A new but different OMC? *European Papers, 3*(1), 257–279.
Rawls, J. (1971). *A theory of justice*. Oxford: Oxford University Press.
Rawls, J. (1999). *A theory of justice* (Revised edition, 2nd edn.). Oxford University Press.
Rifkin, J. (2004). *The European Dream: How Europe's vision of the future is quietly eclipsing the American Dream*. Tarcherperigree.
Rifkin, J. (2011). *The Third Industrial Revolution. How lateral power is transforming energy, the economy, and the world*. Italian edition published by Mondadori (2012).
Roche, S. (2017). Listening to the grassroots. Bottom-up approaches to lifelong learning. *International Review of Education, 63*, 145–152.
Ruiz Vieytez, E. (2016). Cultural traits as defining elements of minority groups. *The Age of Human Rights Journal, 7*, 6–28.
Sacco, P. L. (2009). Cultural policies and local planning strategies: What is the role of culture in local sustainable development? *Journal of Art Management, Law and Society, 39*, 45–64.
Sacco, P. L. (2011). Culture 3.0: A new perspective for the EU 2014-2020 structural funds programming. *European Expert Network on Culture* Paper, April.
Sacco, P. L., Ferilli, G., & Pedrini, S. (2008). System-wide cultural districts: An introduction from the Italian viewpoint. In S. Kagan & V. Kirchberg (Eds.), *Sustainability: A new frontier for the arts and cultures* (pp. 400–460). Frankfurt A.M.: VAS Verlag.
Sarti, M., & St. John, S. (2019). Raising long-term awareness: EU environmental policy and education. In S. St. John & M. Murphy (Eds.), *Education and public policy in the European Union. Crossing boundaries*. Palgrave Macmillan.
Spitzer, M. (2013). *Demenza Digitale. Come la nuova tecnologia ci rende stupidi*, Corbaccio, translated from the original German version: *Digitale Demenz. Wie wir uns und unsere Kinder um den Verstand bringen (2012).*
Stiglitz, J. E. (2002). *Globalization and its discontents*. W W Norton & Co Inc..
Taylor, J. (2013). *Intergenerational justice: A useful perspective for heritage conservation*. In CEROART. Retrieved from https://journals.openedition.org/ceroart/3510

The European Landscape Convention, European Treaty Series - No. 176. Florence, 20.X.2000. https://www.coe.int/en/web/landscape

Tozzi, M. (2012). Intercultural and multicultural education in Europe and the US. In *Languages in a Global World. Learning for better cultural understanding*. OECD.

UNESCO. (Eds.). (2005). *United Nations Decade of Education for Sustainable Development (2005–2014)*. International Implementation Scheme. Paris. UNESCO. Retrieved from http://unesdoc.unesco.org/images/0014/001486/148654e.pdf

UNESCO. (Eds.). (2014a). *Shaping the future we want*. UN Decade of Education for SD. Final Report. Retrieved from http://unesdoc.unesco.org/images/0023/002301/23017e.pdf

UNESCO. (Eds.). (2014b). *Roadmap for implementing the Global Action Programme on Education for Sustainable Development*. Retrieved from http://unesdoc.unesco.org/images/0023/002305/23051e.pdf

UNESCO. (Eds.). (2014c). *The Muscat Agreement*. Retrieved from http://www.uis.unesco.org/Education/Documents/muscat-agreement-2014.pdf

UNESCO. (Eds.). (2016). Education for people and planet: Creating sustainable futures for all. *Global Education Monitoring Report*, 2016.

UNICEF. (1999). *State of the World's Children (1999)*. Retrieved from http://www.unicef.org/sowc99/sowc99a.pdf

Ura, A., & Zangmo, W. (2012). *An extensive analysis of GNH index*. Thimphu, Bhutan: Centre for Bhutan Studies.

Weiss, E. B. (2010). In *Fairness to future generations. Environment: Science and policy for sustainable development* (Vol. 32, 1990).

Wilson, E. O. (1993). Biophilia and the conservation ethic. In S. R. Kellert & E. O. Wilson (Eds.), *The Biophilia hypothesis*. Washington, DC: Island Press.

Chapter 5
Facing Cultural and Education Challenges at the EU Level: Fragmentation and Multiple Solutions

Abstract Global administrative law has gone through a remarkable process of consolidation in the last years. However, such top-down approaches are not facilitating the paradigm shift our society needs under ecological premises. This chapter starts highlighting some parts of the ecological transition which have rarely been assembled, and it tries to explore specific alternative ways of integrating sustainability contents into educational curricula and, more broadly, of moving towards a holistic, ecologically aware notion of education. There is not a unique institutionalised solution to mainstream policy action in culture and education to facilitate social empowerment, trust and a sense of shared responsibility to lead transformations towards a truly ecological transition in Europe. This has favoured many other pathways. We face fragmented normative realities prompting us to fall into the 'illusion' of counting with a wealthy array of multiple solutions to face hard ecological consequences in the Anthropocene, but the results is a 'handful' of rhetorical discourses (see Sect. 5.2). EU action in these fields has shown to be a valid normative level to push for further engagement despite of the prevalence of soft law instruments (see Sect. 5.3). The last part of the chapter focuses on some cases which show that the paradigm shift the book advocates is not just a hypothetical theory: it has been implemented, mainly at local level, in a few best practices experiences. This bottom-up analysis reveals that the marketisation, capitalisation and digitalisation of culture and education can be successfully counterbalanced. Some case studies give evidence of subtle and extended processes of change in Europe contrasting top down approaches and presenting alternative narratives of success in small-scale dimension (see Sect. 5.4.).

M. D. Sánchez Galera, *Educational and Cultural Challenges of the European Sustainability Model*, https://doi.org/10.1007/978-3-030-38716-7_5

5.1 Challenges at EU Institutional Level. Positive Interplay of Global Public Powers?

The EU role was crucial in shaping the Global 2030 Agenda, which is fully consistent with Europe's vision and has now become the world's blueprint for global sustainable development.[1] In the last two decades, EU administrative law has gone through a process of remarkable development and consolidation. This trend first developed as a body of principles and rules aiming at governing, the action of the EU public powers and the action of the national administrations. Subsequently, it has gradually developed in such a way to apply to the several phenomena of organisational and procedural interconnections among national and EU authorities (Chiti, 2011). This is part of wider phenomena. Institutional challenges at the regulatory level, and change of paradigm has been going on at the global level for some time now. The classical construction of States as the only subjects of International law has long been substituted by a more complex understanding, based on the recognition that the subjects of the global administrative order is a broad variety of global public powers as well as private bodies, namely, States, individuals, NGOs, associations, market actors, communities, etc. Thus, today, the dissemination and feedback between global, regional, national and local policymaking arenas is dynamic and rich. This means that, although the change of paradigm fostering sustainability indicated by the most remarkable International agreements claims for transformation,[2] it also means that there is not a unique path.

Today, the various global regulatory systems and the other subjects of the global legal space, contrary to the traditional assumptions of international law scholarship, make recourse to a wider variety of instruments of administrative decision and management. Actually, legal principles, soft law rules, regulations and practices are enriched by a multiplicity of legitimised sources in this complex global governance scenario. In the cultural and environmental sector, this has become a regular practice. Consequently, global administrative law "cannot be conflated in the classical sources of public international law, but it extensively relies on measures of different types, such as institutional practices, intra-institutional rules and private regulation" (Chiti and Mattarella, 2011, p. 2).[3]

As we have seen, the EUSM is part of such global governance dynamism. Therefore, the EU legal regime is also part of global normative strategies, especially

[1]COM (2016) 739 final, Strasbourg, 22.11.2016. *Next steps for a sustainable European future. European action for sustainability*, p. 3.

[2]For instance, The Paris Agreement and the UN 2030 on SD are strengthening the vision of proactive action and protection for present and future generations with equal attention for society, environment and economic interests, and collaborative and responsible action to protect our Planet Earth.

[3]The authors argue further that, the notion of global administrative law thus describes a new legal reality of rules, institutions and practices that the classical understanding of international relations and international legal regimes fails to recognise or underestimates.

the ones referred to the reduction of emissions. Today, EU public policies nurture a well-equipped assortment of sustainability concerns to have an impact on actions that cooperatively conserve our natural environment whilst following economic development. European economic development considers the constraints and limits of our planet and builds social systems that are peaceful and care for equality and human rights, as well as implementing democratic and participatory political arrangements. The strong ecological concerns, climate change policy leadership and the EU sustainability approach described in Chap. 3 of this book seem to have been assimilated by European legal systems generally speaking, even if MS legal systems are far from harmonised, especially if we consider the most social aspects of the multidimensional version of sustainability ambitions, such as those regarding the social welfare sphere, and in particular, the ones related with labour, education and culture, and of course fiscal policies.

In this light, Ursula von der Leyen, has put forward a new political agenda for the next European Commission 2019–2024: A European Green Deal, finally launched the 13th of December 2013 with Poland opting out from the package of strong energy measures.[4] Her agenda intends to foster a shift in long-lasting investments to transform European economies and connect them globally to similar initiatives in the world, in USA and U.K. This is at first instance a financing strategy on issuance of green bonds. The ambitious package of measures is radical and although, it involves transforming economies through green investments (emissions-free transport infrastructure, renewable energies and the most advanced technologies), it should not work if it is to be focused only on financed-related aspects. Indeed, it also contains guidelines to reinforce Europe's social pillar. Thus, new investments from the European social Fund plus (ESF+) should go to education and research. These sectors should be fuelled to reduce intergenerational inequality and social mobility stimulating a sustainable and inclusive growth. Further than that, funds should be democratised by open and accessible mechanisms. Thus, the funds should be invested through a democratic public works agency, which will involve regional, municipal authorities whose decisions will be supported by citizen's assemblies.

The big shift that this Green Deal should bring to the European scene mainly concerns the reinforcement of Europe's Social Pillar that is still drastically weak despite of the most recent political agendas trying to upgrade our unique social market economy. Garben (2017) rightly states that the balance between 'the economic' and 'the social' has clearly been decided in favour of the former in the EU economic policy. The effects of such imbalance are "so wide-ranging and intrusive, subjecting all other policy areas to this singular logic and these one-sided objectives, that it fundamentally affects the overall socio-economic balance in the EU polity, giving decisive precedence to economic concerns over social ones" (Garben, 2017, p. 47). The EU has not signed the European Social Charter[5] and consequently there

[4]Accessible at: https://ec.europa.eu/commission/sites/beta-political/files/political-guidelines-next-commission_en.pdf.

[5]18 October 1961, (ETS No 35). Turin, 18.X.1961, and its protocols. The European Social Charter (revised) of 1996 embodies in one instrument all rights guaranteed by the Charter of 1961, its

exists a clear lack of uniformity in the acceptance of Charter provisions by the EU Member States. This is the result of the choices made by each State Party when expressing its sovereign will based on the Charter acceptance system. This, in my view, is symptomatic of the weak standpoint of the EU in its social policy if we consider that the Charter was established to offer additional support to the European Convention on Human Rights, which stands principally for civil and political rights, and to broaden the scope of protected fundamental rights to include social and economic rights. EU accession to the European Social Charter would be full of advantages in a period of economic turmoil and imbalance concerning the social concerns that were due to be enhanced with the so-called European Pillar of Social Rights (EPSR) proclaimed by the European Parliament, the Council and the Commission at the "Social Summit" in Gothenburg on 17 November. On top of that, understanding the complexity of threats to the social dimension of sustainability in a holistic manner remains challenging because the issues span across many different areas. A strong European social pillar cannot exist without a set of sociocultural values and attitudes behind it. Thus, the political and economic contexts should be embedded in every social concern.

5.1.1 Sustainability Premises Scarcely Set in Education Policymaking

Educational policymaking in this complex picture includes as many challenges as any other sectors, especially those concerning the social dimension of sustainability. However, the additional problem education and cultural challenges face today is perhaps their neglected role as strong sustainability builders. Actually, sustainability without a clear integration of cultural and educational approaches fails. On this light, the EU action for sustainability misses to address holistically SDGs and maps current and future EU action, by placing too much emphasis on the success of other sectorial policies.

---

additional Protocol of 1988 (ETS No. 128) and adds new rights and amendments adopted by the Parties. It is gradually replacing the initial 1961 treaty. Enforcement of the new Charter is submitted to the same system of control as the Charter of 1961, developed by the Amending Protocol of 1991 (ETS No. 142) and by the Additional Protocol of 1995 providing a system of collective complaints (ETS No. 158). At present the 28 EU Member States are part of the "system" of the Charter treaties (the 1961 Charter, the Additional Protocol of 1988, the Additional Protocol of 1995 and the Revised Charter), albeit with differences regarding the commitments they have entered into: nine states are bound by the 1961 Charter (five of which are also bound by the Protocol of 1988) and 19 by the Revised Charter. With the exception of two states, France and Portugal—which have accepted all the paragraphs of the Revised Charter—the others have ratified a greater or lesser number of provisions of either version of the Charter. Only 14 EU Member States have accepted the 1995 Protocol establishing a system of collective complaints. This results in a variety of situations and contracted obligations. See further, https://www.coe.int/en/web/european-social-charter/european-social-charter-and-european-union-law.

In my view, sustainability ambitions could fail if we do not empower people and society at large for real transformation. In todays' knowledge society, the most important instruments to deal with such empowerment are education and culture, and they should help us to revisit all our institutional, legal and ethical concerns, to invert the pathway of top-down regulation to the path of accessibility, solidarity and collaborative action. We should turn our attention from the excessive focus on the culture of digitalisation and think of important role of the humanities to re-think the modern world.

The Earth Charter, the Paris Agreement, the UN 2030 Global Agenda, bring a new opportunity for the world to think of those challenges, and give a stronger consideration not only to educational concerns,[6] but also to strong participatory and collaborative mechanisms for civil society action, as we have seen in the previous chapters. In fact, the renewed global commitment envisaged in SDG 4 in the UN 2030 Global Agenda "may represent an opportunity to rethink educational governance substantially in order to address the challenges arising from the changing education landscape and to implement more effective and ethical education policies" (Locatelli, 2018).

Attention to these topics under the light of ecological and social welfare concerns should still grow drastically among legal scholars and policymakers in Europe. Although the EUSM counts on a robust policy framework on its cultural heritage, in the case of education policy the strength is (still) placed on mobility and exchange; actually, the European dimension of the international education programs has already been diluted in a global perspective and the external dimension of European mobility programs (as a consequence) has been enhanced. Mobility and skills continue to be promoted and internationalisation has supplanted any other policy intervention concerning action in education. "Symptomatic in this respect is that the Commission proposed to bring all education matters for the period 2014-2020 together into a single programme called "Erasmus for All" because of the widespread recognition of the Erasmus brand name as synonym of Union learner mobility" (Grimonprez, 2014, p. 20).[7] This is not negative, but it is a partial intervention.

Most lately, the interest has also been placed on skills, competitiveness and performance. Public education systems are in fact driven by command and control policies to continue to be more concerned with 'performance' and competitiveness, rather than, with equal access and ecological awareness. Grimonprez (2014) argues brilliantly on another missing concern of the education realm. This is the European dimension in education (sensu stricto*).* She adduces that the EU dimension of education is missing because of the unused potential (in substance and in form) of the legal basis provided by Art. 165 (2). She argues that such legal basis, "at the stage of operationalisation, is just focused on mobility" and the European dimension

[6]Educational concerns that are also extremely related to cultural development and promotion.

[7]See further as cited by the author, Proposal "Erasmus for All", Recital 3, adopted as the 2013 Erasmus+ regulation.

"seems to be at risk" (Grimonprez, 2014). In her view, which I totally share, the European dimension is "evaporating into an undifferentiated approach to multilevel citizenship education", mentioning "learning outcomes (knowledge, skills, attitudes, values and active participation) without distinction as to the level or the particular field, and this is obviously extended to the European dimension in citizenship education, where she believes, there is simply a "commitment gap".[8] Furthermore, mobility, research, training at higher education level, and digitalisation seem to cover the whole educational spectrum of the education policy.

These arguments concerning the 'unused potential of Article 165 (2)" should be set in regulatory principles to transform the traditional understanding of education. A proactive approach that is also part of sustainability premises should enrich not only pedagogical discourses but political drive to empower citizens from early age stages. The unused potential of Article 165 of the TFEU, generally speaking, should be taken more seriously by scholars when analysing the political implications of 'populist' movements in todays' European countries demolishing completely the idea of "Europe". Thus, the operationalisation of the current legal basis of education action at the EU level (Arts. 165 and 166), as well as other constitutional provisions that should be integrated and applied together (Art. 2 of the TEU, Art. 9 of the TFEU), should be used in its fullest potential. In fact, the EU values and objectives expressed in Arts. 2 and 3 of the TEU "constitute curricular learning outcomes, referring to "what Europe is about" in a non-partisan, apolitical way" (Grimonprez, 2014),[9] contrasting the scepticism and supporting the idea of developing tools to educate for informed and critical national/EU citizens (Grimonprez, 2014).

Instead, the most current reforms and other initiatives aimed to improve education practices in national policies can be considered as one of the pivotal mechanisms to infiltrate the neoliberal agenda of 'effectiveness' and 'efficiency'. This is most easily perceived at higher education level, where the institutions are increasingly aligned with market forces, and higher education has witnessed a growth of 'marketisation' at postgraduate level. Unfortunately, it is outside the scope of this contribution to provide more detailed analyses of the relevant social dimension of higher education despite of its crucial role for a strong EUSM. The challenges for national authorities to find sustainable solutions for financing higher education are many, while guaranteeing that students of different backgrounds have the right conditions to study and succeed in higher education. Actually, among 43 studied higher education systems by Eurydice,[10] only nine have in place a systematic no-fee policy for first-cycle full-time home students.[11]

[8]Grimonprez (2014), p. 23.

[9]The author is citing Bogdandy et al. (2012), referring to the values enshrined in those constitutional articles of the Lisbon Treaty and influencing apolitical interpretations in every field. "It is possible to designate an EU-specific essence of fundamental rights enshrined in Article 2 TEU".

[10]European Commission/EACEA/Eurydice (2018).

[11]This group includes Denmark, Finland, Sweden, Norway and the United Kingdom-Scotland, as well as Greece, Cyprus, Malta and Turkey. See further, European Commission/EACEA/Eurydice (2018), p. 7 *et seg*.

The EU is openly considering education as a horizontal enabler of SD.[12] Public education systems and public policy in this area should favour a radical institutional change in education that has not happened yet, including targets of financial nature. Education systems must promote the social and cultural change required for sustainable and ecologically healthy futures, addressing institutional changes. Adopting specific regulations to introduce the subject of climate change, or environmental education might help to create awareness but it is not enough. Still, it has been placed little attention to the education policy needs to adapt to current challenges outside the technological needs. We know that the scope of educational activities is immense and education is meant to shape EU's citizens' approaches towards the integration of a strong sustainability model in the next future. In fact, cross-sectorial instruments or policy instruments of other sectors than education are particularly important in the European Union for influencing developments in education sector (Halász, 2013, p. 280). In a recent work, Sarti and St. John (2019) speak of the importance of environmental integration policies towards sustainable development and the resulting environmental education in raising long-term knowledge and awareness. A proliferation of studies and publications on the different experiences of SDE and EE is available today with important insights about raising awareness, and the practical consequences of introducing them into the curriculum. Still, there are also dramatic conclusions coming from those analyses. Jucker (2014) states that 30 years of EE and ESD have shown that abstract knowledge about environmental concerns does not lead to sustainable action.

Talking about a different realm, but addressing European learning experiences I want to refer to the last ET 2020 Working Group on Schools report "*European ideas for better learning: the governance of schools education systems*".[13] This is a clear sign of commitment of the European Commission in a different direction, this is addressing more structural and institutional issues in the education field, but in terms of applied action, the results are slow. This report by the ET 2020 Working Group on Schools is a prime example of the potential for working together across Europe to identify solutions to shared challenges. It affirms the importance of peer learning between European countries and stakeholder organisations, as practised under Education and Training 2020. There is full recognition of the range of changing educational demands, from learners, society and the labour market. The EU is engaging in a long-term commitment showing awareness about the drastic need for educational reforms in Europe. The commitment of the ET 2020 Working Group on Schools goes beyond, mobility, market and skills perspectives and calls for a need to contemporary approaches to teaching and learning and to the governance of school education systems. The European Commission is committed to offering support to EU Member States in raising the quality of schooling for all learners. In fact, the *Council Conclusions on school development and excellent teaching* (2017) the EU council recognises that "[m]aking high-quality, inclusive and equitable

[12]ESPAS (2015).

[13]European Commission (2018).

school education a reality for all leaners is a top priority that influences the EU's social progress and sustainable growth in the future".[14] An evident stress is still placed at first place on 'diversity' within unity in the EU, where MS are fully responsible for organising and developing their own education systems. In the subsidiary role of the EU support, the emphasis goes to cooperation remarks. Thus, cooperation of school education through Erasmus + programme, as having an added value for ensuring quality education.

Following the action framework established by SDG 4, Europe has set through the Skills agenda building on the Education and Training 2020 Strategic Framework what I would call the 'usual staff': a broader learning and exchange programme, and active support to MS in improving the quality of education and training to guarantee greater opportunities for young people. Thus, the focus continues to be on strategies to avoid the number of early school leavers and on tertiary educational attainment, without supporting programs to bring national institutional change in educational programs, curricula, teacher training and cultural integrated programmes, through coordinated action incorporating public funded activities to assimilate activities that promote social and cultural aspects.[15]

Today, Article 9 of the TFEU,[16] that can be described as a 'horizontal clause' should be taken as a yardstick to promote stronger engagement at EU institutional and policy level, on the fields of education and culture under the prospect of sustainability and the UN 2030 Global Agenda. Article 9 states: "In defining and implementing its policies and activities, the Union shall take into account requirements linked to the promotion of a high level of employment, the guarantee of adequate social protection, the fight against social exclusion, and a high level of education, training and protection of human health". It can bring major innovations, going beyond the Lisbon/EU 2020 Strategy, mostly focused on growth and competitiveness of the EU economic system, as well as further development of the internationalisation and mobility program with the EU programme Erasmus+. Articles 165 and 166 of the TFEU as legal bases of education policy have to be read in context and not as absolute barriers to innovative legislation. As such, the potential of Article 165 (and 166) of the TFEU may be greater than suggested (Grimonprez, 2014). In the end, we know that when educational matters should deal with economic competitiveness, rather than social cohesion, empowerment for social transformation and change of consumption habits, the intergovernmental path is always available (i.e., the so-called harmonisation by "stealth"). As much as it is available scientific evidence supporting correlation between citizenship education and

[14]*Council Conclusions on school development and excellent teaching* (2017/C 421/03). In such conclusions, there is an explanation on how EU support can contribute to better and more inclusive schools; to enhanced support to teachers and school leaders; and to education systems that are more effective, equitable and efficient overall.

[15]On this issue, see further, Jagielska-Burduk (2019).

[16]This can really play a crucial role for future development of the EU education policy beyond traditional competencies (Arts. 165 and 166 of the TFEU).

political engagement, as well as the role of education in shared social responsibilities[17] that could help the policy engagement on addressing the enhancement of these topics at national level. However, legal scholars are still turning their attention to different empowerment mechanisms in more sectorial aspects. Bottom-up approaches concerned with educational and cultural activities are indispensable if we want young people, and society in general, to become involved in decision-making at all levels, as actors and stakeholders. In the context of change, intergenerational responsibility needs to be placed at the core of sustainability discussions in Europe and the world, and educational institutions need to contribute to a real change of mindset. Engaging people from early stages of life is crucial.

Another challenging context for education policy regards judicial intervention to enhance the content of the right to education. The context of the Council of Europe in such instances is also a prolific field of cooperation with the EU education policy. If we take the European framework protection of the right to education that is guaranteed by the two main institutions concerned with human rights: the Council of Europe and the EU, we will see the challenging nature of this right (as many other ones), which has not only positive, but also negative implications; namely, Article 2 of Protocol No. 1, which states: "No person shall be denied the right to education. In the exercise of any functions which it assumes in relation to education and to teaching, the State shall respect the right of parents to ensure such education and teaching in conformity with their own religious and philosophical convictions." It is characterised by its negative wording: 'No person shall be denied (...)'. However, this negative formulation, in accordance with the preparatory work, indicates that the 'Contracting Parties' could not recognise such a right to education as this would require them to establish at their own expense, or to subsidise, education of any particular type or at any particular level ("Belgium linguistic case").[18] Still, it cannot be concluded from this that the State has no positive obligation to ensure respect for such a right as it is protected by Article 2 of Protocol 1, States have the obligation of guaranteeing the right (within their jurisdictions), in principle, in accordance with the means of instruction existing at a given time. If the right to education could be 'contracted', it would mean that there is no positive obligation for States to create a public education system. A different matter regards subsidising every kind of private school to satisfy every parent's will. These areas are today an open field for judicial litigation, Article 2 of Protocol 1 of the Convention, when read in accordance with Article 14 and Article 8 of the Convention could still bring controversy.[19] In fact, today such topic, from the legal point of view, triggers questions of equity and social justice concerns remaining controversial with regard to equal access to education,

---

[17]See further, Cernilogar and Coertjens (2011), p. 331 *et seq.*

[18]474/62, 1677/62, 1691/62, 1769/63, 1994/63, 2126/64, (1968) 1 EHRR 252, [1968] ECHR 3, [1967] ECHR 1, *The Belgian linguistic case* is a paradigmatic case regarding the controversial nature of the wording of this right considering the complexities of our societies.

[19]See further the judicial complains in issues of equal access to education, evidenced in the study conducted by Pranevičienė and Margevičiūtė (2015).

and equity considerations. Still, protection and enforcement is also additionally reinforced by other subsequent international agreements, with different legal consequences, such as the UN Convention on the Rights of Persons with Disabilities,[20] and some others.[21] Generally speaking, the international legal framework (especially concerning rights), along with the European-wide education law and policymakers, have created certain "common constitutional principles"[22] providing a balanced set of legal norms that regulate responsibilities of parents and children on the one side and the state on the other (Pranevičienė & Margevičiūtė, 2015).

Either the International Conventions on Human Rights, the EU Convention, or the EU legal framework for the protection of fundamental rights work together to protect and promote human rights at their maximum protection level. Actually, it is important to note that the ultimate mission of the system set up by the European Convention on Human Rights is to determine issues of public policy in the general interest, thereby raising the standards of protection of human rights and extending human rights jurisprudence throughout the community of the Convention States,[23] even if it is possible to find some inconsistencies. The same can be extended to the global protection level despite of the differentiated protection and monitoring mechanisms available. The inconsistencies that have found valid solutions in the past need to be revisited today in view of the problems arising from our dynamic societies and rapid social changes. Today, national and regional governments need to implement adequate financial support for schools of all categories and levels, both state schools and not-for-profit private schools", and this is a hard issue, especially about "equity". It is outside the scope of my study to engage in such discussion following the narrative of 'rights'.

I would confirm that equal access to education has become a key challenge, and although things are changing, there is not a unique EU sounded legal framework for Europe, despite of its last resolution on the *Modernisation of education in the EU* report.[24] Economists like Rifkin had advanced this incipient theoretical approaches based on 'access' and the obsolescence of private property rights two decades ago.[25]

[20]In Europe, the Convention entered into force on the 22 January 2011. It is the first international, legally binding instrument setting minimum standards for rights of people with disabilities, and the first human rights convention to which the EU has become a party. The main elements of the UN Convention are reflected in the European disability strategy, renewed by the EU so-called Social pillar.

[21]Council of Europe: Revised European Social Charter 1996 (Articles 7, 10, 15, 17); Council of Europe: European Charter for Regional and Minority Languages (Article 8); Council of Europe: Framework Convention for the protection of National Minorities (Articles 12, 13, 14).

[22]Glen and De Groof (2012).

[23]*Konstantin Marking v Russia* [GC], § 89, no. 30078/06, ECHR 2012). Indeed, the Court has emphasised the Convention's role as a "constitutional instrument of European public order" in the field of human rights (*Bosphorus Hava Yolları Turizm ve Ticaret Anonim Şirketi v. Ireland* [GC], no. 45036/98, § 156, ECHR 2005-VI).

[24]European Parliament resolution of 12 June 2018 on modernisation of education in the EU (2017/2224(INI)).

[25]Rifkin (2001).

He decided to call this tendency "ecology of culture and capitalism", Rifkin's additional contribution to the notions of aggregate action, extended access, and declining power of private property is the introduction of culture as the "empathy development terrain", this is contextualised within an increasing digitalised society that does not help emphatic relations with others, nor with our cultural contexts. Rifkin discusses how without empathy society cannot function, and he bases his assertions referring to the work of Robert Jay Lifton (1993). Lifton, claims that "we assert our belonging to the community through our capacity for empathy, to find the way of the mind of others with thoughts and feelings",[26] associated to that comes the necessary redesign of the school mission, and the introduction of 'civil education', based on the premise that the first mission of school education is to prepare students to the culture to which they belong and to assume an active role in such ambit.[27] In more recent times, Rifkin (2013), when addressing the conceptual framework of the third industrial revolution he speaks of the need of developing a biosphere consciousness that should be at the heart of the revolutionary change of our educational systems. In Europe, this idea should still be more developed as part of the modernisation plans,[28] but we need to wait and see how future policy plans develop.

There is a high dissemination and influence between international and national policymaking arenas, and innovation policy plans based on curricula changes introducing some sort of 'biosphere empathy' are today prone to be part of policy plans. Actually, changes are in fact led by the many actors at play at the global sphere. The institutional body behind the global governance framework created by the UN 2030 Global Agenda, is already influencing the EU regulatory level as much as the national and local governance level. Thus, at the EU level, there is no need for uniformity of policy patterns. Embedding the paradigm shift (under strong sustainability premises) is what counts for a comprehensive successful future policy approach.

The strong "equity" requirements of the UN Global Agenda 2030 on SD and the different targets enshrined by SDG 4, which even if they are not binding, are part of an international political agreement of coordinated action, need further EU engagement on a more committed role using normative horizontal provisions. Education policies and legal frameworks should be valid instruments to revisit school systems today, as much as judicial claims. There is a need for new judicial "arguments" touching upon old problems with new clothes, such as the crucial aspect of the interpretative function of the Court regarding the recognised limitations in the freedom's parent's educational choices. Today, more than ever we know that to increase inclusiveness and ensure freedom of educational choices, there should be full public funding for independent and alternative (akin to complex social and sustainability needs) education across all European countries.

---

[26]Lifton (1993), p. 214.

[27]Rifkin (2001).

[28]See the *Modernisation of Education in the EU Report, supra.*

The last UNESCO publication (2015b), dealing with challenging education issues on the global community entrenches the global framework of SD Goals. It recognises among the most urgent educational challenges (dedicating them equal importance) the following ones: recognising and responding to the gap between formal education and employment; recognising and validating learning in a world of increasing mobility across borders; professional occupations and learning spaces; rethinking citizenship education in an increasingly globalised world, balancing respect for plurality with the universal values and concerns for our common humanity. Finally, it considers the complexities of national policymaking in education in the context of potential forms of global governance (UNESCO, 2015b, p. 17). The challenges may not be exhaustive, but they underpin the need to re-contextualise foundational principles for the governance of education that are urgently needed for a systemic approach and rapid engagement of public powers to define the axis of education policy by focusing on how knowledge is created, accessed and acquired, validated and used, without abandoning (as it is happening) the educational sector, and with it the cultural one, to the hands of the marketplace and the whims of an increasingly deregulated market.

The 2017 European Commission Report *Reaching out to EU Citizens: A New Opportunity* seems to promote social dialogue with the public by setting out a framework for a more citizen-focused Europe. Introduces the promotion of the European dimension in citizenship education, considering curriculum content and sociocultural relevance. The focus on youth, intergenerational solidarity and education is highlighted as much as the necessary role of education to build 'dialogue' to strengthen communities. According to the Report "Education has the responsibility to respond all at once to the challenges of globalism and complexity, cultural disintegration, the dispersion and fragmentation of both knowledge and communication channels, and the unequal distribution of opportunities throughout European societies" (European Commission, 2017, p. 20).

More recently, as I mentioned before, the European parliament adopted a resolution on the *Modernisation of education in the EU* report.[29] This resolution brings evidence of how global narratives in the education realm are influencing policy discussions for a shift in the curricula design in the right direction. In the decision, there is an excessive concern about digitalisation but the well-being of children is at the heart of a necessary hailed school reform. The European parliament highlights the benefits of school autonomy, affirming that "granting schools more autonomy regarding curricula, assessment and finance has been shown to result in increased pupil performance" (section 42, page 11, 2008). In fact, one of the challenges MS have to face regards the provision of adequate legal frameworks to foster school-based curricula design with activities that foster multidimensional aspects of sustainability, cultural activities and kids empowerment to become active citizens. All of those realms should get a stand.

---

[29]European Parliament resolution of 12 June 2018 on modernisation of education in the EU (2017/2224(INI)).

We know from experience that overly detailed curricula based mostly on academic performance reduce the potential for schools and teachers to innovate. These should be replaced by general objectives and learning outcomes guiding school-based curricula design under the premises of the world changes and the Anthropocene. Section 76, page 14 of the report encourages "the provision of adequate financial support for schools of all categories and levels, both state schools and not-for-profit private schools".[30] This requisite is aligned with the education requirements of the UN 2030 Global Agenda.

5.1.2 Global Change and Worsening of Environmental Conditions Embedded Into Cultural Concerns

Against the instrumental value of education policy for achieving new paradigms in the Anthropocene and accept shared social responsibility, we face the role of the cultural field, which should ideally be another crucial catalyst for empowerment and integration respecting our differences. The cultural sector has a less successful story in the EU as integration builder. Culture's successful story is built around international cooperation for universal (from local to global) enjoyment and respect for diversity.[31] The recognition of the relevance of culture in the EU has not been translated into a comprehensive and coherent legal framework with defined measures and tools aimed at addressing cultural issues transversally. The sector has always been nationally sensitive, and the current status of development of the regulatory body still responds to the exigency to protect national cultural diversities (Art. 167 of the TFEU; Art. 22 of the Charter of Fundamental Rights) preventing the elaboration of well-defined and more courageous European policies.[32] Nonetheless, the implementation of ecological concerns into cultural heritage has increasingly gained attention, as much as the cultural sector itself. Actually, cultural heritage has become a key area of the cultural policy of the EU to strengthen its sustainability model. The political interest in this sector started to be justified by the following list of documents adopted in less than two years starting in May 2014:

- May 2014 Council conclusions on *cultural heritage as a strategic resource for a sustainable Europe.*[33]
- July 2014 Commission Communication *Towards an integrated approach to cultural heritage for Europe.*[34]

[30]Ibidem *supra note.*

[31]See further, Psychogiopoulou (2015).

[32]Degrassi (2008) and Vitale (2011).

[33]2014/C 183/08.

[34]COM (2014) 477 final, the communication maps future cultural heritage actions in European Union policies, programs and activities.

- November 2014 Conclusions on *participatory governance of cultural heritage.*
- November 2014 *Workplan for culture 2015–2018.*[35]
- April 2015 Opinion of the committee of the Regions "*Towards an integrated approach to cultural heritage for Europe*".[36]
- September 2015 Resolution of the European Parliament *Towards an integrated approach to cultural heritage for Europe.*[37]

In such documents, heritage is not only seen as an element of the past, but as an instrument producing social and environmental capital to reach citizens and new audiences, speaking of contemporary needs and inspiring innovation in Europe and beyond. This entire action plan is of course to be followed by concrete support to the creative sectors. It follows a long-term perspective to face the most demanding sustainability challenges. The new creation of a European culture Forum and the European year of Cultural Heritage 2018 is definitely a sign of concrete support to the sector. These are impressive achievements, and the sector is meant to be more dynamic, especially if we consider that we have to look back to the late 1994 to find a formal council conclusion focusing on cultural heritage.

The hallmark was brought by May 2014 Council Conclusions on Cultural heritage as a strategic resource for a sustainable Europe.[38] Heritage is placed at the heart of the EU project, and the aim of the policy plans is to mainstream cultural heritage in national and European policies, as it has been for the environment in the past. The challenge now is to succeed on such integration, coordinated from the top at the EU level, to avoid leaving anyone behind, and hail open governance spaces at localised level by the most appropriate actors. Cultural heritage (tangible and intangible) starts to be transversal and multidimensional, and it is finally considered a strategic resource for a sustainable EU cutting across other significant fields, environment, culture, social cohesion and tourism. Urban contexts have also received major attention after UN 2030 Global agenda and the EU is responding to this trend. Culture should be considered the source of our cities and our identities, for this, the transmission of knowledge is key, as much as keeping alive the wish of every generation to rediscover, renewing sense of belonging and responsibility and place it at the centre of communities for interaction.

Thus, although the cultural heritage policy is primary a matter of national, regional and local competence, the EU must help on building ties, and shared responsibility. The constitutional basis for policy intervention is clear: Article 3 of the TEU, "The union shall.....ensure that Europe's cultural heritage is safeguarded and enhanced" read together with Article 167 of the TFEU "(..) the Union shall

[35]Brussels, 26 November 2014, 15,319/14 CULT 126 AUDIO 66 MI 869 RELEX 907 STATIS 121.

[36](2015/C 195/04).

[37]European Parliament resolution of 8 September 2015 towards an integrated approach to cultural heritage for Europe (2014/2149 (INI)).

[38]Document 52014XG0614(08), Council conclusions of 21 May 2014 on *cultural heritage as a strategic resource for a sustainable Europe.*

encourage cooperation between Member States and (. . .) support (. . .) and supplement (. . .) their action in the (. . .) conservation and safeguarding of cultural heritage of European significance". It is important to build from this normative basis a common policy on the following values: culture to be seen as a shared resource, a common good and a common responsibility. Still, it is important to say that rather than the proactive approach to sustainability premises, the risks and the market interests on cultural heritage have been the main drivers for institutional, policy intervention and market interests in the field.

Global trends have also clearly influenced the EU current stance on an increasing promotion of cultural heritage. The proliferation of bodies and offices and other international agencies operating at the same governance level has largely influenced the policy scenario in the cultural management scenario. There is no longer only vertical International Organisations-States dimension, global public-private partnerships between States and International organisations are increasing. This is taking institutional or procedural form, through Memoranda of Understanding (Closa and Casini, 2016, p. 203). The cultural field is indeed a good example of the interplay of legitimised different governance levels. The system built on the World Heritage Convention, has progressively acquired a significant procedural dimension which is regulated by the UNESCO Operational guidelines for the Implementation of the World Heritage Convention, it fosters new forms of cooperation between international institutions, States, domestic administrators and other actors (Closa and Casini, 2016, p. 214), and it is completely integrated in an inter-legal (horizontal) relationship with the EU legal order. In fact, the global scenario has taken the EU to operationalise its subsidiary competencies into a much more prolific body of normative provisions.

In the different context of the Council of Europe, two landmark conventions in the field of culture have been pioneering the integrated approach that has become vital for the current EU policy. They both introduced at an early date the sustainability paradigm and set a courageous and holistic pathway for sustainable management of landscape in all its manifestations, as well as cultural heritage. An innovative approach of the Conventions that should be highlighted is the integration of the importance of educational initiatives not only to strengthen identity ties with the territory but also to empower people on their management and their conservation for present and future generations. The well-known conventions are: (1) The European Landscape Convention (Florence, 2000); and (2) the Faro Convention. They both interact with the World Heritage Convention from 1992 that included cultural landscapes and recognised their importance for human well-being and community cohesion. They increasingly influence the governance shift dealing with urban and rural planning and integrating the cultural and educational activities needed for a sustainable management.

(1) The European Landscape Convention (ELC) (Council of Europe, 2000), Adopted in Florence (Italy) on 20 October 2000 reinforces the role of cultural landscapes recognised at the international level eight years before. ELC aims at promoting the protection, management and planning of European landscapes

and organising European cooperation on landscape issues. It is the first international treaty to be exclusively concerned with all dimensions of European landscape, and it is a vital point of reference for adopting a comprehensive approach to nature conservation and landscape protection under the paradigm of sustainability. The cultural dimension is also of fundamental importance, because the Convention sets in the idea of landscape as a bridge between nature and culture. Actually, the Convention embodies a crucial contribution to the implementation of the objectives of the Council of Europe in search for Europeans' quality of life and well-being considering not just landscape as isolated phenomena, but its cultural and natural values. It has become from the normative stance a global point of reference. The Member States of the Council of Europe signatory to the European Landscape Convention declared their concern to achieve sustainable development based on a balanced and harmonious relationship between social needs, economic activity and the environment.[39] In fact, themes such as the interpretation of the landscape, democratic participation in its protection and the population's re-appropriation of local areas, as well as the importance of education, empowerment and integrated approaches lie at the heart of the Convention. The field is full of opportunities for interdisciplinary and transdisciplinary collaboration and research. The normative framework set by the ELC recognised the critical links between nature, culture and community for a long-term sustainable development. Prompting for a comprehensive action and integrated urban-rural public policy. Landscape is depicted as a multifaceted resource that should already be integrated into the teaching programs of (compulsory and non-mandatory) education with adequate pedagogical and cultural initiatives.[40] Governance strategies characterised by bottom-up approaches and decentralised style of policymaking stimulating horizontal relations between public and private bodies are increasingly run in protected areas throughout Europe.[41]

(2) The Council of Europe's Framework Convention on the value of Cultural Heritage for Society, best known as the Faro Convention (Council of Europe 2005) should be recalled as a new paradigm for socially and culturally sustainable heritage action. Unlike most heritage conventions, 'Faro' is not concerned with "how to protect heritage, but why: what are the social and cultural benefits, indeed imperatives, in doing so. Faro regards heritage as cultural activity writ large" (Fairclough, Dragićević-Šešić, Rogač-Mijatović, Auclair, & Soini, 2014, p. 10). It highlighted the social and economic benefits of preserving cultural heritage as a prerequisite for achieving sustainable

---

[39]See further Desideri (2015).

[40]It is important to see the challenges that those initiatives bring when facing environmental and cultural homogenisation, as part of the general process of globalisation.

[41]See further, Janssen and Knippenberg (2012).

development and for that purpose its takes the broadest possible definition of cultural heritage and SD.[42] It puts an emphasis on heritage as "process" rather than product that highlights heritage's relevance to sustainability (Fairclough, Dragićević-Šešić, Rogač-Mijatović, Auclair, & Soini, 2014, p. 10). Consequently, Faro takes a people-centred approach, and focuses on the people who construct, use and celebrate heritage. For this reason, it reminds us forcefully of every citizen's right to his or her own heritage and to participation in cultural life. It also enshrines a balance to be drawn between the assertion of these rights balanced by the responsibilities at individual and collective level to respect and protect the cultural heritage and the cultural memory of other groups (Fairclough, Dragićević-Šešić, Rogač-Mijatović, Auclair, & Soini, 2014, p. 10).

Both Conventions, are valid normative frameworks and policy instruments for the integration of cultural and educational concerns under the sustainability paradigm in future sharper public policy action, not only in the context of the European Council member countries, but at global level (due to the novelty and rapid impact of the notion of landscape and heritage understood as "process", both integrated into a sustainability paradigm), the EU level, and also at national and local level. Furthermore, the question of the legitimacy of action under those different normative frameworks has to be resolved smoothly, considering that International organisations and intergovernmental regimes more generally, cannot claim to possess the voluntary consensual mechanisms on which private law systems are usually based. Indeed, legitimacy is founded on the political authority of a given international institution, enhanced by State consensus or at least non-opposition (Closa and Casini, 2016, p. 220).

Thus, although the general regulatory picture seems to be quite adequate the growing awareness in risks related to global change and the continuous worsening of environmental conditions has challenged the effectiveness of past and current EU policies in the cultural and nature conservation policies. New 'alliances'[43] and integrated approaches are mandatory. However, legal scholarship engagement in the field can be scarce with regard to procedural processes needed to activate effective protection mechanisms or empowerment mechanisms of localised nature. Public policy interventions need to be territorialised/localised, but people need awareness, access information and education on their cultural landscapes. Thus, today integration under sustainability premises, especially in the cultural sector, triggering so many different ambits, needs to overcome the traditional separation of protected areas with respect to wider context of global risks, and multi-stake

[42]It covers all forms of cultural heritage put into the context of a shared source of remembrance, understanding and identity. The most relevant part of such notion of cultural heritage is related to the focus on the contribution of this heritage to creativity and social cohesion, and to the ideals, principles and values resulting from the experience of past conflicts and efforts to make progress. The convention highlighted the link between cultural heritage and the development of a peaceful and stable society, founded on respect for human rights, the rule of law and democracy. See further, Fairclough, Dragićević-Šešić, Rogač-Mijatović, Auclair, & Soini, (2014).

[43]See further, Gambino and Peano (2015).

holders gaining relevance at local level. Therefore, the integration of traditional protected areas, and landscape policy interventions should be assimilated following a unique conservation paradigm that needs transdisciplinary interventions, territorial empowerment and regulatory capacities that take stock of considerations, research and experiences at the international level, involving different disciplines, and different institutional bodies (5th IUCN World Parks Congress, Durban 2003), but where 'locals' (local citizens, local institutions) have a definitive role to play. The complexity of devising adequate regulations and institutional frameworks for conservation and promotion of territories, landscapes and protected areas under such integrated foundations, has become one of the major challenges of our European cultural heritage that disciplinary or sectorial policy interventions cannot solve alone.

Another challenging issue regards the stronger bridge that should be built between nature conservation considerations and cultural policy regards. The new report[44] provided by culture 2030 Goal Campaign and coordinated by International Council on Monuments and Sites (ICOMOS) and United Cities and Local Governments (UCLG), advances the cultural dimension of SD as essential for the achievement of 2030 Agenda and the SDGs, but devotes little content to landscapes, biosphere and nature protected areas. It is true that SDG11 and the growing reality of complex urban context need urgent solutions and cultural sector engagement, but the Anthropocene teaches us that nature should not only be a regard of environmental law protection.

In any case, ICOMOS is an important source of key recommendations for future policymaking that is, of course, transversal for every cultural ambit under strong sustainability foundations. The vital policy recommendations identified by the report that should influence policymaking are described as follows: "(a) culture to be from the outset in national development planning frameworks for implementing the SDGs, as well as in their reporting through the Voluntary National Review (VNR) process; (b) the need for wider consultation and participatory exercises in the elaboration of VNRs; (c) the need to develop a wider international community around culture and sustainable development; (d) the organisation of High-Level Meeting devoted to Culture within the next High level Political Forum (HLPF) cycle of reporting (2020-2023); (e) the design and implementation of quantitative and qualitative indicators reflecting the place of culture in sustainable development;

[44]The Report "Culture in the Implementation of the 2030 Agenda: A Report by the Culture 2030 Goal Campaign". The report takes stock of the first four years of SDGs and the 2030 Agenda for the perspective of culture. The background of the report can be found in the campaign "culture2015goal campaign". Leading up to the adoption of the UN 2030 Agenda for SD, several global cultural networks campaigned under the banner "The Future we want includes Culture" for the inclusion of one specific goal devoted to culture, or for the integration of cultural aspects across the SDGs. In the final document of this campaign (23 September 2015: "Culture in the SDG Outcome Document: Progress Made, but Important Steps Remain ahead"), the networks committed to keep their cooperation active. Available at: https://www.icomos.org/en/focus/un-sustainable-development-goals/60720-new-report-culture-in-the-implementation-of-the-2030-agenda.

(f) the importance of cultural contexts in the local implementation of the SDGS and the crucial role played by local cultural actors, institutions and organisations; (g) the need for cultural sectors to strengthen their own efforts towards the implementation of the SDGs, and (h) the commitment to developing partnerships at all levels to strengthen the integration of the cultural dimension in the SDGs".[45]

In Europe, public policymaking in this field, although more fervent in latest years, needs a major interplay of actors, campaigners and instruments available at the different governance level. This concern is crucial for supporting culture and education as sustainability builders. European institutions need to take a major share on redefining the bonds of culture and education with the other sectorial policies. This is particularly relevant concerning heritage promotion and protection in urban contexts and rural settlements (SDG 11); sustainability education (SDG 4), sustainable use of environmental resources (SDGs 6, 7, 13, 14, 15), promotion of sustainable tourism (SDG 8), adoption of sustainable patterns of production and consumption (SDG 12) or mitigation of and adaptation to climate change (SDG 13) in which cultural promotion and educational activities, as well as curricula integration should foster cultural knowledge and empowerment to care for natural resources. More than in others, in these specific contexts, culture and education act as enablers of sustainable development.

The EFACH, which is part of our EUSM, was introduced with the following assertion: "Cultural heritage is a common good passed from previous generations as a legacy for those to come".[46] Sustainability in cultural heritage is one of its five main strands and it comprises several actions. Such actions should be implemented with the support of the European Commission and they are included in this European Framework (2018).[47] An important note is that the EFACH is aligned with the Council of Europe's European Cultural Heritage Strategy for the twenty-first century adopted in 2017 mainstreaming sustainability action, with the UN 2030 Agenda for SD, and with the Sendai Framework for Disaster Risk Reduction 2015–2030.[48]

The cultural sector, and the cultural implications of education needs, are meant to be enhanced by further European action concerning the cross-national and transnational issues that are involved under sustainability premises. The new recently launched "European Green Deal" gives indications of this. Still, the European

---

[45] According to the Report "Culture in the implementation of the 2030 Agenda: A Report by the Culture 2030 Agenda Goal Campaign", p. 93 *et seq*. Available at https://www.icomos.org/en/focus/un-sustainable-development-goals/60720-new-report-culture-in-the-implementation-of-the-2030-agenda.

[46] SWD (2018) 491 final, Brussels, 5.12.2018. Commission staff working document on European Framework for action on cultural heritage.

[47] The European framework for action on cultural heritage, proposes indeed 60 actions to be implemented by the European Commission in 2019 and 2020, focusing on five main thematic areas: (1) Inclusive Europe; (2) sustainable Europe; (3) resilient Europe; (4) innovative Europe; (5) Europe with stronger global partnerships.

[48] https://www.unisdr.org/we/coordinate/sendai-framework.

Green Deal urges action needed to fight climate change and biodiversity crisis at first instance.[49] It has been drafted as EU political priority for the next five years and should further enhance global leadership of the EUSM, especially in these sectors. It means further commitment of common policy action at the EU level and it is supported by growing calls for action by the public in general. "[I]t provides a unique opportunity to scale up and speed up a green and just transition for Europe", but green growth is highest ambition.[50]

5.2 The Complexity of Not Having a Unique Valid Solution

Fortunately, as it has been illustrated above there is growing awareness and increasing policy interest into the education and cultural fields as sustainability builders. This is particularly true regarding the cultural sector.[51] Actually, changes in the cultural sector seem to be easier at the time of implementation thanks to the institutional parties involved. When it comes to education, the limitations are due to the administration stiffness of institutional level tied to the whole sector with detrimental consequences for the end-users, unless harmonisation is agreed on voluntary basis, as it happened with the meta-framework, the European Qualifications Framework.[52]

I have to say that lawyers, especially administrative lawyers, while suggesting theoretical foundations to justify legal intervention in the cultural field by referring to other scientific fields, have not been so worried about suggesting theoretical foundations that could justify an urgent intervention in the educational field, and have not been so prolific on going beyond legal boundaries to discuss problems of social, psychological, or biological nature to explain the need of a new educational system that could help the development of an 'emphatic' relationship with the biosphere to educate current and future generations in an ecological culture, transmitting love for nature and reinforcing the idea that landscape is part of nature, taking distance from anthropomorphic conceptions of landscape.[53]

---

[49]Ursual Von Der Leyen Agenda, "A Union that strives for more. My agenda for Europe", accessible at: https://ec.europa.eu/commission/sites/beta-political/files/political-guidelines-next-commission_en.pdf.

[50]Article published by European Environment Agency, on 16 September 2019 "Making Sustainability happen: new European policies offer a unique opportunity".

[51]See further, the new work plan for culture adopted in Europe. Draft Conclusions of the Council and of the Representatives of the Governments of the Member States, meeting within the Council, on a Work Plan for Culture (2015–2018), CULT 134 AUDIO 69 MI 945 RELEX 980 STATIS 128, accessible at: http://data.consilium.europa.eu/doc/document/ST-16094-2014-INIT/en/pdf.

[52]Recommendation of the EU Parliament and of the Council of 23 April 2008 on the establishment of the European Qualifications Framework for lifelong learning (Official Journal C111, 6 May 2008).

[53]This is the case of the Italian codification of landscape as part of the urban code referred to cultural goods. In fact, it is my opinion that the Italian legal framework has helped permeating this idea by implementing since 2004 (Legislative Decree No. 42 of 22 January 2004, Code of Cultural Heritage

Within the context of cultural action and practice, the cross-sectorial reference is more evident. The intersection with ethnographic, economic, political and natural considerations is constantly present. Legal scholarship in fact has long accepted that the legal notion of cultural property is a "liminal notion", i.e., a notion that legal norms cannot define without referring to other disciplines or sciences (Casini, 2010, p. 18; Giannini, 1976, p. 8), so, its interdisciplinary nature is part of its legal ethos. On education, a similar reasoning could be applied, but education here, is only considered in its public good version. In such version, the outstanding problem of our complex society is the available pedagogical 'forest'[54] without any validated solution. Sometimes, education as a tailor-made 'package' and adjusted to the needs of an 'unsustainable' way of production, (with a promising pedagogical offer) becomes a private good. We need to contrast this, and indeed our power to influence law throughout our aggregate action could be a starting point of departure.

In the meantime, we are left with a dense bid of promising pedagogical offers to face future cultural and educational challenges, and the 'panacea' does not seem to have a unique identified existence yet. José Antonio Marina (2017), with a brilliant study providing a picture of the "pedagogical forest" available out there provides the reader with a roadmap to understand the many promising paths that have rendered the pedagogical field fragmented and (in) operational. Marina claims for transformation by returning to the humanistic approach of the science of learning, without stealing importance to neuroscience and the rest of scientific fields' contributions that can help to identify valid solutions for public education systems today. He suggests the retrieval of the true value of philosophy and its role for a systemic approach that could also help current public policy interventions to introduce courageous and needed urgent changes worldwide. Neuroscience has been long affirming the equal importance of music literacy and physical education but curricula is still focused on traditional subjects and this failing system is feeding the 'marketisation' of necessary activities such as sports and music.

Other research projects have an outstanding value for the way they are depicting the cultural and educational challenges of our world today. Europe of course is part of this picture, but at institutional level, valid solutions are not advanced outside the confines of digital and assessment innovation. The MacArthur Foundation work on 'learning institutions' is a valid example of how educational challenges are depicted at the global level and it is valid for my discussion. The Foundation, in its report *The future of thinking: learning institutions in a digital age*,[55] published by the Massachusetts Institute of Technology argues that we are going through an especial

---

and Landscape, as Mandated by Article 10 of Law. No. 137 of 6 July 2002) an urban code joining cultural heritage laws and landscape protection including them as environmental goods eventually regulated by property law provisions. On 31 March 2016, an updated version of the 2004 Code of Cultural Heritage and Landscape entered into effect in Italy as a consolidated text updated with provisions.

[54]This identification with the Word 'forest' draws on the work of José Antonio Marina (2017) its *Pedagogical forest.*

[55]Davidson and Goldberg (2010).

epistemic moment because learning itself is the most powerful instrument for change. This idea indeed should be an axiom for European cultural and educational challenges of its sustainability model. The book focuses on the customised learning opportunities offered by the internet, but deepening on those opportunities offers a valid study to understand how fundamental aspects of learning institutions are changing without any contrasting 'institutional' power or control. These of course has many benefits for the question of 'access' to learning (long-life based), but also some detrimental effects if we consider the sphere of 'regulation' and 'command and control' traditional approach that has guided and still guides in Europe, educational reforms. Therefore, the big questions are:

(1) Is it prudent to get away with such institutional control? But on the other side;
(2) How can we control it?

The answer to technological acquisition of power is more technology, providing software that contrast excessive access. However, the truth is that the complexity goes beyond disciplinary understanding of learning, and the answer does not seem clear yet. Digital cultural though is imminent in our communities.

Davidson and Goldberg (2010) argue that there are a set of different questions that every educator should be thinking about today. Further, they assert that the modes of learning have changed dramatically over the past two decades (i.e., the sources of information, the ways we exchange and interact with information, how information informs and shapes us), but the fundamental aspects of learning institutions remain remarkably familiar and have been for around two hundred years or more. In fact, conventional institutions of learning are changing far more slowly than the modes of inventive, collaborative, participatory learning offered by the Internet and an array of contemporary mobile technologies. The question is: Are the new learning spaces, mostly internet sites, learning institutions?; and if so, what do these institutions tell us about the more traditional learning institutions such as schools, universities, graduate schools? Their definition of institutions "as mobilising networks" offer a challenge to the insularity of lock-box education, libraries, community centres, or any other civic organisations that define their mission exclusively in terms of their turf, and highlights the possibilities of institutions grounded in distributed and virtual social networks (Wellman et al., 1996).

Reading the book, and these other knowledge experiences, are an incredible learning experience that can drastically shake our own idea of 'learning'. Innovation seems to have not limits through the challenging wake of digital learning experiences and not only. One can remain terrified or just admired by the constant thrill of discovering innovation and facing huge enquiries about the real empowerment of the human side through digital access. I was actually quite disturbed reading the way a five-year-old children can acquire knowledge through the digital instruments by the use of Pokémon:

> A five-year-old masters the equivalent of a third-grade reading vocabulary in order to play online and also customises the game with digital graphic tools that, only a generation ago, would have been considered sophisticated for a professional designer. That five-year-old makes friends online through game play that requires memorising hundreds (the number

> expands every day) of characters with different attributes and skills and learns how to fix, customise, program, or hack a computer in order to participate in this compelling online world of play. You do not have to force a child who is interested in Pokémon to practice at the computer. Technical skills, programming, literacy, social life, aesthetics and design, narrative-making, socialising, the only brake is the parent who worries about the child spending too much time (or money) on Pokémon. Innovation has responded to one parental concern: SoftwareTime has developed a popular program to limit children's time at the computer.

The panorama of pedagogical transformation, innovation is boundless but it is not mainstreamed yet by a systematic roadmap of action in the field to avoid being lightened up by the desire to embrace fragmented bit and pieces of innovation for the sake of innovation. The truth is that there is also a big gap and disconnection between research and educational practice, and sometimes between policy reports (even if nationally based) and educational practice.

If we think of the UK report *The Learning Age a renaissance for a new Britain* presented in Parliament by the Department for Education and Employment in February 1998; or the Canadian report *Towards a learning society, learning economy: An action plan for Canada*, we realise that they all reach the same conclusion, "learning is the key to prosperity, for each of us as individuals, as well as for the nation as a whole" (UK report 1998). Thus, the message is clear: we live in the learning society, we need to learn continuously and constantly, and not only individuals but, institutions, enterprises and society as a whole. The other basic component of these reports regards the transformation of culture. We need a transformation of culture to achieve a learning age. One of the biggest challenges that the UK report highlights is "to get all those who provide learning to make it easier for people to learn, and they outline different solutions that don't go further from outlining basic support to learning needs, recognising institutional change over time, or ensuring flexibility for learning access, as much as high standards of teaching and training. The end result is that these reports do not put forward any valid solution for a systematic governmental approach to education, and how to face the challenges this really poses. They do not even, devise the potential of education for building our sustainable societies, the societies that we urgently need now in terribly condensed urban contexts. The positive side of these contributions and others like the one focused on the "Knowledge-creating culture" that assume that we live in a "knowledge age"[56] advanced by Bereiter and Scardamalia (2014); or the contribution of the Economist study on *Lifelong learning. How to survive in the age*

[56]Bereiter and Scardamalia (2014), explain that 'knowledge age' is a way of saying something very similar to what John Dewey was saying through his long career. "Experience", as Dewey (2007) defined it, has a progressive, feed-forward character like knowledge building. It is growth that enables future growth.

of automation[57] (it is difficult to be exhaustive in this sector)[58] is that they have finally recognised the burgeoning role of education in our societies that cannot be ignored any longer from those who operationalise the education and cultural rights of our constitutions, and the institutional and regulatory body involved. In fact, I personally believe that the abundant literature and increasing focus on how technology is rapidly transforming knowledge and learning, is stealing attention from other more basic concerns with regard to culture and education institutional needs today. There is too much focus on how the education landscape needs a complete remake to address the problem of lifelong learning effectively, abandoning the needed for a reform in our most basic learning institutions.

What emerges from the educational and cultural panorama today according to Marina (2017) is: (1) instability and, (2) contradictory existence full of proliferation of innovative approaches, often without foundational roots, representing all our social, economic and political contradictions of our accelerated society today. This can give perhaps an explanation of why governments, teachers, parents and institutions are all confused and lost about what solution is best. Still the universal learning law is implacable: 'either learning or margination. There is no middle solution'. For that reason, what is clear is that the focus of education is broadened to reach the society as a whole, and lifelong learning is key to build sustainable communities and societies today. Marina (2017) explains how education systems are ubiquitous and educational actors, such as the big technological lobbies and enterprises, everyone in general, have understood that the global education industry can become the big business of this century. Actually, if this economic side of the educational life is what can engage lawyers to think seriously about it, as it has helped to build interest on cultural law, we should not be afraid of this trend. Nonetheless, education and learning are still constitutionally and globally 'sacrosanct' (SDG 4) and we must protect this sacred and common good value.

I believe that if public lawyers do not devote to the educational field as much attention as they have done with the field of media, communication and other forms of cultural creation, we risk ending up in the hands of the market. Marina (2017), provides data about the quantity of money the education industry spends in America, the same data can be found applied to the European context. The money the educational related industry, including government and private expenses, in the global education sectors is a billion dollar industry.[59] It comprises an attractive market for the growing interest of several groups, mainly business ones. Thus, the

[57]Andrew Palmer (14 January 2017), in The Economist magazine. The article provides data and argues about automation of workforce and the advancement of technology and the complex reality we are facing with the increasing need to returning to education, even for the high skilled. They also talk about how the idea of mechanistic relationship between education and wages has taken a knock. The answer is to remain competitive. For that, economies need to offer training and career-focused education throughout people's working lives.

[58]See Marina (2017) for a more exhaustive approach about pedagogical initiatives and the complexity of the teaching and learning field today.

[59]See further Knight (2002); and Psacharopoulos and Anthony Patrinos (2002).

business side of borderless education has grown substantially and it has taken the World Trade Organisation (WTO) to take interest on this type of business, especially higher education. This includes the demand for higher and adult education, especially professionally related courses and non-traditional delivery modes. This is, of course, due to the knowledge economy, lifelong learning education trends and of course the globalised job market. While the demand has been growing, the capacity of the public sector to satisfy the demand has been constantly challenged because of a variety of factors, such as budget limitation, the changing role of governments and increased emphasis on market economy and privatisation. Academic programs and providers are moving across borders and the economic rationale is increasingly driving large part of the international supply of education (Knight, 2002).[60]

However, as we know, education is enshrined as one of the crucial human and social rights for development, and should be generally provided and controlled by the State, and this poses several limitations on the commercial expansion of education traders. National and international recognition of qualifications and the transfer of credit, to access to educational services and to the job market, in some supranational agreements, such as the EU (with the Bologna process) are not new, and are good examples of internationalisation policies without reaching exclusively merchandising concerns but facing the challenges the job market and higher education pose today. We will see how this internationalisation works through the Bologna process in the European context. Instead, limitations that could be identified as 'barriers' to trade at global level will be seen as obstacles that should be suppressed for the sake of the increasing demand on global 'access' to educational services, mainly for the sake of acceding to high quality higher education.[61] On primary and secondary education, the challenges regarding the acquisition of excellence and high quality education in Europe are becoming trendy. In fact, it has been discussed[62] with regard to secondary schools (being equally applicable to primary education) that education at secondary schools is criticised for not serving the interest of society and community, for not teaching children the right behaviour and attitudes towards society and towards nature, for transmitting knowledge and competence that no longer corresponds to the present day society.

Curiously enough, the criticism has rarely been directed at the structure of the system or at its essential characteristics, such as financing, government and management, the way of assessing pupil performance and of certifying qualification. This is one of the major European educational and cultural challenges of its sustainability model. What the European sustainability model needs today is to recuperate the 'legitimacy' of the basic aims of education that have been put forward by the most recent global 'guiding' instrument that enhances the aspirations of a well-established 'right to education', namely: the equality of opportunity, preparing

---

[60]This profit related trend, applies, not only to private stakeholders, but has increasingly implied public institutions.

[61]See further, Knight (2002), Knight (2003), Sauvé (2002), and Egan (2002).

[62]Kallen (1997).

for global citizenship, qualifying for today's global market, contributing to pupil's personality development.

The principle of the state's responsibility for education should be questioned based on the sacred recognition of education as a common good. Why? And why this is so urgent? Today, this is urgent because the predominance of the goals of equality of opportunities and of the pursuit of commonly shared competencies and values has been challenged in favour of other goals, such as individual freedom to determine one's own educational programme and "free enterprise" in providing education (Kallen, 1997). In addition to this, the State has indeed withdrawn from its monopolistic role into the role of a more distant, but vigilant guardian. Although this liberal market economic philosophy has mostly influenced more higher education than primary and secondary education.

In European school systems, the public interest and the pursuit of common goals and values remain the dominant norms, and preserving these values passes first through a process of creating awareness on the urgent policy action to increase the value of 'equality' at every education level. Considering the high redistribution of educational and cultural competencies at local and regional administrations, and to the administrative body (by increasing school autonomy) of schools and principals, we need clear framework laws at national level that mainstream the value of "equality" on providing educational programs integrated in cultural realities promoting strong sustainability concerns that need to be backed up by curriculum design intervention. However, the uncoordinated and fragmented nature of this interventions undertaken by the peripheral powers assigned to the local level or the school autonomy has emerged as a new trend, and it has given some positive consequences, in the sense that the organisation and style of governance and on resource management today in education is very much dependent on such peripheral distribution of administrative tasks that has managed to integrate communities requests, new pedagogical ideas without upsetting the existing structural and administrative frameworks (Kallen, 1997).

The demand for greater diversity of programmes in primary and secondary education (corresponding to today's pedagogical forest)[63] has indeed been satisfied within public education, even if parents and pupils are increasingly becoming 'clients' and 'stakeholders' and this (un) satisfactory answer to today's education challenges is taking place basically based on the instruments of school autonomy (primary and secondary education) and academic autonomy (higher education), deriving from the traditional Constitutional framing of the Educational powers that is common although different from country to country. To refer here to the different EU legal systems framing the education institutional setting would be quite ambitious. Suffices to mention the impossibility to find a unique solution. The same happens with the legislative foundations of education. Whilst educational legislation in Europe usually obeys a typology of hierarchy in which the constitutional text

[63]Ref. Marina (2017).

stands at the top and settles the whole legitimised action framework in the field that goes down to the decrees of implementation.

In nearly all European societies, the Constitution explicitly guarantees the right to education. It stipulates, on the other hand, the responsibility of the State for creating the conditions that enable citizens to benefit from their educational rights. Beyond this broad framework, Constitutions in Europe, in some instances strongly differ in terms of the precise educational guarantees and indications that they contain.[64] Eurydice contains a good data base about the legal frameworks regulating education administration in the different Member States, the topics that have been defining a supranational intervention on how Member States should define their constitutional right to education, regard controversies concerning educational rights of the children of migrant workers, and the educational rights of the 'illegal' immigrant that could be contested based on the different constitutional texts formulations, but also based on the European Court Justice case law. It could be interesting to wait and see if future case law could be built on demands of certain educational services, and administrative interventions at the EU level, through the European court of Justice. This case law could be based on the environmental integration principle (Art. 11 of the TFEU) or even on the more ambitious and overarching principles enshrined in Arts. 2 and 3 of the TEU.

The risk of not having a systematic approach to envisage education exclusively as a common good embracing ecological systemic concerns has many risks in Europe. Some of the risks include the disconnection of current generations from nature and the difficulties to foster a radical institutional change to promote greater bonds with planet Earth and our cultural and natural heritage. All European countries seem to have inevitably increased demand for a diversified and individualised request for educational provisions. This is happening because a paradigmatic pedagogical change has also occurred (Marina, 2017), but the political will, not even at European level is using all its institutional potential to generate more radical changes.

The need to look at these challenges in a holistic manner highlights the importance of an interdisciplinary, and cross-sectorial approach. However, this stance is underused by legal scholarship as much as by policymakers. On this light, the suggested solutions are many but there is not a real change of 'attitude'. Thus, the solutions range from imposing new pedagogies introduced with or without serious curricula transformations, privatisation of education, standardisation of learning process by an increasing introduction of monitoring mechanisms and indicators based on statistics, performance, and standardised test in the traditional knowledge subjects. Taking care of a strong sustainability concerns emerges an enhanced integration of environmental education, and (post) sustainability education; increasing STEM education aligned to the need to provide more technological solutions to global challenges; accelerating digitalisation since early education stages, etc.

Even within the EU, we find an immense variety of pedagogical stances at public education level. The conclusions I have extracted from such a European mosaic, is

[64]For a comparative approach on this topic, see further Kallen (1997).

that drastic political changes, or hard economic crisis, as well as excessive wellbeing and changes in society demands have determined most of the radical leaps in policy intervention in the education field in the last decades.[65] Sustainability concerns, have only determined some limited variations at curriculum level.[66] So, if we think of Lithuania, we see that the educational system has undergone substantial transformation conditioned by the fundamental change of the political situation in the region after the restoration of independence in 1990, the education system was forced to develop denying the former Soviet educational framework (Pranevičienė & Margevičiūtė, 2015), the openness of the system to International and European innovation and policy trends is evident. In fact, Lithuanian National Long-Term Development Strategy, in view of becoming a member of the EU, devoted special attention to education. The education system was foreseen as one of the streamlines of the strategic development of the country. In fact, the main objectives of these rules are to create a system of education based on sustainability, target financing, social responsibility, quality and open society. Consequently, as a long-term planning document, prioritises the political development of education: to increase competence of teachers and lectures, to promote data analysis and self-evaluation based quality culture of education, to develop accessibility and equal opportunities in education, and to encourage life-long learning. Today, the Lithuanian education system is highly modernised and it has a higher than average performance level on digitalisation when compared to other European education systems (Spain, Italy, France, Greece for instance).

In Finland, things have gone so far in the same direction, only in the sense that profound changes in the education system happened because of the economic crisis of the country during the seventies. This took the finish government to invest on human resources to be considered the main wealth of the country. It was the first step of a subsequent investment on the future of the country and its distinctively successful reform of the education system. Finland invested on the training and quality of educators to come out from a crisis that had comported devastation of the country's natural resources. The first stage of the reform was to rely on high quality, well-trained teachers, with strong academic qualifications and master's degree that could train the brains of the future human resources of the country. This was the main shift of their education system transformation.

Pashi Shalberg book *Finnish Lessons 2.0. What can the world learn from educational change in Finland, explains Finnish education system,*[67] with passionate engagement explains the virtues of a courageous reform movement that has become a world model of a real General Education Reform Movement, still, the inspiring vision of Shalberg, wants to tell us that a unique formula for education reform would not work out, and notes that "school reforms are poor travellers. This means that what seems to make an education system perform beyond expectations in one place may not have the same positive effect on school systems elsewhere"

[65]See further, Wang (2013).

[66]See further, Jucker and Mathar (2015).

[67]Shalberg (2015).

(Shalberg, 2015, p. 18). Cultural and institutional contexts are important. The Finnish model began to take shape thanks to the German and Swiss model. Then the idea of an equitable, comprehensive school system came from neighbouring countries, especially from Sweden. Today, such models are going through different experiences and holding different expectations for transformation.

The Swedish school system has become today highly privatised, and Germany has extremely focused on vocational training education. Unfortunately, the scope of this study is to suggest the conceptual basis for a future line of research and policymaking in a different direction and cannot go further on explaining details on the variety of education systems. However, OCED data and the existing literature on the field can be useful in this regard.

I am making the part for substantial changes driven by growing concern on our shared responsibility towards future generations, the planet Earth and responsible citizens. We need to build a civil economy.[68] Civil economy and responsible citizens needs educated citizens. Thus, what we need now is a paradigmatic change at institutional level guided by serious implementation of the targets contained by the SDG4 and the enshrining of education as a common good for a start.[69] Otherwise, the fear is that the promotion of internationalisation of public education could be increasingly discussed in international trade fora such as the WTO rather than at International Education ones. As it has been argued elsewhere, the education community (still) needs to define and propose its own preferred internationalisation model based on the desirability of internationalisation for the sake of enriching education and generating research synergies in a cooperative logic that prioritises cultural exchanges (Verger, 2010).

Still, the global arena and the internationalisation trends of higher education are relevant for national competitiveness to the extent that it informs national policy agendas, and the cooperative logic is often surpassed by the logic of power. Sustainability has become the new marketing tool to gain alternative market portions of the green economy. These challenges are unfortunately part of our sustainability challenges if we do not leave behind (just) economic concerns. For a sustainable future, education underpinned by sustainability values must be at the forefront of future agendas, and in higher learning institutions education (which are the ones more at risk of 'marketisation') should aim at imparting sustainability values and norms by giving emphasis to collaborative efforts as well as encouraging practices that promote sustainability in a more 'transdisciplinary' spirit.

I suggest that we should bear in mind three key aspects for future policymaking:

(1) The assumption that the paradigm shift towards holistic approaches, the child centred approach, needs to be articulated in relation with the natural world in the Anthropocene;

[68] See further, Bruni and Zamagni (2015).

[69] See further, Locatelli (2018).

(2) This change of paradigm has already been embedded in most pedagogical approaches in Europe even without unsettling the current institutional structures. There is a need to re-orient educational institutions management, especially in their cultural and educational role to build sustainability. As opposed to the pedagogical field, this change of paradigm has not been fully embraced by policymakers, and consequently there is little concern around these topics by legal scientists. Nonetheless, there are certain Member States addressing (sometimes quite rhetorically) sustainability in future re-organisation of the educational content, things are not happening everywhere at the same rhythm, but the proliferation of the new governance mechanisms that are now part of the EU sustainability model may support future transformations at public level.

(3) SDG 4 launched by the Global Agenda, could be a valid model for building on further regulation and institutional reform in Member States' education institutional bodies. It might also help to extend the scope of the right to education and guide judicial decisions to shape a more homogenised content of such constitutionalised right throughout Europe, particularly referred to controversial contexts such as the one referred to 'equality' 'access', vocational and lifelong learning, etc.

5.2.1 SDG 4 and Curriculum Reorientation to Face Educational Challenges, But Not Only

The topic of how to face future challenges in our sustainability model by introducing substantial changes throughout the whole institutional existence of our current education models cannot be exhausted here, but we definitely need to depart 'somewhat' by providing some conceptual ingredients for further disquisitions about how to introduce changes at institutional level through legal mechanism (existing or new ones) in the most significant phases of our learning and teaching processes to foster sustainability values that are part of the Constitutional ethos of the EU. Unfortunately, even if I may mention pedagogical questions, the relevance of referring to them relates to the importance of contributing to a discussion about the legal and institutional reforms required by this field, which need to be founded on pedagogical roots, empirical research, evidence and experiences that go beyond the scope of this study, but are instrumental to it.

The contributions for change of our cultural surrounding and our educational systems have all insisted on the necessity to assimilate the implacable and plain law of our 'learning societies': "In order to survive people, enterprises and society as a whole demand to learn at least at the same speed with which the word around us is changing, but in order to progress we must learn at a higher speed than our surrounding" (Marina, 2017).

Neil Postman (2011), who has been an eclectic communication theorist, and shared a progressive vision of education (such as John Dewey), praised the influence of education to shape societal communities. He has contributed to the task of redefining the sense of education and pedagogy today by founding an educational reform on the construction of new 'narratives' based on a confrontational view affirming that current education systems are aimless because of a 'crisis of its current narratives'. His provocative work is entitled *The End of Education*. He suggests a new narrative based in (different stories), "new gods" (without religious sense) founded in the necessary conservation of the planet, cultural diversity and language. For this purpose he suggest the necessary creation of a new knowledge structure with a directing principle, the conservation of the planet, and then go on to create a new data base to foster the history of civilisation and culture freed from the faulty narratives in which he includes economic utility, consumerism, technology and multiculturalism. Although he stands as a referent for the American educational context, his discourse is universal, but in the array of suggestions about the "gods that may serve" as better narratives for new pedagogical foundations (touching upon nature conservationism-spaceship, ethics, cultural diversity, and linguistic concerns) I find one of the arguments behind the "Gods that may serve" that could be applied to our European narrative. He calls it the American experiment, not exempted from patriotism he devotes a whole chapter to "the American experiment" suggesting a new narrative for that. Briefly, his idea is to consider "America" a work in progress, encompassing government, economics, history, etc.

Within the European context would not be a question of changing narrative, but of creating one in which the European project passes as a work in progress in which we all need to take a responsible share. This is an inspiring work about the need of changing our current pedagogical foundations, without any particular or excessive attention to the digitalisation trend of education that worries educators today and has occupied a significant part of his work.[70] He does go to the heart of the main challenges: changing our pedagogical foundations and direct them to embrace at first instance a sense of responsibility towards the care for the Earth; to go on to speak of the many other challenges, such a 'multiculturalism', emblematic part of our European societies today. Postman does not support any available pedagogy and neither goes on as far as to devise a roadmap of how to formulate a plan or a political strategy for change. Still, his thoughts are valid, for its inspirational nature for curriculum change, and his thoughts are valid to me to introduce the difficulty of changing narratives within a context that has to do with philosophical, anthropological, historical, cultural and linguistic concerns. A complex context that touches upon different cultural concerns, and stages of education and learning.

My conceptual framework should depart from the wording of SDG 4. The 2030 Agenda, with its own dedicated Goal 4 devoted to the topic of education, aims at

[70]Postman (2011). Postman has a different work devoted to this topic, *Technolopoly: The surrender of Culture to Technology*. See further, Postman (1992); it can be retrieved from: www.collier.sts.vt.edu. In such work, Postman attempts to describe when, how and why technology became a particularly dangerous enemy. In his introduction, he describes the essence of his work, Postman criticises that the uncontrolled growth of technology destroys the vital sources of humanity and it creates a culture without moral foundation (Postman, 1992, p. xii).

ensuring inclusive and equitable quality education and promote lifelong learning opportunities for all. All the educational (and cultural) ambitions (and challenges) of humankind are included in the wording of this Goal.

Education 2030, founded on the principle of the Right to Education, goes beyond past attempts to ensure access to basic education, as set out in the 'Education for All'[71] goals and the education-related Millennium Development Goal 2 of 2000–2015. Sustainable Development Goal 4 has 10 targets encompassing many different aspects of education. There are seven targets, which are expected outcomes,[72] and three targets, which are means of achieving these outcomes.[73] There are also existing indicators such as participation rate in different education levels and forms, extent to which citizenship education and sustainable education are mainstreamed at all levels in curricula, teacher education, student assessments, scholarships access, and also a proportion of youth and adults with relevant skills in information technology and communication (ITC) and entrepreneurship, etc.[74] All are valid indicators to measure the success of such ambitious goal at global scale.

The Global Agenda 2030 and the SDGs would fall under the category of agreements adopted by the UN. The fact that once more education is placed at the forefront of the current UN development together with the many challenges that threaten the future of our global community gives evidence of its relevance for the future of human kind despite of how much is overlooked in terms of its decisive role for transformation. Cultural issues and the power of culture to address the ambitious goals of the SD Agenda have also been disregarded. Still, the governance mechanisms and the invitation for collaboration and global engagement at every action level implies that not only UN members should be taking concrete legal action (learning by experience) after such ambitious agenda, but regional organisations, national, local institutions, stakeholders and civil society should be highly involved and accountable.

[71]The Education for All (EFA) movement is a global commitment to provide quality basic education for all children, youth and adults. At the World Education Forum (Dakar, 2000), 164 governments pledged to achieve EFA and identified six goals to be met by 2015. Governments, development agencies, civil society and the private sector are working together to reach the EFA goals. UNESCO coordinates these partners, in cooperation with the four other convenors of the Dakar Forum (UNDP, UNFPA, UNICEF and the World Bank). UNESCO remains the leading agency and focuses its activities on five key areas: policy dialogue, monitoring, advocacy, mobilisation of funding, and capacity development.

[72]There are seven outcome targets: 4.1. Universal primary and secondary education; 4.2. Early childhood development and universal pre-primary education; 4.3. Equal access to technical/vocational and higher education; 4.4. Relevant skills for decent work; 4.5. Gender equality and inclusion; 4.6. Universal youth literacy; 4.7. Education for sustainable development and global citizenship.

[73]Three means of implementation: 4.a. Effective learning environments; 4.b. Scholarships; 4.c. Teachers and educators.

[74]UN Knowledge Platform. Targets and Indicators. Available on line: https://sustainabledevelopment.un.org/sdg4.

The specific targets of SDG 4 are accompanied by indicators to monitor progress, change and continuity that enable monitoring bodies to measure the path of development. Within SDG4, they describe the way in which a given unit (pupil, school, country or region) is progressing in relation to a specific target. SDG 4 indicators are multifaceted and many require new methodologies and calculation methods, as well as considerable changes to national systems reporting data both nationally and internationally (UNESCO, 2018a).

Beyond its impact on democracy, education at every learning level is a key driver of economic and societal development, and this is embedded in SDG 4 targets. Moreover, the relationship between education and other dimensions of sustainable development, as well as its important interaction with other goals, cannot be overlooked. Still, despite its potential as a driver for the attainment of other goals it is indeed ignored specially by legal scholarship because of the lack of evidence and knowledge on the pathways by which education influences other sectors of development. This in fact has been evidenced by the last monitoring reports including contributions from the highest-level engagement of the academic and the political world in every field of action (TWI2050, 2018, p. 33).

The first target of SDG 4 stipulates the provision of 12 years of free public primary and secondary education of which at least nine years should be compulsory. This is related to the long-established foundational principles of education as a human right and as a public good, underlying the primary responsibility of the State in ensuring the right to education for all, in safeguarding social justice and in the public interest in education (Locatelli, 2018). According to this requirement, States are expected to directly provide the institutional and the financial resources. This is well engrained within the European context, especially during mandatory education. Still, it remains a big challenge for European Education system in the basis of providing 'quality', new curriculum reform, equality, and equal access; and of course for the EU external and development policy.

The new proactive role of the 2030 Agenda for SD on education's function to promote sustainable development lies in the way SDG 4 addresses 'education' in its multiple applied contexts. I hope the bulk of requirements that have reached consensus at global level could foster more legal scholarship attention. The Agenda widens the focus to education levels outside the traditional frame of compulsory education, including early childhood education and care (Indicator 4.2.2), secondary, post-secondary and tertiary vocational education (Indicator 4.3.3) and adult education (Indicator 4.3.1).

This reveals the evidence of the educational challenges in our complex dynamic societies. Ensuring inclusive, quality education at all these levels remains a challenge for the European sustainability model. Target 4.2 reaffirms the importance for all children of receiving a strong 'foundation' through early childhood education and care. The OECD (2015) has identified the growing need of measuring equity with regard to access to quality services on all these extended areas of the learning processes, and has been focused on developing data on faithful indicators' results, especially for the relevance with regard to equity concerns.

The notion of equity is essential to us because it is linked to a normative framework of fairness, which may differ across countries and cultures, but it is mandatory under European constitutional traditions. The main indicator chosen to measure equity across the SDG 4 agenda is the parity index. It is defined as the ratio between the values of a given indicator for two different groups, with the value of the likely most disadvantaged group in the numerator. These measuring instruments could proof ineffective as indicators for eventual reform or urgent policy action in the European context, let alone the wider spectrum of development.[75]

Regarding non-compulsory education, target 4.3 focuses on participation in technical, vocational and tertiary levels of education and training. Each of these programmes plays a crucial role in preparing students for the labour market, and as it has been argued to increase social European cohesion, and solidarity to be applied in our external policy. Participation of 15–24 years-old in technical-vocational programmes in secondary, post-secondary, non-tertiary and short-cycle tertiary education varies widely across countries, and has strong associations with both gender and socio-economic status.[76] Target 4.4 refers to skills for work, actually, skills could be considered as the ultimate goal of education policy, and it does not concern simply providing access to all levels of education, it entails to ensure that all students gain the necessary skills to guide them through life (OECD, 2018a). Target 4.4 refers to skills for work. In today's increasingly digitalised economies, literacy and numeracy skills may not be sufficient to prosper in the labour market; but an excessive focus on technical and computational skills have excessively shadowed other urgent concerns with regard to a strong sustainability model investing in other issues skill-related (i.e., integration of social and civic services in the education programme, cultural concerns, social care, nature related services, etc.). The indicators (such as global indicator 4.4.1) associated to target 4.5 are actually drafted to measure the "proportion of youth and adults with information and communications technology (ICT) skills, by type of skill" (OECD, 2018a),[77] but this target is also concerned with resources, which for our conceptual approach are crucial. Ensuring equitable participation and skills acquisition relies on the availability of resources. This explains why Target 4.5 aiming at eliminating all discrimination in education contains three financing-related indicators, each of which tackles education expenditure from a different angle.[78] Target 4.6 aims at ensuring universal literacy and

[75]See further information on measuring inequity in education, at UNESCO *Handbook on Measuring in Education* (UIS, 2018b).

[76]See further, OECD (2018b).

[77]This indicator has been developed according to the definition of the International Telecommunications Union in the framework of the Partnership on Measuring ICT for Development, see further (ITU, 2014).

[78]Target 4.5 By 2030 aims at eliminating gender disparities in education and ensure equal access to all levels of education and vocational training for the vulnerable, including persons with disabilities, indigenous peoples, and children in vulnerable situations. Expenditure for student data is presented for OECD and partners countries by the report on 'Education at glance' (OECD, 2018a). In fact, the thematic indicator 4.5.4 on "Education expenditure per student by level of education and source of

numeracy, target that is underpinned by the contemporary understanding of literacy as a continuum of proficiency levels in a given context.[79]

The key target concerning the major educational challenge of the European sustainability model is entrenched in target 4.7: "Education for sustainable development and global citizenship". I have discussed in a separate article how to implement SDG into the curriculum (Sánchez Galera, 2018) To implement successfully SDG 4.7 (Considering that National realities now are striving for a change), namely, to which extent (i) global citizenship education and (ii) education for sustainable development, including gender equality and human rights, are mainstreamed at all levels in: (a) national education policies, (b) curricula, (c) teacher education and (d) student assessment (in the last place).

> The target aims at ensuring that all learners acquire the knowledge and skills needed to promote sustainable development, including, among others, through education sustainable development and sustainable lifestyles, human rights, gender equality, promotion of a culture of peace and nonviolence, global citizenship and appreciation of cultural diversity and of culture's contribution to sustainable development.[80]

Target 4.a aims at building and upgrade education facilities that are child, disability and gender sensitive and provide safe, non-violent, inclusive and effective learning environments for all. This target addresses the need for adequate physical infrastructure and safe, inclusive environments that nurture learning for all, regardless of background or disability status.

Target 4.b aims at substantially expand globally the number of scholarships available to developing countries, in particular least developed countries, small island developing States and African countries, for enrolment in higher education, including vocational training and information and communications technology, technical, engineering and scientific programmes, in developed countries and other developing countries, to be reached by 2020. The reasoning behind this target is based on the vital role Scholarship programmes play in providing opportunities for young people and adults who would otherwise not be able to afford to continue their education.[81]

---

funding" provides a meaningful way to measure the availability of resources in a country. This indicator alone cannot measure the quality or equitability of education in a country, but it serves as a useful reference point. The report OECD suggests that increased data availability, such as disaggregation by students' socio-economic status or location of schools, for example, would provide more relevant information to measure target 4.5 (OECD, 2018a, p. 33).

[79]It goes beyond the understanding of a simple dichotomy of 'literate' versus 'illiterate', to refer to functional literacy and numeracy skills extended to all children and adults.

[80]www.sdg4education.2030.org.

[81]According to this target, where developed countries offer scholarships to students from developing countries, these should be structured to build the capability of the developing country. While the importance of scholarships is recognised, donor countries are encouraged to increase other forms of support to education. In line with the SDG 4—Education 2030 focus on equity, inclusion and quality, scholarships should be transparently targeted at young people from disadvantaged backgrounds. See further, https://www.sdg4education2030.org/the-goal.

Target 4.c, which is to be reached by 2030, is aimed at a substantial increase of the supply of qualified teachers, including through international cooperation for teacher training in developing countries, especially least developed countries and small islands developing States, this is based on the understanding of crucial role of teachers to achieve all the SDG 4 targets.[82]

Five other goals refer to the SDG 4, and show the almost exhaustive approach that the Agenda has devoted to education as an integrative and crosscutting goal defining welfare and well-being:

- Health and well-being (SDG 3 target 3.7)
  By 2030, ensure universal access to sexual and reproductive healthcare services, including for family planning, information and education, and the integration of reproductive health into national strategies and programmes
- Gender equality (SDG 5 target 5.6)
  Number of countries with laws and regulations that guarantee women aged 15–49 years access to sexual and reproductive health care, information and education
- Decent work and sustainable growth (SDG 8 target 8.6)
  By 2020 substantially reduce the proportion of youth not in employment, education or training.
- Responsible consumption & production (SDG 12 target 12.8)
  By 2030 ensure that people everywhere have the relevant information and awareness for sustainable development and lifestyles in harmony with nature. This target is particularly challenging for Europe that has an ambitious plan for its circular economy without providing any guiding program to be introduced into educational institutions at primary and secondary education level.
- Climate change mitigation (SDG 13 target 13.3)
  Improve education, awareness raising and human and institutional capacity on climate change mitigation, adaptation, impact reduction, and early warning. Italy is the first country to announce a compulsory subject on climate change to be introduced.

Let us say that the new 'narratives' suggested by Postman are relevant here, but the contextual role given to culture is not indifferent, considering how little 'wording' has been devoted to it in the Global Agenda, and the overlooked leading role of cultural institutions for the accomplishment and awareness enhancement of the agenda. SDG 4.7 stands as a yardstick for a guided institutional reform required by the foundational concerns of our education systems which is currently completely disconnected from nature, cultural institutions and our responsibility towards it. But another big educational challenge remains the training of qualified teachers, the human resources component remains one of the most important elements that cannot

[82]It requires urgent attention, with a more immediate deadline, because the equity gap in education is exacerbated by the shortage and uneven distribution of professionally trained teachers, especially in disadvantaged areas. As teachers are a fundamental condition for guaranteeing quality education, teachers and educators should be empowered, adequately recruited and remunerated, motivated, professionally qualified, and supported within well-resourced, efficient and effectively governed systems. See further, https://www.sdg4education2030.org/the-goal.

be shadowed by promising (digital) teaching methods such as the one experimented in a Slum at Kalkaji in Delhi by Sugata Mitra placing a computer (the so-called "Hole in the wall") in a wall and observing some days later that kids had acquired advanced knowledge in different topics just on their own.

How should we start devising an institutional reform? The answers could be many at practical level, but for a functional theoretical approach I have decided to suggest this action 'template' to apply SDG 4.7. We need first:

(1) Exploration about how the concept of sustainable development with all the SDG fits into our legal systems;
(2) advocacy and communication activities to stimulate awareness and active participation (among associations of national and local public administrations, public and private universities, research centres, organisations member of international organisations dealing with SDGs, etc.). Especially relevant is the role of associations of stakeholders working in the field of culture and information;
(3) *memorandum* of understanding among all the involved parties and the government for a detailed action plan; and finally.
(4) introduction of a policy scenario that offers a strategic plan for educators, teachers, educational institutions, schools at every level, research centres, stakeholders, and society as whole. The final result (should) and could be a well-designed curriculum integrating the 17 SDG.

Defining concrete action in education is challenging considering how much our society is changing. The challenge passes not only through the implementation of a compulsory global curricula implementing the 17 SDG, although this, undoubtedly, lies at the basis of embedding education in the other SDGs, the challenge is also instrumentalising education as part of the complex process of development itself that aims at building a long lasting heritage for humanity, and its future cultural patterns. The problem is that States have never been interested on reaching consensus about the possibility to fulfill in a coordinated manner the right to education. Nor there has been an interest on a harmonised or standardised curriculum. Instead there is a growing formalisation of the trend for standardised student assessments[83] and analyses of sectorial competences throughout the world. In my view, they become useless assessment tools if they are not concretely used to strengthen national curricula and institutional teaching and learning instruments. Indicators could also be of little use if we do not use best practices (even if only based on better achievements) to improve national systems based on successful experiences elsewhere.

Effective, accountable and inclusive institutions and public administrations are another critical part to implement the SDGs. This is particularly true for education and cultural concerns. The 2030 Agenda's vision calls for more coherent action across a wider scope of issues and the engagement of a broader range of stakeholders than ever before, but needs implementation of the SDGs requiring a nationally long-term vision with the engagement and localisation of accountable institutions. On the

[83]Such as the famous PISA (Programme for International Student Assessment).

way to achieve this, we will identify some concrete action led by cultural and educational institutions (later in this chapter) at local level.

The current EU framework for action in the cultural field provide for integrated and crosscutting policy action, involving bottom-up approaches in which citizen's participation has become strategic. In Europe, multiple realities are acting as examples of transformation drawing on current legal frameworks that without having introduced big systemic transformations provide the right legal basis for increasing school autonomy and localised educational administrations, cultural action and enhanced role of cultural institutions to foster strong sustainability practices. In fact, cultural institutions, according to the given context and economic resources are more prompt today to change and to provide substantial pedagogical influence to spread strong sustainability and collaborative practices introducing into the public education system private and third sector stakeholders in order to improve the pedagogical offer. However, this of course is not enough because we need a systemic change with strong public policy engagement and coordinated action from Europe pushing the integration of education and cultural heritage and research for sustainable development. It is time to claim strong policy intervention at national level, not exclusively restricted to short sighted political wills dwarft in rhetorical action frameworks and not implemented strategies at national and EU level.

5.2.2 *From Higher Education to Early Childhood. The Overarching Culture of a Strong Sustainability Model Failing to Reach Educational Institutions?*

We tend to forget that since national educational systems were first organised in the eighteenth century legislation has been used to enforce a variety of educational policies, and this has also happened at supranational level in Europe, and in many federal systems were national laws provide just the basic framework for regional or local legislation and policies. In fact, most countries have relied on statutory and delegated legislation to bring about educational change. Consequently, the twentieth century witnessed the intensification and diversification of education legislation throughout the world for various purposes, including the reorientation of educational systems for nation building or rebuilding after the World Wars, the development of education and curricular reforms in response to social change, including globalisation, and the promotion of special national goals or tasks (Law, 2007). Still, in the sociology of law literature there is a broad spectrum of views on the relationship between law and social change. In fact, an instrumentalist view of law to bring change can be criticised for leaving aside other relevant factors such as cultural, political or economic issues.[84] The discussion has been more prolific when applied

[84]Law (2007) gives bibliographic evidence of the different views. He explains that one extreme of the spectrum views the law in terms of legislation and judicial decisions that are both a source and route of social change, and he refers to the works of Anleu (2000) as an instrumentalist view.

in development contexts and national building in more recent times within the Asian-Pacific region.[85] Still a discussion about the role of law to mainstream change today cannot be separated from cultural issues. Nonetheless, the development of education and curricula reforms in response to social change is an international trend that has also influenced some curricula modification in EU Member States to introduce innovation concerning mainly, environmental education, digital issues and the enhancement of scientific areas with detriment of 'humanist' subjects. In reality, the use of law as a top-down exercise to influence educational change has been largely criticised,[86] and can be hardly disapproved today because of the need of obtaining support of all the educational parties involved, teachers, trainers, school directors, managers, policymakers, stakeholders, and families. Today, we should not be afraid to affirm that there are many factors influencing transformations, and the instruments available could be many.

On the light of the varied availability of factors influencing transformation, Kosta (2019) reminds us that "as the countries of the world move toward meeting the UN 2030 SDGs, the importance of Higher education Institutions (HEIs) as drivers and enablers of sustainability has been labelled up".[87] This should not be a surprise, considering that HEIs are more prompt for change and innovation than Primary and Secondary School Institutions. It is important to acknowledge how much of the effort has been focused on HEIs and driven by them to accomplish the ambitious 2030 Agenda and, generally speaking, to spread and reach sustainability concerns or cultural heritage ones. Their role on developing the skills of the locality where they are established and the appraisal of their role to create links and relationships with various stakeholders and communities creating interconnections and interdependencies between higher education society and economy (Jongbloed, Enders, & Salerno, 2008) has strengthened their leading role in the education sector in national public policies and the global agenda (SDSN, 2018). However, the focus on HEIs is insufficient to mainstream all the desired efforts for committed educational models needed to achieve sustainable development.[88]

At the moment there are countless initiatives to foster sustainability at higher education level, but for the purpose of this study it suffices to mention a few of them. The value of the many initiatives is the indication that things are changing and awareness has grown. People at that level of education, management and action are engaged with sustainability concerns even if the policy horizon may appear fragmented. There is the Higher Education Sustainability Initiative (HESI) within

---

Podgórecki (Podgórecki, 1974; Podgórecki, 1985) would be at the other extreme, deeming law as a passive force of change and recognising both, the rising reliance on and the limitations of using law to effect social change.

[85]See Pan and Law (2006), and Law (2007).

[86]See, Lieberman (1997), and DeMitchell and Fossey (1997).

[87]Kosta (2019).

[88]See further, Fleaca, Fleaca, and Maiduc (2018).

the UN ambit,[89] and as part of a European initiative, we can find the European University association initiative[90] on the belief that universities facilitate social, environmental and economic development for being strong institutions accountable to society and platforms of knowledge creation contributing to all the knowledge areas and culture spread, especially at local level. Unfortunately, there is no space here to discuss other HEI initiatives in other regional parts of the world. Actually, their major accomplishment is that universities are closely connected to their regions, playing a crucial role not only in educational concerns, but also, in innovation, culture, health (university medical hospitals), poverty alleviation, and civil life of their local communities (Oppong, 2018). Being also major employers, they make considerable economic contributions to their regions and bring solutions to urgent challenges, through partnerships, research, training, local engagement, internationalisation, etc. Universities are in the process of recognising the need for shifting and transforming established structures and practices in research, teaching, and operations to meet the sustainability challenges of the twenty-first century.[91]

One important domain of HE transformation as a knowledge platform for our sustainable societies is the emergence of international education programs in 'sustainability', with a strong sustainability approach, especially valuable when introduced in business' education programs (Molthan-hill, 2017). What is eventually the success of these programs? Their general learning objectives comprehend the following:

(1) Increasing the capability of the students to work across national, geographical and cultural boundaries;
(2) Recognising the cultural, historical, epistemological and ethical context of perceiving sustainability problems and developing solution options; and.
(3) Drawing on a pool of internationally-sourced solution ideas that can, when adapted, be transferred to different local contexts.

However, what is the value added of the role of higher education institutions in Europe? They have a conspicuously public role to contribute to the 'shaping of the European Identity' and the European culture not exempted of responsibility. To meet this public responsibility, as well as they have historically received generous

[89]It is a partnership between United Nations Department of Economic and Social Affairs, UNESCO, United Nations Environment, UN Global Compact's Principle for Responsible Management Education (PRME) initiative, UN University, UN-HABITAT, UNCTAD and UNITAR, was created in 2012 in the run-up to the UN Conference on SD (Río + 20). With commitments from over 300 universities from around the world, HESI accounted for more than one-third of all the voluntary commitments that were launched at Rio + 20. Through its strong association with the UN, HESI provides higher education institutions with a unique interface between higher education, science and policymaking Sustainable Development Knowledge Platform: sustainabledevelopment.un.org.

[90]See further, http://bit.ly/EUA and SDGs.

[91]There is abundant research evidencing the leadership of HEI in sustainability, see further, Gough and Longjurst (2017), Caniglia et al. (2017), Gunesakara (2004), Fleaca et al. (2018), Molthan-hill, Puntha, Darmasasmita, and Simmons (2015), Ávila et al. (2017).

amounts of government funding, they are now receiving European funding, whilst keeping their institutional and academic autonomy. Their social responsibility is scrutinised through laws and policy framework accountable to government, and governing bodies (Neave, 2000), but their autonomy, and the academic freedom is far more under-scrutinised than it is at any other educational institutional ambit (primary, secondary, etc.). Thus, the public service function of university has been evidenced based on the contribution that universities make to the solution of major problems faced by local communities and by society a large (OECD-CERI, 1982, p. 10). Their autonomy and their burgeoning position at the scale of educational institutions render them particularly influential.

Nonetheless, if we want to mention two of the dangers of the leading role of higher education for our sustainable future supporting the cooperative societies that we need ahead of us, I should remark 2 things about their negative side: (1) One, is the risk of higher education institutions to play part of the 'marketisation' of education in many different ways. On the other hand, the fact that is not a compulsory education level, and the far reaching consequences of their contribution to improve the social, economic, and cultural conditions of their communities, shadows such 'merchandising' side; (2) The second danger is the fragmented and uncoordinated nature of the sustainability initiatives that may emerge from one single institution and 'die' afterwards. Many of those initiatives despite of their valuable contribution are not helping to change institutional structures, especially when considering educational institutions (such as primary and secondary education).

A relevant shift is offered by the growth of transdisciplinary research which has emerged within academic practice, however we need to take such 'practice' which belongs to the epistemology of education to the entire institutional structure considering the 'universality' of education at every level and the need to identify fundamental problems that are neglected in the pedagogical realm but should be taught in the future. They should be taught for the sake of transformation and to build a 'sustainable future' for our children, grandchildren and great grandchildren. We can say with Edgar Morin (1999) that "*[I]f we want this earth to provide for the needs of its inhabitants, human society must undergo a transformation. The world of tomorrow must be fundamentally different from the world we know as we step into the 21st century and the new millennium*".

The role of the universities has also been criticised for helping to enlarge global knowledge and contribute to the so-called academic knowledge instead of creating local knowledge and empowerment (Chatterton and Goddard, 2000); but this eventually could also change by creating awareness and local empowerment from the university context, in fact this is the heart of the matter of 'transition network'[92] initiatives, which are already a real movement in some parts of the world; and it should be the successful introduction of 'transdisciplinary' methodology in well-

[92]See further, transition network (2018); David Fleming, Chamberlin, and Hopkins (2016), Jain and Jain (2008), and the experience of Swaraj University available at: http://www.swarajuniversity.org.

established scientific fields. Universities have their share on transformation, by empowering local knowledge, local culture, and transition to sustainable cultural production and consumption patterns by integrating the compulsory education world into its mission of spreading and creating knowledge. They should foster integration avoiding the drastic moves towards ‘marketisation’ and ‘elitism’. Academic work could often help ‘transformation’ initiatives to spread over as it is already the case (Göpel, 2016), but it is still insufficient because of its disconnection from other educational structures and, often, from the cultural institutions.

Thus, in any case, the big share is clearly to stimulate changes from earlier spheres of learning. Institutional change, policy intervention and transdisciplinary research should be focused on designing transformations from early childhood development. The emphasis, considering the need for systematic research, should be placed urgently at this lower stage of education (early childhood, primary and secondary education, informal education, etc.), and the policy path is already open. However, welfare policies, as well as alternative governance structures opening the path for third sector and organised group of citizens’ initiatives, should be provided with the right legal instruments to obtain funding, the right infrastructures, fiscal aid and sufficient policy attention for long-term overarching interventions.

One of the most significant advances in the understanding of human capital over the lifecycle has been in the area of early childhood development (Sachs, 2015). Sachs puts emphasis on the instrumental nature of the scientific knowledge gained concerning the early stages of human development to build on new channels to prepare human to the challenges of what he calls the age of sustainable development. Obviously, the human capital was always there, a couple of decades ago, early childhood development “was on the formal education system, with little understanding of the crucial importance of the preschool environment, including health nutrition, physical safety, and preschool preparation of children ages 0-6” (Sachs, 2015, p. 256). It has taken some statistics, and data based on neurological, medical, nutritional, pedagogical and other scientific studies to understand the importance of those early years of human development.[93]

What we need now for these early phases of growth is the articulation of a context-specific theory of change focusing on human development outcomes to force public expenditure, inspired by sustainability principles (SDGs) to bring tangible results for children, and the generations to come. The importance of child lens for achieving SDGs has been advanced by UNICEF (2017) without providing an institutional approach trying to appeal to an interdisciplinary audience of experts and policy advocates who could be interested on further adaptation of SDG framework to the national context. The emphasis is placed on public actions to achieve better child outcomes through the interlinked influence of family, community, policies and institutions. UNICEF and the most recent research on human

[93]Evidence has widely shown that the early years play a pivotal role in determining future performance and breaking the vicious circle of socio-economic inequality. See further data, (OECD, 2017).

development have provided a definition of a child-centred approach to development that has been missing for decades. This approach should be complemented contextually (always with a view to a positive planning and increment resources) with empirical research based on the successful experiences of promoting outdoor education and some sustainability akin pedagogical approaches that not only keep the child at the centre, but also his or her relationship with nature that is inextricable, and should be extended through the approach to education in other phases of development and compulsory schooling (i.e., primary, secondary education).

The main conceptual leap that future institutional and systematic approaches should consider about these early stages of education embraces the theory of life cycle skills formation under which fundamental skills acquired in early years produce and foster skills later in life (Heckman, 2008).[94] This is especially true when applied to and in relationship with the natural environment and the contribution of early childhood education to a sustainable society (UNESCO, 2008) that is part of the whole approach to education for sustainable societies fostered by UNDESD[95] already discussed. The financial resources should be spread up for these interventions.

Growing bibliographical and scientific data is available to justify structural institutional interventions with adequate financial resources to transform educational institutions in those relevant early life stages. This is one crucial effective way to construct a just and sustainable world. We need to pay major attention to education from the earliest stages of development. As I mentioned before the growing awareness about the crucial role of the early years of development is not a modern trend, it has been supported by scientific research in the areas of physical development, anatomy and physiology, and psychological development, cognitive, psychosocial and personality building (UNESCO, 2008). This has prompted a flow of interdisciplinary research departing from the discoveries on the evolution of the brain and on the evolution of the individual from sensorimotor stage to pre-operational stage before the age of seven. Government should not only devote public investment that should be reinforced in all areas of education holistically, it should also re-orientate the teaching and learning program contents towards strong sustainability models to be applied at every education level.

Thanks to a major integration of scientific data of interdisciplinary nature, with regard to the learning and teaching offer (early childhood, primary, secondary, adult

[94]On top of that, the UNICEF (2017) report provides arguments about the wealth of evidence suggesting that "public returns on investments in children are high, particularly when policy ensures that the most disadvantaged children are benefiting from the provision. The effects of Early Childhood Education programmes are a good example. The High quality of these programmes produce long-term improvements in school success and school attainment; some are also found to be associated with reduced delinquency and crime in childhood and adulthood, better employment chances and higher earnings.

[95](2005–2014) that has been renewed by the overarching education goal of the UN 2030 Agenda for SD.

and literacy as life-long learning opportunity), policymakers could have better and more proficient available data for lawmaking. In addition, because of the diversification of bottom-up approaches influencing educational and cultural change, there is room to encourage action and by providing the right governance framework at local level to mainstream action by different stakeholders whose role should not be limited to reinforce the already well-established public educational offer. Stakeholders and local communities should attempt to include other formal, informal and non-formal settings considering the demographic increase in our European urban areas, and the lack of institutional resources.[96]

Unfortunately, there are not enough engaging works (especially within the field of law, or the sociology of law) aimed at giving clear evidence of how crucial the role of education is to achieve a sustainable future, nor about how its function is important for a responsible engagement in our civic contexts to build collaborative societies and create more and more awareness for the protection of our natural resources. Human scale culture and community experiences are taking the floor leading academic discourses on 'transformation',[97] also SDGs transformation role, but these (still) niche realities that are gaining importance, especially in economic science, do not delineate either a clear path to face cultural and educational challenges for the future of a strong sustainability model.

The cultural 'software' rooted in economic and social transformation running with experiences such as 'transition towns' in the UK (one of the most popular degrowth movements), would definitely create the 'humus' for further research to design theoretical frameworks valid for the European sustainability model that could help more radical shifts within the area of education. However, those changes that need to be systematic and overarching are not a reality yet.[98] I intend to give my share on this although some efforts in systemic change and integration of SD education into teaching and learning curricula are already extended.[99]

---

[96]The analytical tools when referring to the European context become more concerned with the quality of the provision of early childhood services already well established, but still not fully re-oriented towards integrating sustainability principles based on cooperation, enhanced understanding of our dependency from the limited resources of the planet Earth, equality, social cohesion, etc. When we refer to the developing world, the gap is still very wide, and it is difficult to imagine universal access to basic social services to envisage participation in social, economic and cultural development. We must bear in mind that poverty renders in a drastic manner, education and health provisions harder, and these conditions continue to provoke bigger population growth.

[97]Göpel (2016) and Fleming et al. (2016).

[98]See for instance, what is happening in India: http://www.swarajuniversity.org/.

[99]See further, Jucker and Mathar (2015).

5.2.3 Complex Reality and the Educational Engagement: From Edgar Morin Thought to the Laudato Si' **Contrasted with** *Environmental and (Post) Sustainability Education*

Despite its conceptual vagueness, SD has helped the world to reach consensus on a global agenda and define new strategies that are instrumental to face old and new problems. Vagueness is never a good friend to define concrete action for 'transforming the world' according to what the 2030 Agenda envisages. Still, education (and culture entering from the 'back door') seem to be an effective widely accepted basis for future transformation. As early as 1996, Delors Commission (UNESCO, 1996) in a report entitled: *Education Treasure Within*, placed education at the heart of society and it tackled on the most disrupting topics of our complex societies. It devoted most of the report to devise specific policy directions on the different education stages. The ideas that were launched with such report are still vivid and correspond the same educational and cultural needs that our society needs today. The emphasis was given to the education as expression of affection for children and young people "whom we need to welcome into society, unreservedly offering them the place that is theirs by right there in- a place in the education system, to be sure, but also in the family, the local community and the nation". It introduced the all-embracing idea of the "learning society" that has helped to broaden education throughout a life-time and the concept of learning throughout life thus emerges as one of the keys to the twenty-first century, without diminishing the strong policy concern to 'basic education' which is the basis of a good use of the potential resources offered by education under a long life perspective. Therefore, nothing can replace the formal education system where each individual is introduced the many forms of knowledge that helps him or her through life. Not by chance, learner-centered pedagogies are the guiding paradigm today, the problem is that are (still) not human centered (!). This has taken pedagogical theorist to design new learning 'clusters', enquiry-based learning or collaborative learning, which are particularly suitable in giving the learner an active role and promoting the application of key skills and attitudes. This has been so, to permit knowledge and skills being developed to change in tune with the world of the twenty-first century and adapt better to our learning society. That is why curriculum reforms introducing environmental or sustainability concerns with specific subjects or learning programs, is crucial (and helpful), but not enough. A new pedagogical paradigm in our learning society needs the right policy pillars for society transformation preserving solidarity, social justice and future generation principles. To achieve this, we need to build a dialogue between legal scholars and pedagogical theorists and communities.

European Member States' education systems need a more integrated approach to education in this sense. Thus, we need legal scholars engagement and in communication with pedagogical needs. European education systems need a whole institutional reform to create the basis, at least, for what the Delors Commission called the four pillars of education: (1) *Learning to live together*, by developing an understanding of others and their history, traditions and spiritual values; (2) *learning to know;* (3) *learning to do*; (4) *learning to be*, which was the dominant theme of the Edgar Faure Report *Learning to Be: the World of Education Today and Tomorrow*, (UNESCO, 1972). The Delors Commission draws on the precedent report on light of the contemporary relevance of such pillar, but adds a further imperative: "none of the talents which are hidden like buried treasure in every person must be left untapped" (UNESCO, 1996).

The reform strategies suggested by the Delors Commission are universally valid and give some guiding policy instruments of crucial relevance:

(1) Long-term approach of the required reforms, stressing the fact that too many reforms one after another can be the death of reform, but this unfortunately has been the opposite of what it has been happening in many European States (i.e. Spain, Italy, France, Greece, Poland, Lithuania); The Finnish education system with its well-known reform in the seventies stands as a model of education that complies with the four pillars of this report and the guises of innovation under the complexities of today's societies. Finland by investing into the development of its human resources to activate its economic growth, brought into life a well-designed economic system that upgraded the social, cultural and material status of educators and this was considered a matter of priority to foster a high quality education system.
(2) The second reform strategy of the Delors Commission regards the local community and the relevant part of teachers. The parties involved in strategies contributing to the success of educational reforms are, first, the local community, including parents, school heads and teachers; second, the public authorities; and third, the international community. Local community participation has not traditionally been part of our European educational reforms. In this respect, the Delors Commission stressed the value of a cautious measure of decentralisation in helping to increase educational establishment's responsibilities and their scope for innovation (UNESCO, 1996).[100]
(3) A third guiding suggestion that is highly relevant and urgent today for the improvement of education "requires policy makers to face up squarely to their responsibilities. They cannot leave it to market forces or to some kind of self-regulation to put things right when they go wrong" (UNESCO, 1996).

This important requirement of policymakers' action takes us to the validation of subsequent UNESCO reports, such as the Edgar Morin seven lessons on education,[101] that today are re-gaining attention. Two antidotes are suggested by the idea of education as common good, and by the transdisciplinary methodology that should be applied to fragmented and reductionist knowledge and to the 'paradigm of disjunction and separation' that Morin is presenting:

[100]On this, see further the contribution of Iso Amagi, "Upgrading the quality of school education", in the epilogue to the Report (UNESCO, 1996).
[101]Morin (1999).

(1) the need to define the role of the State in Education (UNESCO, 2015a);
(2) Identification of fundamental problems that are overlooked or neglected in education, and should be taught in the future introducing a paradigm compatible with complex knowledge that are at the basis of his transdisciplinary vision of thought, and the idea of learning about learning, including the learner into his knowledge. (Morin, 1999).

Today the challenges posed by cultural diversity run the risk of turning into "clashes of civilizations" and need to be faced by our educational systems as part of 'sustainability' policies that embed transversal policy concerns. According to Morin (1999), the education of the future needs to grasp the realities and problems that are global, transnational, multidimensional, transversal, polydisciplinary, and planetary. He defines the complexity we face as the "bond between unity and multiplicity".[102]

The value of Morin's document lies on the conceptual basis provided for a new educational reform fostering human developing in a complex society. He advances the idea of understanding human development as a joint development of individual autonomies, community participation and a sense of belonging to the human species (Morin, 1999, p. 25). The thinker, deals explicitly with what he calls 'somatic' diversities (superficial differences) language, myths, rituals and ethnic cultures that, he argues continue to hide the common bio-anthropological identity. In his thought emerges the idea of the necessity of a new paradigm based on a spiritual planetary sense of belonging, going beyond superficial cultural diversities. In his view, our constant focus on differences has helped humanity to build barriers, and education is the key to demolish such fences in our societies. UNESCO has indeed given a specific value to his theoretical contribution on 'complex thought' and its relevance for the education of the future.[103]

Today there is a converging scientific, intellectual and spiritual thought that places an emphasis on 'complexity' and the importance of redefining the mission of 'education' in a world going through a deep ecological crisis. If we take the *Laudato Si'* Encyclical (Pope Francis, 2015), we find a variety of places in which the Encyclical intersects, from time to time, with ecological culture as opposed to a failing anthropocentric culture, for an epistemology of complexity and for the denunciation of the so-called "technocratic paradigm"; many other places of thought in the Encyclical converge with the 'Morinian' approach of inter-poly-transdisciplinarity as an antidote to fragmented and reductionist knowledge and to the 'paradigm of disjunction and separation'. It is surprising to find in paragraph 79 of the Encyclical a conceptual reference to 'open systems', recalling Von Bertalanffy 'systems theory', a theory which is spread today in ecological science and presented as the right scientific model to face the complexities surrounding

[102]He introduces the issue of 'general intelligence' instrumental to his idea of complexity and quotes the words of H. Simon expressing that the "human mind is a G.P.S. (General Problems Setter and Solver)". Morin argues that, contrary to what is widely believed, developing general aptitudes of the mind improves the capacity to develop particular and specialised skills (Morin, 1999, p. 15).

[103]See Morin (1999).

ecological problems. There is a strong message against the anthropocentric model that situates man at the top of the hierarchy and explains how the ideal of harmony, justice, fraternity and peace in Jesus' message is at the opposite side of such model[104] and the Encyclical places a strong emphasis on this.

In paragraph 116, we read: "Many times the" Promethean dream "of domination over the world has been transmitted which has given the impression that the care of nature is a weak thing. Instead the correct interpretation of the concept of the human being as lord of the universe is that of understanding him as responsible administrator" (Pope Francis, 2015, para. 116).[105]

Of particular significance is the statement that links the ecological crisis to the crisis of humanity in the age of modernity: "If the ecological crisis is an emergence or an external manifestation of the ethical, cultural and spiritual crisis of modernity, we cannot delude ourselves to heal our relationship with nature and the environment without healing all fundamental human relations (...) In fact we cannot propose a relationship with the environment regardless of that with other people and God. It would be a romantic individualism disguised as ecological beauty and an asphyxiating imprisonment in immanence" (Pope Francis, 2015, par. 119).

Here there is a clear message about the spiritual essence of man, and the ecological culture against anthropocentric culture, that is converging today in every sphere of thought and spreading all over the political and philosophical debates in search of a common purpose to save the planet. That is why we should be aware that the momentum has arrived, and Europe has a specific mission on this on the transition towards a strong sustainability model.

The value of the encyclical thought for the European sustainability model lies on the call for awareness of complexity aligned to the most relevant conceptual approaches (included Edgar Morin), to face our cultural and educational challenges. The text has also a sounded strong critical attitude against technocracy. Actually, it strongly criticises the institutional, political, economic focus on the 'prevailing technocratic paradigm" that renders human kind "naked and unprotected in front of his own power that grows constantly without having the means to keep control of it" (Pope Francis, 2015, par. 101), and has not helped policy approaches to address true challenges. There is a hard criticism to our financial systems, and my ending note about the Encyclical's contribution regards Chapter VI devoted to "Education and Ecological Spirituality". The Chapter refers to the Earth Charter and the need to develop a universal consciousness to render possible the abandonment of our destructive phase. There is a specific claim for an alliance between humanity and environment that should be reached through educational and cultural means. In fact, it is clear that "awareness about the seriousness of our current cultural and ecological crisis has to be translated into new habits" (Pope Francis, 2015, para. 209).

---

[104]The Encyclical text introduces the Biblical citation of Jesus: "You know that the rulers of the Gentiles lord it over them, and their high officials exercise authority over them. Not so with you. Instead, whoever wants to become great among you must be your servant" (Mt, 20, 25–26).

[105]In fact, Chapter III is devoted to the "Crisis and consequences of Modern Anthropocentrism".

As opposed to these holistic approaches suggesting paradigmatic solutions mainstreamed by education and culture focused on a spiritual ecology and community concerns that help to face the 'complex' problems of our time there has been a parallel action (arriving at earlier times) concerning the need of environmental education (EE), and later on concerning education for sustainable development (ESD). The aims established by EE and ESD were focused primarily on the following: (1) awareness; (2) Knowledge; (3) Attitude; (4) skills; (5) Evaluation ability; (6) Participation. Such goals are recognised by the landmark text for recognition of the importance of environmental education emerging in 1975 with the Charter of Belgrade adopted by UNESCO.[106]

The Charter of Belgrade established a conceptual framework for environmental education worldwide for the first time. It included an assessment of the global environmental situation and a statement of goals for environmental action. The need for worldwide environmental education programs was discussed and the guidelines to implement environmental education were included. The Charter gave a follow-up to the Recommendation 96 of the Stockholm Conference on the Human Environment call for the development of environmental education as one of the most critical elements of an all-out attack on the world's environmental crisis. The Charter specified that this new environmental education must be broadly based and strongly related to the basic principles outlined in the UN Declaration on the New International Economic Order.

This functionalist approach on environmental education emerging out from the Charter has evolved with more or less success worldwide in the education systems internationally. The audiences to which the Charter was addressed included[107]: (1) The formal education sector: including pre-school, primary, secondary and higher education students as well as teachers and environmental professionals in training and retraining; (2) The non-formal education sector: including youth and adults, individually or collectively, from all segments of the population such as the family, workers, managers and decision-makers, in environmental as well as non-environmental fields. However, this sort of approach is insufficient to change cultural patterns and to empower citizens for today's societies.

Within the EU context, there has been, as part of the 'environmentalisation' process of the EU sectorial policies, an evolution of environmental education for an effective implementation of EU's environment policy that has developed incessantly since the seventies following the global trends. In fact, in 1988, the Council of Ministers adopted a Resolution and argued that the objective of environmental education was:

[106]Adopted by the UNESCO-UNEP International Workshop on Environmental Education at Belgrade, 13–22 October 1975.

[107]According to the text, UNESCO-UNEP (1975).

> To increase the public awareness of the problems in this field, as well as possible solutions, and to lay the foundations for a fully informed and active participation of the individual in the protection of the environment and the prudent and rational use of natural resources.[108]

In 1993, the European Parliament reinforced this approach in a Resolution that called on Member States and the Commission to: 'include the environmental dimension in all aspects of education at all levels' and to 'emphasise the fundamental role of schools and their teachers in the development and implementation of policy". In addition, the Fifth European Community Environment Programme sought to advance the importance of the principle of environmental integration in all other policy areas as a key factor in bringing about the behavioural changes required for sustainability.[109]

In this framework,[110] information and education have become important components, complementing legislation and market-based instruments with the ambition to foster ecological transition, but this has not helped EU policy to face the educational and cultural challenges addressing them as the crucial architects of its sustainability model with the end purpose of achieving an ecological transition reinforcing other strategic plans concerning energy, transport, consumption and production (circular economy), and technology. There is evidence coming from the Scottish school education reality in environmental education, supported by the comparative report on environmental education in the educational systems of the EU (Stokes, Edge, & West, 2001) that "even where local authority policies are in place, provision in schools remains patchy and heavily reliant on the interests and will of a small number of committed teachers" (Nixon, Sankey, & Simmons, 1999).[111]

In the contemporary global society, the questioning of neoliberal rationality and the progress in all the dimensions that support the proposal of SD, systematic and global, must be assumed and agreed, in a collaborative and transversal way by all the actors involved, from international organisations, governments, large local businesses and small businesses, universities and schools until reaching the various productive sectors, social entities and the commitment of all citizens (Stiglitz, 2006). This would help to increase, not only ecological identities, but also other economic reasoning rooted on solidarity economy aimed at the common good that little by little has helped to settle a more integrated version of environmental education: Education for SD (ESD).

If we turn our attention to the International Agreements adopted under UNESCO's auspices, UNESCO has been promoting ESD since 1992. From 2005 to 2015 led the UN Decade for ESD and it has now launched its follow up, the Global Action Program (GAP) launched by UNESCO (2014) on ESD, which should

---

[108] Resolution of the Council and the Ministers of Education meeting within the Council on Environmental education of 24 May 1988, *OJ C 177, 6.7.1988, pp. 8–10.*

[109] See further, Stokes et al. (2001).

[110] Stokes et al. (2001), Jucker and Mathar (2015) offer relevant comparative study on environmental education and education for sustainability in the educational systems of the EU.

[111] See the case of ECOLOG, reported in the case studies of this book, further down in this chapter.

have a crucial role defining further action on what ESD involves.[112] ESD empowers people to change the way they think and work towards a sustainable future. UNESCO "aims to improve access to quality education on sustainable development at all levels and in all social contexts, to transform society by reorienting education and help people develop knowledge, skills, values and behaviours needed for sustainable development" (UNESCO, 2014). UNESCO's message on what ESD involves puts emphasis on the 'transformation of society', but then, it seems to be quite reductionist when it speaks that it is all "about including sustainable development issues, such as climate change and biodiversity into teaching and learning".[113]

Therefore, what emerges from the international panorama is that despite global understanding of that sustainable development claims for change in the cultural patterns of relationships between humans and human beings with nature, our cultural and educational institutions have not entrenched such understanding. Educational programs have not been modified in an integral manner, there have been curriculum amendments aiming at introducing education for sustainability (EfS) but the lack of a holistic approach to knowledge is embedded on the way EfS has been introduced in school or university curricula around the world.[114] Although, as we have seen there are efforts that go on the opposite direction most recently, those efforts have been mostly limited to the HEI context.

On top of that, there is a lack of consensus on how to reach binding global agreements on education. Neither UN nor UNESCO can do much about it, since the agreements are, in the last resort, purely voluntary, and both organisations are bound by their constitutions not to intervene in matters that are essentially within the domestic jurisdiction of any state. Still, an important conclusion emerges from the study of the loads of international agreements: The success is directly related to the high consensus reached on international agreements in the field of environment law, as much as international development agreements. The various declarations of the international community have given evidence of how declarations relating to the environment and social development have been relatively free of controversy, and the Paris agreement on Climate Change shows how this continues to be the norm. Moreover, the ethics of sustainability that were put at the heart of Earth Charter, found consensus on education for sustainable development as an ethical requirement for a strong sustainability model, even if legal scholars have paid little attention to such document.

---

[112]The GAP on ESD, the follow-up programme to the Decade of ESD seeks to generate a scale-up ESD and to accelerate progress towards sustainable development. The GAP aims to contribute to substantially to the 2030 Agenda, through 2 objectives: (1) Reorienting education and learning so that everyone has the opportunity to acquire the knowledge, skills, values and attitudes that empower them to contribute to a sustainable future; (2) Strengthening education and learning in all agendas, programmes and activities that promote SD.

[113]See further, Education for SD retrieved from: https://en.unesco.org/themes/education-sustainable-development.

[114]Parker (2008).

Outside the intergovernmental level, but suggesting concrete institutional action to give answers to some of the concerns already highlighted in the encyclical *Laudato si', Pope Francis, recently announced an important event for the construction of more fraternal a*nd inclusive world: "A Global Compact on Education".[115] This is indeed the first initiative of this kind at global level, focused on human kind, not Earth centered, but including Earth system concerns. The choice of education as the ground on which to make a Global Pact is considered as a priority to "*unite efforts in a broad educational alliance, to form mature individuals capable of overcoming division and antagonism, and to restore the fabric of relationships for the sake of a more fraternal humanity*".[116] The Global Compact on Education is aligned with SDG 4, but goes beyond it, claiming for a "new humanism" within the extreme fragmented reality we live now. The axiom behind the message of the Pope is: "transformation is not possible without education". The Alliance pursued by the Global Education Pact claims for human "networks" of action, and this is the key for future challenges, of ecological and human kind.

Pope Francis invites the representatives of major religions, international organisations, and various humanitarian institutions in the academic, economic, political and cultural sectors to subscribe an alliance to rebuild the global educational pact and hand over a solid and fraternal common home to the younger generations. My question is: Is this utopic?

I believe that the value of creating human connections, fostering awareness and building truly human bounds to support education initiatives can be more effective than multiplying legal commands. However, our fragmented reality does not help.

At the educational policy level, important shifts need to be done. However, global awareness on how to shift from traditional teaching models is still required. We need to accept that such pedagogical shift is as indispensable as it has been an agreement to keep under control our levels of atmospheric pollution.[117] We have never tried to reach consensus on a multilateral legislative instrument that would create a subject on global citizenship (including climate change, biosphere concerns) of transdisciplinary nature. There have neither been popular initiatives to press governments to

---

[115]See further, https://www.educationglobalcompact.org/. The event is scheduled to take place in Rome on 14 May 2020, on the fifth anniversary of the encyclical *Laudato si'*. It will follow a series of thematic seminars relating to the areas of human rights, the science of peace, and dialogue between religions, as well as the issues concerning the educational pact between the young people and adults, the pact with nature and the environment, democracy, economy, international cooperation, aspects of informal education, and those concerning migrants and refugees.

[116]Pope Francis speech on 14 September 2019 (Vatican news reporting, Pope's message) available at http://www.unitedworldproject.org/en/workshops/pope-francis-a-global-pact-for-education/.

[117]One of the most universal steps that reached educational field lately concerns the 'technology integration agenda'. Meaning, it is a curriculum integration with the use of technology involving the infusion of technology as a tool to enhance the learning in any content area or multidisciplinary setting. To integrate technological skills worldwide the world community, public and private bodies, have struggled to introduce pedagogical tools and financial instruments to empower learners and train educators. Consensus at the political level has been reached in an incredibly fast growing manner for this matter, and the same can happen with the ethical concerns of sustainability.

define relevant learning objectives and learning contents by "introducing pedagogies that empower learners, and urge their institutions to include sustainability principles in their management structures".[118] This would definitely touch the sensibilities of nation States. Accordingly, it seems highly unlikely that there will be one globally recognised and permanent definition of "sustainable development" but the high consensus and collaboration we have reached to create the emerging field of 'sustainable development law' and 'policy' has proven to be a helpful tool for identifying and evaluating common features of effective solutions for sustainability and the interests of future generations.[119] The most recent emphasis on transformations driven by sustainability, changing paradigm in the economic thought,[120] need still to be grasped by legal scholars and help them to contribute to an institutional reformation of the education system (including teachers, spaces, goals, assessments, etc.), but the path is widely opened now. The Pope is opening an alternative path for a global alliance that needs (in fact) more engagement than just intergovernmental action.

Turning the attention back to other policy alliances, the GAP with its five priority areas aligned with SDG4[121] has an ambitious 'transformation' agenda that is perfectly valid for a start in any regional context. It could be really successful at European context. It offers a concrete roadmap for action in the following areas: (1) Policy support; (2) whole institutions approaches; (3) educators; (4) youth; (5) local communities. In fact, the GAP suggests the establishment of national coordination mechanisms to monitor such priority areas. Within the European context, a similar roadmap could be promoted by the EU agency on Education, Audiovisual and Culture Executive Agency (EACEA).[122] The role of the EACEA could be promoted from the institutional coordination needs required by the implementation of the UN 2030 Agenda and the SDG 4. Considering the complex administrative law landscape we are facing with the increasing growth of soft law, and the current needs of internal market integration, especially in topics concerning sustainability topics, such as energy, food, environment, agriculture, transport and the urban contexts, etc., the neglected role of the EACEA could be endorsed in the light of its necessary coordination role for strengthening the EU sustainability model touching upon the cultural and educational foundations.

Still, The EACEA role is of course missing as opposed to what is happening in other sectors, such as energy, given the increasing 'agentification' process going on

---

[118] Sánchez Galera (2020).

[119] The global policymaking processes during three decades, since the 1972 Declaration of the UN Conference on the Human Environment in Stockholm, followed by the summits in Rio de Janeiro and in Johannesburg, states have not focused on finding an agreement on one definition for sustainable development, rather, they have focused on developing greater global consensus on how to achieve sustainability.

[120] Göpel (2016).

[121] UNESCO 37 C/Resolution 12.

[122] https://ec.europa.eu/info/departments/education-audiovisual-and-culture_en.

at the EU level addressing "cross-border functional dimensions"[123] that are need for sustainability and climate change concerns that are at the forefront of the EU Agenda. EACEA could have a renewed role creating networks of best practices following the GAP suggested roadmap, and helping Member States to build long lasting policies coordinating all the policy levels at play.

Unfortunately, the gap between policy rhetoric and school practices in environmental education has not only persisted but probably has increased over the past 20 years, given the contested advent of education for sustainable development (ESD) as the dominant international policy discourse in this area, and a growing focus in schools on didactic teaching in traditional content areas resulting from narrowly defined accountability measures in many national educational policies.[124]

Nevertheless, in my opinion we need to wait and see the impact of the GAP on future educational and cultural transformations addressing the five suggested priority areas. Europe needs to build more awareness on its coordinating role for the transformation of our societies. Europe could strengthen policy intervention through the coordinating role of the European agencies in the pertinent areas with which I am dealing, as it has happened with the Agency for the Cooperation of Energy Regulators (ACER) in the realm of energy policy. In the end, it is all a question of Member States political will. Lack of effective action in these fields, is part of a bigger humanity crisis, touching upon every policy realm that can no longer be disconnected: "[A]ll areas of study need to be encouraged to review their capacity for joined-up analysis and propositional thinking in order to make their appropriate contributions to: reduction of human impact on local and global ecologies; mitigation of current effects; and political, social, economic adaptation to predicted future conditions that are easier thanks to the integration of knowledge" (Parker, 2008).

Still, these existing contributions, either in their more ontological form (Morin, *Laudato si'*) or, alternative practical and curricular interventions (Environmental education, ESD, EfS), have a lot to offer to our societies. They provide knowledge building on sustainability and support the need for greater social justice. They are contributing to evolved forms of ethical development and ecological understanding that are necessary for better project analysis and future policy planning leading to solidarity actions. This also means a boost of citizen participation in development management, and an equitable distribution of resources and services to resolve social injustices meeting human rights and needs. Nevertheless, cultural patterns are still evolving and despite of the lack of complete 'transformation' of our educational institutions, it is possible to affirm that EE, ESD and EfS in any form are still the most valuable tools our society needs to start changing such cultural patterns.

[123]See further on this, Simoncini (2018). Administrative ReHart Pub. Ltd.

[124]Stevenson (2007).

5.2.4 *Education and Knowledge as Common Goods. Humanity's Global Purpose*

Goal Four of the 2030 Agenda for Sustainable Development, which aims to "ensure inclusive and equitable quality education and promote lifelong learning opportunities for all" is grounded, as we have already argued, in long-established foundational principles of education as a human right and as a common good (UNESCO, 2015b, p. 5).

The re-contextualisation of education and knowledge[125] as a global common good is extremely relevant today, considering the cultural and educational challenges of our 'learning society'. In fact, UNESCO recommends the re-contextualisation of education in the light of this rapidly changing reality by suggesting rethinking the normative principles that guide educational governance: in particular the right to education and the notion of education as a public good. Considering the ambitious scope of the Global Agenda and the already discussed SDG 4, it is important to find an answer to the following question: "To what extent does the right to education, and the principle of public good, apply also to non-formal and informal education, which are less institutionalised, if at all?" (UNESCO, 2015b, p. 11).

The authors of UNESCO document on "Rethinking Education" puts forward that both, knowledge and education, should be considered *common goods*. This implies that the creation of knowledge, as well as its acquisition, validation and use, are common to all people as part of a collective *societal endeavour that reinforces* the concept of aggregated action that we have put forward in these lines. Actually, "the notion of common good allows us to go beyond the influence of an individualistic socio-economic theory inherent to the notion of 'public good' (often interchanged). Today it is important to emphasize participatory processes and collective actions in defining "what is a common good, which takes into account a diversity of contexts, concepts of well-being and knowledge ecosystems" (UNESCO, 2015b, p. 11).

In a context of growing privatisation and marketisation, the redefinition of 'education and knowledge' within the conceptual boundaries of a common good is highly pertinent and necessary. Unfortunately, education, despite of rhetoric inclusion in every 'dancing ball', is neglected in the sense of not offering a clear answer to the implications of globalisation for national policies and decision making. This sector, indeed, needs an entire redefinition in which the public sector appears as the main actor, but not the only one, all the stakeholders and the civil society involved need a concrete place in such structural redefinition. In fact, for Locatelli (2018, p. 11) is essential to develop new approaches likely to integrate the notion of education as a public good with the fundamental social and cultural components of education which are often disregarded within standardised approaches. Today it is essential to consider education as part of the domain of the public sphere where

[125]Understood as the "information, understanding, skills, values and attitudes acquired through learning-is central to any discussion of the purpose of education" (UNESCO, 2015b, p. 11).

transparent and participatory processes can take place (Locatelli, 2018, p. 6). She suggests the legal frameworks of education as a public good and as a common good "as a sort of continuum in line with the aim of developing democratic political institutions that enable citizens to have greater voice in the decisions that affect their well-being" Locatelli (2018, p. 11). Furthermore, the author stresses the socio-philosophical interpretation of common goods, to remark that the concept of 'common goods' is preferable to that of commons as the latter seems hardly applicable to goods and services such as education which necessarily requires public institutions to play an important role in their governance (Locatelli, 2018).

In this light, also a set of financial resources has to be bound to such ends with a long-term view in addition to a sustainable budget planning, counting mostly (with emphasis added when related to education) on public money. In addition, there should be an action plan for institutional transformation based on the broad availability of the current governance mechanisms fostering broad participation of society actors in the education and cultural domain.

The notion of commons is valid to foster broader participation. It has already been discussed as part of the EU sustainability model types of governance, and the question of 'access', is part of the 'new ecology of law' if we look at the change of paradigm from a legal scientist view, or simply as a breach of the traditional public and private divide that in the cultural and educational spheres have been increasingly gaining room. Within the economic context, the paradigm shift is presented confronting market capitalism to the collaborative commons.[126] When referring to the education context, embedded in the essence of 'sustainability concerns' and the education policymaking needs in a complex world, the UNESCO (2015a) has joined this debate by reformulating the whole problematic of education in today's complex societies on the light of education as a global 'common good'.

It is possible to affirm now that natural resources common are the most studied types of commons in the last decades since the 1970s (Ostrom, 1990). However, lately other types of commons, such as digital and information commons have prominently increased (Benkler, 2006; Hess, 2008; Hess & Ostrom, 2007). At the beginning of this millennium, the drastic spread of digital technology and open access to digitalised instruments, particularly in the wealthiest parts of the world, has given as a result: "(...) large sections of the population capable of communicating and collaborating in online settings and engaging in activities of cultural creativity" (Fuster Morell, 2013, p. 284). Within this context, there is growing interest among law scholars in the expansion of intellectual property in the neoliberal frame. This has led them to take legal action to protect creativity and the public domain. It has also helped scholars to develop the idea of "intellectual commons" and the Creative Common Licenses has been introduced with the aid of Lawrence Lessig (2004). Creative Common Licenses enabled sharing and developing derivative work from

[126]Foundational theoretical roots of how to foster a paradigm change for the commons is also rooted on Gorgescu-Roegen (1971) thought, and Polany's conceptual approach to 'transformation' explained by Göpel (2016).

existing materials and then adopted to support online collaboration. This trend gave a boost to new 'free culture' expressions emerging with the aim of collaboratively creating cultural content and generating universal access knowledge.[127] Still, Fuster Morell (Fuster Morell, 2010; Fuster Morell, 2013) explains by shedding light into on line creation communities (OCCs) that although OCCs started with a 'commons' logic and processes based on self-governance and collaboration, such processes were co-opted to serve a corporate logic because they depended on an infrastructure of providers that followed a corporate logic (Fuster Morell, 2013, p. 279). In fact, the author suggests that there is "a necessity to understand the complexity and interaction of the regulation of both platforms and infrastructure if we are to preserve the values and logic of the commons, which would allow future generations to main control over the creation of digital resources" (Fuster Morell, 2013, p. 287), especially if dealing with cultural and educational matters in the light of preserving universal access to what should be protected as common good.

Nevertheless, the digital environment is undergoing constant and rapid changes, this added to all the economic interests behind the expansion of digital technology make it difficult to make future predictions, so it is not so clear whether the commons logic will have a well-established future, or if the corporate model will keep control of the collaborative production in the digital environment. More awareness in this sense and full engagement of legal scholarship to the expansion of commons in this field is needed. On training materials in an eventual transformation of the education sector in the light of sustainability concerns, integrating climate change awareness courses, and more transversal teaching materials to train teachers (at first instance), and learners, should be available. Open data coordinated by a European agency is still needed in such concerns.

The expansion of the collaborative common discourse associated to digital means and referred to the educational and cultural spheres is very much needed in Europe, addressing issues that go beyond the current concerns of intellectual property. Locatelli (2018) offers an excellent conceptualisation of its interpretation and historic evolution, and it can well re-frame an institutional shift of governance applied to the cultural and educational discourses within the European context.

5.2.5 *Europe of Knowledge or Knowledgeable Europe? Too Much Attention to Innovation Through Digitalisation*

The digitalisation of Europe involves much more than providing universal broadband, free Wi-Fi and a flow of big data. The digital economy, brought by the new economic paradigm, is dramatically changing the way we organise economic life on the planet, will revolutionise every commercial sector, and disrupt the workings of

[127]See further, Fuster Morell (2013). The most important example that the author cites in the context of digital commons is *Wikipedia*, founded in 2001.

every industry (Rifkin, 2016).[128] Rifkin argues that to grasp the ongoing economic change of paradigm we need a deep understanding of the technological forces that have given rise to new economic systems throughout history. There are three elements interacting with each other to enable a system to operate as a whole: (1) new communications technologies; (2) new sources of energy and; (3) new modes of transformation.[129] His focus is quite restricted to the evolution of the economic activity and he has a quite a positive vision of the future based on an equally important narrative aligned with the economic change of paradigm, namely, a new 'biosphere consciousness'. He explains how the human race is beginning to perceive the Earth as its indivisible community. In his view, each of us is beginning to take on responsibilities as stewards of the planetary ecosystems that sustain all forms of life. However, how is Europe addressing such institutional transformation to gain such competences?

It has been noted that the phrase "Europe of Knowledge" is a veritable 'complex and malleable term' (Elken, Gornitzka, Maassen, & Vukasovic, 2011, p. 5). In fact, whilst it is possible to trace its political and supranational origin to the European Commission's, 1997 Communication "Towards a Europe of Knowledge" (European Commission, 1997),[130] national and supranational policy actors have interpreted the term differently since then. In the 1997 Communication we see the EU executive referring to the Europe of Knowledge as 'an open dynamic European educational area' (European Commission, 1997, p. 2); in 2000 the term was used to refer to 'Europe of Innovation and knowledge', as a synonym for the European Research Area (ERA) (European Commission, 2000); it has also been contrasted 'the Europe of knowledge' to the "Europe of the Euro" (Sorbonne Joint Declaration 1998). Chou and Gornitzka (2014, p. 8) discuss the following visions associated with the Europe of knowledge: 'as the basis of knowledge-based economy' [or society]; as an instrument for invigorating and increasing the competitiveness of European science; and as a tool for informed policymaking and implementation'.[131]

The construction of an open and dynamic European 'educational area' was the overarching plan of the 'Europe of Knowledge' in its 1997 version. These were the guiding principles on which this Communication was based:

> The gradual construction of an open and dynamic European educational area is the guiding principle on which this Communication is based. In a rapidly-changing world, our societies must offer all citizens greater opportunities for access to knowledge, irrespective of their age or social circumstances. This is why the notion of an educational area needs to be understood in the broadest possible sense, both geographically and temporally. It provides the framework for mobilising the effort to make a reality of the idea of lifelong learning, which was at

[128]The third industrial revolution that Rifkin (2015) envisages for Europe, fosters a digitalised communication internet converging with a digitalised renewable "Energy internet" and a digitalised, automated "transportation and Logistics Internet" to create a super "Internet of Things" infrastructure.

[129]See further, Rifkin (2013).

[130]COM *(97) 563 final,* 12 November 1997.

[131]See further, Chou and Ulnicane (2015).

the heart of the European Year devoted to this theme in 1996. Three dimensions of the European educational area should be emphasized:

- Knowledge. In order to be able to take an active part in the current processes of change, the citizens of Europe will be able to develop their fund of knowledge continually, thus expanding and renewing it on a lasting basis.
- Citizenship: This educational area will facilitate an enhancement of citizenship through the sharing of common values, and the development of a sense of belonging to a common social and cultural area. It must encourage a broader-based understanding of citizenship, founded on active solidarity and on mutual understanding of the cultural diversities that constitute Europe's originality and richness.
- Competence: Developing employability through the acquisition of competencies made necessary through changes in work and its organisation. This means that it is necessary to promote on a lifelong basis creativity, flexibility, adaptability, the ability to 'learn to learn' and to solve problems. These are the conditions we must meet in order to overcome the now rapid obsolescence of skills. Activities must be developed which help towards anticipating needs and towards the evolution of job profiles.

The idea was to enhance the newly introduced provisions of lifelong learning. This broad and systemic approach offered by this first EU Communication on 'Knowledge' has been subsequently cut down to concentrate on education challenges related to market integration needs and the job market requirements in an enlarged Europe, leaving behind the enhancement of citizenship founded on active solidarity and on mutual understanding of the cultural diversities that constitute Europe's originality and wealth. "The Europe of Knowledge" includes the goal of building the European Higher Education area through the Bologna process, aiming at boosting mobility, scientific cooperation, research and innovation. However, the proliferation of opportunities has not taken Europe to become a more 'knowledgeable' place. The consequences are slightly paradoxical. Knowledge has been instrumental to its contribution to economic development, and technological leadership. This has brought with it a devaluation of the more 'humanistic' and 'intellectual' purposes of Knowledge. "On a more paradigmatic level, it has led to the instrumentalisation of knowledge –its valorisation only or primarily in terms of its contribution to economic growth, and the consequent devaluation of other, more "traditional" purposes, such as self-awareness, development and intellectual pursuit for its own sake, which some critics associate with the Humboldtian model of university" (Bacevic, 2013).

What is clear is that in Europe, 'the research cooperation policy' has been and it is essential for European integration. The paradox is that Knowledge has mostly been associated with 'innovation'. Thus, the Europe of knowledge has become too much focused on innovation and digitalisation at every cost. At the same time, the increasing speed of globalisation of higher education, has led to the growing construction of knowledge as a commodity. Consequently, this trend has not improved access to knowledge or knowledge production. Information technology in education has been a horizontal priority of EU education policy, and this was recognised at community level as a priority earlier than in most MS. There were introduced a significant number of specific programmes relating to the new information technology in education, supported by the European Commission (Halász,

2013, p. 273). The same can be said for the EU promotion of cooperation between education and business that has been a permanent priority of community policies in education. Consequently, it has been claimed that "[a]lthough a "Europe of knowledge" hints at a shared space where everyone has the same (or similar) access and right to participate in the creation and transmission of knowledge, this is hardly the case" (Bacevic, 2013). The privatisation of education and research has become a natural consequence of innovation entrenched in the same ethos of lifelong learning, vocational training and higher education offer in Europe.

Actually, such privatisation of education, based on the growing construction of knowledge as a market item, something that can be bought and sold, has not only changed the entire ethos related to knowledge production, it has also brought very tangible consequences for financing higher education and vocational training in general. This trend has consequently introduced changes in the working conditions for those professionally engaged in the sector of higher education and vocational training. What is clear, considering such commodification tendency of lifelong learning in general, is that accountability mechanisms, performance measurements and quality assurance are not favouring the democratisation of knowledge, but they have been surely fostering its digitalisation at every cost.

The Digital Agenda presented by the European Commission forms one of the seven pillars of the Europe 2020 Strategy. It sets objectives for the growth of the European Union (EU) by 2020. It proposes to better exploit the potential of Information and Communication Technologies (ICTs) to foster innovation, economic growth and progress. Sustainability concerns are only a minimum part of collective awareness platforms for sustainability and social innovation (CAPS) that are initiative pioneers new models to create awareness of emerging sustainability challenges and of the role that each and every one of us can play to ease them through collective action. Thus, if we want to give a name to the sustainability concerns of the digital agenda that it is at the core of the Europe of knowledge, we must affirm that we are not in front of a more knowledgeable Europe. We should still find the right balance between the most prominent components of knowledge: education and culture on one side, and innovation and digitalisation on the other side. We must devote our policy agendas to invigorate education programs and cultural approaches (that should be integrated) to face the challenges of nature conservation, inclusion, and inequality. Instead, we are embracing the understanding of knowledge as constant technological development, obscuring its greedy market and human domination purposes on the promise of building more knowledge. Bacevic (2013) argues that higher education and research policies developed in Europe arriving at the edges of excessive focus on technological innovation, are hidden in a "neutral language that promises equality, efficiency and prosperity", thus, indeed giving effective content to these terms is a challenging task for a 'knowledgeable' Europe willing to provide a strong European sustainability model.

In fact, the introduction of 'sustainability' concerns into the equation of "the Europe of Knowledge" and the Lisbon Strategy has had at the forefront the idea of leading an industrial transition (third industrial revolution) that is taking place worldwide and where there is a predominance of 'green developmentalism'[132] fed by 'green' concerns. The transition is pretty much focused on market solutions to environmental concerns, just related to job market interests, and industrial production concerns, often reinforcing the claim of European and global elites to the greatest share of the Earth's biomass and all that relates to it. In this context, knowledge has not become a paradigm to force urgent systemic and equally accessible education programs, it has been a display place for tailor made courses in private institutions, or alternative ways of learning beyond the borders of public education offer.

The aim of the Lisbon Strategy, launched in March 2000 by the EU heads of state and government, was to make Europe "the most competitive and dynamic knowledge-based economy in the world, capable of sustainable economic growth with more and better jobs and greater social cohesion". The message was clear: competitive and dynamic knowledge for 'green developmentalism', and this has clearly had drastic consequences for educational and cultural reforms, just focused on more proliferation of standardised texts (PiSA), and enhanced focus on communication practices of core importance for a European Knowledge society that needed to be simultaneously competitive and inclusive. The EU has tried to keep up with the latest technological innovations associated with digital practices with the goal of establishing a digital Europe. Thus, instead of strong sustainability concerns aligned with culture, ethic and humanistic concerns prevailing over digitalisation the opposite has been true. The balance that needs to be drawn to lead action according to scientific evidence has not been highlighted enough, at least in what regards the early stages of education development, where digitalisation has even proved to be detrimental according to scientific evidence (Spitzer, 2013). The risks of the digitalisation agenda have not been sufficiently spread, and the lack of reference to neuroscientific results contrasting detrimental effects of digitalisation in those countries where digital technology is more accessible is a sign of political and social mistreatment of the actual facts.

This means that the 'green' concerns and the idea of knowledge that has been spread through the Lisbon Strategy were not providing the right roadmap to face all the European challenges posed by today's learning societies. The EU Climate change leadership cannot be based only on air pollution regulation and a complete package of Energy measures rendering the EU market more competitive addressing goals and objectives at industrial, production, consumption and research level. Society engagement on the low carbon economy, through cultural and educational activities depending on resources and geopolitical circumstances must be crucial. The Paris agreement, as we already mentioned, acknowledges the need of big educational foundations behind climate change action. In fact, in Europe from very early times, the HE sector has been the first one to get engaged at institutional level to support transdisciplinary knowledge and solutions, integrating Earth's system approaches and fostering cultural activities to create public awareness. HEI

[132]See further McAfee (1999).

have trained and educate students in climate change education for more than one decade, it also engages students in research activities as a way of learning science, understanding climate change, contributing to climate change studies and participating in several local and international workshops, seminars and conferences,[133] but courageous institutional action has not been undertaken yet. It is only recently that the Italian education minister has announced that Italian public schools would soon require students in every grade to study climate change and sustainability, a step that could put Italy at the forefront of environmental education worldwide. The lessons, at first, would be taught as part of the student's civic education, and will eventually become integrated throughout a variety of subjects. This that can be seen as an important reform with a vital impact for education for sustainability, needs other institutional endorsement.

The systemic institutional reform that education systems need in Europe is supported by the strong legal basis offered by Article 3.3 of the TEU as part of Europe's constitutional framework. This structural reform of educational and cultural institutions should be positioned at the head of 'EU future plans' without rhetorical discourses. Of course, the progression of these new challenges associated with the 'marketisation' of ideas and knowledge, and the complexity of our urban contexts, calls for a greater degree of integration between the fields of education, training and youth policy. Horizontal EU policies in the education field supporting equity, fighting against school failure, supporting the integration of children with special needs, immigrants and ethnic minorities as well as the introduction of climate change lesson as a mandatory schools subject in all European schools at all levels should be put at the forefront of present and future political agenda. On top of that horizontal policies should facilitate children transition from school to work in a changing society that is not only challenged by digital innovation.

Actually, although it is evident that in the past decade, EU research policy has become more central to the EU's political ambitions and its instruments are expanding in scale and scope, recently there has been apprehension over the EU's R&D efforts, such as the Framework Programmes, and their adequacies in meeting European and global 'grand challenges' (Langfeldt, Godø, Gornitzka, & Kaloudis, 2012).[134] The importance of addressing contemporary educational challenges through the right 'pedagogical' innovation contents is crucial for current and future educational policy, and this has been fairly acknowledged by OECD and research efforts (Paniagua & Instance, 2018). Thus, today some basic 'clusters' are already recognised as necessary innovation knots: blended learning, experiental learning, embodied learning, multiliteracies and discussion-based teaching. However, our political agendas seem to be focused on computational needs and computational thinking as the only innovative 'cluster' of our immediate pedagogical needs, more

[133]Sanni, Adejuwon, Ologeh, and Siyanbola (2010).

[134]The authors are concerned with how European-level and national research efforts interact is a key condition for enhancing Europe's research competitiveness and responsiveness.

focused on the acquisition of competitive and measurable skills for leadership than on equipping society with the right value needs for 'transformation'.

5.3 Is It Easier to Face Challenges at European Union Level?

I am dealing with a conceptual approach to education that involves complete social transformation and aims at a change of paradigm going beyond cultural and conceptual fragmentation. Accordingly I want to start this section with a little paragraph from the works of the Spanish philosopher Ortega y Gasset (1944) that is clearly up to date, even if his message does not mention the words 'transformation' and even if the text contains just some of the essential hints of what Ortega wanted to transmit when dealing with the "mission of the university". His starting point is the idea of general culture with the basic function of the university, akin to Plato's idea of culture and education and what the mission of a cultured man should be in the society that he had to help building. The Spanish philosopher writes the following:

> Culture is the vital system of ideas of a period. It makes not a particle of difference whether these ideas, or convictions, lie partly or wholly in the province of science. Culture is not science. It is characteristic of our present culture that a great part of its content proceeds out of science; but in other cultures this has not been the case, nor it decreed anywhere that in ours it will always be so to the same degree as at present.
>
> Compared with the medieval university, the contemporary university has developed the mere seed of professional instruction into an enormous activity; it has added the function of research; and it has abandoned almost entirely the teaching or transmission of culture (Ortega y Gasset, 1944, p.57).

Now, if this is a truism that is still validly applicable to the higher education field, the same has not been discussed when related to other educational stages (education subsystems) equally important for a real transition to a strong sustainability model. Ortega goes on to argue:

> When one considers that the European countries have deemed it admissible to grant professional titles and prestige to magistrates and doctors without making sure that these men have a clear idea, for example, of the physical conception we now have of the world, and an equally clear idea of the character and limitations of the marvellous science by which that concept has been attained-we need not be surprised that affairs have come to such a pass in Europe (Ortega y Gasset, 1944, p. 59)

Ortega goes on criticising the fragmentation of knowledge, arguing that "Europe is broken into pieces" representing such fragmentation (p. 61). In fact, his arguments cannot be more up to date than when he says: "[I]ndeed, the crumbling away of Europe which we are witnessing is the result of the invisible fragmentation that the European man has progressively undergone".

I believe that this problem persists in Europe today. As we have seen above, the understanding of the change of paradigm is explained by UNESCO (2015a) by reaffirming the 'humanistic approach to education' and emphasising how "[a] humanistic and holistic approach to education can and should contribute to achieving a new development model" in formal education. This humanistic approach has implications for the definition of the learning content and pedagogies, as well as for the role of teachers and other educators. It is even more relevant today given the rapid development of new digital technologies. Thus, what happens is that, in Europe we urgently need to invert the (in) balance between innovation based on digitalisation and innovation grounded on the culture of democracy, human rights, citizenship, ecology, shared responsibility and active citizenship.

This imbalance needs to be corrected because it is true that it is easier to face cultural and educational challenges at supranational (European) level, in the sense that the transfer, dissemination and feedback between the European and the national policymaking arenas is always more enriching than facing challenges alone. Across Europe, new policy ideas about education have driven major restructuring projects that dismantled older forms of schooling and welfare provisions (Alexiadou & Lundhal, 2019). The same can be said about culture. Furthermore, the cross-sectoral aspect of culture and education policies flow more naturally at European level, and education remains an area of public policy naturally linked to the rest. In this light, policy formation, and ideas about education and schooling are the product of international concerns that will surely affect national education and cultural questions. Both fields, education and culture have been influenced by the flux of international actors and solutions.

Still, in Europe, the knowledge economy has represented the paradigm underpinning education reforms. Sustainability concerns have been entangled into this paradigm rather than guiding it. Thus, although Europe has not been indifferent to the idea of education for SD, yet, the result is a fragmented scenario of isolated initiatives that mirror somehow the UN commitment to what is called the UN Decade of Education for Sustainable Development (2005–2014), aiming at the integration of "the principles, values and practices of sustainable development into all aspects of education and learning", but they do not reach it yet. There is evidence that the nations of Europe have developed many distinctive and innovative features on this regard (Jucker & Mathar, 2015), but an unanimous decision to strive for a systemic transformation of education systems in Europe, starting by an important shift on financial resources is far from reality.

The danger is that the rapid internationalisation and Europeanisation processes of education and cultural policy can exclusively regard innovation linked with digitalisation, market strategies and neoliberal values, which are already reflected in a culture of performativity, accountability, measurement and the effectiveness of outcome-based education.

But Europe's shift in its education policy is ready to promote precisely defined norms, values and discourses in the field of education engaged with education for sustainability, and more concretely with a more humanistic approach to education integrating the concept of 'shared responsibility' for future generations (Göpel, 2011). Lifelong learning opportunities reaching all education stages and affecting other policy matters can easily be engaged with ecology, community building and future generations' concerns; going beyond 'meta-frameworks' (qualifications), despite that European formal competences on education and culture are limited. A European education and cultural space, has already emerged in which a coherent range of themes, technologies and discourses are being established, and through which global and European processes are transforming education policy, cultural policy and education systems. Still, education remains an under-financed and under-prioritised sector at national and European level. On top of that, there is a clear gap between the role granted to education in the latest sustainability strategies, documents and stakeholder discussions at the EU level (as well as global level)[135] on the one hand, and the priorities expressed by institutional action in fields that do not have a direct impact on the overall human wellbeing.

Nevertheless, we should not overlook the importance of a European intervention for some positive 'transformation' in the educational and cultural policy, despite of its many critical aspects. The 'Europeanisation' of education might help to foster the transformation of our societies more easily than it can be done at national, or local level. Good practices, coordinated approaches, and information exchanges find at the EU level the right knowledge platform to push MS towards policy transformation and extending good practices.

Two important steps have governed the 'Europeanisation' in education whilst increasing Eurosceptic political trends in the public sphere that are holding back some more advanced processes of European integration: (1) The OMC; and (2) The Europe 2020 "strategy for smart, sustainable and inclusive growth", where education is featured prominently as a priority under the clothes of 'developing an economy based on knowledge and innovation' and as one of the five headline targets.[136]

Such important steps in the field of education prove that things are changing in a field that has been closely associated with national historical roots. It also means that even, if developments in education governance are mostly referred to the HE and vocational training level, not often concerning investments on human capabilities,[137] social policies are getting more prominent roles. Therefore, enhanced EU policy action in such fields does not necessarily mean that the EUSM is suddenly rooted in some sort of virtuous education model providing the receipt for institutional reform to face the challenges of our complex world, but the truth is that the crucial pillars of EU policy in education: lifelong learning education (including all the education stages) and mobility,[138] have created a new paradigm that is gradually gaining

---

[135]See further, Bengtsson, Barkat, and Muttarak (2018).

[136]The EU has set 5 targets as part of the European 2020 Strategy: (1) Employment; (2) Research and Development −3% of the EU's GDP to be invested in R&D; (3) Climate Change and energy sustainability; (4) Education- (a) to reduce the rates of early school leaving below 10%; (b) at least 40% of 30–34-year-olds completing third level education; (5) Fighting poverty and social exclusion-at least 20 million fewer people in or risk of poverty and social exclusion. See further, http://ec.europa.eu/europa.eu/europe2020/europe-2020-in-a-nutshell/targets/index_en.

[137]Sen (1999).

[138]The first common objective of the strategic framework for European Cooperation in education and training (ET 2020) refers to, "Making lifelong learning and mobility a reality".

ground in the member countries policy decisions partly because of the use of the community policy instruments supporting implementation (Halász, 2013, p. 275).[139]

The virtue of this new paradigm (gaining ground in MS) relies on the capacity of the EU to promote particular policy agendas and ideas for reform, present solutions to what they identify as common problems across national boundaries, and promote solutions through soft forms of governance instead of legislation. However, the work to be done is still enormous considering major changes in society and States interdependence heightened by globalisation. The initiatives of the Council of Europe in co-operation with the European Union are crucial for both instances, education and culture taking account of future generations and common goods as key factors to be prioritised to face future challenges.[140]

Gornitzka (2018) identifies the Lisbon process as a landmark for European Education Policy when EU heads of state publicly stated the EU's ambition to become the most competitive knowledge-based economy in the world. She argues that this put education for the first time at the crossroads with the EU's economic and social policy, triggering immediate visibility of the education sector at EU policy level. Consequently, the Commission's Directorate General Education and Culture (DG EAC) pushed the education sector's contribution to the Lisbon Strategy 2000[141] as we already mentioned. In fact, the role of the DG EAC was also crucial for the process of setting up the OMC, which would mean a change of attitude towards European coordinating efforts among European Ministers of Education that had been invited by the Lisbon European Council to formulate future goals boosting EU's transition to the knowledge economy.[142] This initiative, unfortunately, at least in part, is an attempt to 'restructure' educational provisions around market approaches to educational systems and organisations in ways emphasise a new set of educational imperatives linked to standardised measures of educational performance (Hall, Grimaldi et al., 2015).

It is outside the scope of these lines to delve into the early years of history of European education policy,[143] formerly and firmly based on "the idea of closed national systems, founded on the basic principle that the particular character of

[139]The key components of the lifelong learning policy of the EU are specified by Halász (2013, p. 275): (1) valuing learning; (2) information, guidance and counselling; (3) Investing time and money in learning; (4) bringing together learners and learning opportunities; (5) Basic skills; (6) innovative pedagogy.

[140]See further, (Farrell, 2011).

[141]European Council Conclusions of 23–24 March 2000.

[142]Gornitzka (2018), refers to three main strategic objectives adopted by the 2001 Lisbon Council concerning (European Council Conclusions of 23–24 March 2001: (1) quality and effectiveness of education, access to education and opening up national education and training systems to society and "the wider world". This would turn into a ten-year work programme containing 13 specified objectives. Cf. Council and Commission, *Detailed work programme on the follow-up of the objectives of education and training systems in Europe*, 14 June 2002 (European Council Conclusions of 15–16 March 2002).

[143]On this point, see further St. John (2019), p. 21. It gives an account of development policies since early European financed programs (COMETT, ERASMUS, LINGUA, etc.. . .) to other regulatory

education systems in the Member States should fully respected, while coordinated interaction between education, training and employment systems should be improved" (Gornitzka, 2018).[144] It suffices to say that cooperation and internationalisation have increased over the years at the EU level, and some scholars have argued that changes in the education policy sector have to some extent been institutionalised.[145] The OMC mechanism is an important evidence of such institutionalisation that should be considered a positive top-down administrative structure facilitating 'transformations' of EU education systems. Gornitzka (2018) explains how the inception of the OMC into EU education policy was from the start marked by the active role of the Commission's DG, which acted as a procedural and ideational entrepreneur for creating and maintaining OMC. She argues that quantified aspects of the OMC process, such as indicators and benchmarks, have been deeply institutionalised. Actually, indicators for development also gained a strong position when a specific Centre for Research on Education and Lifelong Learning (CRELL) was established as part of the Commissions' Joint Research Centre, and the legal basis for Eurostat's education statics was strengthened (Gornitzka, 2018, p. 247).

These development hints are important, because on an eventual top-down coordinated transformation of EU educational systems based on a more systemic approach, there should be a claim for: (1) education for sustainability, (2) European (global) citizenship; (3) the integration of humanistic concerns and; (4) the idea of education as a common good. The current role of European education policy in the knowledge society is not indifferent, and the governance architecture of the OMC has already opened the floor for coordination on education policy areas, such as "access to education, approaches to teaching and learning basic skills, funding and organisational issues, counselling, information and communication technology and so on" (Gornitzka, 2018).

When the OMC was introduced, brought some changes to the education and cultural field in Europe; and both, the Education and Training 2020 program and the recent Employment Reports published by the Commission and the Council, emphasise the need to 'pursue reforms' (further) that will modernise education systems and "Rethink Education" to face future challenges which for Europe clearly converge with the strengthening of its sustainability model including and integrating other cross-sectoral policies such as climate change, the economic and social consequences of the global financial crisis, declining water and energy resources, shrinking biodiversity, threats to food security and health risks. Thus, the desire to produce more 'impact' of the 2020 program on national education systems in relation to other policies is explicit, and the instruments of governing and monitoring this impact are being refined.

---

policies in the form of mutual recognition of degrees and the provision for migrant worker's children (described as a the result of functional or 'economic spillover').

[144]Gornitzka refers to the works of Huisman and Van Der Wende (2004).

[145]See further, Walkenhorst (2008), p. 567.

In such positive view, it is possible to say that a wider integration process over the last years has shaped a European model of education with distinct features, a process that has been intensified and formalised since 2000, and the OMC has contributed to this formalisation process. The European knowledge economy agenda has disrupted nationally embedded and institutionalised practices and norms in education, learning and cultural issues. In this process, I want to highlight that the amount of actors involved in this institutional changes has grown: governments, research, science sector, entrepreneurs and society at large. Today, MS are more concerned with the need to be aligning themselves behind a set of concrete common challenges and objectives.

The success of the Lisbon Strategy urged important reforms (draft joint interim report on the implementation of the detailed work programme on the follow-up of the objectives of education and training systems in Europe). Perhaps the most remarkable policy step that can be easily overlooked concerns the concept of 'lifelong learning'. It dissolves boundaries between schooling and workplaces and between universities and commercial organisations. Nowadays policy and technologies are constantly active and seek to discipline the learner in continuous self-improvement under the premises of competition, into a neo-liberal perspective. Thus, the shift from education to learning signalled in the Lisbon agreement and in the Europe 2020 targets has had considerable implications for governing future action. However, it does not necessarily mean that those implications are just positive transformations of our education systems. Countries like Sweden, have taken over the years decisive steps into privatisation and marketisation of education that are a relevant consequence of the new lifelong learning perspective and digitalisation demands.

The most recent European Strategy and Policy Analysis System (ESPAS, 2015)[146] project aims at helping the EU to manage today's complexity, by identifying the main global trends, assessing their implications and reviewing the resulting challenges and policy options confronting decision-makers. Education, has not been ignored (ESPAS, 2015), but the focus is mostly on educational concerns related to HE level and innovation associated to digitalisation. In effect, the report points that Europe will remain a leading area of research and development (R&D), despite the fact that its knowledge and high technology sectors account for a mere 30% of GDP in Europe compared with 40% in the United States and Japan (and currently 20% in China, but growing).[147] There is a specific suggestion for a more systematic and comprehensive approach needed for relationships between business, regulators, public and private sectors and education that could lead to the development of a new innovation model. However, the path to be followed needs a renewed policy and research agenda accompanied by political consensus for its implementation.

[146]See further, https://ec.europa.eu/epsc/sites/epsc/files/espas-report-2015.pdf.

[147]Reference source provided by the ESPAS 2030, National Science Foundation (NSF), Science and Engineering Indicators 2012, 2012.

Most innovation in cultural and education issues continues to be focused on raising European competitiveness in digitally based improvement. The research program framework Horizon 2020 is endorsed based on its relevance for important public-private partnerships that are addressing social innovation and societal challenges at every level. However, research programs promoted at the EU level are privileging more intelligent, accessible and large-scale networks. The advanced and controversial 5G technology is put at the forefront of the digital agenda today to reach European leadership, but a serious campaign 'educating' people on the criticalities, or impact on human health of such advance technology has not been taken yet.

My concern is that more public awareness on critical aspects related to health and negative effects are needed because the challenges posed by the technological revolution also sharpens inequalities. Another basic concern, regards other pressing challenges of the European social sphere. At the moment, aging in Europe seems to be more problematic in recent policy analyses than educational and cultural needs. Therefore, another basic concern for European social welfare, apart from the inequalities growing out of digital access, is demographic change. Economic pressure should increase under current healthcare and pension conditions with the current demographic change. European population is ageing fast and the risk of drastic fall in the active population is latent. The direct consequence of this risk is that European Union Member States' financial situations will be more onerous in the near future, surely sacrificing financial resources for education and cultural institutions. It is difficult to find politicians that believe that further investments in education and cultural policies are mandatory to equip our present societies with right 'cognitive empowerment'[148] to combat aging problems too. Whatever leads coordinated and long-sighted political agendas to integrate ways of supplying responsible patterns of social action should be welcomed and encouraged.

A positive improvement of the European context is that holistic approaches are starting to proliferate and be more evident.[149] Demographic challenges and the metrics integrated to the measurement of this issue will also assist policy agendas, and these elements are definitely advanced in the fora discussing, *The Role of Education in enabling the sustainable development agenda.*[150] In this context, Wolfgang Lutz emphasise that "in empirical studies the effects of improvements in education on a range of different desirable outcomes, it is important to distinguish between education flows (schooling) and the gradually changing education attainment stocks (human capital of the adult population)".[151] In reality, "the distinction between education flow and the stock of education outcomes in the form of enhanced human capital at later stages in life is very important for understanding and

[148]Term referred to education by Wolfgang Lutz in its foreword "Universal education as the root cause of sustainable development" in Bengtsson et al. (2018).

[149]Bruni and Zamagni (2013), and Hopkins (2011).

[150]Bengtsson et al. (2018).

[151]According to Lutz, in his foreword to the book of Bengtsson et al. (2018).

identifying the benefits of education".[152] On top of that, the democratisation of governance mechanisms available today and the conceptual framework for political and legal action, as well as the institutional implications fostered by the Global Agenda 2030, when they are not just concerned with monitoring mechanisms are providing constructivist approaches of which Europe is not indifferent.

On the relevance of Education policy at European level, the intergovernmental process towards establishing the European Higher Education Area ("The Bologna Process") and the EU's "Copenhagen Process" for vocational education and training were added to this European policy area to include the whole range and forms of education. This demonstrates that cooperation around common objectives is always possible even in nationally sensitive areas. Today, after all these experiences, plus the addition of the *Europe of knowledge*, *Europe 2010* and subsequently *Europe 2020*, the complexity of the Europeanisation process of education and cultural policies (including harmonisation of national qualifications and Pisa tests), as well as the high amount of interests involved, could hamper, not only a stronger integration process, but also the need to push and strive for financial and institutional change in these sectors. Anyhow, Ministers of Education have gained experience in coordination practices that were unthinkable only two decades ago. Education and culture have reached the status of cross-sectoral policies[153] that once seemed to be reserved to economic or environmental concerns.

The transmission of common European values based on democracy, human rights, ecological concerns and shared responsibility, have also been put forward as a challenge for the EU (Mokrosch & Regenbogen, 2015) and in the same light, Grimonprez (2014) makes an important contribution with an interesting legally based approach that criticises the unused potential of Article 165 of the TFEU to deal with the European dimension of citizenship education. She offers evidence by presenting research supporting the assumption that citizenship education has an impact on active citizenship, which is crucial for many social and democracy aspects valid for a strong EU sustainability model. She affirms that "[t]he European Parliament, the Council and the Commission also confirm the role of education in this respect. In *Groener*, the European Court of Justice (ECJ)[154] considered that "[t] eachers have an essential role to play" in a policy of cultural and linguistic diversity. The Council of Europe is firmly convinced that education plays a central role in promoting human rights, democracy and the rule of law. Education is increasingly

---

[152]Ibid.

[153]Before the Lisbon European Council, the European Employment Strategy (EES) had already included lifelong learning as an area of cooperation. National Ministers of Education were nudged towards defending the educational domain. Under the EES, decisions with implications for core educational issues were not decided by European ministers of education, but by national ministers running the employment portfolios, and prepared by DG Employment and not DG EAC.

[154]*Groener v Minister for Education* (379/87) [1989] E.C.R. 3967; [1990] 1 C.M.L.R. 401 at [20]. Grimonprez (2014) also draws attention to an American case where the US Supreme Court also mentioned the importance of education: *Pierce v Society of Sisters* 268 U.S. 510 (1925).

seen as a defence mechanism against the rise of violence, discrimination or intolerance" (Grimonprez, 2014).[155]

Within the context of Europe, the paradigm change of a strong EU sustainability model that needs to be aligned with educational and cultural issues seems to have permeated in scientific discourses, research and policy agendas. Still, on its implementation, too much focus has been placed on higher education, vocational training and aspects of responsibility, and accountability, and on the means by which schools ought to be governed with prominence of the control of the 'output' side of education by (mainly) quality controls, standardised testing and evaluations etc. These have been the central political issues aiming at rendering the current education model 'highly competitive' for a 'smarter Europe', without addressing the matter of a building a "knowledgeable" European space.

The aim of a 'knowledgeable' European space should be building a stronger humanistic and holistic perspective integrating Earth system approaches since the earliest educational stages, and this goes beyond the concept of education for sustainability, to embrace other systemic transformations. Thus, the paradoxes of the European policy advancements in education and cultural policy (Europeanisation), at supranational and intergovernmental level, consist on the fact that these policy areas are permeating certain superficial aspects of the paradigm shift under sustainability basis, but they are leaving behind three basic concerns:

(1) Developing the materials for school formal education, pointing out a good direction for a holistic and transformative Education for SD based on innovative didactic approaches (e.g., outdoor learning) from early education stages.
(2) A conceptual approach to education based in a humanistic content rooted in our cultural identity. Indeed, at European level, since the 'Lisbon Strategy' and "Education and Training 2020" what prevails is a 'measurable' concept of lifelong learning aiming at rendering European education systems more competitive.[156]
(3) The integration of culture, from its smallest to its largest existence, encompassing a high concern for the Earth system once we have assumed the consequences of the Anthropocene for our planet. This involves assigning a crucial role to culture as a strong builder of the EU sustainability model, integrating cultural heritage in education programs according to what it was invoked in the Resolution of the Council of 16 November 2007 on a *European Agenda for Culture*, when promoting the transversal role of culture.[157]

---

[155]The author refers to the "Council of Europe Charter on Education for Democratic Citizenship and Human Rights Education", Recommendation CM/Rec (2010)7, p. 35.

[156]The European policy level, with its Lisbon Strategy and the Europe 2020 targets has disrupted in educational policies of MS without providing a focus for an enhancement of education practices in today's complex societies, if not for addressing competitive performance regimes of transnational nature.

[157][2007] OJ287/1, para 7.

As a result, if it is true that too much focus has been placed at higher education level, at least we must hope for further upheaval of our European sustainability model through education at this education stage. It is perhaps a dream to think that big worldwide (and ambitious) plans like the UN Decade for the ESD could work at a smaller scale, such as the EU regional level. Maybe we just need to start reinforcing what HE institutions and HE level initiatives are doing. Indeed, this is the strongest departing point of our EUSM represented by higher education institutions. Thus, we can say with Ortega that "*(..) the University, once again, will come to be what it was in its grand hour: an uplifting principle in the history of the western world*" (Ortega y Gasset, 1944, p. 99).

5.4 Case Studies Offering a Glimpse on How Things Should Go

These case studies will be used to widen the depicted conceptual framework that has been deployed in these lines. The case studies that I have chosen show transformations in the educational and cultural fields embedding a strong sustainability model and integrating: social justice, future generations rights, subsidiarity, new welfare, common good, learning and teaching communities. Such transformations give evidence of how small is indeed beautiful (Schumacher, 1973). Still, change is always difficult today because it runs counter to most of the deeply engrained neo-liberal and modern myths. In fact, we can say with Jickling (2017) that "criticism of market-driven, outcomes-oriented, factory production, industrial or efficiency curricula provide clues to systemic barriers to transformative educational experiences". Instead, new educational experiences that are not only based on the integration of technology in our current learning environments, are needed to foster collaboration and involvement to enhance the idea of learning as a community effort and to open new venues for the promotion of a responsible culture.

5.4.1 Examples of Paradigm Shift in the Education Sector: Senza zaino *Experience and* ECOLOG

In higher education context, the experiences are many, and have different entities. However, making change happen at other institutional levels, as we have seen through the theoretical setting, is not easy. Pedagogical innovation is crucial but deep changes need legal frameworks and institutional support. Nowadays networks are critical in this process, emphasising the transformation of cultural patterns and practice. For both policy and practice, it is useful to consider pedagogy in the space that lies between broad principles and specific teaching methods and practices at local level. This is why case studies on specific innovative pedagogies should not be neglected in this research agenda. These specific cases have a crucial role to push for systemic changes. In fact, the OECD published in 2010 a study about the *Nature of Learning: Using Research to Inspire Practice.*[158] The study identified seven principles of learning that have been pivotal for promoting OECD further research addressing pedagogical challenges. The seven principles of learning are actually contained in the case studies that I presenting. They are the following: (1) Make learning central, and encourage engagement and awareness in students of their own learning strategies; (2) Ensure that learning is social and often collaborative; (3) Be highly attuned to motivations and the emotions involved in learning; (4) be acutely sensitive to individual differences, including in prior knowledge; (5) Be demanding for each learner but without excessive overload; (6) Use assessments consistent with the main goals for learning, with a strong emphasis on formative feedback; (7) Promote horizontal connection across learning activities, across subjects, and across in-and out-of-school learning.

The following experiences are born as isolated experimental projects in schools that are part of the national education system. Meaning, they are both part of the public education systems and they are public funded education initiatives, departing in small-scale basis and developing as network programs at national level. In 2017, they were both selected within the framework of the OECD project of *innovative pedagogies for powerful learning-Networks*, among 25 projects worldwide for innovative approaches in teaching. I had chosen these two cases representing 'innovative pedagogical' approaches before knowing that they had actually been selected as snapshots of innovative pedagogy by the OECD.[159] Thus, according to how things are going in Europe within the education field, the OECD could (ideally) help to better respond to educational challenges and concerns by the diffusion of inspiring best practices. As I have argued, there are slow systemic changes, scarce funding for educational and cultural initiatives in general unless projects are backed up by technological lobbies. International bodies such as the OECD have also fostered the international prominence of evaluation tests (OECD-PISA test), so the need for the culture of evaluation continues to be strongly emphasised. From my personal research, it has emerged that European States have augmented the role of their national agencies for evaluation pushing the ongoing creation of national standards that should reach standardised international evaluation standards (OECD-PISA tests). In addition to this detrimental trend, the need for a new culture of evaluation has been strongly emphasised. Unfortunately, fashionable neo-liberal key themes have been put at the centre of the education debate: meritocracy,

[158] Dumont, Instance, and Benavides (2010).

[159] It means that well-documented reference can be found about these two cases and some others at the OCED library date base. These two case studies are accessible at: https://read.oecd-ilibrary.org/education/teachers-as-designers-of-learning-environments_9789264085374-en#page210.

excellence, etc.. . . . .providing the instruments for the privatisation of education, and widening the educational offer for the sake of 'excellence' creating inequalities.

However, the projects I am going to write about are giving little importance to innovation through the integration of technology, or excellence standards. They are both very little focused on students' evaluations. They are, instead, fostering change and implementing paradigm changes creating transversal competencies adequate to prepare young people to become lifelong learners with a deep awareness of the learning process and a broad set of social skills. They are human centred creating the means for equity and accessible holistic education. They have a strong focus on community creation. A community that must include teachers, school-heads, learners and parents. They are, both of them, public initiatives. The key step in this sort of initiatives is the 'school autonomy'. The negative point is always the lack of appropriate financial means. This is of course also because of their bottom-up nature: The process of innovation is undertaken by teachers, masters' schools and learners themselves. They have created teaching 'networks' that allow monitoring and evaluating mechanisms. They are all in all best-practices samples for teachers and policymakers to innovate and inspire others.

(2.1) **The experience/idea of "*senza zaino. Per una scuola Comunità*"** (Without Backpack for a Community School) came from a school principal in Lucca, Tuscany (Italy).[160] The principal invited other teachers and experts in the project, beginning in 2002, to create classrooms as innovative environments.[161] The innovative teaching proposal entered for the first time in a small town school in Tuscany (Lucca) thanks to the Italian education system reform introducing 'school autonomy'. This autonomy reform was framed within a wider restructuring of public administration more generally. The main change of this public management (called 'weak' site-based management by Grimaldi and Serpieri (2010)) was that schools were entitled to greater room for manoeuvre in relation to financial, organisational and educational issues, although not for human resources management. In fact, the *senza zaino* project has the problem of teachers' mobility, which is an old structural problem of the Italian education system. This is some trained teachers might not have permanent positions, whereas others not trained might have their permanent position in a school belonging to the network.

Senza zaino is a network of schools mostly located in small towns and country areas in Tuscany, but they are also elsewhere in Italy. They are a network of 35 Italian schools.[162] The school organisation is profoundly different from the other Italian schools. The central values of the school that are taken from the presentation of the project itself are three: (1) responsibility, (2) community

---

[160] Marco Orsi. He has been interviewed for portraying this 'innovative' education experience in this study. See further for reference, Orsi (2015).

[161] Paniagua and Instance (2018).

[162] See reference at: http://www.oecd.org/education/ceri/ITA.TUS.002.pdf.

and (3) hospitality.[163] In fact, this school project substitutes the backpack with a light folder or a bag to carry just one piece of homework. Its pedagogy is mainly inspired by the Montessori method, but also linked with current research and innovative pedagogical instruments such as: learning environments, learning as an emotional and physical fact, sustainable teaching and learning, collaborative work for both teachers and pupils, cross-curricular competencies, multiple intelligences, learning styles and personalisation, formative and authentic assessment.[164]

The project revolves around two closely interacting dimensions: 'hardware' of physical spaces and materials, and the 'software' of pedagogical strategies and methods. *Senza zaino* substitutes a small bag for the heavy school backpack, where all the classrooms are provided with functional furniture and tools to implement innovative approaches. Every classroom is multipurpose, with different work areas with large tables, where students can work individually, in pairs, in groups or with the teacher depending on the learning aims. The traditional class setting disappears offering a multidimensional space where the autonomy of the child to manage its own learning should come out facilitated by the teacher. Creativity and handcraft based activities are put at the forefront of transversal teaching in addition to theatre, music and other lab experiences that are offered according to the available funding. The *senza zaino* schools represent different school types, but not all; namely, early childhood, primary schools and secondary schools. There is ample room for the teacher to design its best teaching method. Even if teachers must adopt a curriculum defined by the adaptation of national guidelines, the learner will always remain at the centre of the pedagogical experience. The three fundamental school values, the four features (global approach to persons, global approach to knowledge, global approach to relationships, and global approach to the environment) and ten statements[165] describing the main pedagogical instruments of this teaching and learning method are basic for the elaboration of the "global curriculum handbook". This is a collaborative product setting tools aimed to class management, day planning, activities planning, resources and management that can be used by the whole network of schools.[166] The schools are (regularly) public funded but they also count with family funds for every student in addition to the annual quota of ministerial funds. Other eventual funding can be raised participating to tenders of local and national institutions and with activities organised by the school community.

[163] www.senzazaino.it.

[164] See further, Orsi (2006, 2015).

[165] (1) children's autonomy and responsibility affecting proficiency learning; (2) problem-solving; (3) focus on body and senses; (4) multiple intelligences and differences in every child; (5) students and teachers involved in school planning; (6) teachers work in a professional community; (7) several didactic tools develop several ways of teaching; (8) well-organised spaces; (9) parent's participation as part of the community; (10) authentic assessment fosters student's improvement.

[166] See further, Orsi (2006).

The network assessment results show that *senza zaino* students have more autonomy and high levels of empathy and collaboration than students following traditional public education schools.[167]

(2.2) The **ECOLOG** is an initiative which has taken place in Austria as part of the action program and network for the greening of schools and promoting education for sustainability.[168] It was developed as early as the mid-1990 (1996) following the development of Austrian's schools autonomy, by a team of Austrian teachers as part of the international project "Environment and school initiatives" (ENSI) network.[169] It is a national support system for individual schools that promotes this sustainability approach through regional networks and regional governments.[170] Networks arise in this context as alternative ways of coordination to fill structural gaps after administrative decentralisation and taking over functions traditionally assigned to the hierarchy (Rauch, Pfaffenwimmer, & Dulle, 2016). Overall coordination is ensured by the Institute of Instructional and School Development at the University of Klagenfurt in partnership with the Federal Ministry of Education.

Key practices of the ECOLOG action program include:

- Project-oriented teaching and learning. Head teachers play a crucial role through what it has been described as "official" support of the project through actions such as putting sustainability on the agenda of teachers' conferences seminars, and training sessions;
- Communication and openness is a vital element allowing schools common understanding of ESD and allowing a wide range of issues to be included and fostering creativity and innovation along the lines of ecologically aligned projects triggering many different topics (such as health, consumption, resources, etc.. . . .)
- Focal topics and school development plans issued annually;
- Student involvement;
- Aligning teaching development and school development;
- Systematic reporting, cross-case-analysis of the reports of the regional network and evaluation;
- Inquiry-based learning on real-life issues apparent at the school and local levels.

---

[167] In 2009, the Faculty of psychology of Florence conducted a research project in ten schools senza zaino on collaborative, pro-social and empathic behaviour, evidence of the study can be retrieved from: www.isomar.it/file/empatiaprosocialitapprendimento-1.doc.

[168] Austrian network "Ecologising schools" (ECOLOG).

[169] Originally, ENSI was set up as a research and development project of OECD's centre for Educational Research and Innovation (CERI), but as a result of a reorganisation of OECD all decentralised networks became independent in 2002 and ENSI is now an association under Austrian law based at the Ministry for Education and Women's Affairs in Vienna. The ENSI network is financed by its members and through its own project work. See further, in Affolter and Mathar (2016), p. *12 et seq.*

[170] See further, Rauch and Pfaffenwimmer (2015).

At the heart of the ECOLOG project, we find a participatory approach. This is the most important element for success and community creation. Schools analyse the ecological, technical, and social conditions of their environment and, from these results, define objectives, targets, and/or concrete activities and quality criteria, to be implemented and evaluated. Students, as well as all the other stakeholders of a school, should be involved in a participatory way, and collaboration with authorities, businesses, and other interested parties is encouraged by the coordinating body and creating synergies. This initiative covers all school types: primary, secondary, higher secondary schools, as well as vocational schools and higher vocational schools. The areas of concern on which the network is focused include among others: natural resources (water, energy, land, etc.), reduction of emissions (waste, traffic, etc.), spatial management, learning processes and the culture of learning (communication, etc.), health promotion and opening the school to the community. The annual evaluation reports and the network synergies allow constant creativity and innovation according to society needs under the premises of ecological transition. In fact, since the early 1990s, the Austrian vocational education and training system and curricula have been developed in support of SD and the transition to a green economy thanks to the coordinating efforts of network.

The synergies among the members of the network and the advisory and development role of the network of representatives of university colleges of teacher education strengthen the flux of information. It fosters events, seminars, training, publications and collaborations with the regional science networks, with other international projects and facilitates the existence of monitoring mechanism, evaluation and a wealth of up-to date teaching materials. This is a guarantee for the quality development of schools and offers qualified teacher training in connection with the most updated materials coming from a wide range of sources. School reports that are issued annually take the form of school development plans. They are a helpful tool for planning and future enhancement of ECOLOG's schools mission. In addition to this, schools that are living out a sustainable culture can influence the surrounding communities by spreading good practices.

Constant monitoring results are other crucial element of network development. The appraisal results have always been performed with quantitative and qualitative methods enabled by coordinating bodies.[171] The outcomes have shown that participation in ECOLOG improves understanding of environmental education and ESD issues, supports commitment and offers space for students in concrete activities associated with ecological transition and community building.

[171]On this topic, see further, Rauch et al. (2016), pp. 21–32.

5.4.2 *Examples of Paradigm Shift in the Cultural Sector:* Julie's Bicycle *and Other* Urban Initiatives

Under this heading, two different cases will illustrate two paradigmatic realities that represent the experiences that society needs to implement change and a strong ecological transition. (1) The first experience regards the relevant role of cultural institutions for sustainability awareness and people's empowerment. It is a case that deals with the incorporation of a cultural narrative (creativity, arts, emotions, etc.) in a wide society context; (2) the second experience explores alternative governance models behind community-run examples of heritage-reuse that are successful urban regeneration[172] archetypes for heritage sites, which involve and benefit local communities.

(1) I have chosen **Julie's Bicycle** experience among many other similar experiences representing today the same pattern: fostering ecological awareness and social change through cultural initiatives run by cultural institutions through cultural narratives' tools (such as creativity, inspiration, emotions, arts, music, shows, etc.). This is a London-based charity born more than ten years ago to offer support to the creative community to act on climate change and environmental sustainability. Alison Tickell, the founder and current CEO of Julie's Bicycle,[173] founded this organisation in 2007 to help the music industry to reduce it ecological impact and develop new ideas in accordance with sustainability challenges. Since then, it developed to influence the whole cultural sector and today it is considered a leader organisation hosting a long-lasting marriage between sustainability and the creative world.
According to their public website, they believe: "the creative community is uniquely placed to transform the conversation around climate change and translate it into action". Thus, "they provide the creative community with the skills to act, using their creativity to influence one another, audiences and the wider movement". To achieve this, they run a prolific programme of events, free resources, seminars, webinars, and public speaking engagements that contribute to national and international climate change policy development.

They are deeply engaged with the arts and cultural sectors, working together with many different organisations and independent professionals across the UK and internationally to embed environmental sustainability into their different actions. They support the Paris Agreement goal to limit global warming to 1.5 degrees Celsius through their action. They focus on energy, which is the major source of carbon emissions for the cultural sector. For this purpose, they encourage companies to use the Creative Green Tools (formally the IG tools) which are a free set of carbon calculators developed by this organisation

---

[172]The notion of urban regeneration, in the Anglo-American context where it was adopted in the late 1980s is rigorously connected to tackling environmental, cultural and social issues in urban policies.
[173]Since 2015 in concomitance with the COP21 Julie's Bicycle.

specifically for the creative industries to make it easy to measure any organisation's key environmental impacts (from the energy use of the building, to the waste generated, to the travel, materials impact). These indicators are used by over 3,000 organisations across 50 countries to understand the environmental impacts of cultural buildings, offices, outdoor event, tours and productions.[174] They represent benchmarks for sustainability achievement worldwide.

Two key objectives define their mission in today's society:

- Advocate to and for culture to publicly inspire action on climate change and sustainability. They aim at equipping cultural professionals and artist with the knowledge and confidence to speak out and together on sustainability issues.
- Support the Paris Agreement, decarbonisation and energy transition.

Since 2015, they promote COPtimism. It is a movement engaging the creative community in conversation about culture and climate change. They coined the term 'COPtimism' to focus on the hope that followed the historic outcome of the 2015 COP21 Climate change talks. It is inspired by former Executive Director of the UNFCCC, Christian Figueres' approach centred on "relentless optimism".

Julie's bicycle gives substantial and influential voice to the creative sector of society representing bottom-up approaches that equip society at large with a set of values founded on sustainability and climate change awareness. It empowers, influences and inspires urgent action on climate change and sustainability transition through culture.

(2) The urban initiative in **Bratislava's Old Market Hall**. *Alianca Stará Tržnica* is an NGO managing a historic building in the centre of Bratislava, the Old Market Hall. It belongs to the municipality,[175] but the municipality closed down the building after years of unsuccessful attempts to keep the market alive. The City had tried to run the place as a mono-functional market, but there was only about six stalls left inside, and all the others were closed down. The market was suffering losses although the tenants were there for the whole week but they did not generate revenue for the market hall. The reason behind this failure was the narrow focus: "a market hall had to be a market hall". However, Mazur (2017, p. 182) affirms that there was no market for a market hall in Bratislava any more. Thus, *Alianca Stará Tržnica* (NGO) proposed a new kind of redevelopment project to the City. Therefore, considering that there was no market for a market hall for seven days a week, they deliberated to have a market there one day a week, and have six days of new programming which could subside the market. The urban regeneration and management proposal was prepared by a team of experts from different disciplines to cooperate elaborating a new program for the building. The result was a multifunctional place with a blend of

[174]This info can be retrieved from their public website: https://www.juliesbicycle.com/news/introducing-the-creative-green-tools.

[175]For more detailed information about this particular Project and, more data about community finance and the cooperative civic projects, see further, Patti and Polyák (2017).

activities mixing some initiatives not generating solid revenue with those that can generate it to compensate and subsidise the former ones. The Old Market Hall has been a non-profit project since 2013. They created a special programme with a flexible forum where anyone could put any content they wanted according to specific needs and functions. Thus, during the week when there is not enough people to attend markets, the building is used as a concert hall, a ballroom for companies, a conference hall, or a workshop space. The market is run on Saturdays when people have time to go. Mazur explains how the whole project was introduced as a sustainable and financially separate project from the municipality. According to the agreement, they do not receive any subsidies or financing from the city, but they pay a symbolic one euro rent per year for the building, and have to invest in the renovation of the market hall. The economic plan is working out so far getting a large portion of the revenue from about 16 private events per year. There is a great demand due to a specific situation in Bratislava. During the first years, the necessity to rise revenues from private events is evident considering that the need to invest in the regeneration of the space was clearly a mandatory need for its future sustainability. In the future when the building will need less structural regeneration, and building investment's needs will decrease, expecting a surplus of money, the need for private events will be lessened, the possibility to offer more public events will grow. The concept behind *Stará Tržnica* is that the prices for the tenants are slightly reduced when compared to market prices,[176] because they do not do it for profit. Therefore the business that are run inside the market hall have a social value, and not only. I have chosen this example to illustrate a civic space that can work outside the mainstream public or commercial sector, reinvesting revenues and profit into their own activities at the service of an extended community, creating significant social and cultural value in the city, at odds with the urban trends dominated by the financialised real estate market and commercial predispositions.

This urban initiative belongs to a more gigantic social movement that is boosting an important social shift outside traditional set up division between public and private administration. The shift is happening under the premises of sustainable transformations where civic society play an increasing role in creating inclusive, accessible and well-managed communication systems of decision making. This social movement is led by local-based community initiatives, citizens' initiatives, or NGOs experimenting new forms of solidarity, collaborative and civic economy, in urban or rural contexts; new governance and welfare provisions.

In some instances, this civic collaboration has been initially inspired by constitutional provisions. This is the case of an association called laboratory of

---

[176]The way of supporting them is to lower the rent, or to allow them to deduct certain investments they did, from the rent over the course of ten years.

subsidiarity *(labsus)*[177] operating in Italy. The platform behind this initiative has helped to spread the idea of building "a new model of society characterised by the presence of active citizenship, understanding this as autonomous, caring, responsible citizens, allied with the government in taking care of all the common goods" and it is facilitated by Civic collaboration formalised through 'civic' pacts with standardised regulatory tools. *Labsus* gives voice to the principle of horizontal subsidiarity introduced by an Italian constitutional revision law in 2001. Today the Italian Constitution Art. 118, last paragraph reads as follows: "State, Regions, Metropolitan Cities, Provinces and Municipalities favour the autonomous initiative of citizens, individual and associated, for carrying out activities of general interest, based on the principle of subsidiarity". This new rule recognised citizens' capacities and capabilities to act autonomously in the general interest providing the legal basis for an institutional support of their efforts, based on the idea of "responsible subsidiarity". Today the collaboration agreements are 203, with projects that are increasingly spreading for the use of cultural heritage.[178]

In other instances in the same territory, under the same sustainability premises, with different inspiration but equal results and similar regulatory tools, the social initiatives are born adapting to the urban environment the design principles for the governance of the 'commons' located by the Economic's Nobel Prize Elinor Ostrom to the urban context. Since 2011, the city of Bologna initiated a policy process to introduce collaboration as a methodology for governing the urban commons. The central regulatory tool of the Bologna regulation on Public Collaboration for the Urban Commons is the pact of collaboration. Since the approval of the Regulation, 280 pacts of collaboration have been signed (labgov.city).[179] This idea is associated to the "shared responsibility" concept (Sacconi, 2011) and it is also correlated to initiatives such as the 'gift economy' and the more international movement 'transition initiative' headed by transitionnetwork.org that engages a myriad of communities worldwide craving for a green transition of a localised nature. Unfortunately this movement can marginally be mentioned here (Transition Network, 2015): "Transition is a movement of communities who are engaged in real life, real time experiments. (. . .) ordinary people creating, bit by bit, resilient and sustainable cultures all across the world (. . .)". For these communities, research and learning are important (. . .).[180]

[177]See further, https://www.labsus.org/.

[178]This data is published on the association web page "list of collaboration agreements", retrieved from, https://www.labsus.org/i-regolamenti-per-lamministrazione-condivisa-dei-beni-comuni/.

[179]See further, https://labgov.city/explore-by-lab/bolognalab/.

[180]Retrieved from, https://transitionnetwork.org/about-the-movement/what-is-transition/research/tn-research/.

References

Affolter, C., & Mathar, R. (2016). Environment and school initiatives- ENSI: A precious network for thirty years! In W. Lambrechts & J. Hindson (Eds.), *Research and innovation in education for sustainable development*. Vienna: CoDeS, ENSI.

Alexiadou, N., & Lundhal, L. (2019). The boundaries of policy learning and the role of ideas: Sweden, as a reluctant policy learner. In U. Stadler-Altmann & B. Gross (Eds.), *Beyond erziehungswissenschaftlicher Grenzen. Diskurse zu Entgrenzungen der Disziplin*. Verlag Barbara Budrich.

Anleu, S. L. R. (2000). *Law and social change*. London: Sage.

Ávila, L., Leal-Filho, W., Brandli, L., Macgregor, C., Molthan-hill, P., Özuyar, P. G., et al. (2017). Barriers to innovation and sustainability at universities around the world. *Journal of Cleaner Production, 164*, 1268–1278.

Bacevic, J. (2013). Europe of knowledge: Paradoxes and challenges. *Green European Journal, 6*. Accessible on line at: http://greeneuropeanjournal.eu

Bengtsson, E. L., Barkat, B., & Muttarak, R. (Eds.). (2018). *The role of education in enabling the sustainable development agenda*. Oxon: Routledge.

Benkler, Y. (2006). *The wealth of networks*. New Haven: Yale University Press. Available at: www.benkler.org/Benkler_Wealth_Of_Networks.pdf

Bereiter, C., & Scardamalia, M. (2014). Knowledge building and knowledge creation: One concept, two hills to climb. In S. C. Tan, H. J. So, & J. Yeo (Eds.), *Knowledge creation in education*. Singapore: Springer.

Bogdandy, A. V., Kottmann, M., Antpöhler, C., Dickschen, J., Hentrei, S., & Smrkolj, M. (2012). Reverse Solange-protecting the essence of fundamental rights against EU Member States. *Common Market Law Review*, 49, 489, 512.

Bruni, L., & Zamagni, S. (2013). *Handbook on the economics of reciprocity and social enterprise*. Edward Elgar Publishing.

Bruni, L., & Zamagni, S. (2015). *L'economia civile*. Il mulino.

Caniglia, G., Luederitz, C., Groß, M., Muhr, M., John, B., Keeler, L. W., et al. (2017). Transnational collaboration for sustainability in higher education: Lessons from systematic review. *Journal of Cleaner Production, 168*, 764–779.

Casini, L. (2010). "Italian hours: The globalization of cultural property law", *NYU Jean Monnet Working Paper*, n.11.

Cernilogar, K., & Coertjens, M. (2011). The role of education in shared social responsibilities. In *Towards a Europe of shared social responsibilities: Challenges and strategies*, Trends in Social Cohesion, No.23. Council of Europe Publishing.

Chatterton, P., & Goddard, J. (2000). The Response of higher Education Institutions to Regional Needs. *European Journal of Education, 35*(4), 475–496.

Chiti, E. (2011). "EU and global administrative organizations". In E. Chitti & B. G. Mattarella (Eds.), Global *Administrative Law and EU administrative Law*, Berlin.

Chiti, E., & Mattarella, B. G. (Eds.). (2011). *Global administrative law and EU administrative law*. Berlin: Springer.

Chou, M. H., & Gornitzka, Å. (2014). *Building the Knowledge economy in Europe: New constellations in european research and higher education governance*. In *New Constellations in European research and higher education governance. series new horizons in European politics*. London: Edward Elgar.

Chou, M. H., & Ulnicane, I. (2015). New horizons in the Europe of knowledge. *Journal of Contemporary European Research, 11*(1).

Closa, C., & Casini, L. (2016). *Comparative regional intregration. Governance and legal models*. Cambridge: Cambridge University Press.

Dakar. (2000). *The Dakar framework for action: Education for all: Meeting our collective commitments* (including six regional frameworks for action)-World Education Forum in Senegal 26–28 April 2000. UNESCO Digital Library

Davidson, C. N., & Goldberg, D. T. (2010). The future of thinking. Learning institutions in a digital age. In D. John & C. T. MacCArthur (Eds.), *Foundation reports on digital media and learning*. MIT Press.

Degrassi, L. (2008). La fruizione dei beni culturali nell'ordinamento Italiano e Comunitario2, in Degrassi, L. *Cultura e istituzioni. La valorizzazione dei beni culturali negli ordinamenti giuridici*. Giuffrè, Milano, pp. 137–203.

DeMitchell, T. A., & Fossey, R. (1997). *The limits of law-based school reforms: Vain hopes and false promises*. Lancaster: Technomic Publishing Co.

Desideri, C. (2015). Legal frameworks for nature conservation and landscape protection. In R. Gambino & A. Peano (Eds.), *Nature policies and landscape policies. Urban and landscape perspectives* (Vol. 18, pp. 77–84). Cham: Springer.

Dewey, J. (2007). *Experience and Education*. New York: Simon and Schuster. First Published in 1928 by Kappa Delta Pi.

Dumont, H., Instance, D., & Benavides, F. (Eds.), (2010). *The nature of learning: Using research to inspire practice*. Paris: OECD Publishing. Accessible at: https://doi.org/10.1787/9789264086487-en

Egan, A. (2002). *Wither Education?: Human rights law versus trade law*. Right to education.org. Available on line at: http://right-to-education.org/content/strategy/whiter_education.html

Elken, M., Gornitzka, Å., Maassen, P., & Vukasovic, M. (2011). "European Integration and the transformation of higher education", *report, department of educational research*, Oslo, Norway. Available from https://www.uv.uio.no/iped/forskning/prosjekter/eie-utd2020forprosjekt/HEIK-Utd2020-Part1-EI_and_transformation_of_HE.pdf

ESPAS. (2015). *Global trends to 2030: Can the EU meet the challenges ahead?*

European Commission. (1997). *Towards a Europe of knowledge. Communication from the Commission to the Council, the European Parliament, the Economic and Social Committee and the Committee of the Regions,* COM (97) 563 final, 12 November 1997.

European Commission. (2000). Communication from the commission to the council, The European Parliament, The economic and social committee and the committee of the regions, *Social Policy Agenda*. COM (2000) 379 final.

European Commission. (2017). *Reaching out to EU Citizens: A New Opportunity,* October 2017,a report by Luc Van den Brande. Accessible at: https://ec.europea.eu/commission/sites/beta-political/files/reaching-out-to-citizens-report_en.pdf

European Commission. (2018). *European ideas for better learning: The governance of school education systems*. Produced by the ET 2020 Working Group Schools; The final report and thematic outputs of the ET 2020 Working Group Schools, Directorate-General Education, Youth, Sport and Culture, European Commission. Accessible at: https://www.schooleducationgateway.eu/downloads/Governance/2018-wgs6-Full-Final-Output.pdf

European Commission/EACEA/Eurydice. (2018). *National Student Fee and Support Systems in European Higher Education-2018/2019*. Eurydice –Facts and Figures. Luxembourg: Publications Office of the European Union.

Fairclough, G., Dragićević-Šešić, M., Rogač-Mijatović, L., Auclair, E., & Soini, K. (2014). *The Faro Convention, a new paradigm socially-and culturally-sustainable heritage action*? Available at: https://journals.cultcenter.net/index.php/culture/article/view/111

Farrell. (2011). (coord), *Towards a Europe of social responsibilities: Challenges and strategies*. In Trends in Social Cohesion, no. 23. Council of Europe Publishing.

Fleaca, E., Fleaca, B., & Maiduc, S. (2018). Aligning strategy with sustainable development goals (SDGs): Process scoping diagram for entrepreneurial higher education institutions (HEIs). *Sustainability, 10*(4), 1032.

Fleming, D., Chamberlin, S., & Hopkins, R. (Eds.). (2016). *Surviving the future: Culture, carnival and capital in the aftermath of the market economy*. Chelsea Green Pub. Co.

Florence. (2000). *European Landscape Convention of the Council of Europe*, 20th October Florence (Italy) and came into force on 1 March 2004 (Council of Europe Treaty Series).

Fuster Morell, M. (2010). *Governance of online creation communities, provision of infrastructure for the building of digital commons*. Florence: Mimeo, European University Institute.

Fuster Morell, M. (2013). Intergenerational justice and digital resources: Is there a future for digital commons? In S. Bailey, G. Farrell, & U. Mattei (Eds.), *Protecting future generations through commons*, Trends in Social Cohesion, No. 26. Council of Europe Publishing.

Gambino, R., & Peano, A. (Eds.). (2015). *Nature policies and landscape policies. Towards and alliance, in Urban and landscape perspectives* (Vol. 18). Springer.

Garben, S. (2017). The constitutional (Im)balance between 'the market' and 'the social' in the European Union. *European Constitutional Law Review, 13*, 23–61.

Giannini, M. S. (1976). "I Beni culturali" in *Riv. Trimmestrale di Diritto Pubblico*, pp. 5 et seg.

Glen, C. L., & De Groof, J. (2012). Introduction to volume two: V. In C. L. Glen & J. De Groof (Eds.), *Balancing freedom, autonomy and accountability in education* (Vol. 2). Wolf Legal Publishers.

Göpel, M. (2011). Shared responsibilities and future generations: Beyond the dominant concepts of justice. In O. C. Farrell (coord), *Towards a Europe of social responsibilities: Challenges and strategies*, in Trends in Social Cohesion, no. 23 (pp. 135–156). Council of Europe Publishing.

Göpel, M. (2016). *The great Mindshift. How a new economic paradigm and sustainability transformations go hand in hand*. Springer.

Gorgescu-Roegen, N. (1971). *The entropy law and the economic process*. Cambridge, MA: Harvard University Press.

Gornitzka, A. (2018). Organising soft governance in hard times. The unlikely survival of the open method of coordination in the EU Education policy. *European Papers, 3*(1), 235–255.

Gough, G., & Longjurst, J. (2017). Monitoring progress towards implementing sustainability and representing the UNSDGs in the curriculum at UWE Bristol. In *Implementing sustainability in the curriculum of universities*. Manchester Metropolitan University.

Grimaldi, E., & Serpieri, R. (2010). The reforming trajectory of the Italian educational system: Site-based management and decentralisation as a challenge for democratic discourse. *Journal of Educational Administration and History, 42*(1), 75–95.

Grimonprez, K. (2014). The European dimension in citizenship education: Unused potential of Article 165 TFEU. *European Law Review, 1*.

Gunesakara, C. S. (2004). The third role of Australian universities in human capital formation. *Higher Education Policy Management, 26*(3), 329–343.

Halász, G. (2013). European Union: The Strive for Smart, Sustainable and Inclusive Growth. In Y. Wang (Ed.), *Education Policy Reform Trends in G20 Members* (pp. 267–288). Springer.

Heckman, J. (2008). Schools, Skills and Sypnapses. *Economic Inquiry, 46*(3), 289–324.

Hess, C. (2008). *Mapping the new commons*, Conference governing shared resources: Connecting local experience to global challenges, the Twelfth Biennial Conference of the International Association for the Study of Commons, Cheltenham, Available at: http://dlc.dlib.indiana.edu/dlc/handle/10535/304

Hess, C., & Ostrom, E. (Eds.). (2007). *Understanding knowledge as a commons: From theory to practice*. Cambridge, MA: MIT Press.

Hopkins, R. (2011). *The transition companion: Making your community more resilient in uncertain times*. Vermont: Chelsea Green Publishing.

Huisman, J., & Van Der Wende, M. (2004). *On cooperation and competition. National and European policies for the internationalisation of higher education*. Bonn: Lemmens.

ITU. (2014). *Manual for measuring ICT access and use by households and individuals*. International Telecommunication Union.

Jagielska-Burduk, A. (2019). Cultural heritage, education and research in the European Union. In A. Jakubowski, K. Hausler, & F. Fiorentini (Eds.), *Cultural heritage in the European Union. A critical enquiry into law and policy*. Leiden: Brill | Nijhoff.

Jain, M., & Jain, S. (Eds.), (2008). Reclaiming the gift culture. In *Artwork: Sunny Gandhrva Shikshantar*. The Peoples' Institute for Rethinking Education and Development. Accessible in: www.swaraj.org/shikshantar

Janssen, J., & Knippenberg, L. (2012). From landscape preservation to landscape governance: European experiences with sustainable development of protected landscapes. In T. Piacentini &

E. Miccadei (Eds.), *Studies on environmental and applied geomorphology* (pp. 241–266). Rijeka: InTech.

Jickling, B. (2017). Education revisited: Creating educational experiences that are held, felt and disruptive. In B. Jickling & S. Sterling (Eds.), *Post-sustainability and environmental education* (pp. 15–30). Switzerland: Palgrave Studies in Education and the Environment.

Jongbloed, B., Enders, J., & Salerno, C. (2008). Higher education and its communities: Interconnections, interdependencies and a research agenda, in higher education. *The International Journal of Higher Education Research, 56*(3), 303–324.

Jucker, R. (2014) *Do we know what we are doing? Reflections on learning, knowledge, economics, community and sustainability.* Cambridge Scholars Publishing.

Jucker, R., & Mathar, R. (Eds.). (2015). *Schools for sustainable development in Europe. Concepts, policies and educational experiences at the end of the UN decade of education for sustainable development*. Switzerland: Springer.

Kallen, D. (1997). *Secondary education in Europe: Problems and prospects.* The Council of Europe Publishing.

Knight, J. (2002). Trade in Higher Education Services: The implications of GATS. In *The observatory on borderless Higher Education.* London, UK, Retrieved on line from: (www.obhe.ac.uk)

Knight, J. (2003). "GATS, trade and higher education. Perspective 2003. Where are we?". Report published by *The Observatory on borderless Higher Education.* London

Kosta, K. (2019). *Institutional sustainability assessment.* In Filho L (Ed.), Encyclopedia of Sustainability in Higher Education. Accessible at: https://doi.org/10.1007/978-3-319-63951-2_196-1

Langfeldt, L., Godø, G., Gornitzka, A., & Kaloudis, A. (2012, February). Integration modes in EU research: Centrifugality versus coordination of national research policies. *Science and Public Policy, 39*(1), 88–98.

Law, W. W. (2007). Legislation and educational change: The struggle for social justice and quality in China's compulsory schooling. *Education and the Law, 19*(3–4), 177–199.

Lessig, L. (2004). *Free culture: How big media uses technology and the law to lock down culture and control creativity.* New York: Penguin Press.

Lieberman, M. (1997). *The teacher unions: How the nea and the aft sabotage reform and hold students, parents, teachers and taxpayers hostage to bureaucracy.* New York: Free Press.

Lifton, R. J. (1993). *The protean self: Human resilience in an age of fragmentation.* New York: Basic Books.

Locatelli, R. (2018). "Education as a public and common good: Reframing the governance of education in a changing context", in *Education Research and Foresight Working Papers,* UNESCO.

Marina, J. A. (2017). *El Bosque Pedagógico y como salir de él,* Editorial Ariel, Barcelona.

Mazur, J. (2017). *Starña Tržnica. New purpose for a public building.* In D. Patti, & L. Polyák (Eds.), *Funding the Cooperative City. Community finance and the economy of civic spaces.* Vienna: Cooperative City Books. A pdf of this publication can be downloaded at cooperativecity.org, open data distributed as part of the Horizon2020 eutropian project.

McAfee, K. (1999). Selling nature to save it? Biodiversity and green developmentalism. *Environmental and Planning D: Society and Space* (1). Accessible at: https://doi.org/10.1068/d170133.

Mokrosch, R., & Regenbogen, A. (2015). Can values education promote cohesion in Europe? Considerations on the example of the EU values of freedom, equality, solidarity and human dignity. In H.-J. Blanke et al. (Eds.), *Common European legal thinking*. Switzerland, Accessible at:: Springer. https://doi.org/10.1007/978-3-319-19300-7_20

Molthan-Hill, P. (Ed.). (2017). *The business student's guide to sustainable management: Principles and practice. Principles of responsible management education.* Abingdon: Routledge.

Molthan-hill, P., Puntha, H., Darmasasmita, A., & Simmons, E. (2015). Food for thought: A university-wide approach to stimulate curricular and extra-curricular ESD activity. In W. Leal-Filho, U. Azeiteiro, S. Caeiro, & F. Alves (Eds.), *Integrating sustainability thinking in science and engineering curricula.* World sustainability series (pp. 31–48). Cham: Springer.

Morin, E. (1999). *Seven Complex Lessons in Education for the future*. Accessible at: https://unesdoc.unesco.org/ark:/48223/pf0000117740

Neave, G. (2000). *The universities' responsibilities to society*. Oxford: Pergamon.

Nixon, J., Sankey, F., & Simmons, M. (1999). Education for sustainability in Scottish secondary schools: Boundary maintenance or professional reorientation? *Environmental Education Research, 5*(3), 305–318.

OECD. (2017). *Education at a glance 2017: OECD Indicators*. Paris: OECD Publishing.

OECD. (2018a). *The Education Sustainable Development Goal*. Education at a Glance 2018: OECD Indicators.

OECD. (2018b). *How is the tertiary-educated population evolving?*, Education indicators in Focus, No. 61. Paris: OECD Publishing. https://doi.org/10.1787/a17e95dc-en

OECD-CERI. (1982). *The university and the community: The problems of changing relationships*. Paris: OECD.

Oppong, C. K. (2018). The nexus between universities and local development. *Current Research Journal of Social Science, 9*(2), 21–27.

Orsi, M. (2006). *A scuola senza zaino. Il metodo del curricolo globale per una scuola comunità*. Trento: Erickson.

Orsi, M. (2015). *L'ora di lezione non basta. La visione e le pratiche dell'ideatore delle scuole senza zaino*. Quaderni di "Rivista dell'Istruzione", Maggioli Editore.

Ostrom, E. (1990). *Governing the commons: The evolution of institutions for collective action*. London: Cambridge University Press.

Pan, S. Y., & Law, W. W. (2006). Legalising education: The role of law in the regulation and deregulation of China's private education. *Education and the Law, 18*(4), 267–283.

Paniagua, A., & Instance, D. (2018). *Teachers as designers of learning environments: The importance of innovative pedagogies*, Educational Research and Innovation. Paris: OECD Publishing. Open access at: https://doi.org/10.1787/9789264085374-en

Parker, J. (2008). Its life Jim – But not as we know it': The unique contribution of development education to 'Big Picture' sustainability education with a focus on climate change. *Policy and Practice: A Development Education Review, 6*, 95–100.

Patti, D., & Polyák, L. (Eds.). (2017). *Funding the Cooperative City. Community finance and the economy of civic spaces*. Vienna: Cooperative City Books. A pdf of this publication can be downloaded at cooperativecity.org, open data distributed as part of the Horizon2020 *eutropian project*

Podgórecki, A. (1974). *Law and society*. London: Routledge and Kegan Paul.

Podgórecki, A. (Ed.). (1985). *Legal systems and social systems*. London: Croom Helm.

Pope Francis. (2015). *Laudato Si'. Sulla cura della casa comunes*. Lettera encíclica, EDB.

Postman, N. (1992). *Technolopoly: The surrender of culture to technology*. See further, Vintage. It can be retrieved from: www.collier.sts.vt.edu

Postman, N. (2011). *The end of education: Redefining the value of school*. Vintage.

Pranevičienė, B., & Margevičiūtė, A. (2015). Challenges to the implementation of institutional reform in the Lithuanian general education system. *Baltic Journal of Law and Politics, 8*(1), 106–138.

Psacharopoulos, G., & Anthony Patrinos, H. (2002). *Returns to investment in Education: A further update*. World Bank Research Paper 2881. Washington, DC: World Bank.

Psychogiopoulou, E. (2015). "The Cultural Open Method of Coordination". In Psychogiopoulou, E. (Ed), *EU Cultural Governance and the European Union. Protecting and Promoting Cultural Diversity in Europe*, Pallgrave MacMillan.

Rauch, F., & Pfaffenwimmer, G. (2015). Education for sustainable development in Austria: Networking for innovation. In R. Jucker & R. Mathar (Eds.), *Schooling for sustainable development in Europe. Schooling for sustainable development* (Vol. 6). Cham: Springer.

Rauch, F., Pfaffenwimmer, G., & Dulle, M. (2016). The Austrian network "Ecologising Schools" (ECOLOG). In W. Lambrechts, J. Hindson (Eds) *Research and innovation in education for sustainable development* (pp. 21–32). Vienna: Environment and School Initiatives.

Rifkin, J. (2001). *The age of access: The new culture of hypercapitalism.* TarcherPerigree.

Rifkin, J. (2013). *The third industrial revolution. How lateral power is transforming energy, the economy, and the world.* Griffin.

Rifkin, J. (2015). *The zero marginal cost society: The internet of things, the collaborative commons, and the eclipse of capitalism.* MPS.

Rifkin, J. (2016). How the Third Industrial Revolution Will Create a Green Economy. *New Perspectives Quarterly, 33*(1), 6–10.

Sacconi, L. (2011). From individual responsibility to shared social responsibilities: Concepts for a new paradigm. In G. Farrell (coord.), *Towards a Europe of shared social responsibilities: Challenges and strategies*, Trends in Social Cohesion, No. 23 (pp. 35–80). Council of Europe Publishing.

Sachs, J. D. (2015). *The Age of Sustainable Development.* New York: Columbia University.

Sánchez Galera, M. D. (2018). "Sustainable development: "The hedgehog" or "the fox" of the European integration dream?. A closer look to its social dimension", In P. Masala (Ed.), *La Europea social alcances, desafíos para la construcción de un espacio jurídico de solidaridad*, CEPC.

Sánchez Galera, M. D. (2020). Compulsory education and its role in sustainable development. In W. Leal Filho, A. Azul, L. Brandi, P. Özuyar, & T. Wall (Eds.), *Quality education. Encyclopedia of the UN sustainable development goals.* Cham: Springer.

Sanni, M., Adejuwon, J. O., Ologeh, I., & Siyanbola, W. O. (2010). Path to the future for climate change education: A university project approach. In F. W. Leal (Ed.), *Universities and climate change. Climate change management.* Berlin, Heidelberg: Springer.

Sarti, M., & John, S. K. S. (2019). Raising long-term awareness: EU environmental policy and education. In S. K. S. John & M. Murphy (Eds.), *Education and public policy in the european union. Crossing boundaries.* Pallgrave McMillan.

Sauvé, P. (2002). Trade education and the GATS: What's in, What's out, What's all this fuss about. *Higher Education Management and Policy, 14*(3).

Schumacher, E. F. (1973). *Small is beautiful: A study of economics as if people mattered.* New York: Harper Perennial.

Sen, A. (1999). *Development as Freedom.* Oxford: Oxford University Press.

SDSN Australia/Pacific. (2018). *Getting Started with the SDGs in Universities. A guide for universities, Higher education institutions and the academic sector.* Retrieved from: ap-unsdsn.org

Shalberg, P. (2015). *Finnish Lessons 2.0 what can the world learn from educational change in Finland?* (2nd ed.). Teachers College, Columbia University.

Simoncini, M. (2018). *Administrative regulation beyond the non-delegation doctrine: A study on EU agencies.* Hart Pub. Ltd.

Spitzer, M. (2013). *Demenza digitale. Come la nuova tecnologia ci rende stupidi*, (Italian translation from the original title: *Digitale Demenz: Wie wir uns und unsere Kinder um den Verstand bringen* 2012), edited by Corbaccio.

St. John, S. K. (2019). Tracing the roots: The origins and evolution of European Union education policy. In S. K. St. John & M. Murphy (Eds.), *Education and public policy in the European Union. Crossing boundaries* (pp. 21–46). Switzerland: Pallgrave Macmillan.

Stevenson, R. (2007). Schooling and environmental/sustainability education: From discourses of policy and practice to discourses of professional learning. *Environmental Education Research, 13*, 2. Retrieved from: https://doi.org/10.1080/13504620701295650

Stiglitz, J. E. (2006). *The great divide: Unequal societies and what we can do about them.* New York: W. W. Norton & Company.

Stokes, E., Edge, A., & West, A. (2001). "Environmental Education in the Educational Systems of the EU", *Synthesis Report*, Centre for Educational Research, London School of Economics and Political Science. Retrieved from http://www.medies.net/_uploaded_files/ee_in_eu.pdf

Transition Network. (2015). In R. Hopkins (Ed.), "21 Stories of Transition: how a movement of communities is coming together to reimagine and rebuild our world", *Transition movement's contribution to COP21* (the 21st Conference of the Parties). Retrieved from: transitionnetwork.org

TWI2050-The World in 2050. (2018). *Transformations to achieve the Sustainable Development Goals. Report prepared by The World in 2050 initiative*. Laxenburg, Austria: International Institute for Applied Systems Analysis (IIASA), Retrieved from, www.twi2050.org also available at: http://pure.iiasa.ac.at/15347

UNESCO. (1972). *Convention concerning the protection of the world cultural and natural heritage*, Adopted by the General Conference at its seventeenth session, Paris. Retrieved November 16, 1972, from https://whc.unesco.org/archive/convention-en.pdf

UNESCO. (1996). Learning: The treasure within; report to UNESCO of the international commission on education for the twenty-first century (highlights), ED.96/WS/9. Available from https://unesdoc.unesco.org/ark:/48223/pf0000109590

UNESCO. (2008). In I. Pramling Samuelsson, & Y. Kaga (Eds.), *The contribution of early childhood education to a sustainable society*.

UNESCO. (2014). *World Conference on Education for Sustainable Development,* Aichi-Nagoya, Japan, 10-12 November 2014.

UNESCO. (2015a). *Global action programme on education for sustainable development as follow-up to the United Nations decade of education for sustainable development after 2014*.

UNESCO. (2015b). *Rethinking Education: Education as a common good, France*. Accessible at: http://www.unesco.org/new/fileadmin/MULTIMEDIA/FIELD/Cairo/images/RethinkingEducation.pdf

UNESCO. (2018a). *Quick Guide to Education Indicators for SDG 4*. Retrieved from http://uis.unesco.org

UNESCO. (UIS 2018b). *Handbook on Measuring in Education.*

UNESCO-UNEP. (1975). International Workshop on Environmental Education at Belgrade, 13–22 October.

UNICEF. (2017). Zlata Bruckauf and Sarah Cook, "Child-centred Approach to Sustainable Development Goals in High-income Countries: Conceptual issues and monitoring approaches", *Office of Research-Innocenti Working Paper*, WP-2017-06. Retrieved from: www.unicef.irc.org

Verger, A. (2010). WTO/GATS and the global politics of higher education. In P. Altback (Ed.), *International studies in higher education*. New York: Routledge.

Vitale, C. (2011). The protection of cultural heritage between the EU legal order and the global legal space. In E. Chiti & B. G. Mattarella (Eds.), *Global Administrative Law and EU Law*. Berlin: Springer.

Walkenhorst, H. (2008). Explaining change in EU education policy. *Journal of European Public Policy, 15*, 567.

Wang, Y. (2013). *Education policy reform trends in G20 members*. Springer.

Wellman, B., Salaff, J., Dimitrova, D., Garton, G., Gulia, M., & Haythornthwaite, C. (1996). Computer networks as social networks: Collaborative work, telework, and virtual community. *Annual Review of Sociology, 22*, 213–238.

y Gasset, J. O. (1944). *Mission of the university*. (trans: Nostrand, H. L.). Princeton, NJ: Princeton University Press.

Chapter 6
Conclusions

Abstract This conclusive chapter reaffirms some of the main arguments dealt during these pages and suggests that our aspirations for SD require us to resolve common problems and tensions and to recognise new horizons in our research and policy agendas. We need new conceptual approaches for education and culture as the main builders of the EUSM. Otherwise SD challenges will remain. Numerous laws, policy documents, economic measures, research papers, policy announcements and articles have been produced over the past two decades calling for public and private bodies and institutions to give greater focus to the integration of social, economic and environmental sustainability to face future challenges. However, public and private interventions addressing sustainability have been occurring at intervals and at various locations and instances rather than all together. As a consequence there has been much less attention given to the foundations of transforming some of our existing public and private institutions in order to ensure that a real integration of sustainability is successfully initiated. Education must find ways of responding to such challenges taking into account alternative knowledge systems often rooted in local realities with universal validity. Moreover, traditional economies need to be transformed into modern 'knowledge' economies helping to foster a system model that embeds the challenges of the desirable cultural transformation.

Europe is at a crossroads mainly because the cultural and educational challenges of its (economic) development project have been fairly neglected. The internal and external challenges of the EUSM comprise geopolitical imbalances in the energy transition, threats to economic and social cohesion, growing cultural diversity, increasing social and political complexity, uncertain political trends at national levels, the climate crisis, and last but not the least, endangered legitimacy and trust. The EU is in the midst of complex and interconnected transformations at all levels. The EUSM is a global leader on environmental protection, not only in line with the Paris climate agreement but with biosphere protection and regulatory challenges identified by the Global Agenda, but we are facing crucial and unprecedented social threats. On top of that, understanding the complexity of menaces to the social dimension of sustainability in a holistic manner remains challenging because the issues span across so many areas: the scientific and technological

M. D. Sánchez Galera, *Educational and Cultural Challenges of the European Sustainability Model*, https://doi.org/10.1007/978-3-030-38716-7_6

basis of environmental problems, the sociocultural values and attitudes behind them, and their political and economic contexts that should be embedded in every social concern.

In the context of ever-increasing globalisation and ecological perils for the Earth, Europe has a strong responsibility as a global actor. Its sustainability model is under pressure. We are experiencing, more than ever, radical transformations that need to be led in the right direction. Governance, democracy, social welfare, and basically educational and cultural institutions need to be mainstreamed into the unique model of integration Europe is exporting to the world under strong sustainability premises but mainly focused on growth, despite of its inclusive governance processes, finding new equilibrium between diversity and unity in this globalising world.

Despite the Anthropocene risks, the political disrupts and the pressing social problems, Europe remains a civilisation project characterised by a rich institutional infrastructure and cultural heritage strongly equipped to face future challenges, but these infrastructures are still insufficient and cultural and natural heritage need further public policy attention. The European economic project is still imbalanced with the social market idea enshrined in the Lisbon Treaty. Only a social economic community that is also culturally empowered and truly focused on youth, intergenerational solidarity, education and biosphere empathy can strengthen the EUSM and lead to sustainable and cohesive European societies.

Urban spaces, consumption practices, and commercial models have become aggressive and complex. The need for new learning spaces, not exclusively provided by digital innovation is mandatory. In this context, solidarity practices and organised community based initiatives have become important for living convivially and disempower the 'marketisation' and the overarching digitalisation trends. The role of education, cultural values, ethical values, heritage and the study of humanities is fundamental in all this. The Anthropocene and the risks it poses to the planet Earth and societies, generally, need more than global consensus on transnational environmental protection and strong sustainability concerns. Environmental education, ESD or EfS initiatives integrated into educational national policies are not enough, although they are vital for awareness, as well as International conventions. The Anthropocene needs new 'narratives' and the right learning and cultural initiatives to empower the widest spectrum of social actors. The 'traditional' learning environments are radically changing becoming more competitive, fragmented, technologically distant and multifaceted, but digital transformation is just one of the many challenges of the new emerging deontologies.

Following this reasoning, we need new forms of governance and action, in addition to new physical places of dialogue and accessible communication and information, as well as a variety of new and old actors in the public scene to find stronger connections with citizens, people needs and communities. Education needs a radical change if Europeans want to renew their long-term vision project under the premises of sustainability, solidarity and 'shared sovereignty'. Not only education as a common good, (public good) should dominate public policy discourses, but a more democratic institutional framework in which citizens are not indifferent to the future political project and share common responsibilities towards future generations is required.

The French philosopher Edgar Morin spoke of 'planetary crisis' and the need 'to change civilisation' to address the complexity of today's world. Moreover, the various crises Europe faces are indeed symptoms of a broader, systemic crisis. New consensus are needed departing from important international experience as the Earth Charter, and other international Conventions. Stakeholders and active citizens have reached the right momentum for effective action leading to the transformation the UN 2030 Global Agenda is claiming assisted by its 17 SDGs.

Our aspirations for sustainable development require us to resolve common problems and tensions and to recognise new horizons in our research and policy agendas. Unsustainable patterns of economic production and consumption contribute to the global warming, environmental degradation and an upsurge in natural disasters. Moreover, while international human rights frameworks have been strengthened over the past several decades, the implementation and protection of these norms today still remain a challenge aligned to sustainability requirements. Education must find ways of responding to such challenges taking into account multiple worldviews and alternative knowledge systems, as well as new frontiers in science and technology such as the advances in neurosciences and the developments in digital technology, placing them at the service of human needs contrasting the devastating human attack to our natural resources. However, legal scholarship has extensively neglected attention to the strong digitalisation challenges, and the market pressure and power of the digitalisation industry is predominantly overshadowing its negative effects for human wellness and childhood neurological development. The church is rightly and timely reacting under the guidance of the Pope claiming for a Global Pact focused on education concerns. Thus, rethinking the purpose of education and the organisation of learning has never been more urgent for our public institutions.

Traditional economies need to be transformed into modern 'knowledge' economies helping to foster a 'sustainability model' that embeds the challenges of the desirable cultural transformation. Economists have been suggesting human well-being and other objectives beyond GDP measures of economic growth, and our legal systems have been moving away from a carbon-based energy system at a quite high speed at European level. However, we are missing any kind of planning for an educational reform or biosphere education integrating in such improvements the promotion and re-connection with our natural and cultural heritage.

Nonetheless, the upheaval and redemption of such complexity to face sustainability challenges in these sectors seems to be a 'transdisciplinary' rather than disciplinary approach; and this realm, for legal scientists is completely unexplored. In fact, sustainability science that has already emerged as a recognised scientific field an inclusive field drawing from transdisciplinary methodology to face complex questions, still misses a significant amount of legal contributions. In legal science, the trend that could most validly bring solutions and transformations, regards the recognition by jurists that human laws are not out there, separate from their interpreters, and that the process of their emergence is probably no less complex than the discovery of a "law of nature". A valid suggestion drawing on this assumption is indeed the already mentioned call for "ecolegal literacy" that is urgent to face one of the great challenges of this time, “building and nurturing sustainable communities: Social, cultural and physical environments in which we can satisfy our needs and aspirations without diminishing the chances of future generations”.[1] This approach is founded on systems thinking rather than on an outdated mechanistic way of thinking that could help us to “become aware of our own power to influence law throughout our aggregate action” (Capra & Mattei, 2015, p. 28). What the EUSM ultimately needs is citizens and communities’ awareness and engagement at every life stage to overcome today’s humanity crisis reaching beyond global environmental degradation in order to privilege care for others, responsibility, active participation and morals.

Reference

Capra, F., & Mattei, U. (2015). *The ecology of law. Toward a legal system in tune with nature and community*. Berrett and Koehler.

[1]Capra and Mattei (2015, pp. 28–29). See further the way they describe how a sustainable community is designed.

The manufacturer's authorised representative in the EU is Springer Nature Customer Service Centre GmbH, Europaplatz 3, 69115 Heidelberg, Germany. If you have any concerns regarding our products, please contact ProductSafety@springernature.com

Printed and bound by CPI Group (UK) Ltd, Croydon, CR0 4YY
30/09/2026
02225644-0019